Deltora Quest

デルトラクエスト

Volume 2

Story by Emily Rodda

Manga by Makoto Niwano

Translated by Mayumi Kobayashi

Lettered by North Market Street Graphics

KC
KODANSHA COMICS

Deltora Quest volume 2, is a work of fiction. Names, characters, places, and incidents are the products of the author's imagination or are used fictitiously. Any resemblance to actual events, locales, or persons, living or dead, is entirely coincidental.

Original story by Emily Rodda

A Kodansha Comics Trade Paperback Original

Published in the United States by Kodansha Comics, an imprint of Kodansha USA Publishing, LLC, New York.

Publication rights arranged through Kodansha Ltd., Tokyo.

First published in Japan in 2006 by Kodansha Ltd., Tokyo.

ISBN 978-1-935429-29-6

Printed in the United States of America

www.kodanshacomics.com

9 8 7 6 5 4 3 2 1

Translator: Mayumi Kobayashi
Lettering: North Market Street Graphics

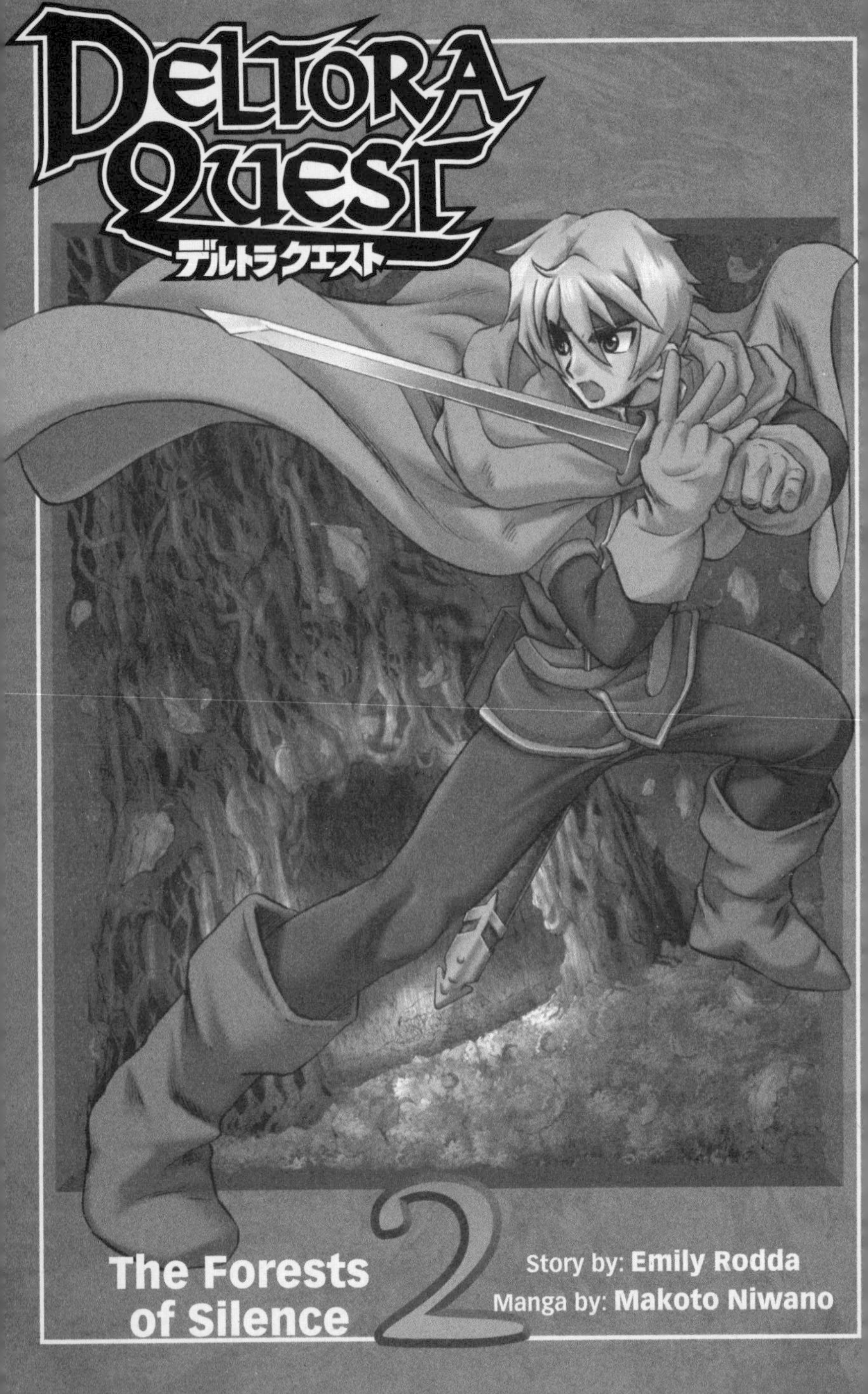
DELTORA QUEST
デルトラクエスト
2
The Forests of Silence
Story by: Emily Rodda
Manga by: Makoto Niwano

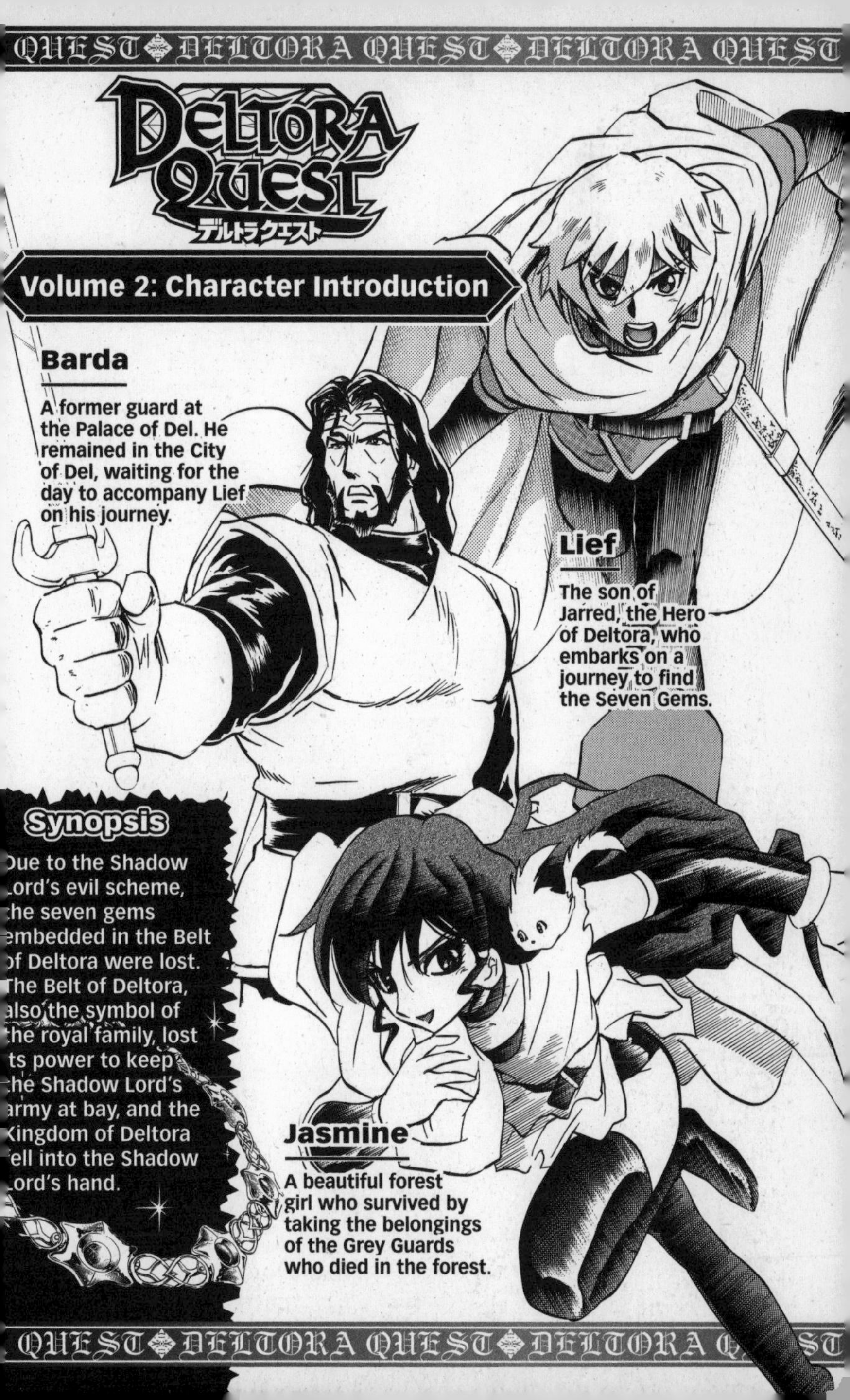
QUEST DELTORA QUEST DELTORA QUEST
DELTORA QUEST
デルトラクエスト
Volume 2: Character Introduction
Barda
A former guard at the Palace of Del. He remained in the City of Del, waiting for the day to accompany Lief on his journey.
Lief
The son of Jarred, the Hero of Deltora, who embarks on a journey to find the Seven Gems.
Synopsis
Due to the Shadow Lord's evil scheme, the seven gems embedded in the Belt of Deltora were lost. The Belt of Deltora, also the symbol of the royal family, lost its power to keep the Shadow Lord's army at bay, and the Kingdom of Deltora fell into the Shadow Lord's hand.
Jasmine
A beautiful forest girl who survived by taking the belongings of the Grey Guards who died in the forest.
QUEST DELTORA QUEST DELTORA QUEST

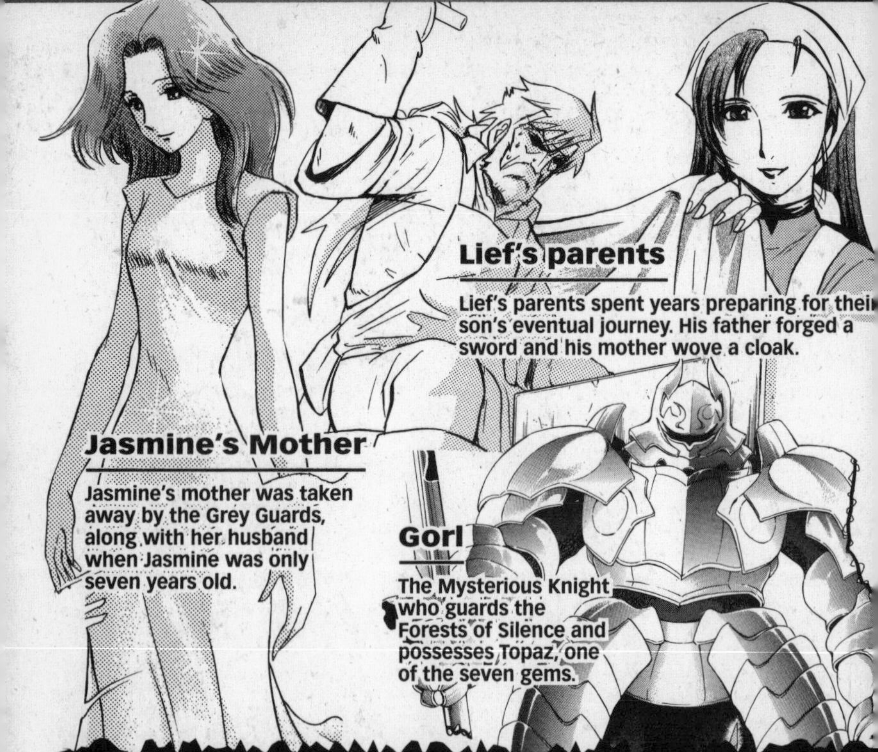

Lief's parents

Lief's parents spent years preparing for their son's eventual journey. His father forged a sword and his mother wove a cloak.

Jasmine's Mother

Jasmine's mother was taken away by the Grey Guards, along with her husband when Jasmine was only seven years old.

Gorl

The Mysterious Knight who guards the Forests of Silence and possesses Topaz, one of the seven gems.

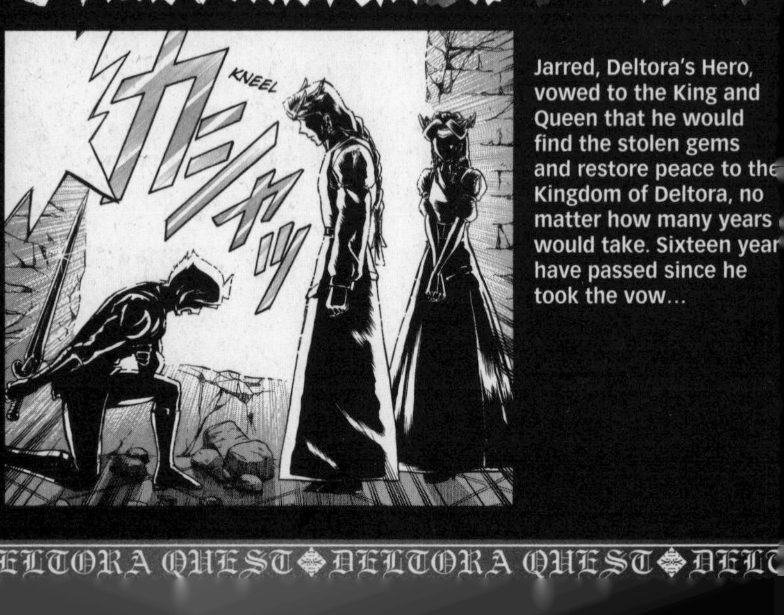
KNEEL

Jarred, Deltora's Hero, vowed to the King and Queen that he would find the stolen gems and restore peace to the Kingdom of Deltora, no matter how many years it would take. Sixteen years have passed since he took the vow...

DELTORA QUEST

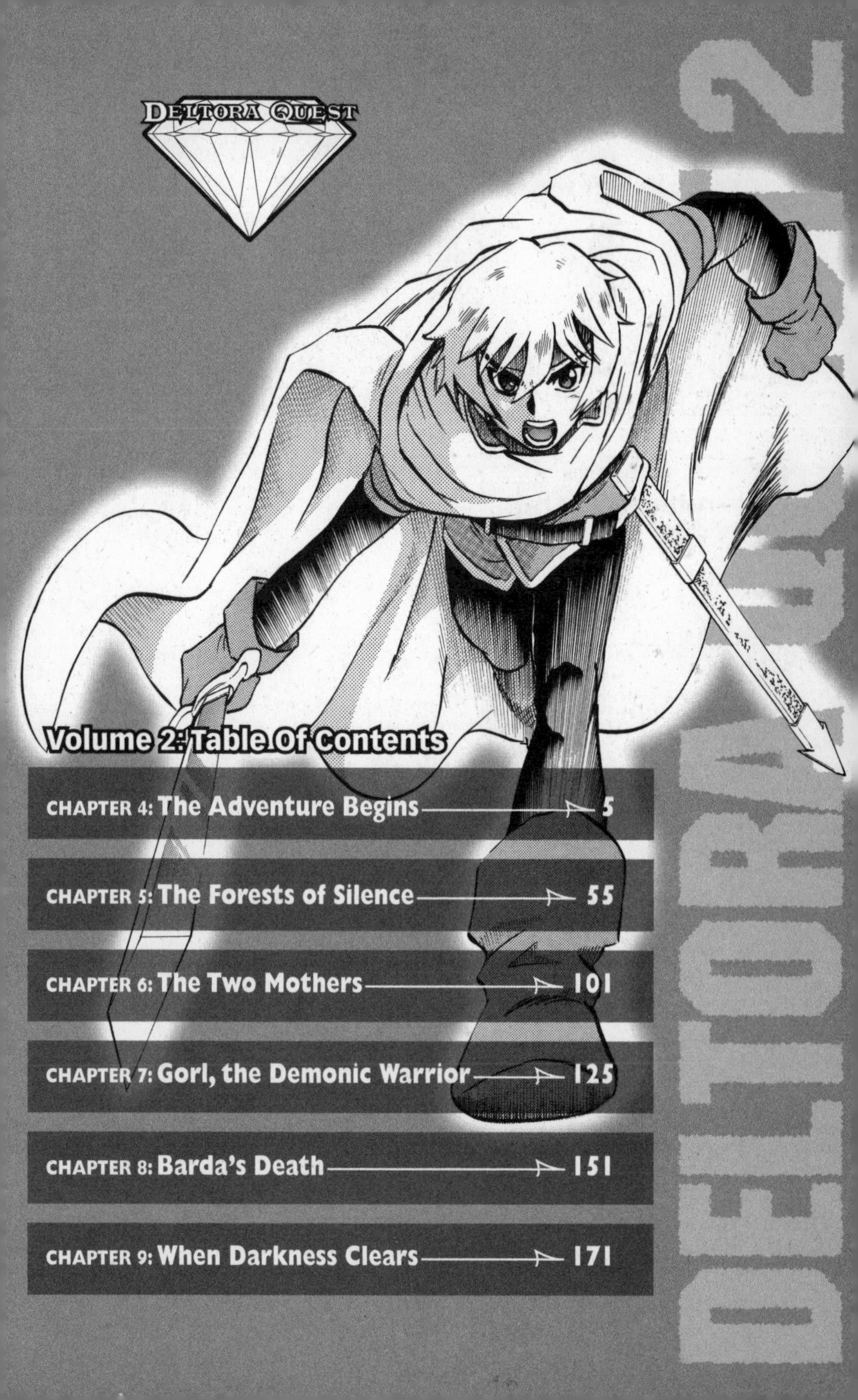

Volume 2: Table Of Contents

Chapter 4:
The Adventure Begins

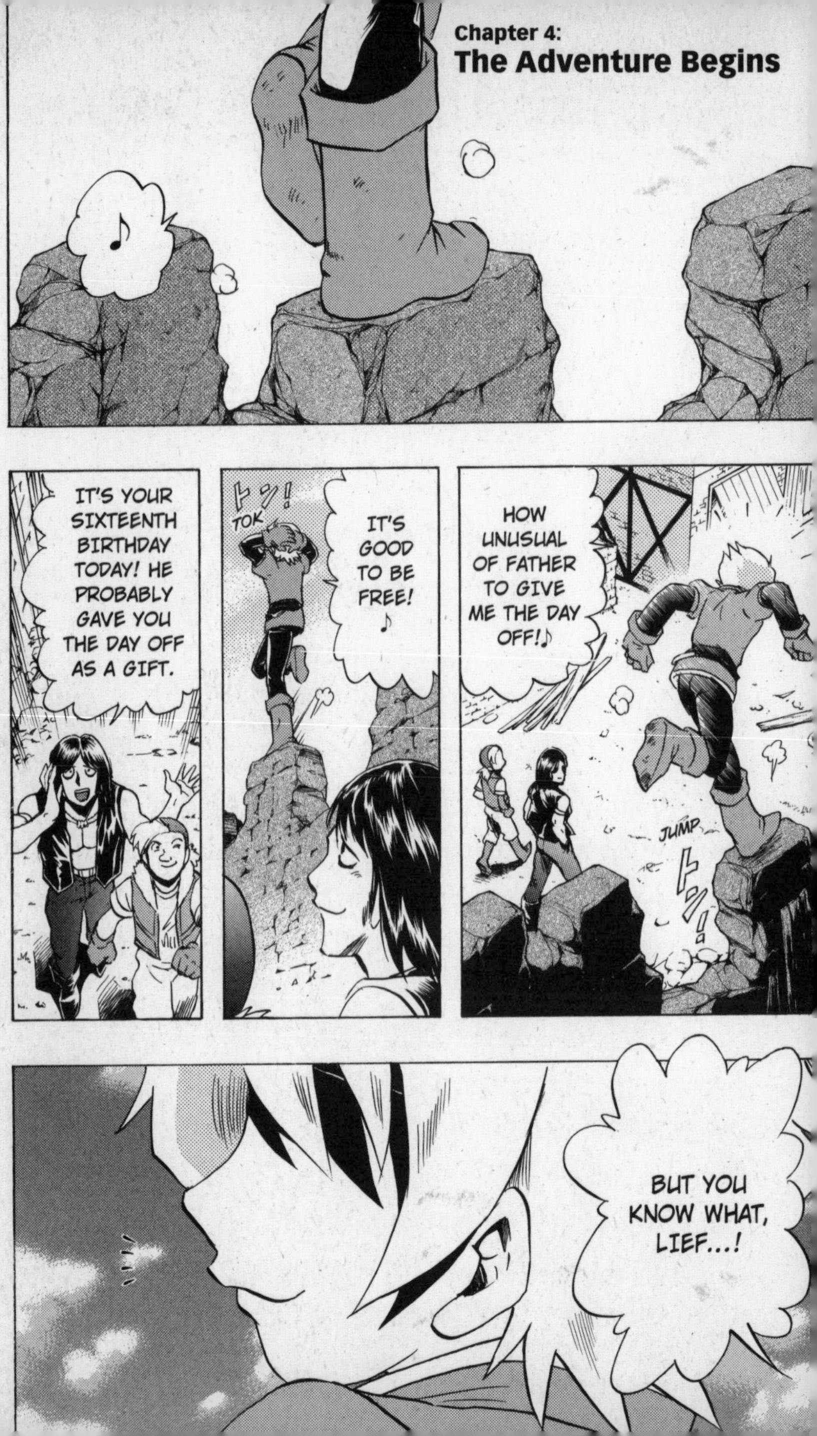
♪
HOW UNUSUAL OF FATHER TO GIVE ME THE DAY OFF!♪
JUMP
トッ!
トッ!
TOK
IT'S GOOD TO BE FREE! ♪
IT'S YOUR SIXTEENTH BIRTHDAY TODAY! HE PROBABLY GAVE YOU THE DAY OFF AS A GIFT.
BUT YOU KNOW WHAT, LIEF...!

Chapter 4: The Adventure Begins

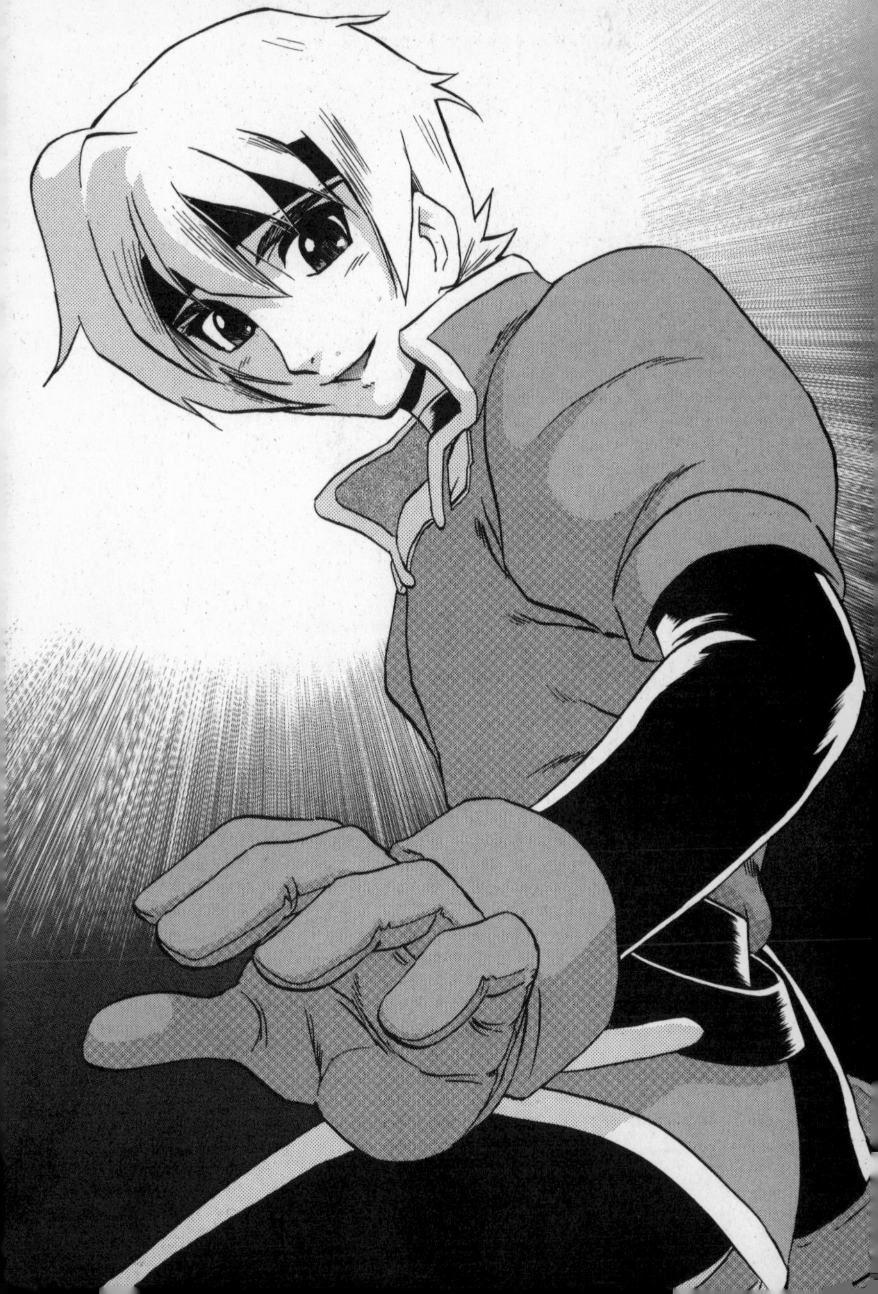

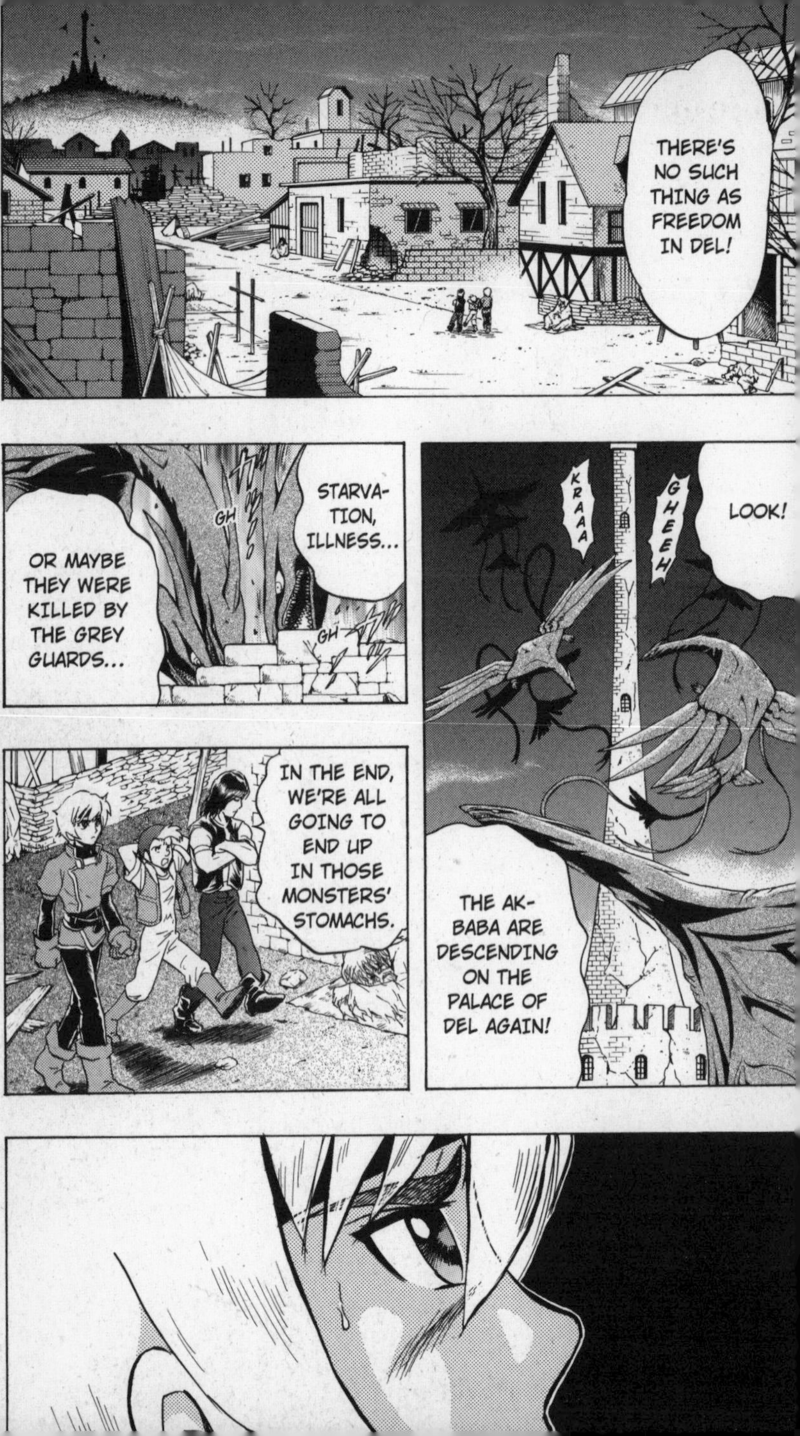
THERE'S NO SUCH THING AS FREEDOM IN DEL!
LOOK!
GHEEH
KRAAA
THE AK-BABA ARE DESCENDING ON THE PALACE OF DEL AGAIN!
STARVATION, ILLNESS...
GH
GH
OR MAYBE THEY WERE KILLED BY THE GREY GUARDS...
IN THE END, WE'RE ALL GOING TO END UP IN THOSE MONSTERS' STOMACHS.

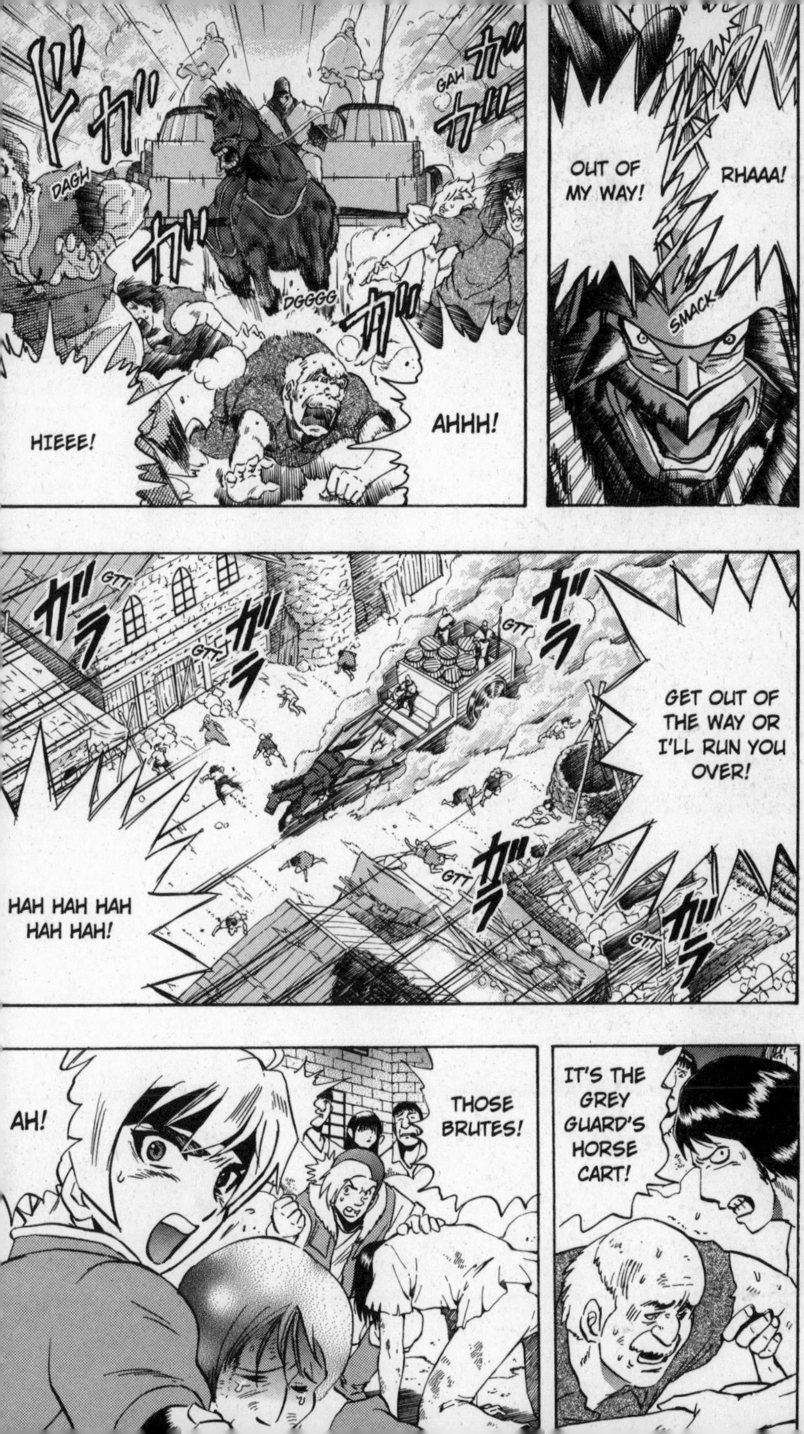
RHAAA!
OUT OF MY WAY!
SMACK
GAH
DAGH
DGGGG
AHHH!
HIEEE!
GTT
GET OUT OF THE WAY OR I'LL RUN YOU OVER!
HAH HAH HAH HAH HAH!
IT'S THE GREY GUARD'S HORSE CART!
THOSE BRUTES!
AH!

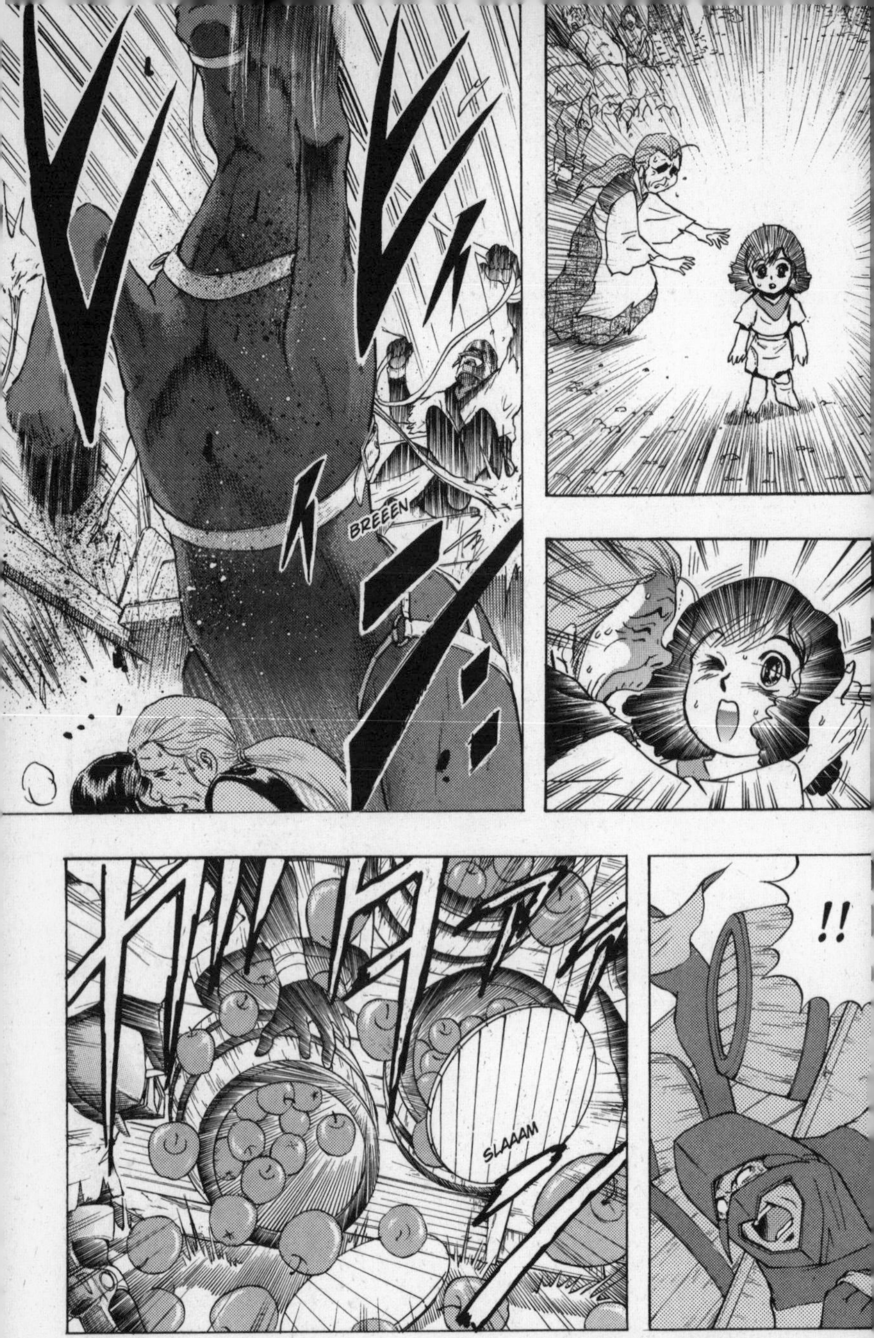
BREEEN
!!
SLAAAM

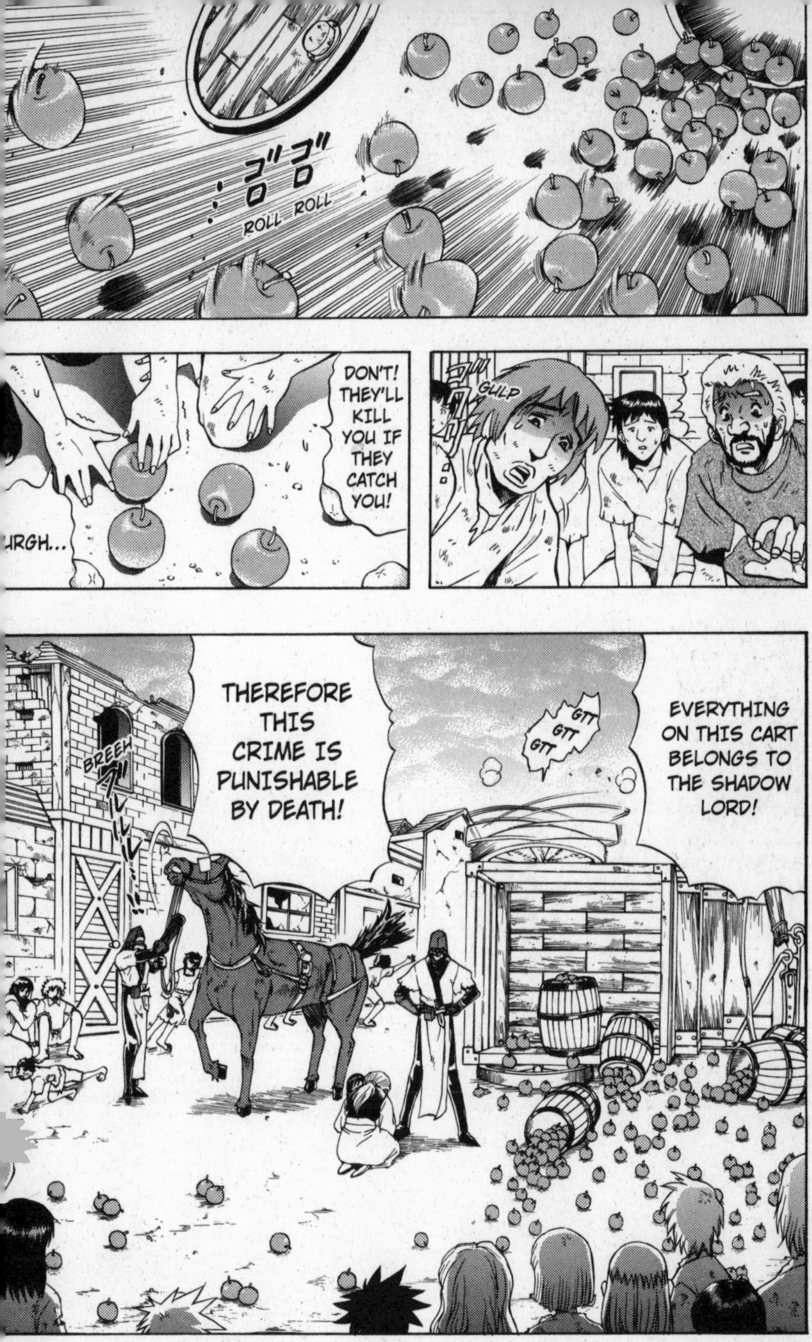
ROLL ROLL
GULP
DON'T! THEY'LL KILL YOU IF THEY CATCH YOU!
URGH...
EVERYTHING ON THIS CART BELONGS TO THE SHADOW LORD!
GTT GTT GTT
THEREFORE THIS CRIME IS PUNISHABLE BY DEATH!
BREEH

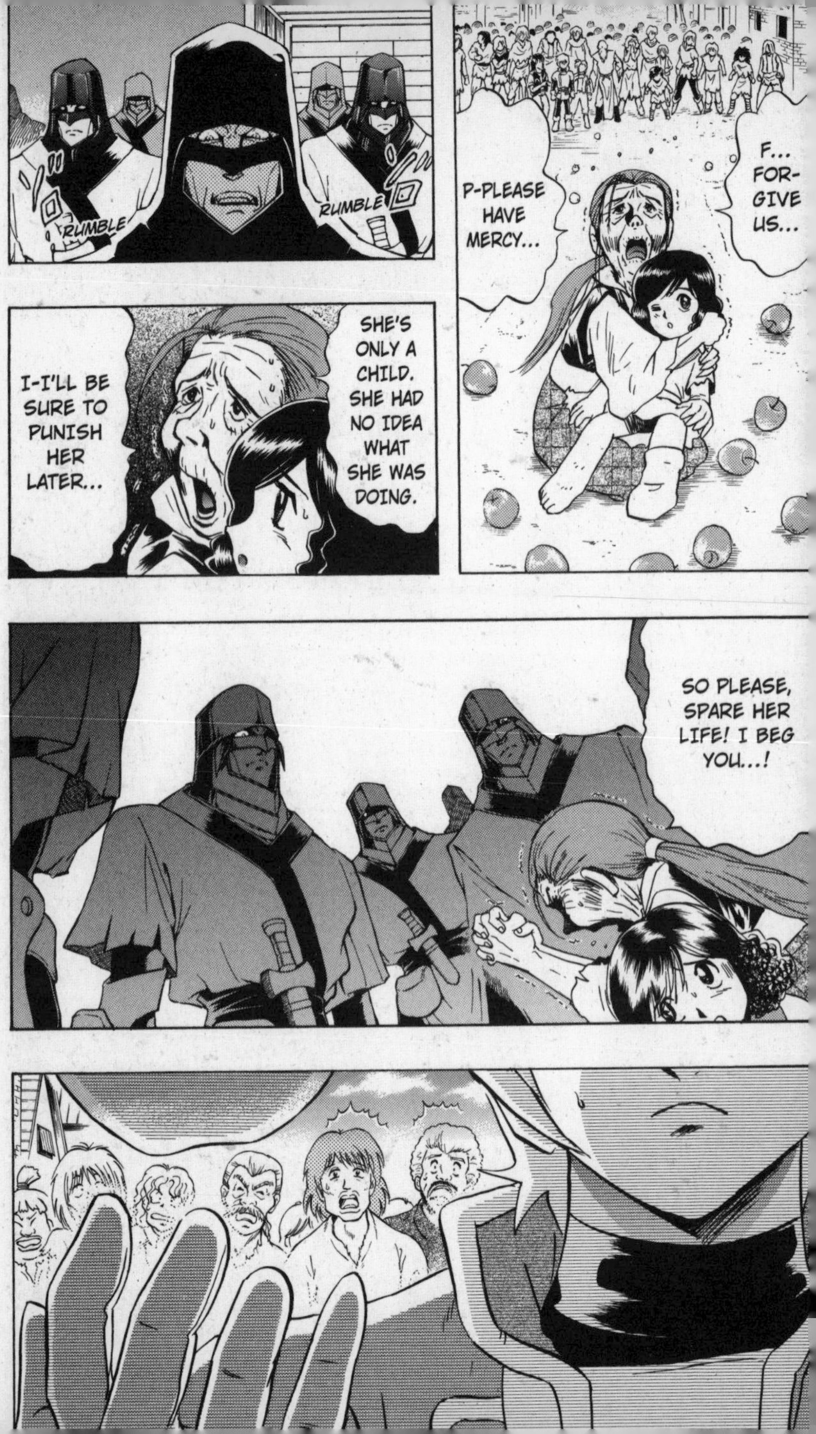
F... FOR-GIVE US...
P-PLEASE HAVE MERCY...
RUMBLE
RUMBLE
SHE'S ONLY A CHILD. SHE HAD NO IDEA WHAT SHE WAS DOING.
I-I'LL BE SURE TO PUNISH HER LATER...
SO PLEASE, SPARE HER LIFE! I BEG YOU...!

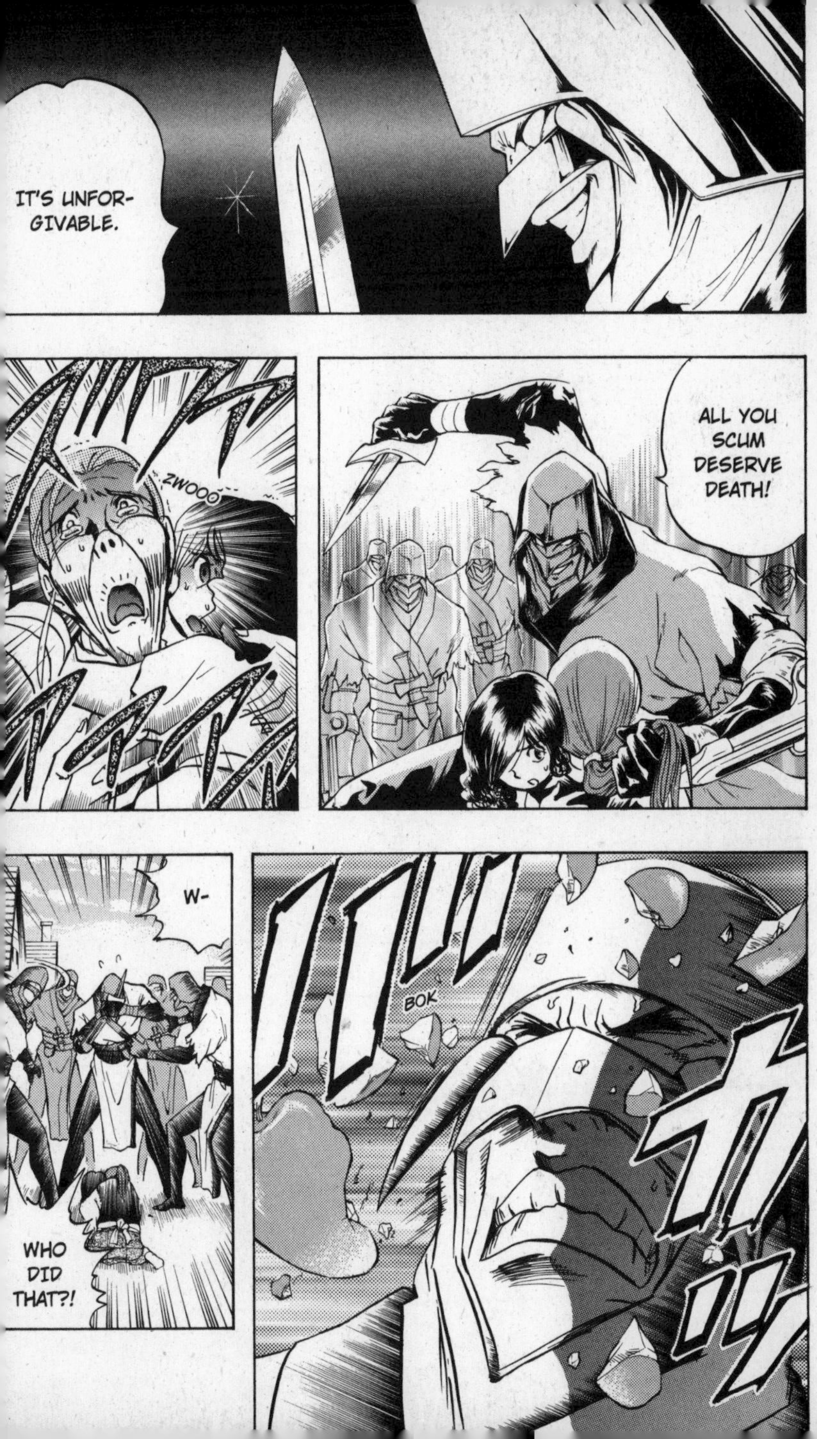
IT'S UNFOR-GIVABLE.
ALL YOU SCUM DESERVE DEATH!
ZWOOO
BOK
W-
WHO DID THAT?!

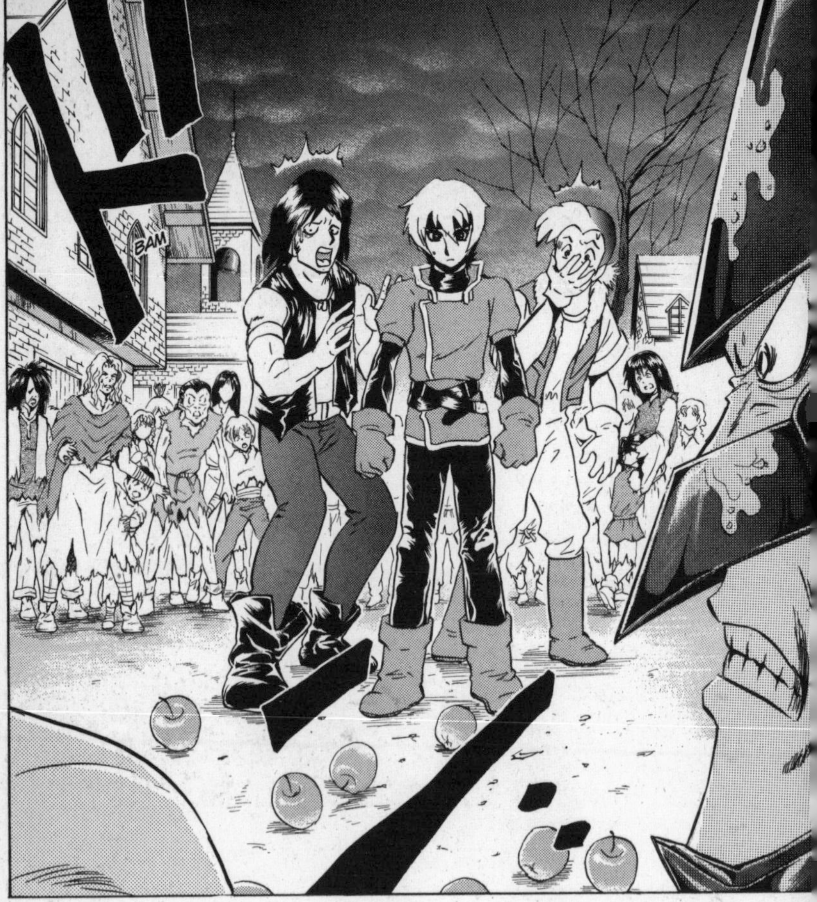
BAM
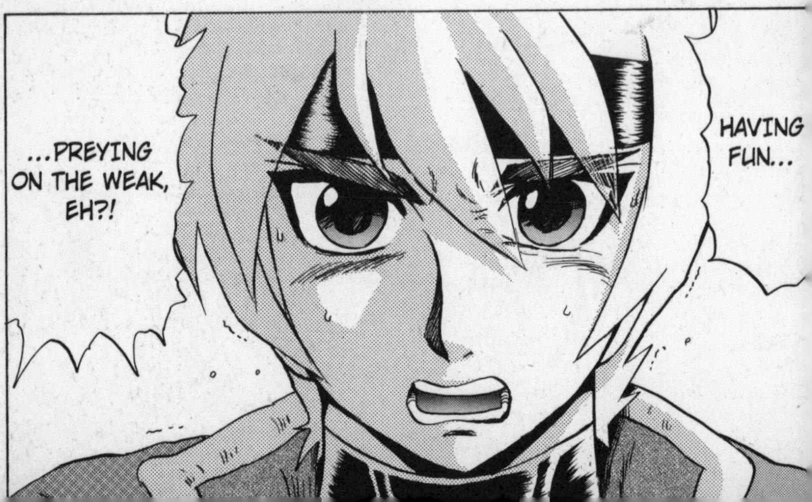
HAVING FUN...
...PREYING ON THE WEAK, EH?!

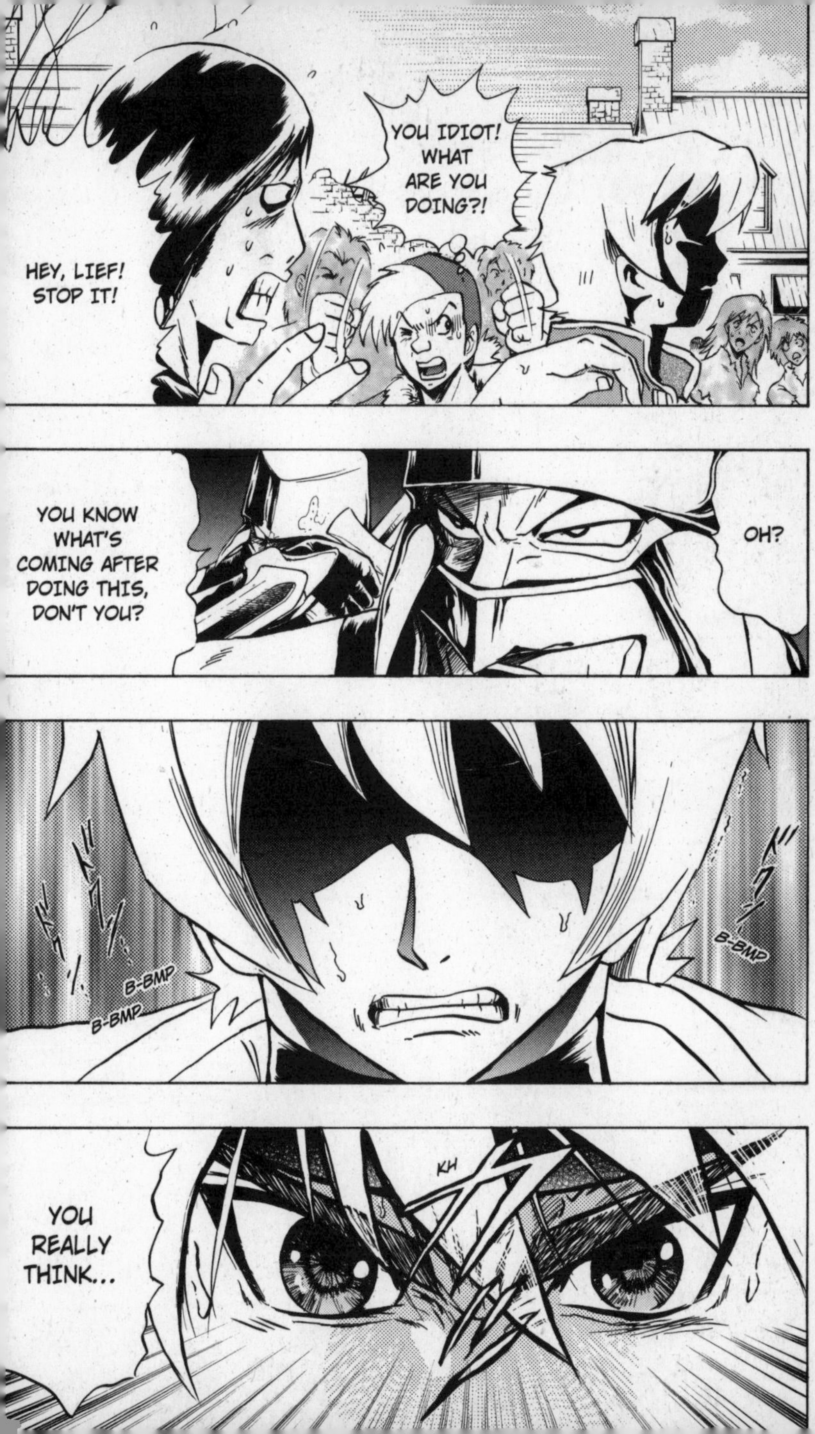
YOU IDIOT! WHAT ARE YOU DOING?!
HEY, LIEF! STOP IT!
OH?
YOU KNOW WHAT'S COMING AFTER DOING THIS, DON'T YOU?
B-BMP
B-BMP
B-BMP
KH
YOU REALLY THINK...

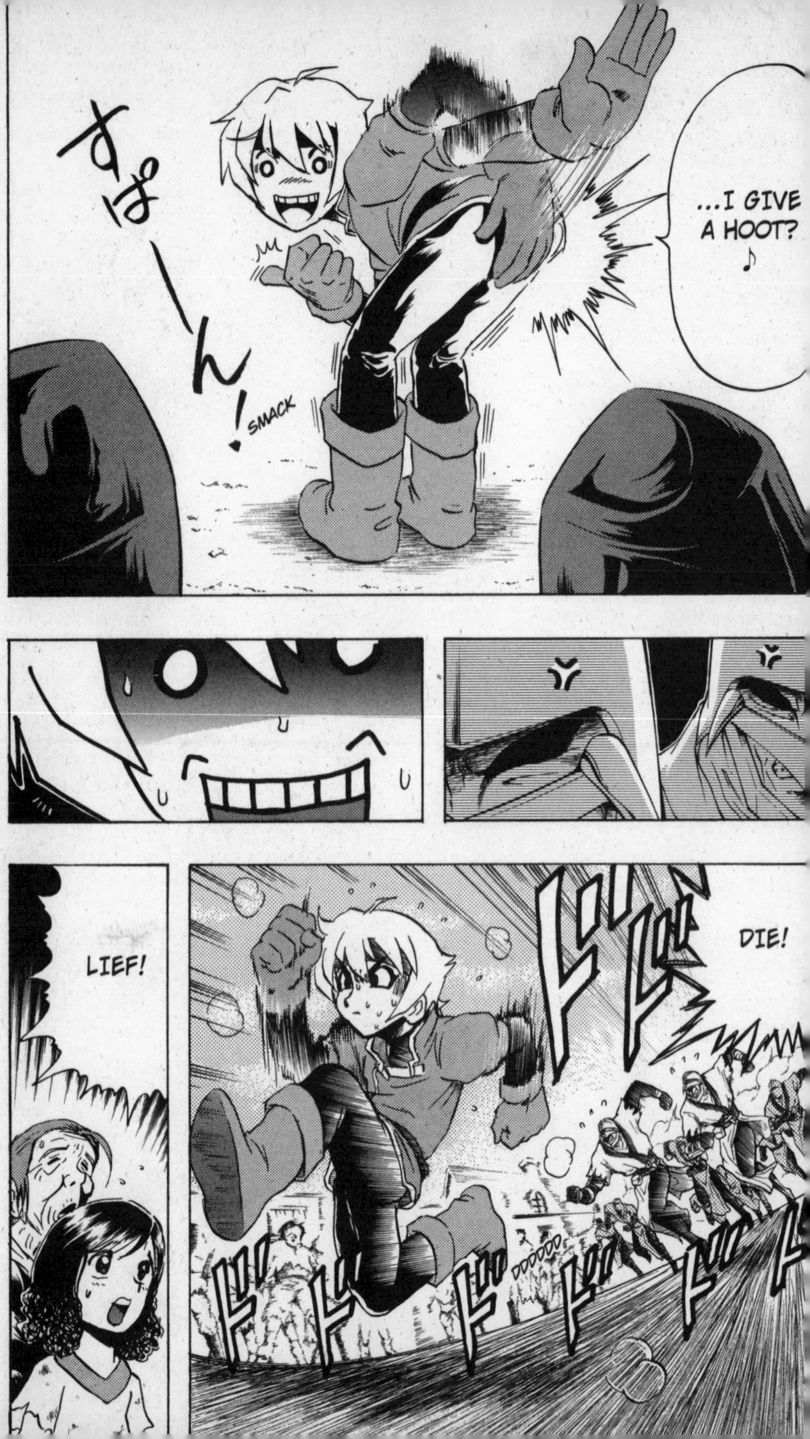
...I GIVE A HOOT? ♪
すぱーん!
SMACK
DIE!
DDDDDD
LIEF!

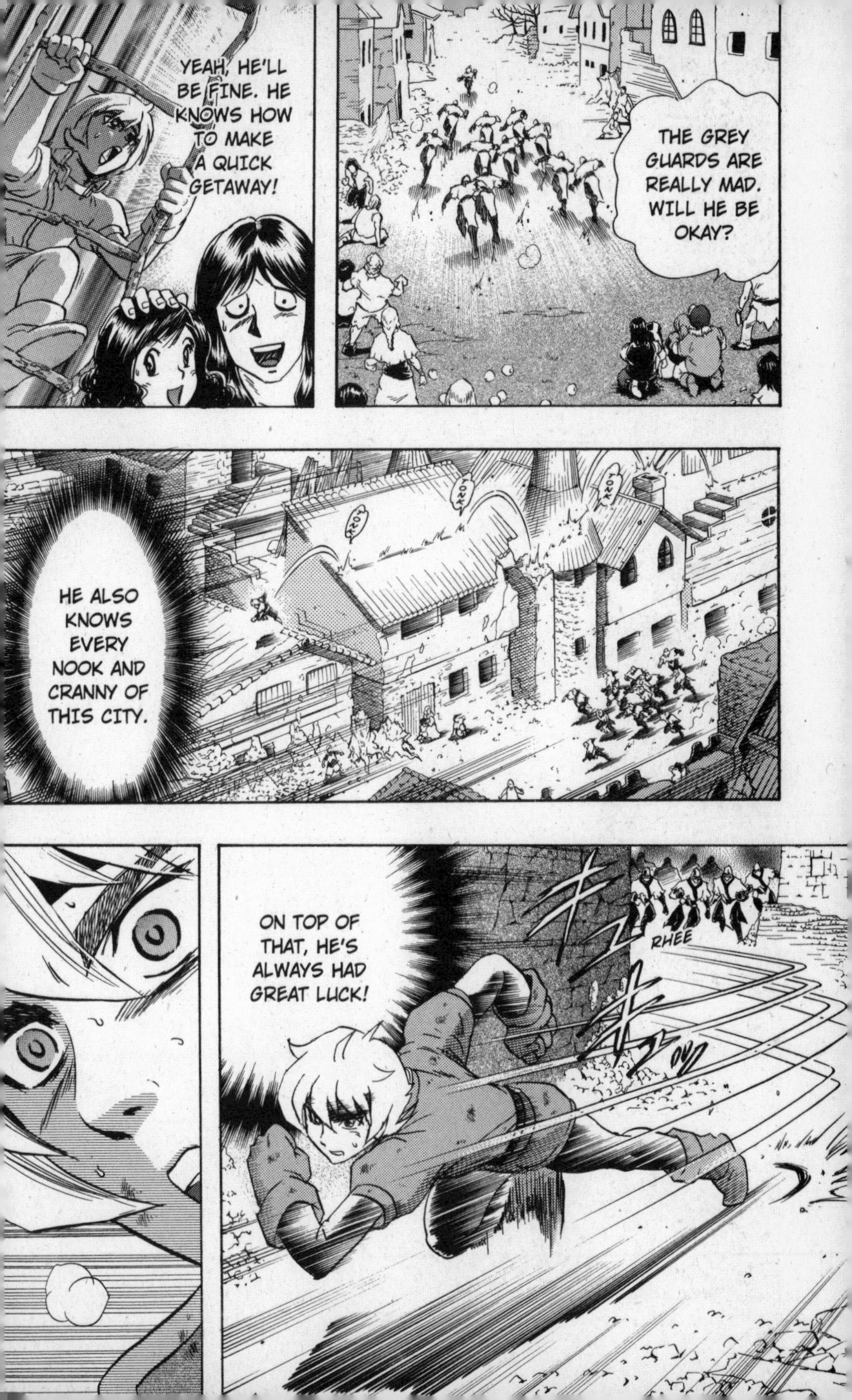
THE GREY GUARDS ARE REALLY MAD. WILL HE BE OKAY?
YEAH, HE'LL BE FINE. HE KNOWS HOW TO MAKE A QUICK GETAWAY!
TONK
TONK
TONK
HE ALSO KNOWS EVERY NOOK AND CRANNY OF THIS CITY.
RHEE
ON TOP OF THAT, HE'S ALWAYS HAD GREAT LUCK!

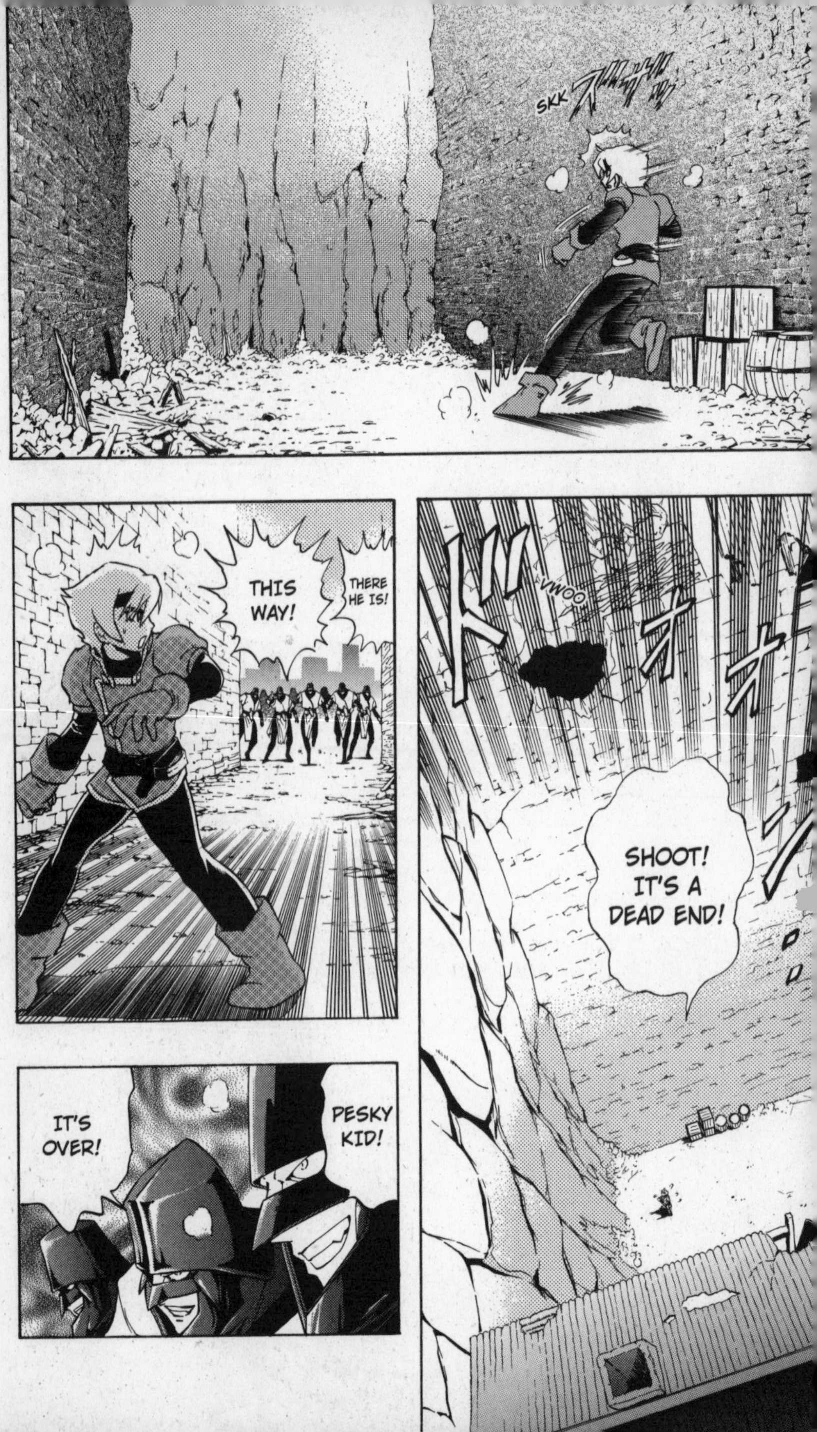
SKK
VWOO
SHOOT! IT'S A DEAD END!
THERE HE IS!
THIS WAY!
PESKY KID!
IT'S OVER!

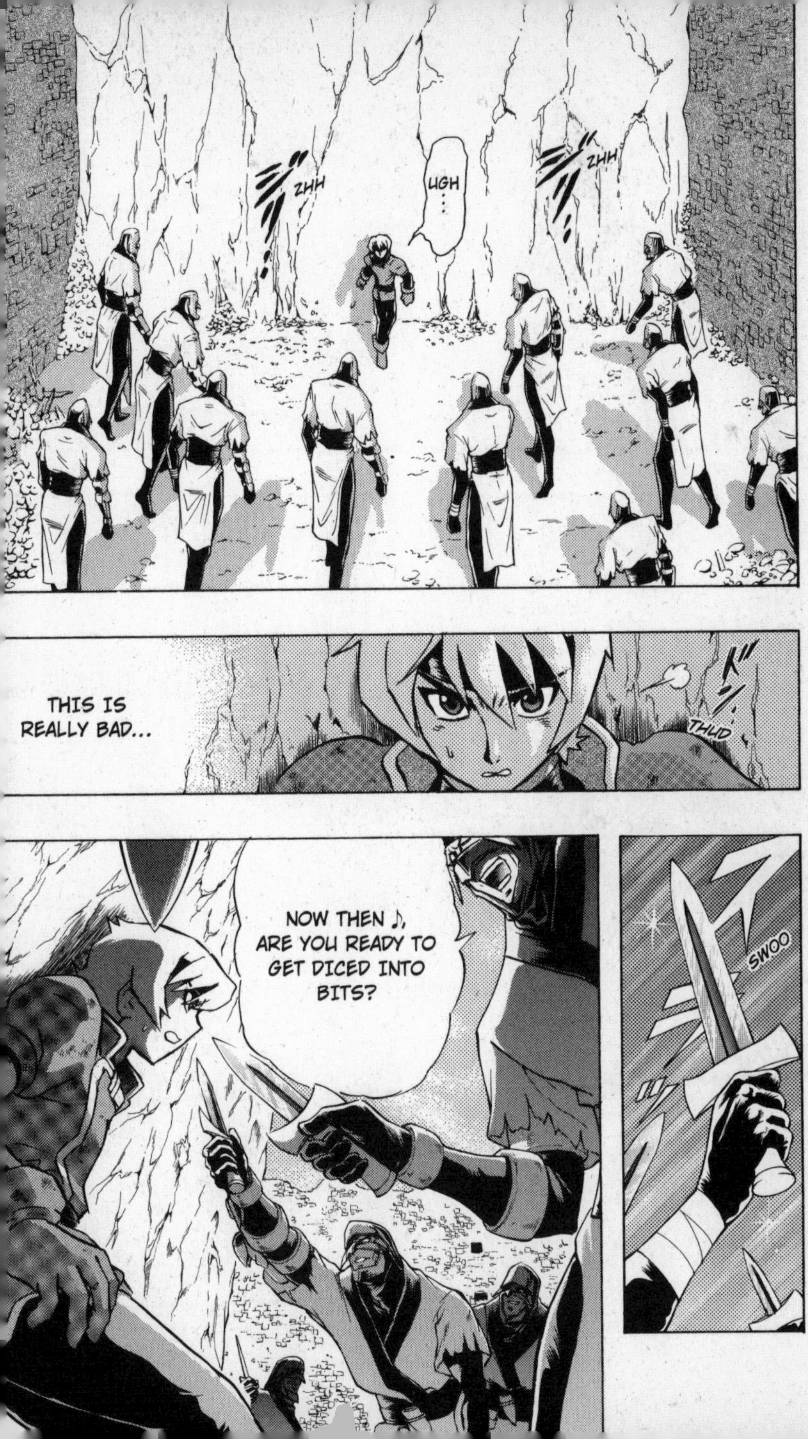
ZHH
UGH...
ZHH
THUD
THIS IS REALLY BAD...
SWOO
NOW THEN ♪, ARE YOU READY TO GET DICED INTO BITS?

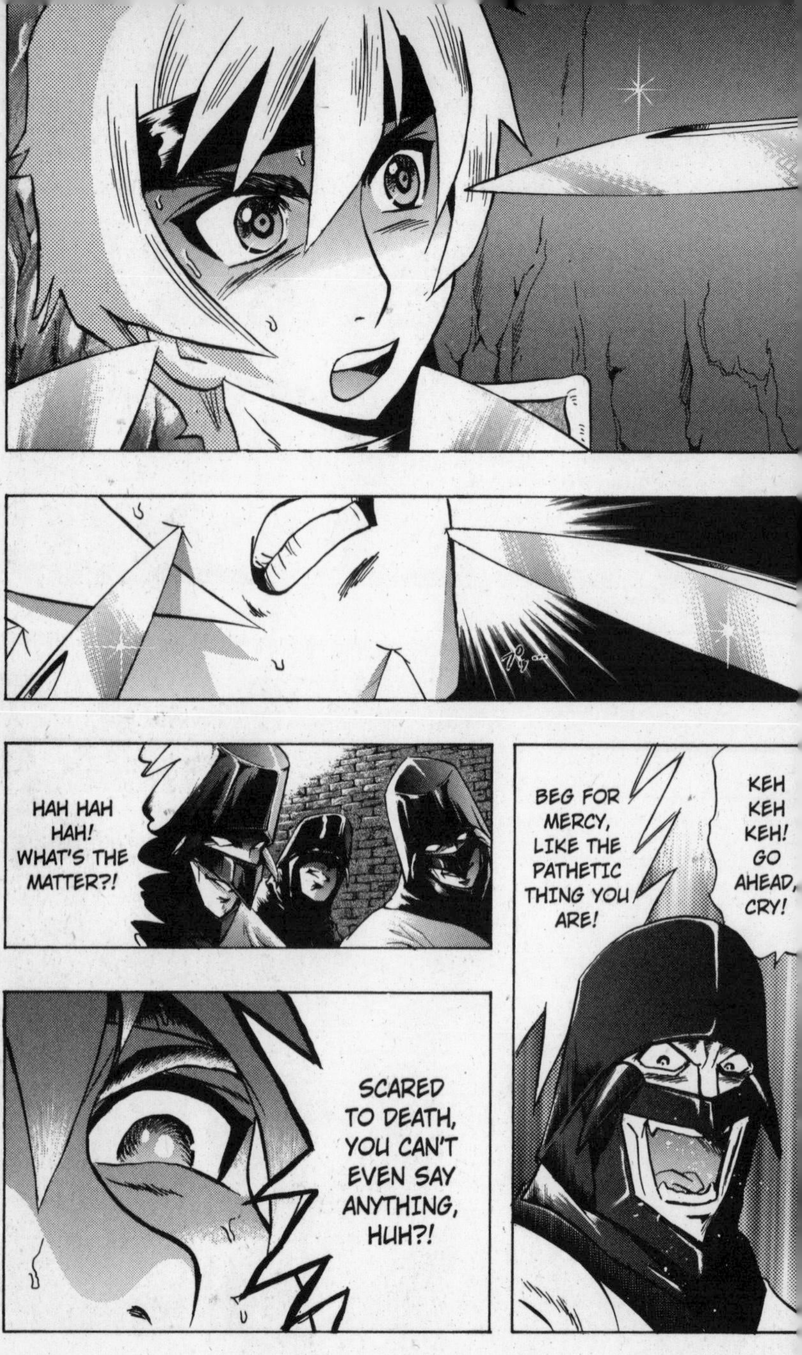
KEH KEH KEH! GO AHEAD, CRY!
BEG FOR MERCY, LIKE THE PATHETIC THING YOU ARE!
HAH HAH HAH! WHAT'S THE MATTER?!
SCARED TO DEATH, YOU CAN'T EVEN SAY ANYTHING, HUH?!

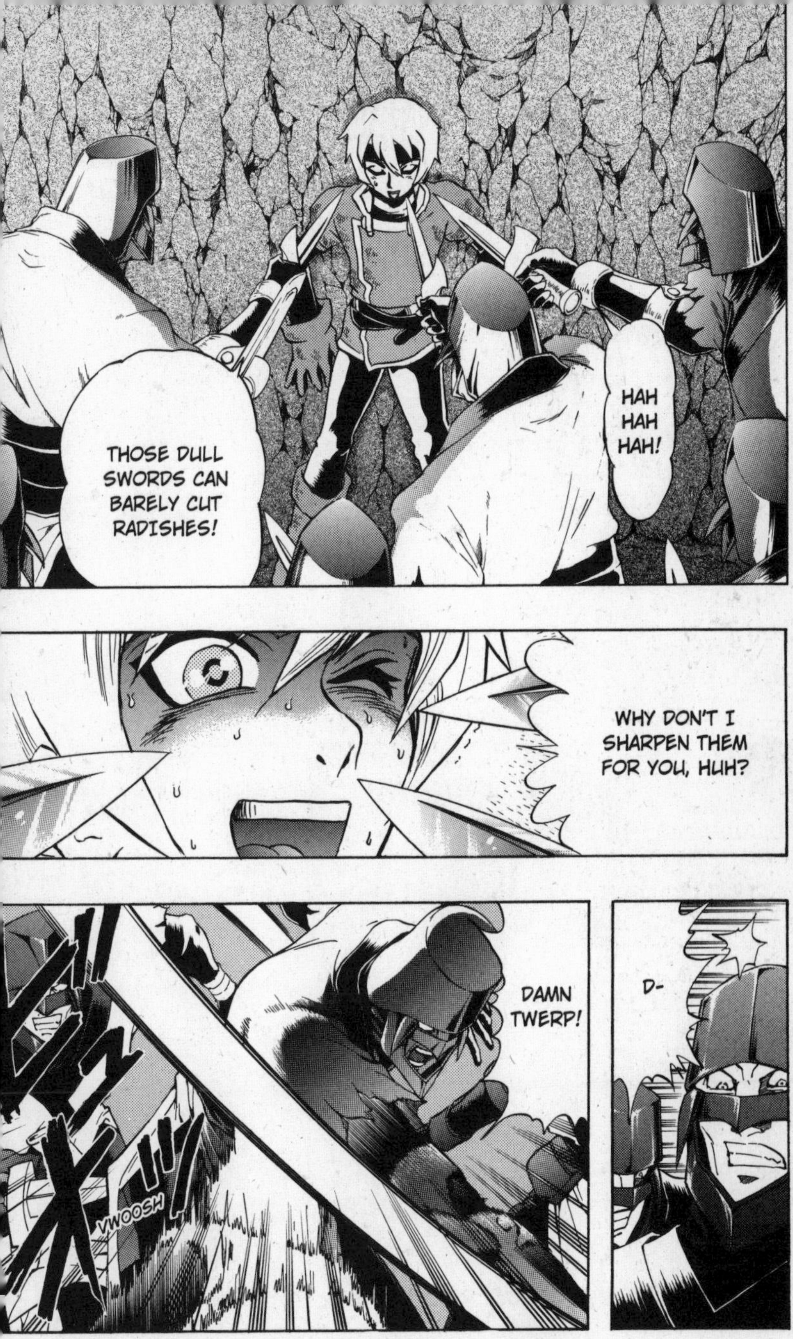
HAH HAH HAH!
THOSE DULL SWORDS CAN BARELY CUT RADISHES!
WHY DON'T I SHARPEN THEM FOR YOU, HUH?
D-
DAMN TWERP!
VWOOSH

AWE-
SOME!

JUMP

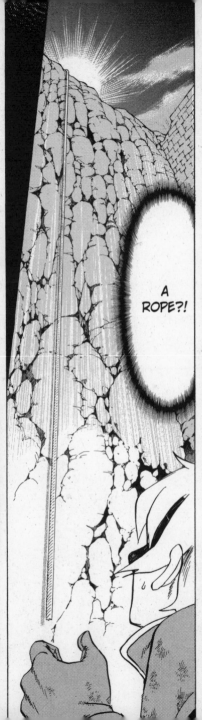

A
ROPE?!

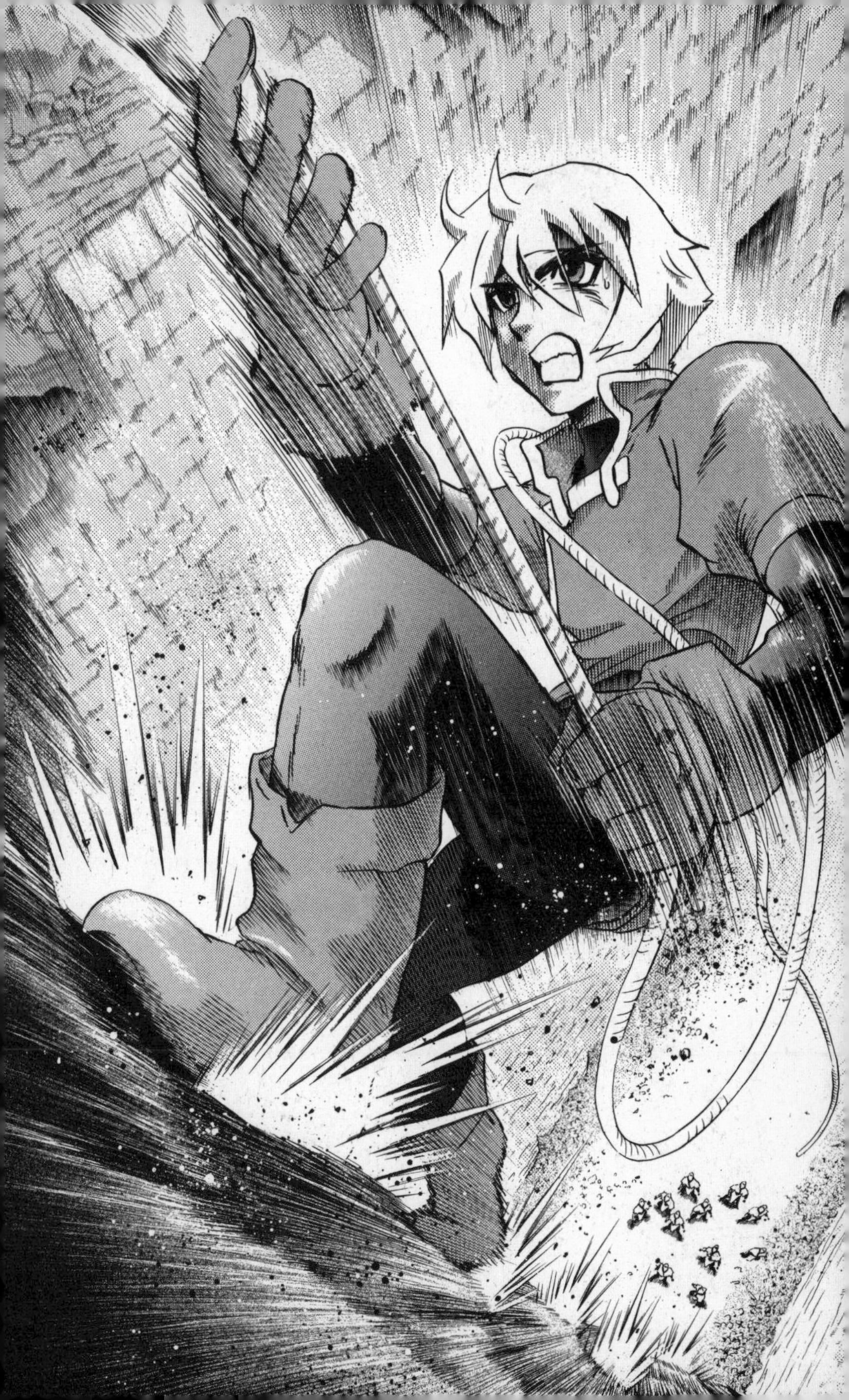

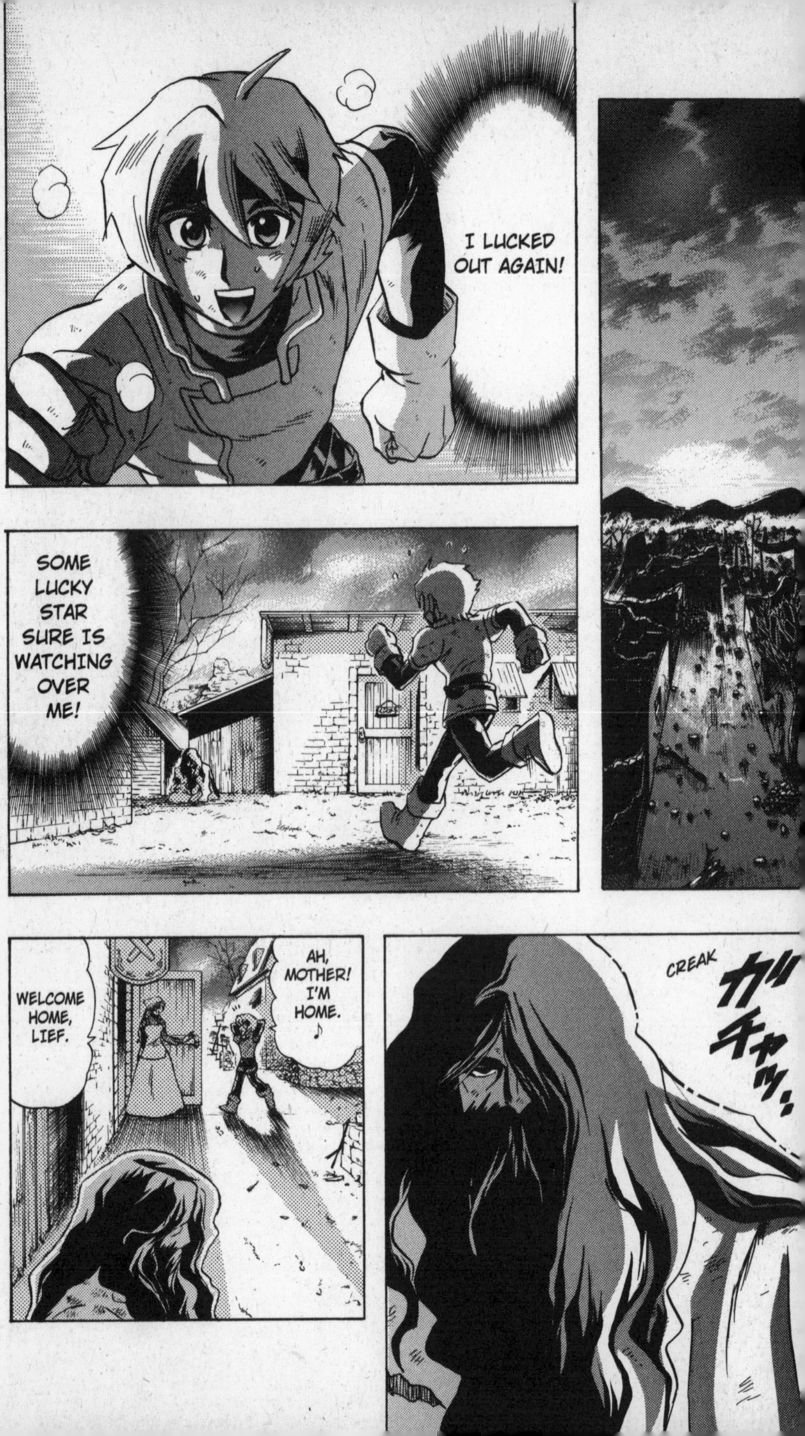
I LUCKED OUT AGAIN!
SOME LUCKY STAR SURE IS WATCHING OVER ME!
CREAK
ガチャッ
AH, MOTHER! I'M HOME. ♪
WELCOME HOME, LIEF.

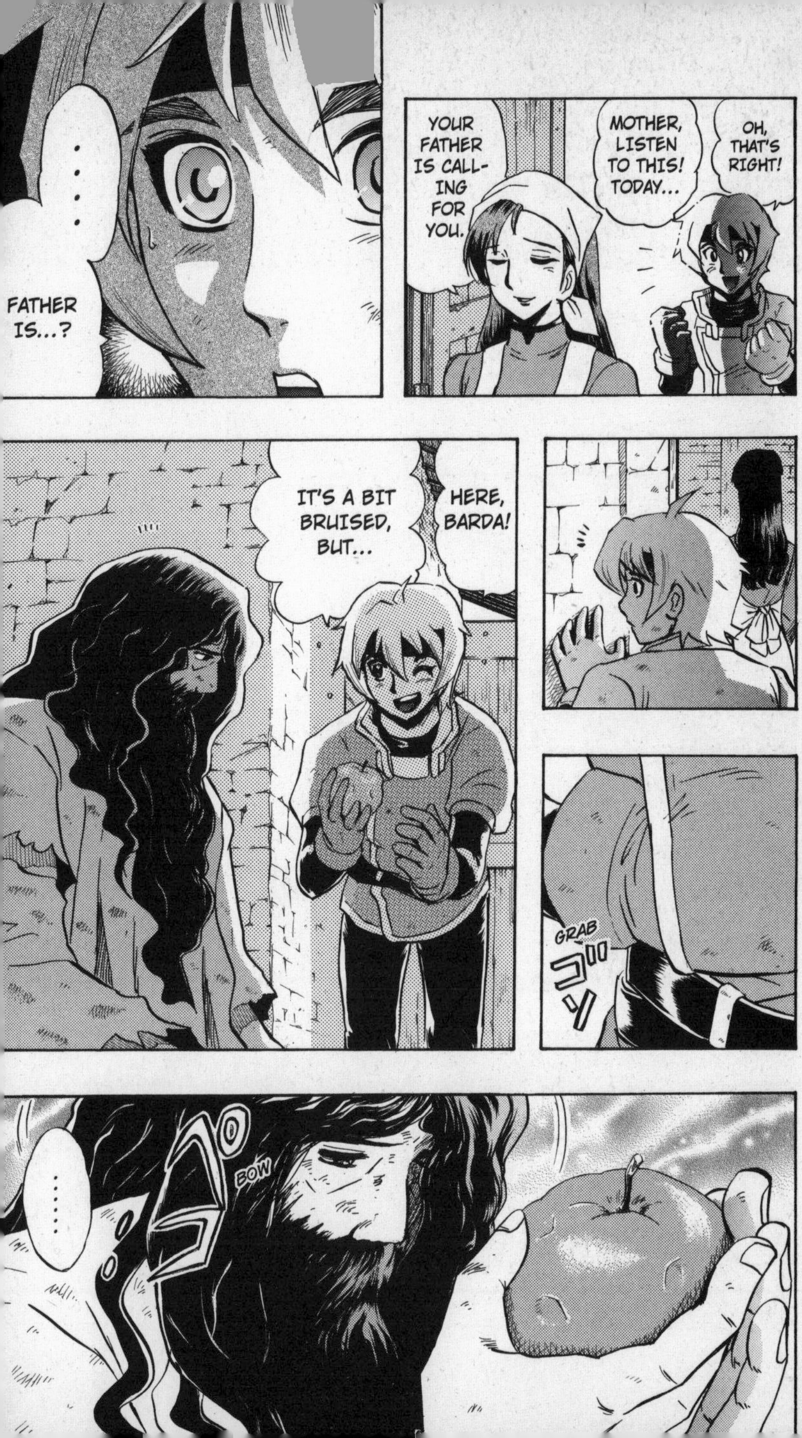
OH, THAT'S RIGHT!
MOTHER, LISTEN TO THIS! TODAY...
YOUR FATHER IS CALLING FOR YOU.
......
FATHER IS...?
GRAB
HERE, BARDA!
IT'S A BIT BRUISED, BUT...
BOW
......

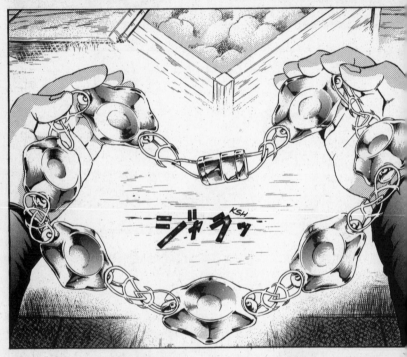

ジャク KSH ッ

25

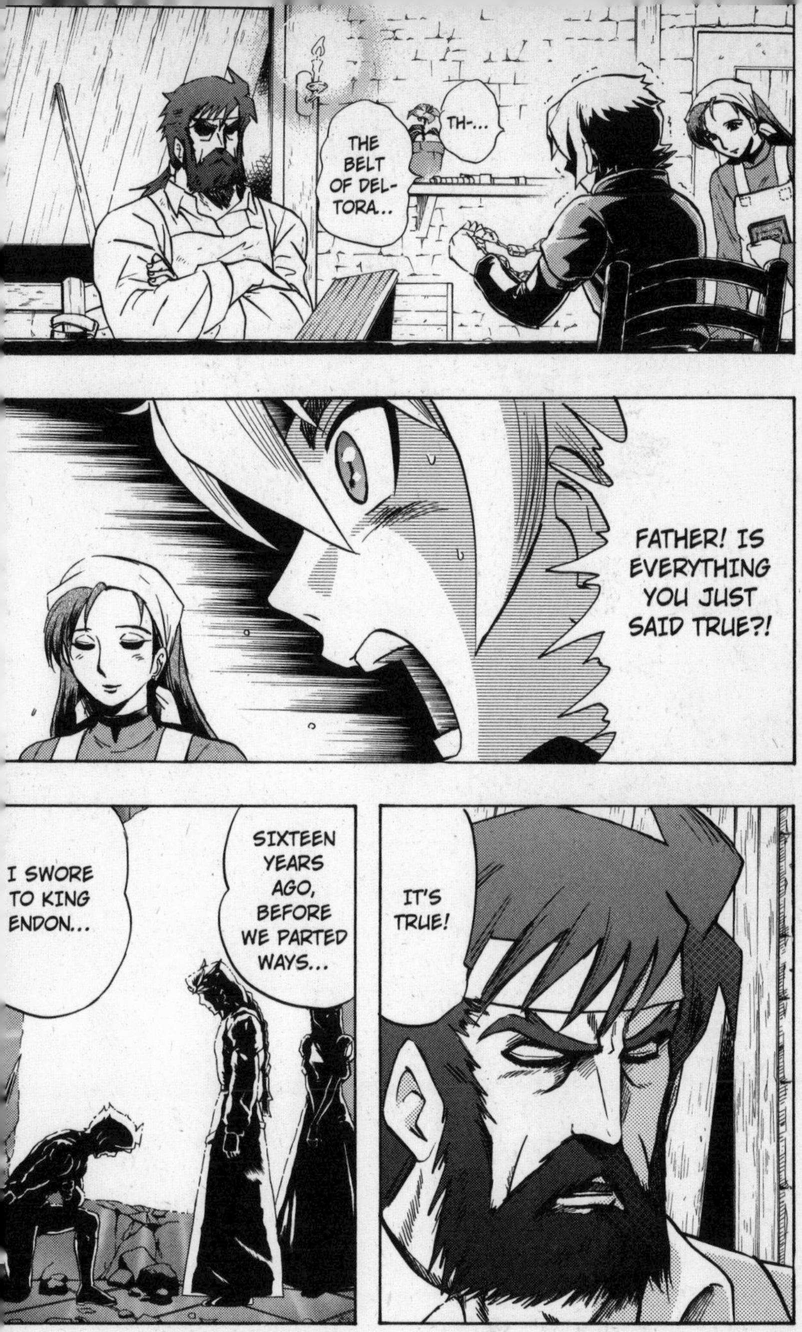
TH-...
THE BELT OF DEL-TORA...
FATHER! IS EVERYTHING YOU JUST SAID TRUE?!
IT'S TRUE!
SIXTEEN YEARS AGO, BEFORE WE PARTED WAYS...
I SWORE TO KING ENDON...

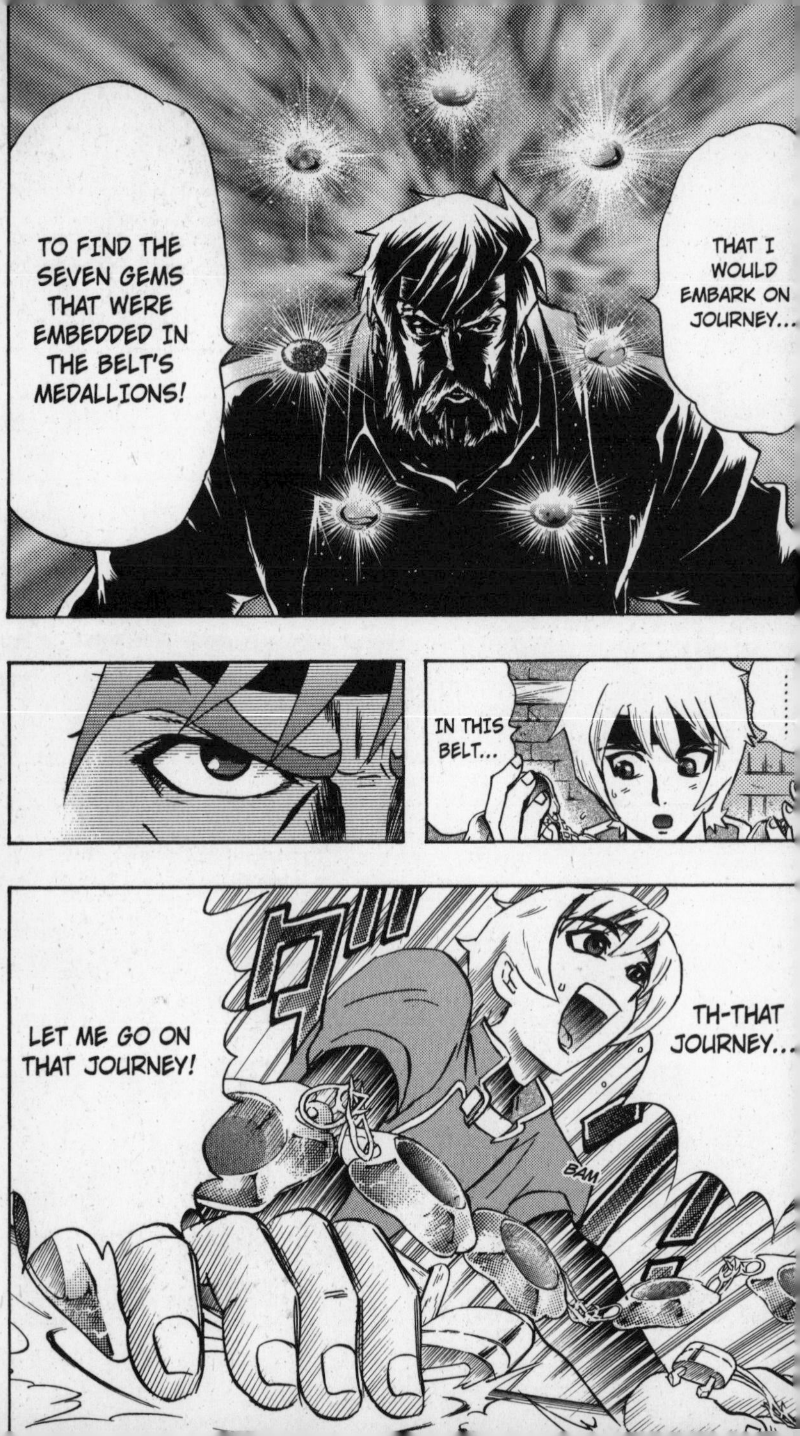
THAT I WOULD EMBARK ON JOURNEY...
TO FIND THE SEVEN GEMS THAT WERE EMBEDDED IN THE BELT'S MEDALLIONS!
......
IN THIS BELT...
TH-THAT JOURNEY...
LET ME GO ON THAT JOURNEY!
BAM

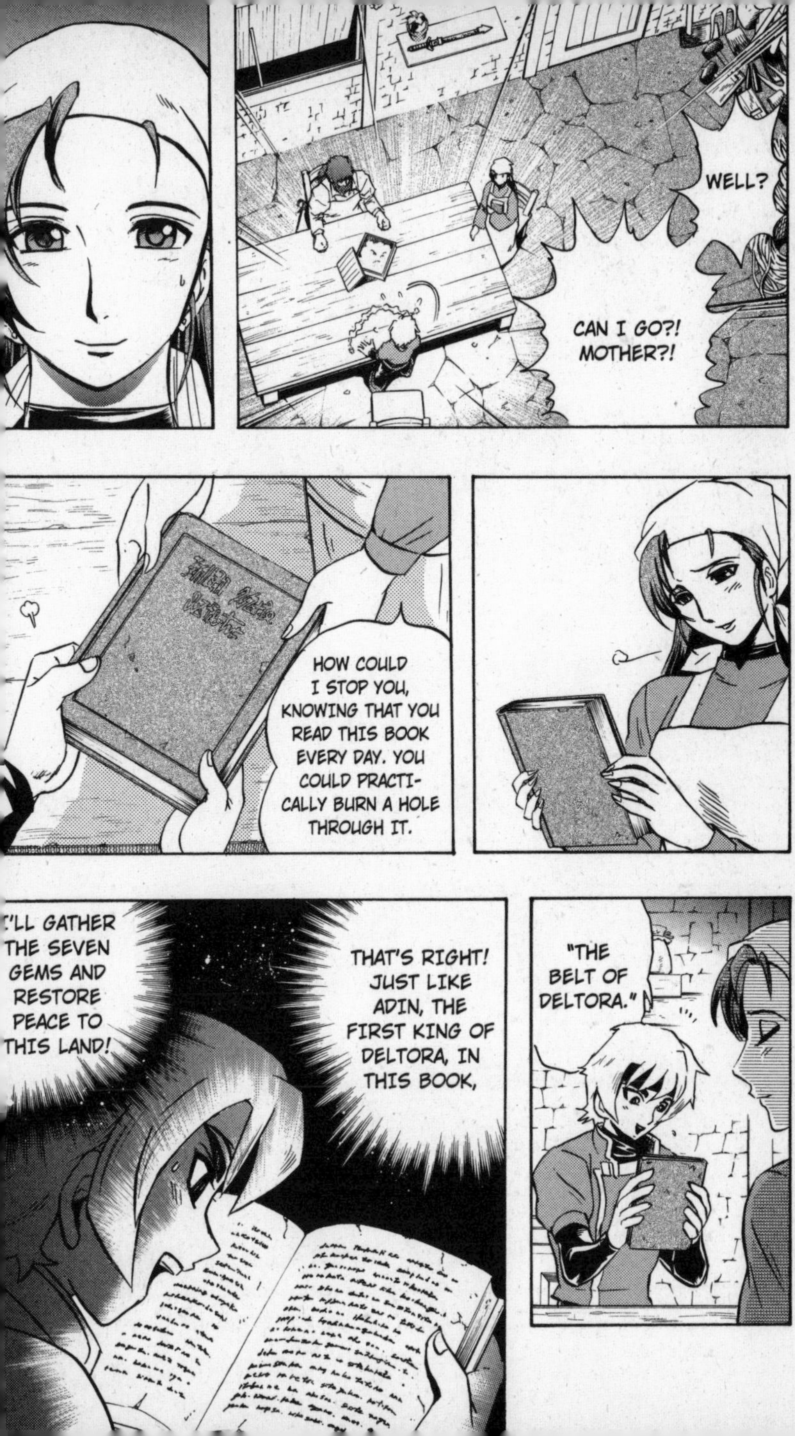
WELL?
CAN I GO?! MOTHER?!
HOW COULD I STOP YOU, KNOWING THAT YOU READ THIS BOOK EVERY DAY. YOU COULD PRACTI-CALLY BURN A HOLE THROUGH IT.
"THE BELT OF DELTORA."
THAT'S RIGHT! JUST LIKE ADIN, THE FIRST KING OF DELTORA, IN THIS BOOK,
I'LL GATHER THE SEVEN GEMS AND RESTORE PEACE TO THIS LAND!

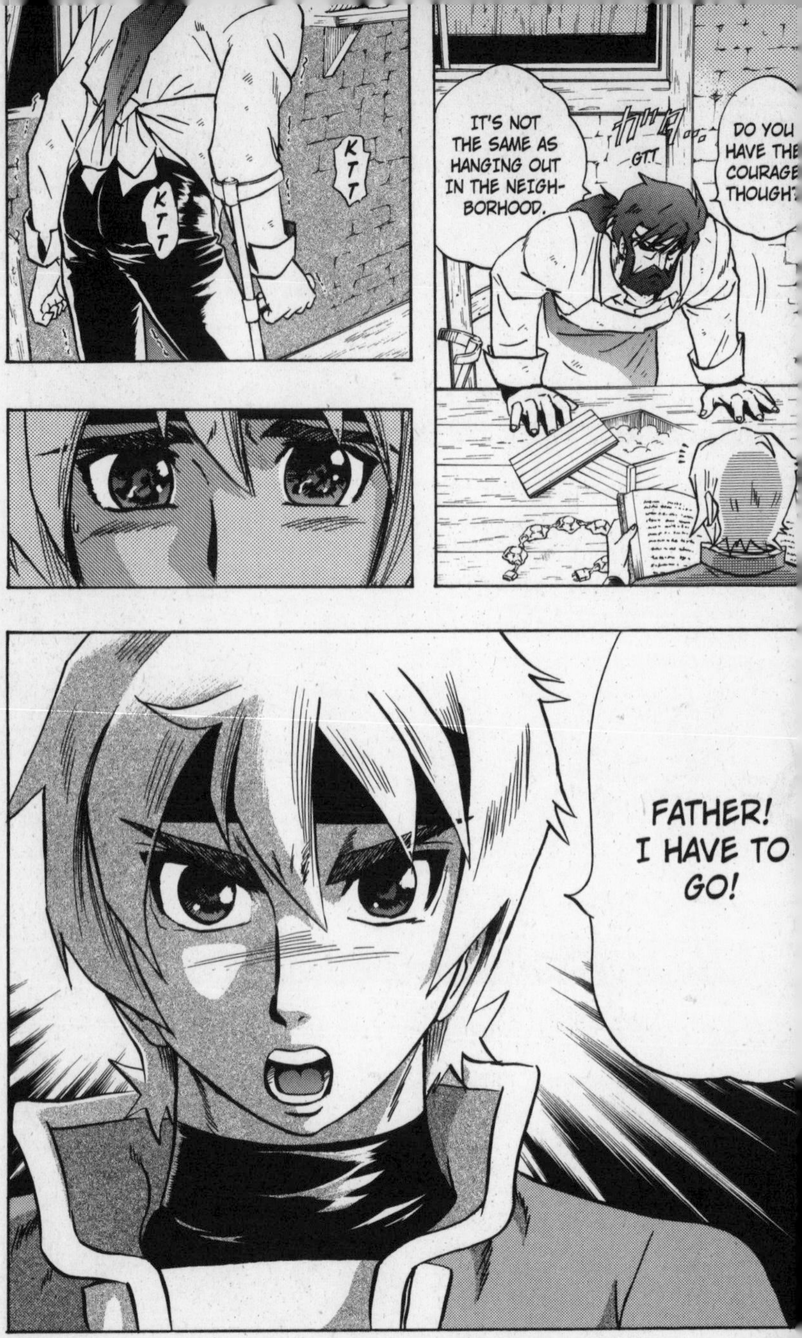
DO YOU HAVE THE COURAGE THOUGH
GTT
IT'S NOT THE SAME AS HANGING OUT IN THE NEIGH-BORHOOD.
KTT
KTT
FATHER! I HAVE TO GO!

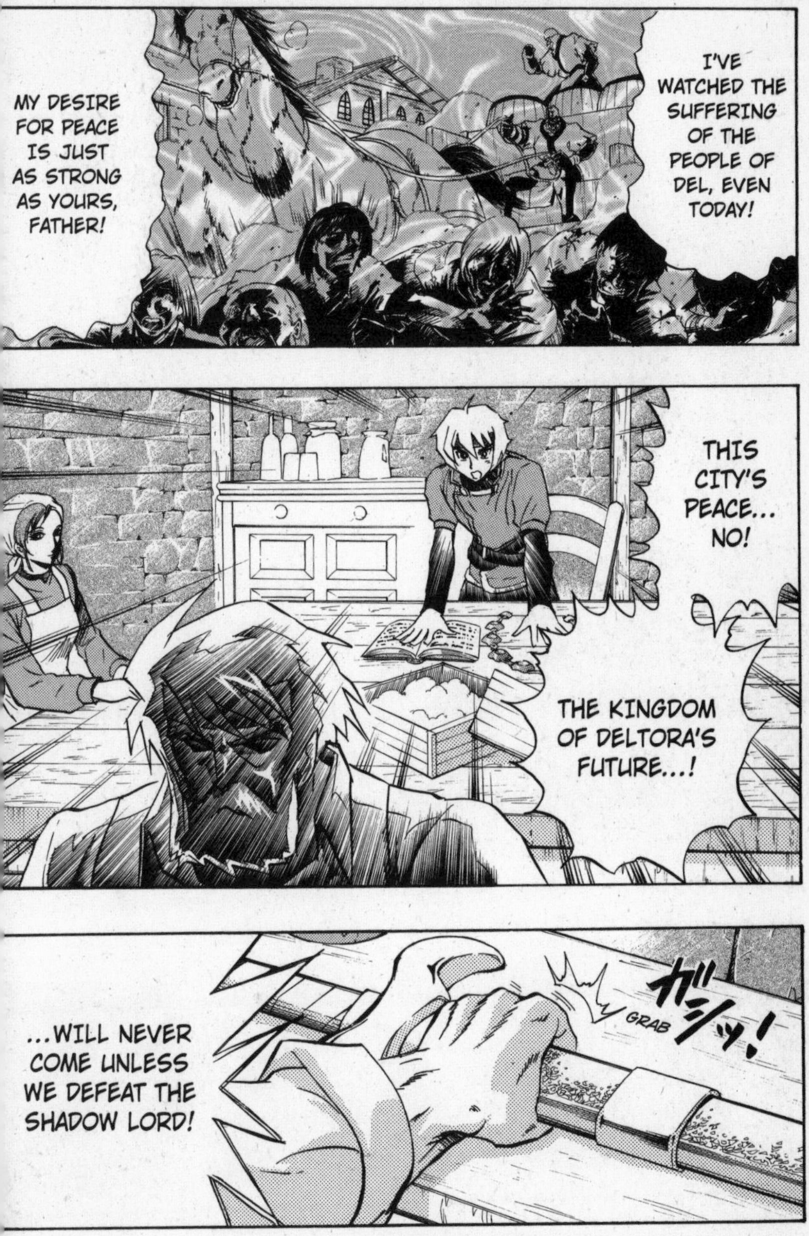
I'VE WATCHED THE SUFFERING OF THE PEOPLE OF DEL, EVEN TODAY!
MY DESIRE FOR PEACE IS JUST AS STRONG AS YOURS, FATHER!
THIS CITY'S PEACE... NO!
THE KINGDOM OF DELTORA'S FUTURE...!
ガシッ!
GRAB
...WILL NEVER COME UNLESS WE DEFEAT THE SHADOW LORD!

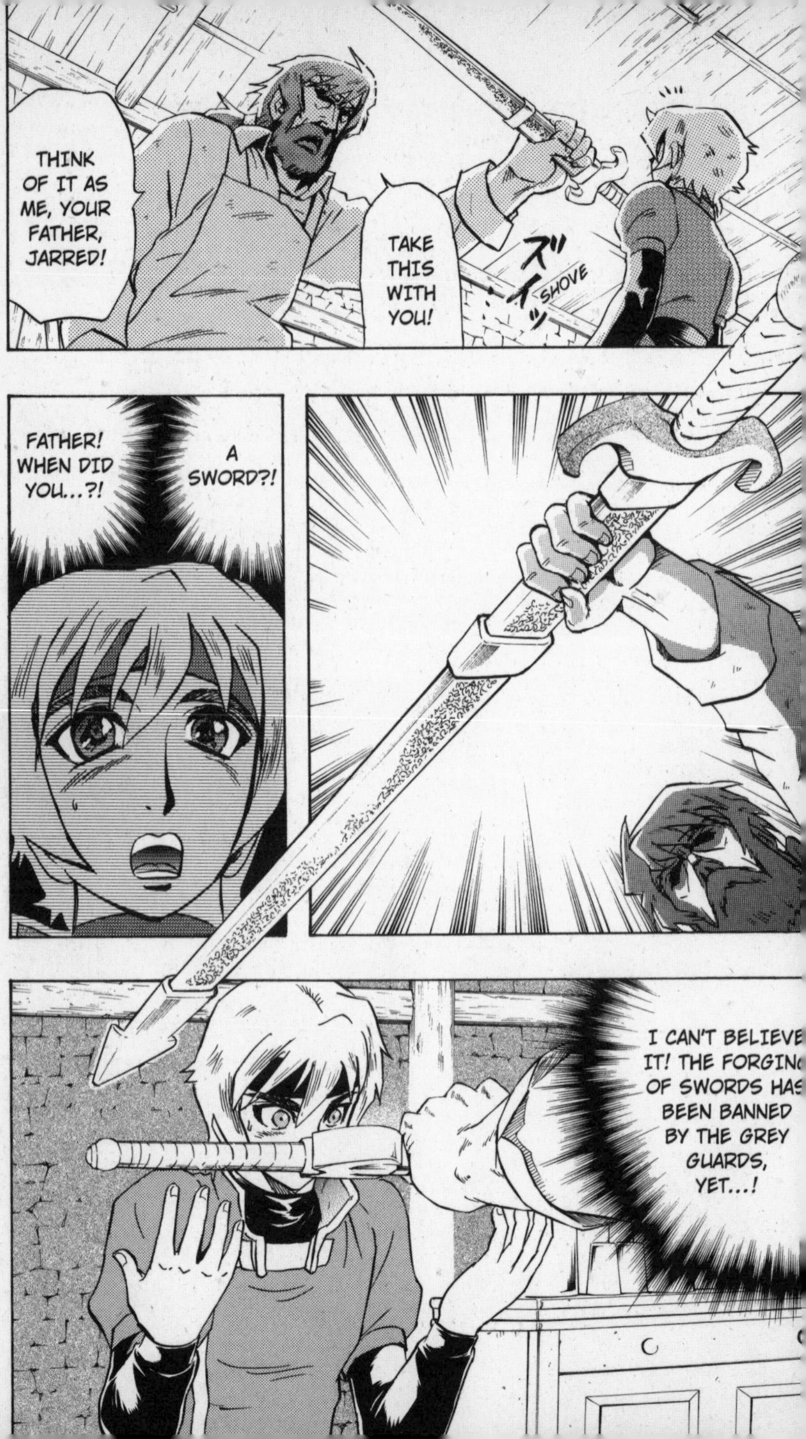
TAKE THIS WITH YOU!
ズイッ SHOVE
THINK OF IT AS ME, YOUR FATHER, JARRED!
A SWORD?!
FATHER! WHEN DID YOU...?!
I CAN'T BELIEVE IT! THE FORGING OF SWORDS HAS BEEN BANNED BY THE GREY GUARDS, YET...!

WHO WOULD HAVE IMAGINED THAT I WOULD OWN A SWORD!

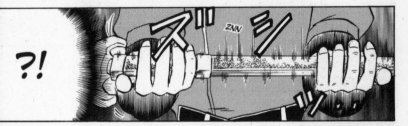

?!

ZNN

A-A REAL SWORD...

SNK

IT... IT'S HEAVY!

KSH

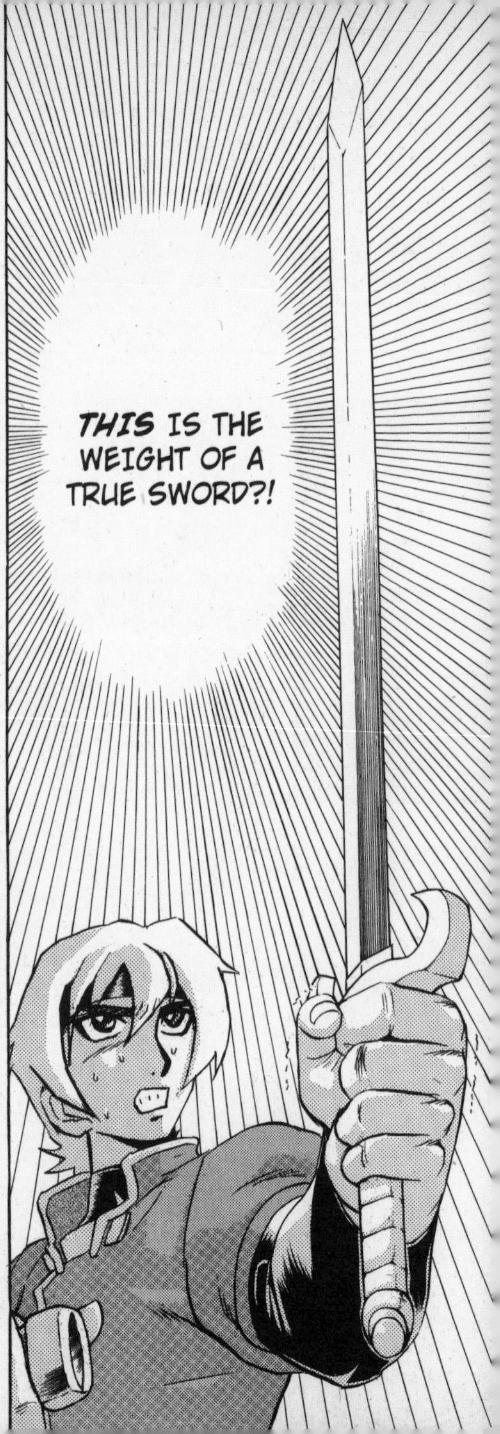
THIS IS THE WEIGHT OF A TRUE SWORD?!

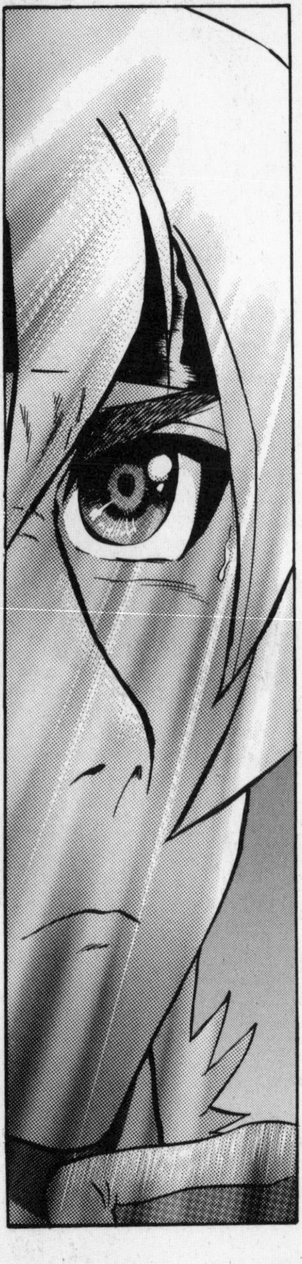

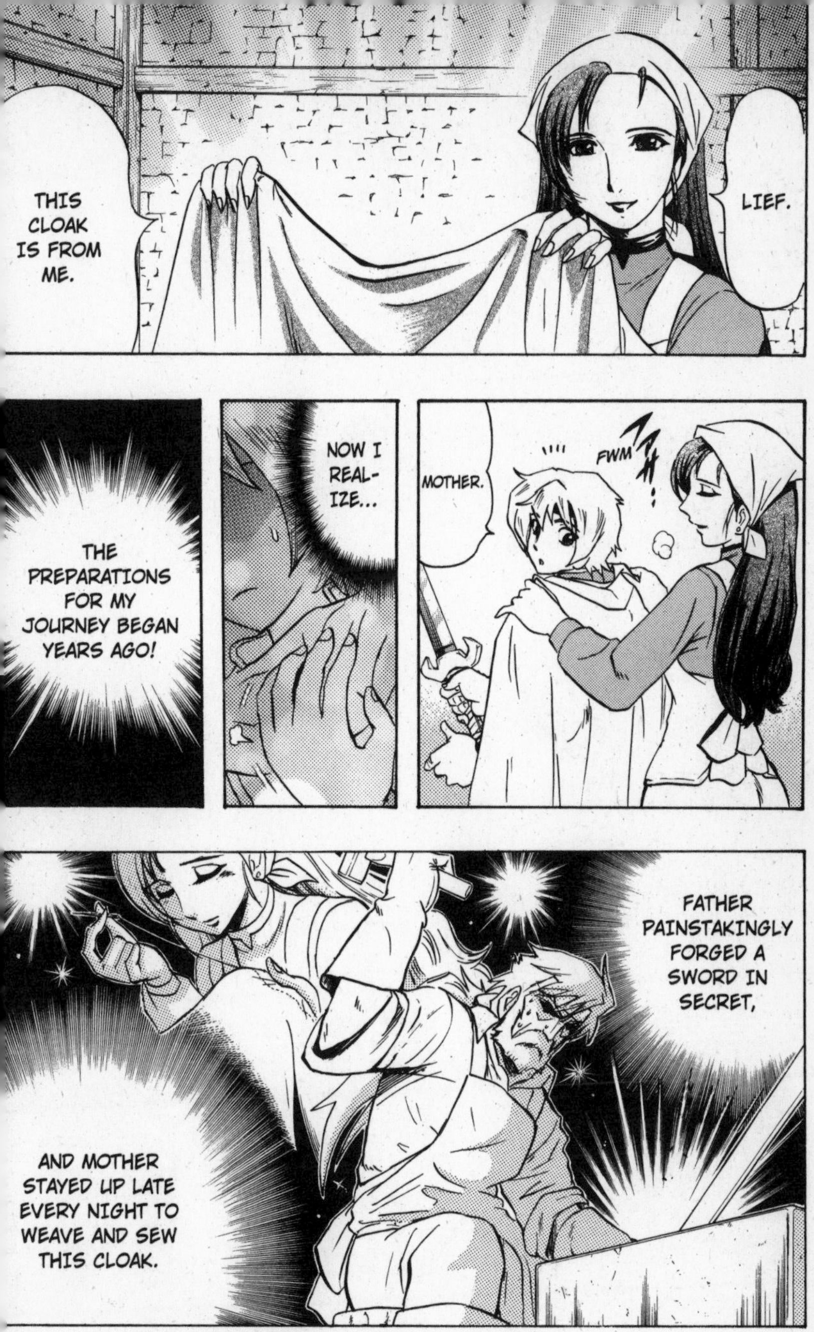
LIEF.
THIS CLOAK IS FROM ME.
FWM
MOTHER.
NOW I REAL-IZE...
THE PREPARATIONS FOR MY JOURNEY BEGAN YEARS AGO!
FATHER PAINSTAKINGLY FORGED A SWORD IN SECRET,
AND MOTHER STAYED UP LATE EVERY NIGHT TO WEAVE AND SEW THIS CLOAK.

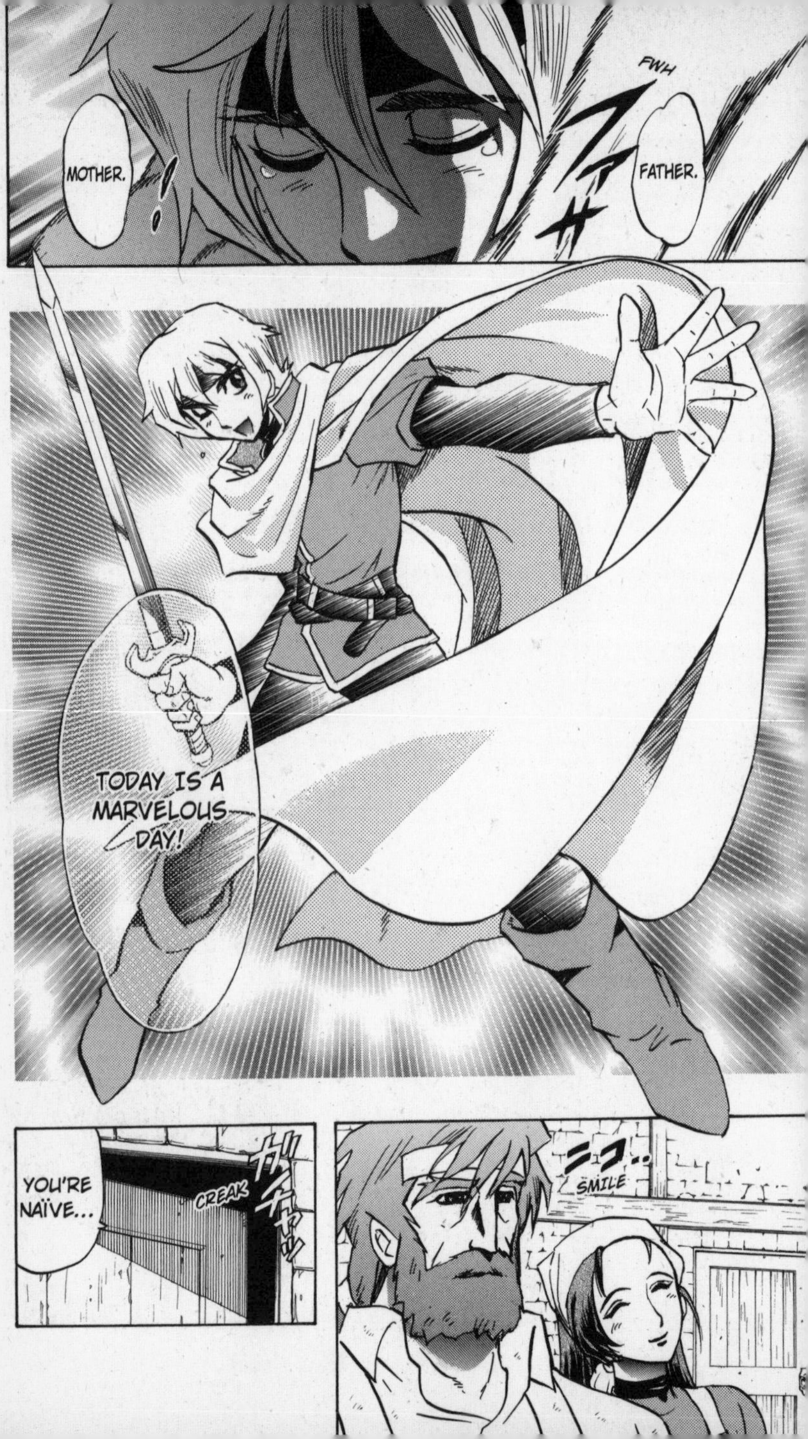
FWH
FATHER.
MOTHER.
TODAY IS A MARVELOUS DAY!
SMILE
CREAK
YOU'RE NAÏVE...

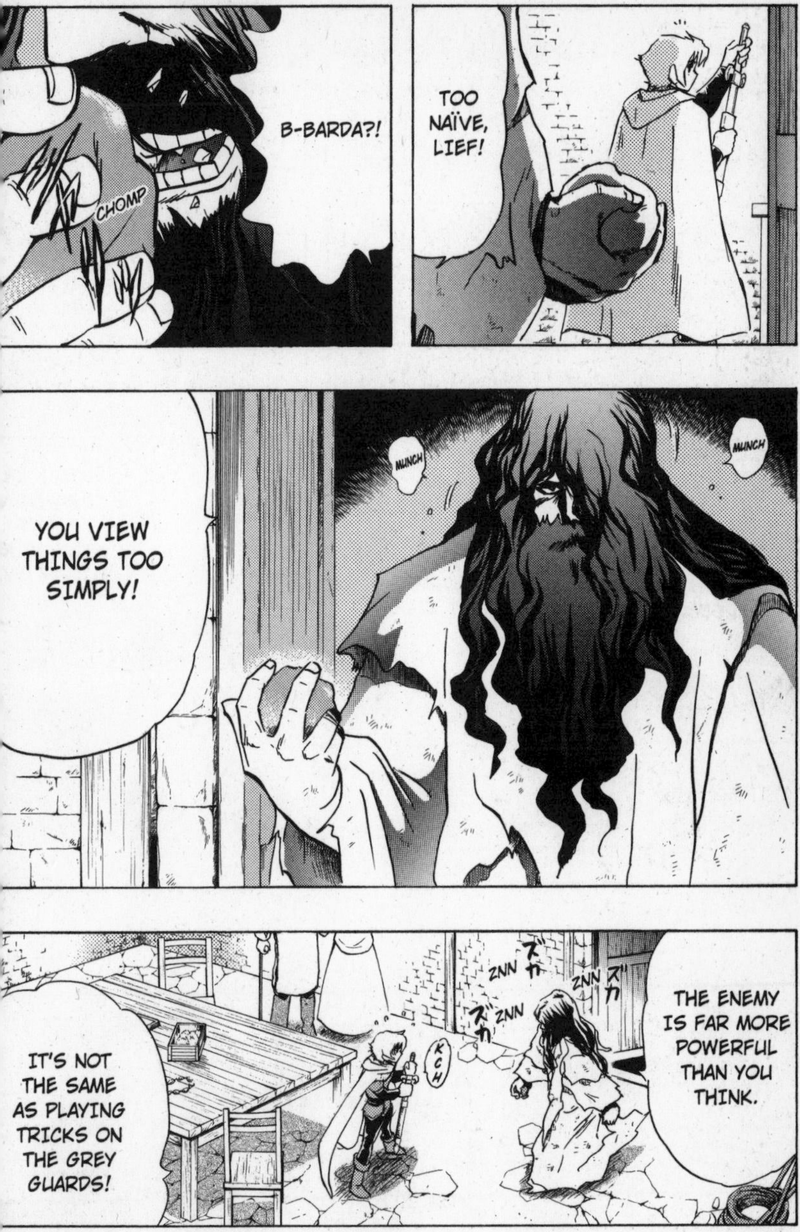
TOO NAÏVE, LIEF!
B-BARDA?!
CHOMP
MUNCH
MUNCH
YOU VIEW THINGS TOO SIMPLY!
THE ENEMY IS FAR MORE POWERFUL THAN YOU THINK.
ZNN ズカ
ZNN ズカ
ズカ ZNN
KCH
IT'S NOT THE SAME AS PLAYING TRICKS ON THE GREY GUARDS!

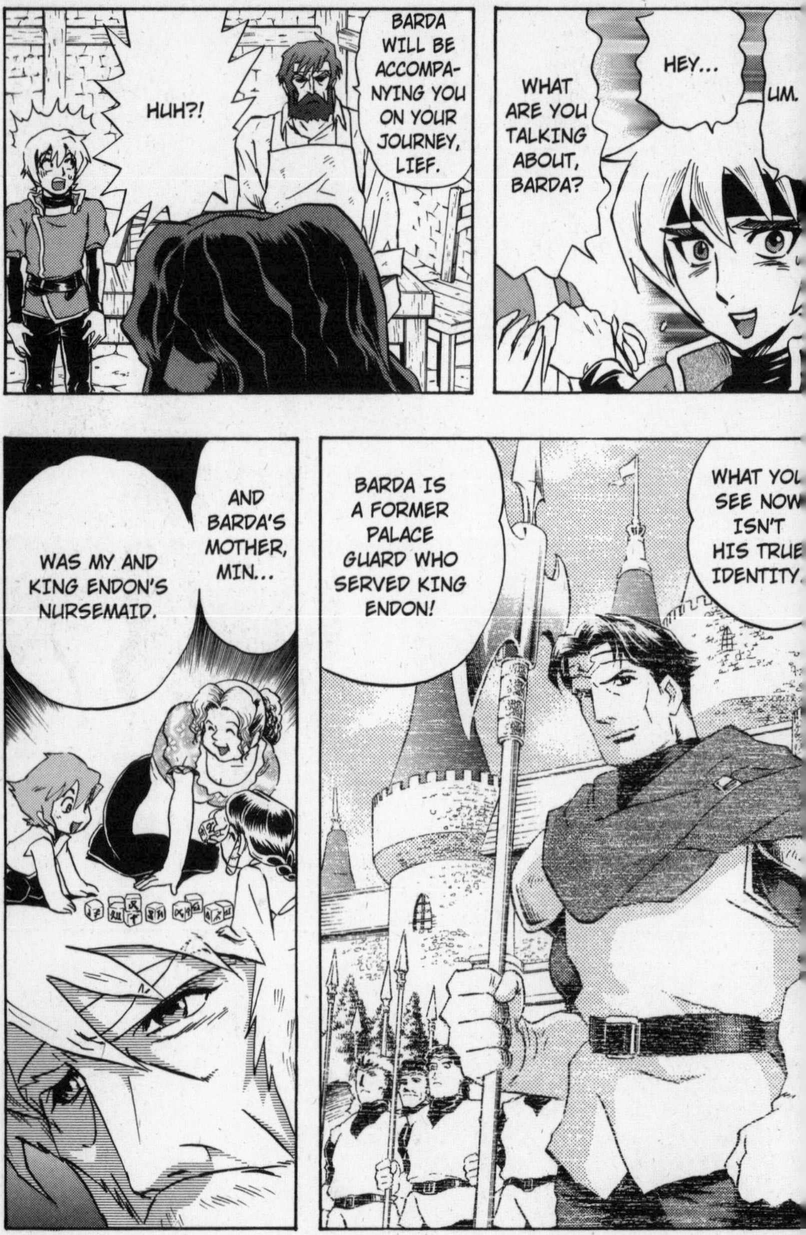
UM.
HEY...
WHAT ARE YOU TALKING ABOUT, BARDA?
BARDA WILL BE ACCOMPANYING YOU ON YOUR JOURNEY, LIEF.
HUH?!
WHAT YOU SEE NOW ISN'T HIS TRUE IDENTITY.
BARDA IS A FORMER PALACE GUARD WHO SERVED KING ENDON!
AND BARDA'S MOTHER, MIN...
WAS MY AND KING ENDON'S NURSEMAID.

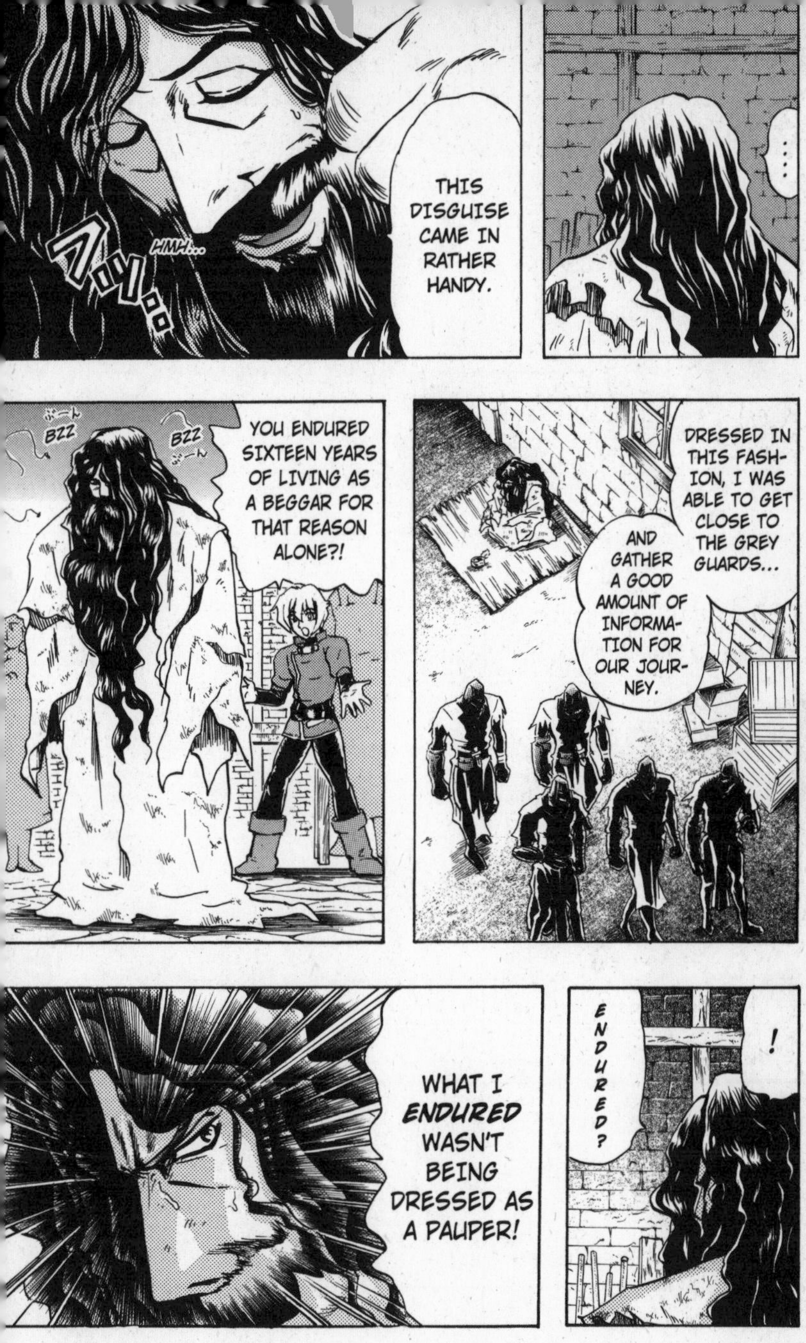
....
HMH...
THIS DISGUISE CAME IN RATHER HANDY.
DRESSED IN THIS FASHION, I WAS ABLE TO GET CLOSE TO THE GREY GUARDS...
AND GATHER A GOOD AMOUNT OF INFORMATION FOR OUR JOURNEY.
BZZ
ぶーん
BZZ
ぶーん
YOU ENDURED SIXTEEN YEARS OF LIVING AS A BEGGAR FOR THAT REASON ALONE?!
!
ENDURED?
WHAT I *ENDURED* WASN'T BEING DRESSED AS A PAUPER!

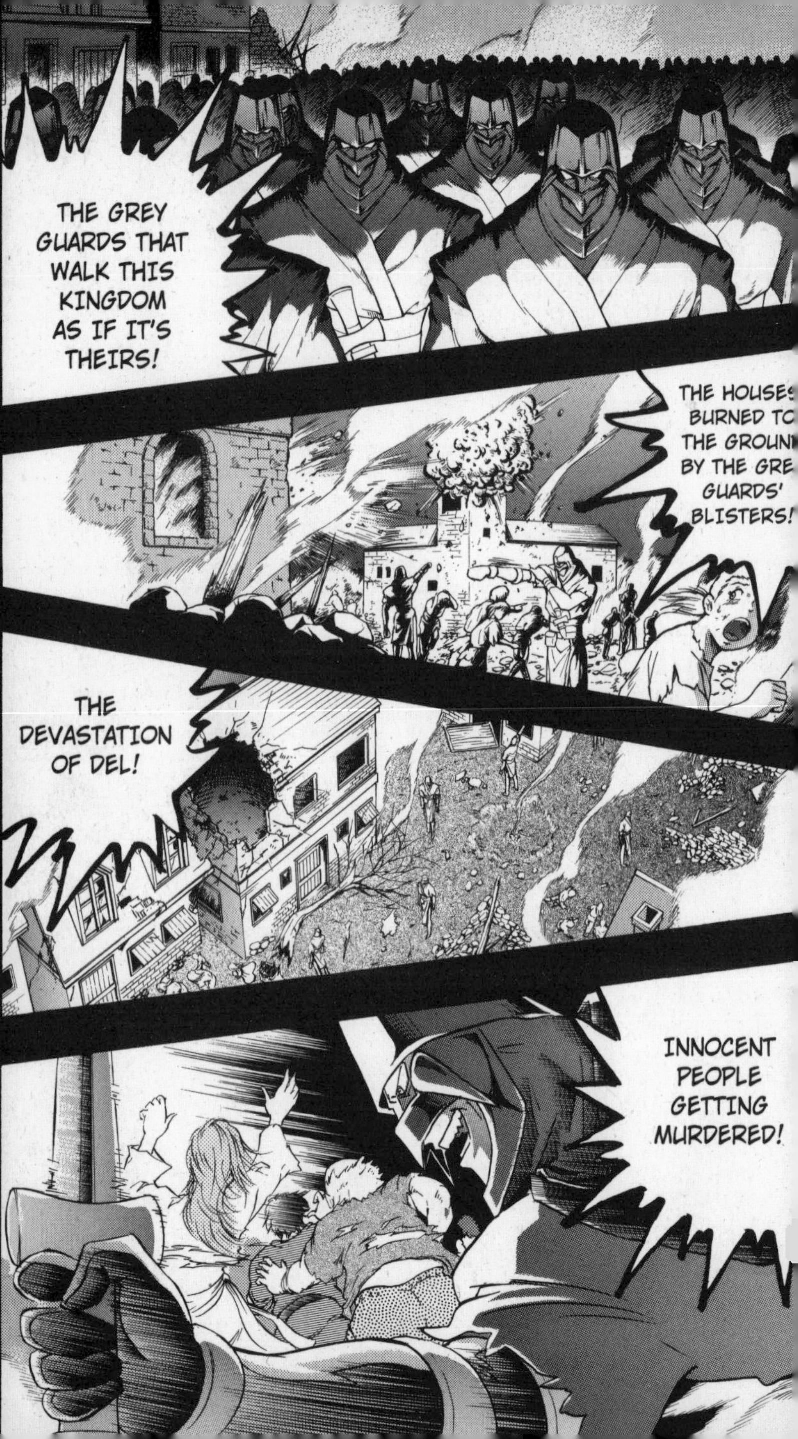
THE GREY GUARDS THAT WALK THIS KINGDOM AS IF IT'S THEIRS!
THE HOUSES BURNED TO THE GROUN BY THE GRE GUARDS' BLISTERS!
THE DEVASTATION OF DEL!
INNOCENT PEOPLE GETTING MURDERED!

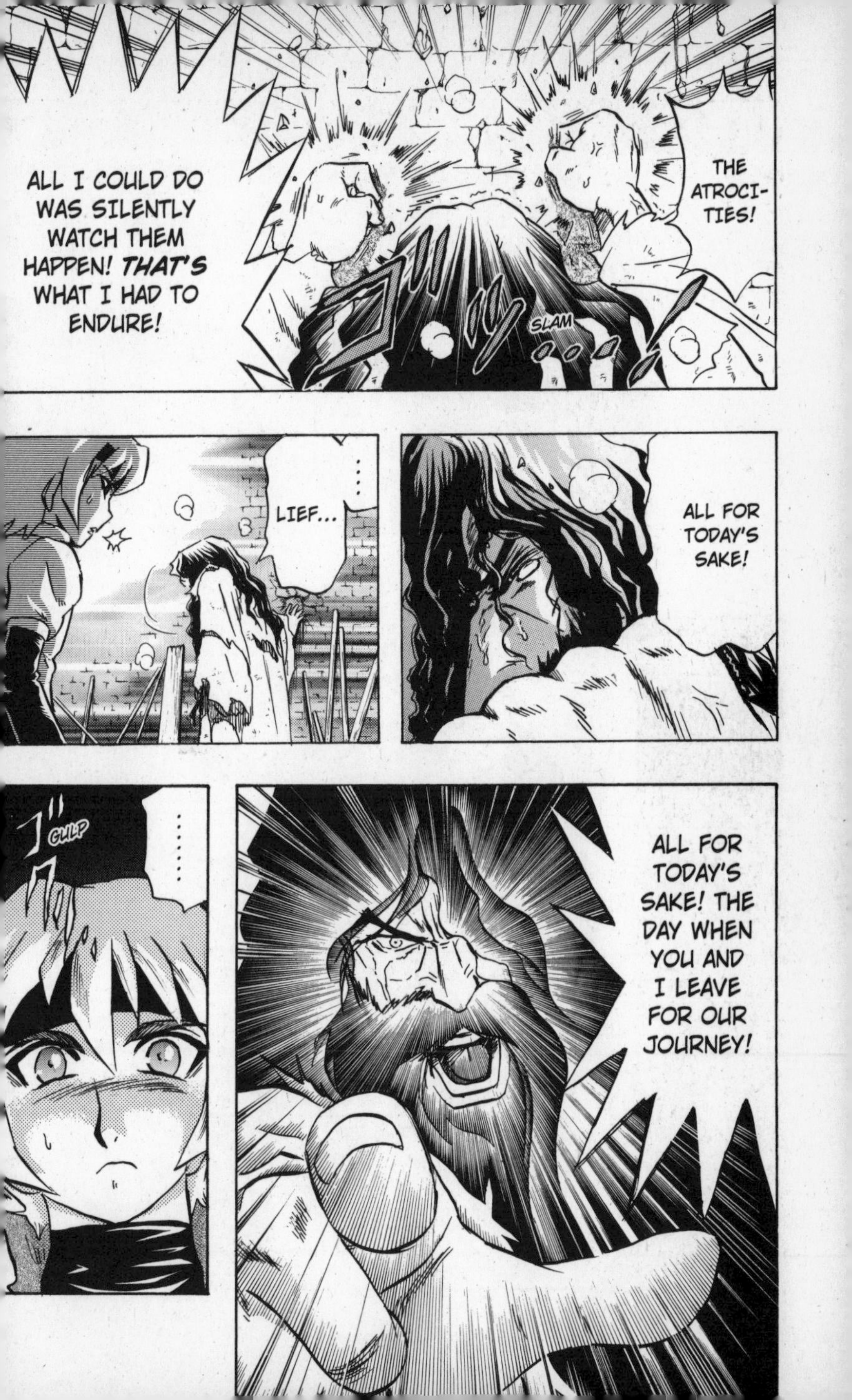
THE ATROCITIES!
ALL I COULD DO WAS SILENTLY WATCH THEM HAPPEN! *THAT'S* WHAT I HAD TO ENDURE!
SLAM
ALL FOR TODAY'S SAKE!
......
LIEF...
ALL FOR TODAY'S SAKE! THE DAY WHEN YOU AND I LEAVE FOR OUR JOURNEY!
......
GULP

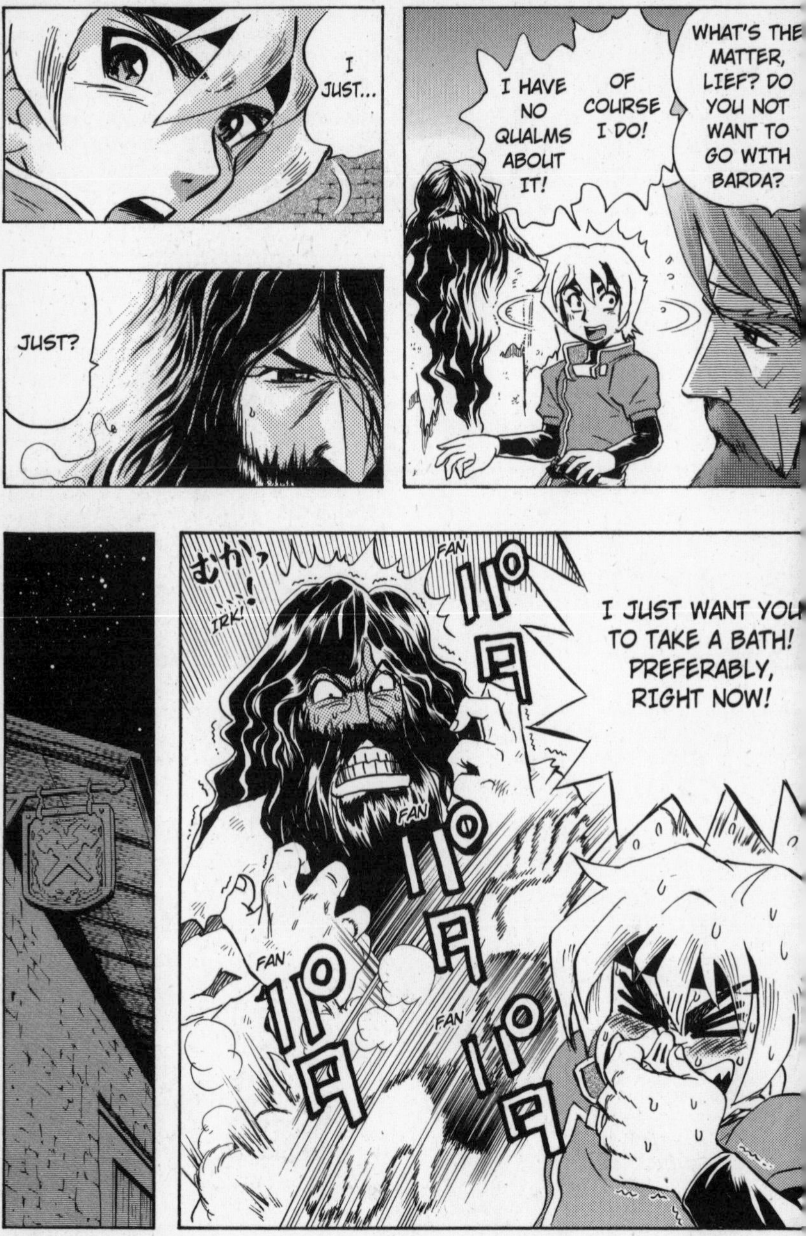
WHAT'S THE MATTER, LIEF? DO YOU NOT WANT TO GO WITH BARDA?
OF COURSE I DO!
I HAVE NO QUALMS ABOUT IT!
I JUST...
JUST?
I JUST WANT YOU TO TAKE A BATH! PREFERABLY, RIGHT NOW!
FAN
むかっ!
IRK!
FAN
FAN
FAN

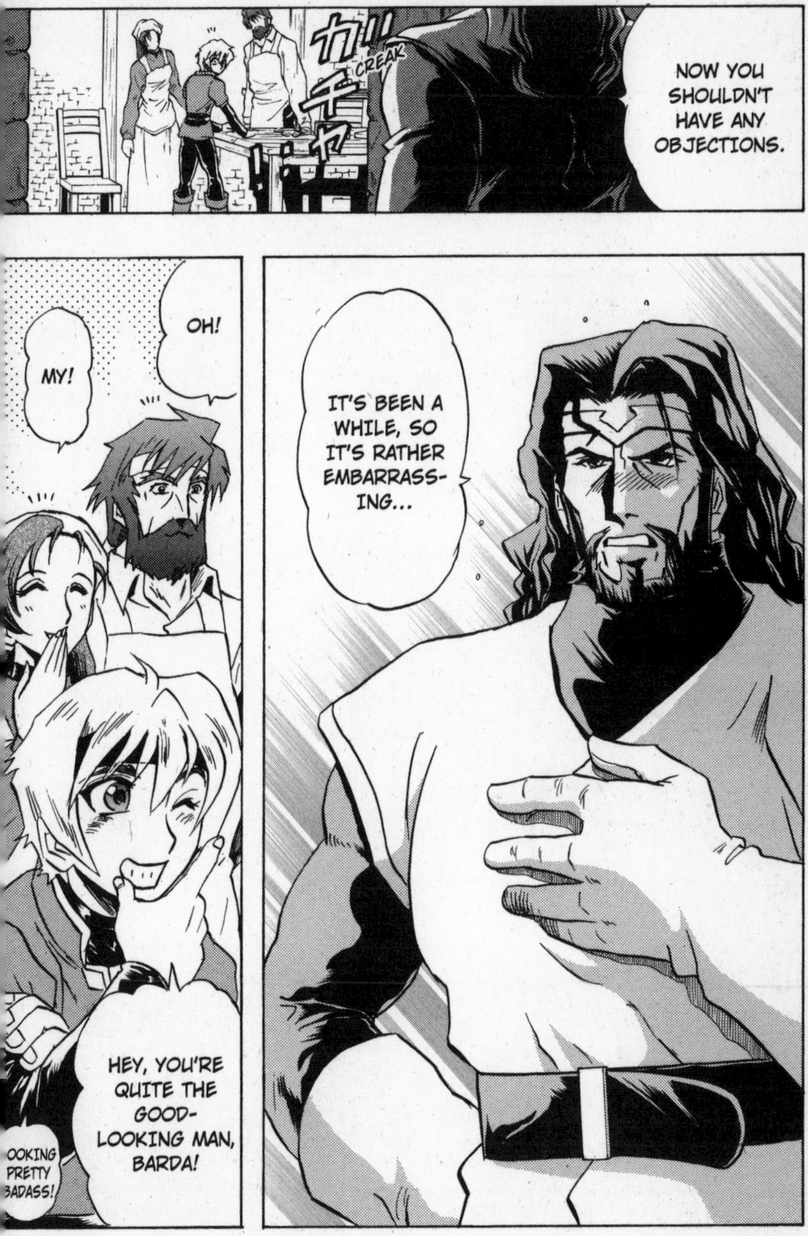
NOW YOU SHOULDN'T HAVE ANY OBJECTIONS.
CREAK
IT'S BEEN A WHILE, SO IT'S RATHER EMBARRASS-ING...
OH!
MY!
HEY, YOU'RE QUITE THE GOOD-LOOKING MAN, BARDA!
OOKING PRETTY BADASS!

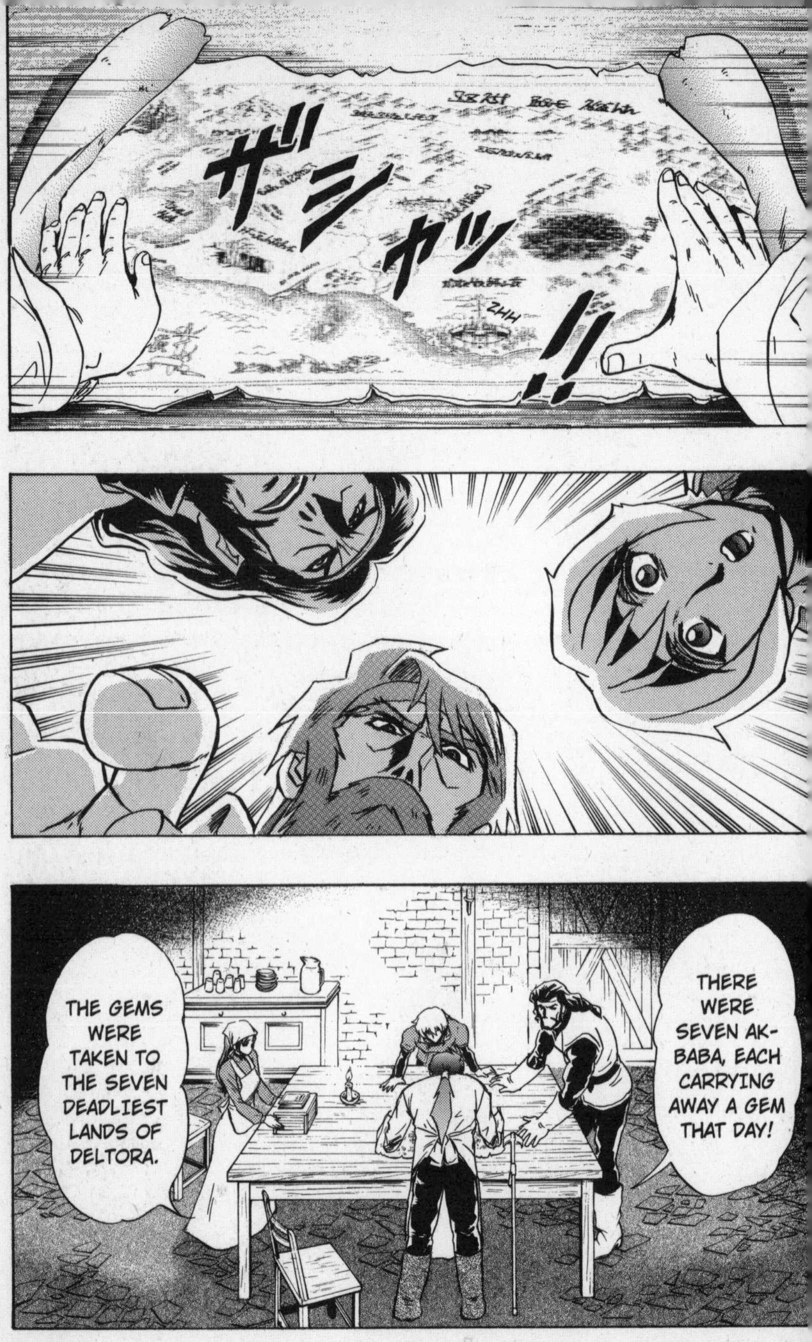
ザシャッ!!
THERE WERE SEVEN AK-BABA, EACH CARRYING AWAY A GEM THAT DAY!
THE GEMS WERE TAKEN TO THE SEVEN DEADLIEST LANDS OF DELTORA.

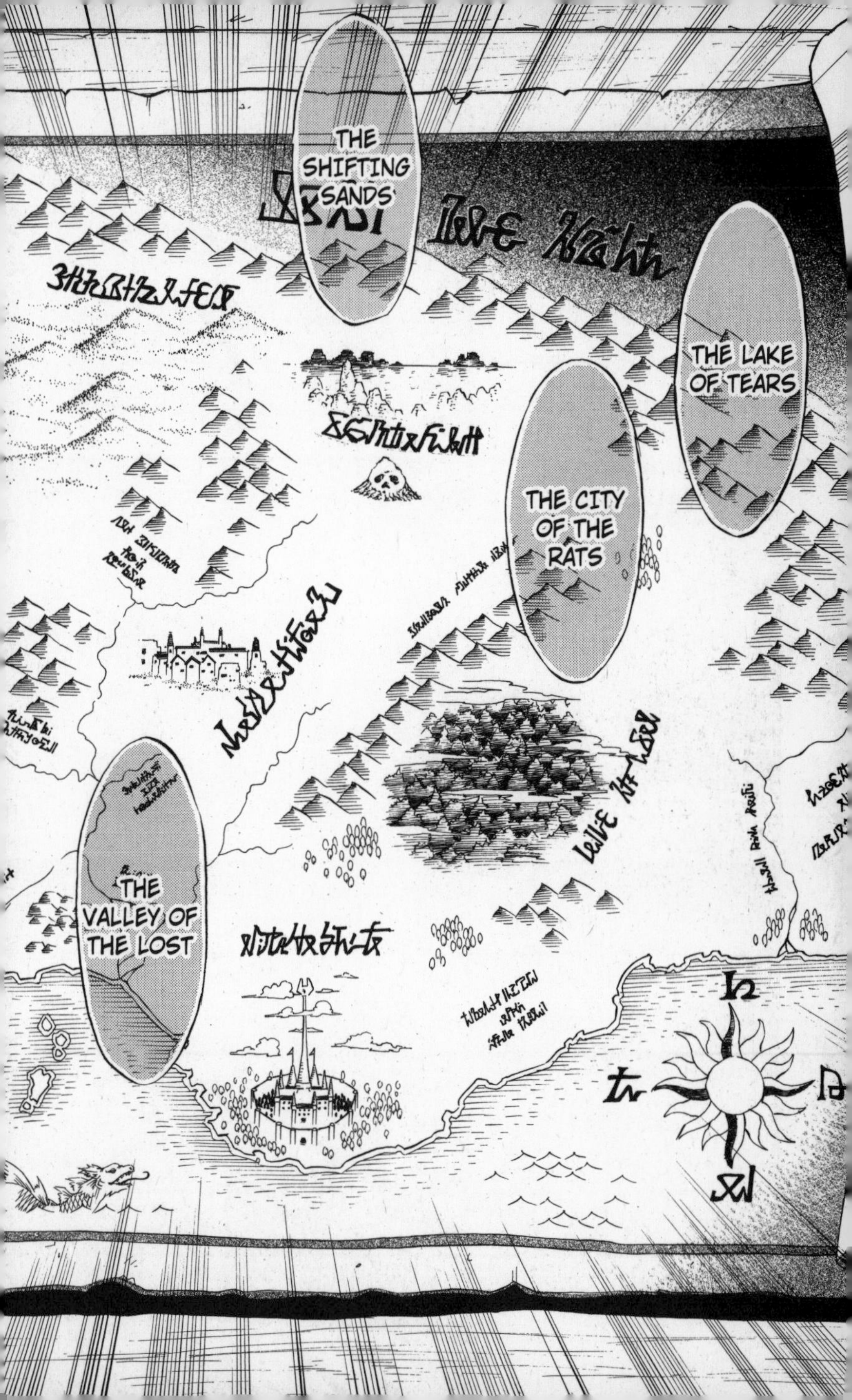

THE SHIFTING SANDS
THE LAKE OF TEARS
THE CITY OF THE RATS
THE VALLEY OF THE LOST

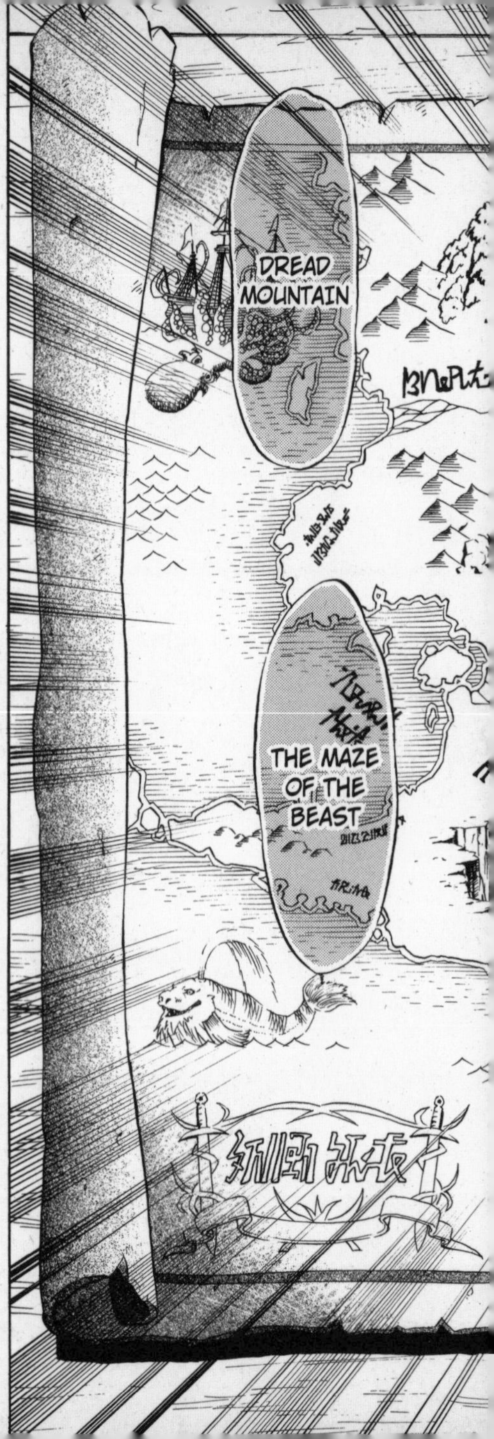
DREAD MOUNTAIN
THE MAZE OF THE BEAST
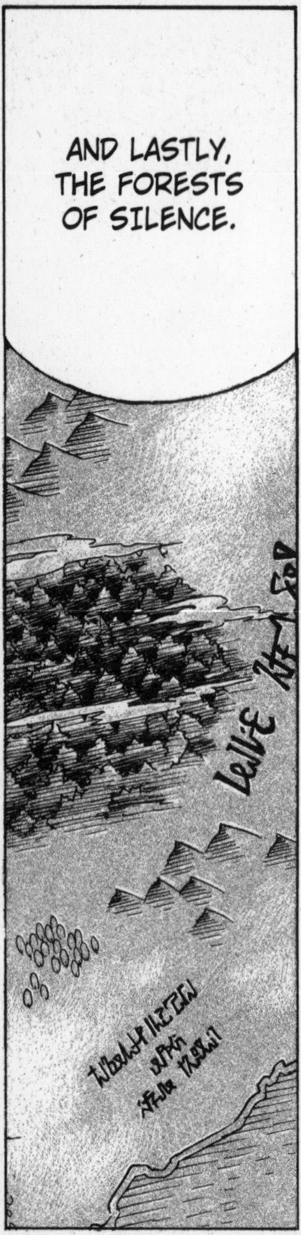
AND LASTLY, THE FORESTS OF SILENCE.

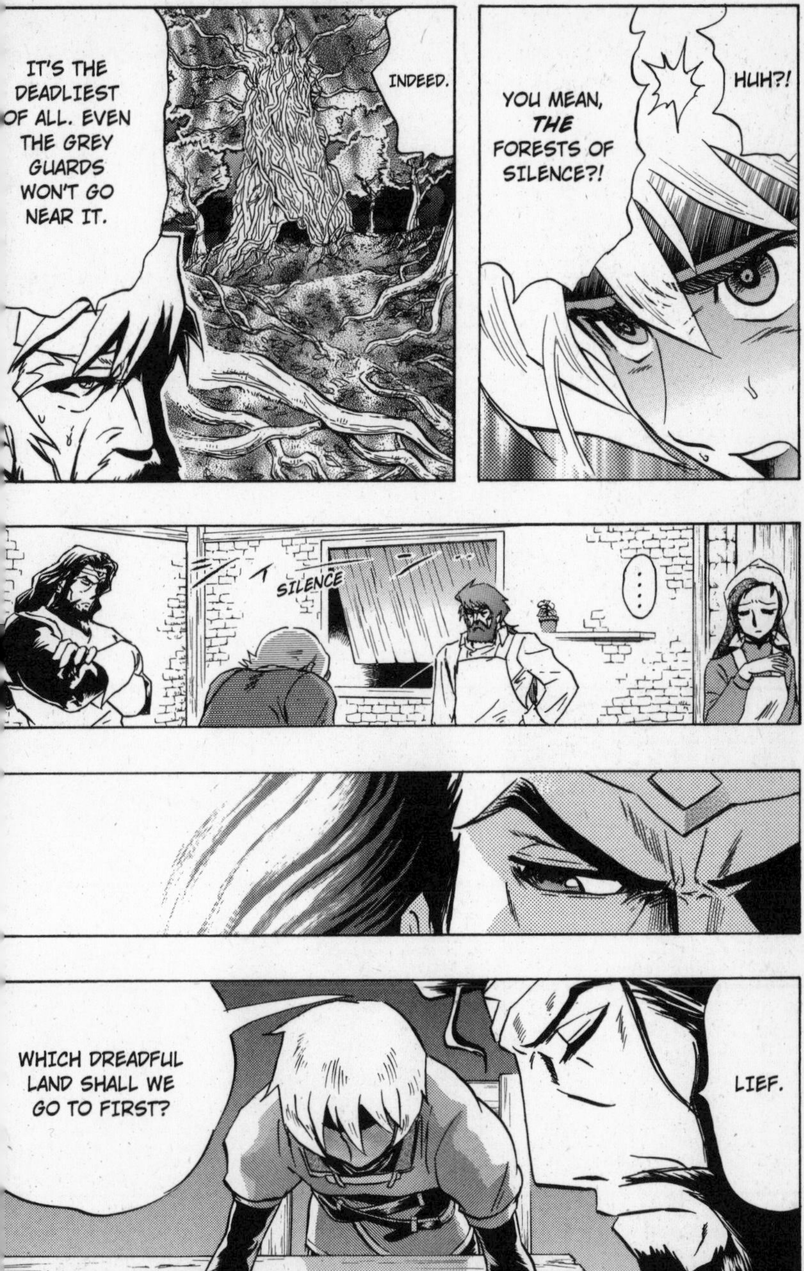
HUH?!
YOU MEAN, *THE* FORESTS OF SILENCE?!
INDEED.
IT'S THE DEADLIEST OF ALL. EVEN THE GREY GUARDS WON'T GO NEAR IT.
....
SILENCE
LIEF.
WHICH DREADFUL LAND SHALL WE GO TO FIRST?

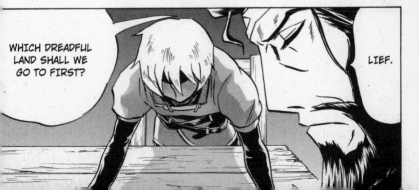

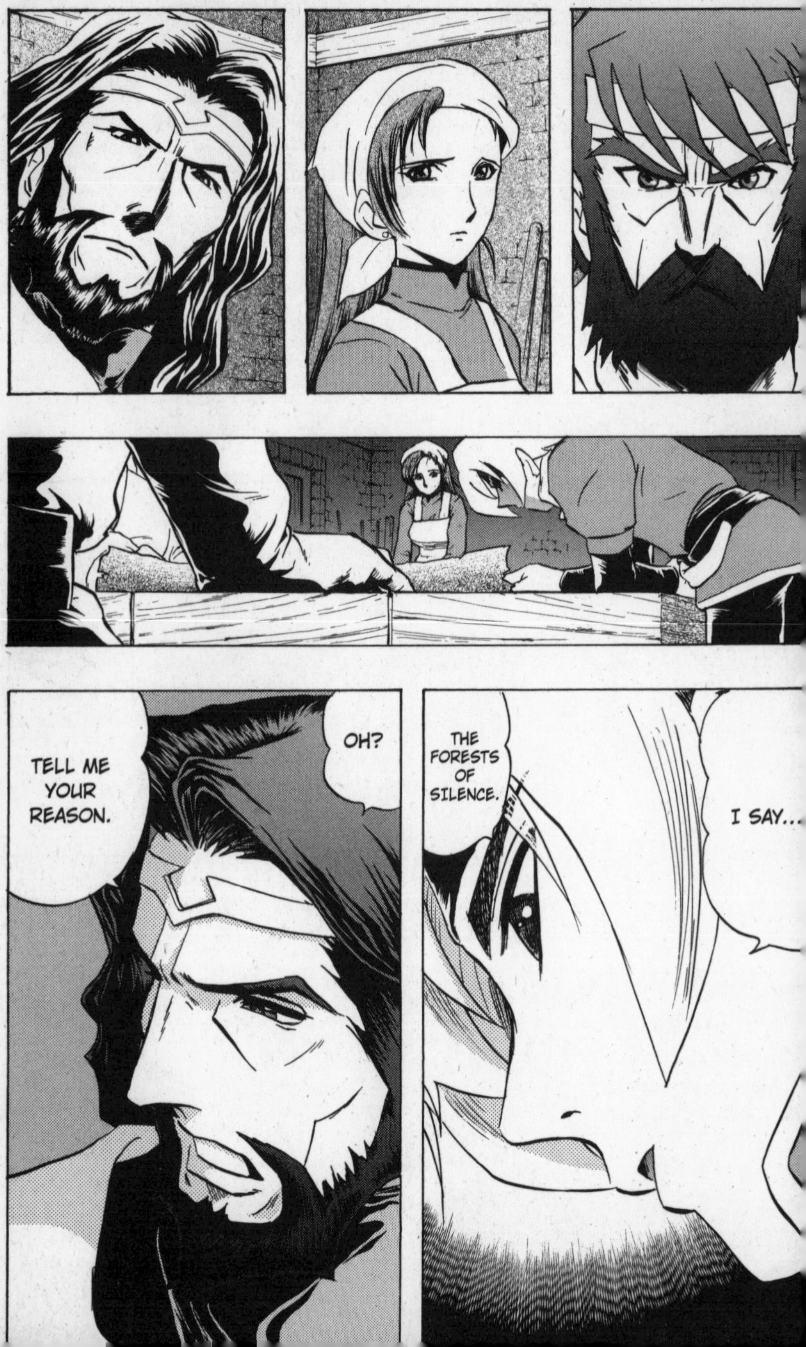
I SAY...
THE FORESTS OF SILENCE.
OH?
TELL ME YOUR REASON.

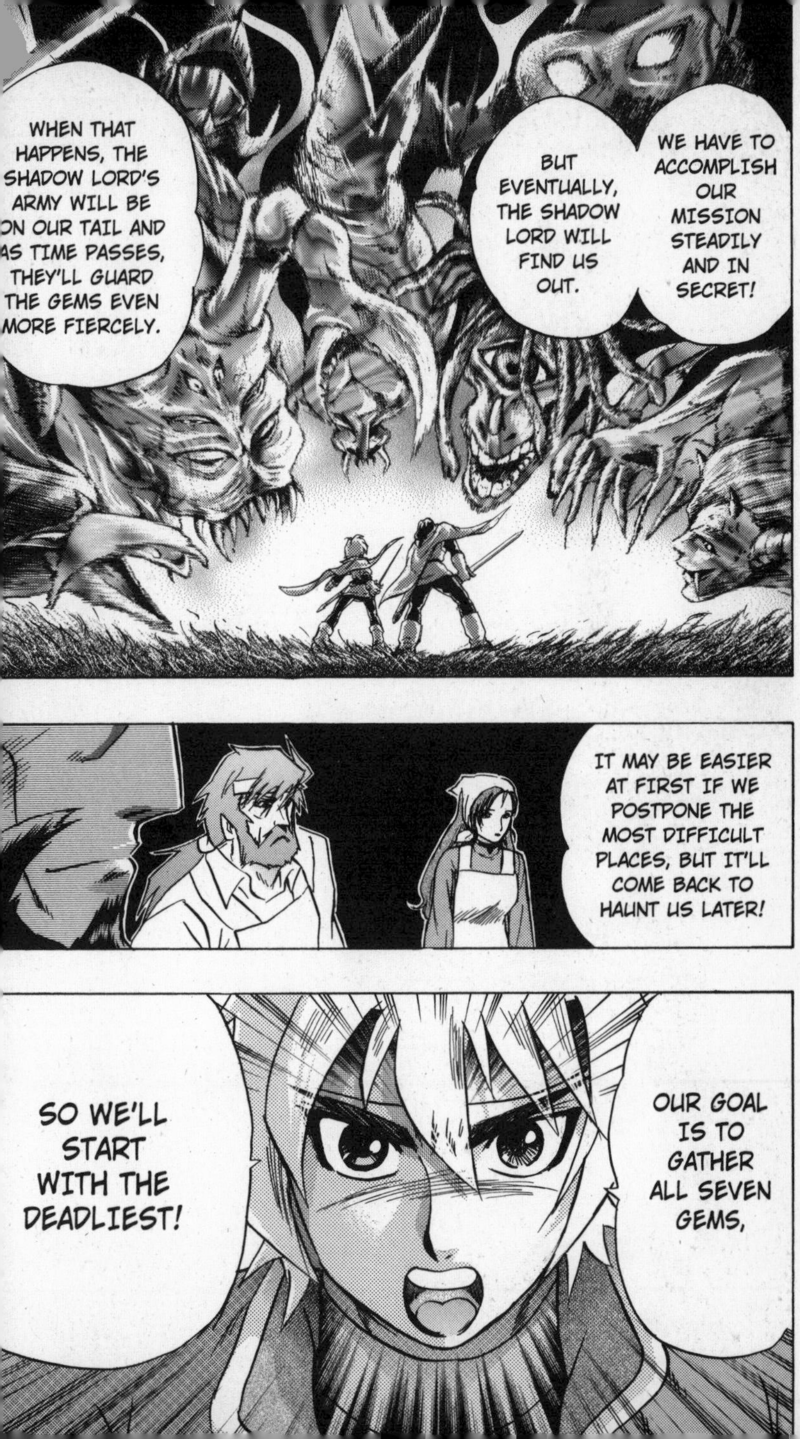

WE HAVE TO ACCOMPLISH OUR MISSION STEADILY AND IN SECRET!
BUT EVENTUALLY, THE SHADOW LORD WILL FIND US OUT.
WHEN THAT HAPPENS, THE SHADOW LORD'S ARMY WILL BE ON OUR TAIL AND AS TIME PASSES, THEY'LL GUARD THE GEMS EVEN MORE FIERCELY.
IT MAY BE EASIER AT FIRST IF WE POSTPONE THE MOST DIFFICULT PLACES, BUT IT'LL COME BACK TO HAUNT US LATER!
OUR GOAL IS TO GATHER ALL SEVEN GEMS,
SO WE'LL START WITH THE DEADLIEST!

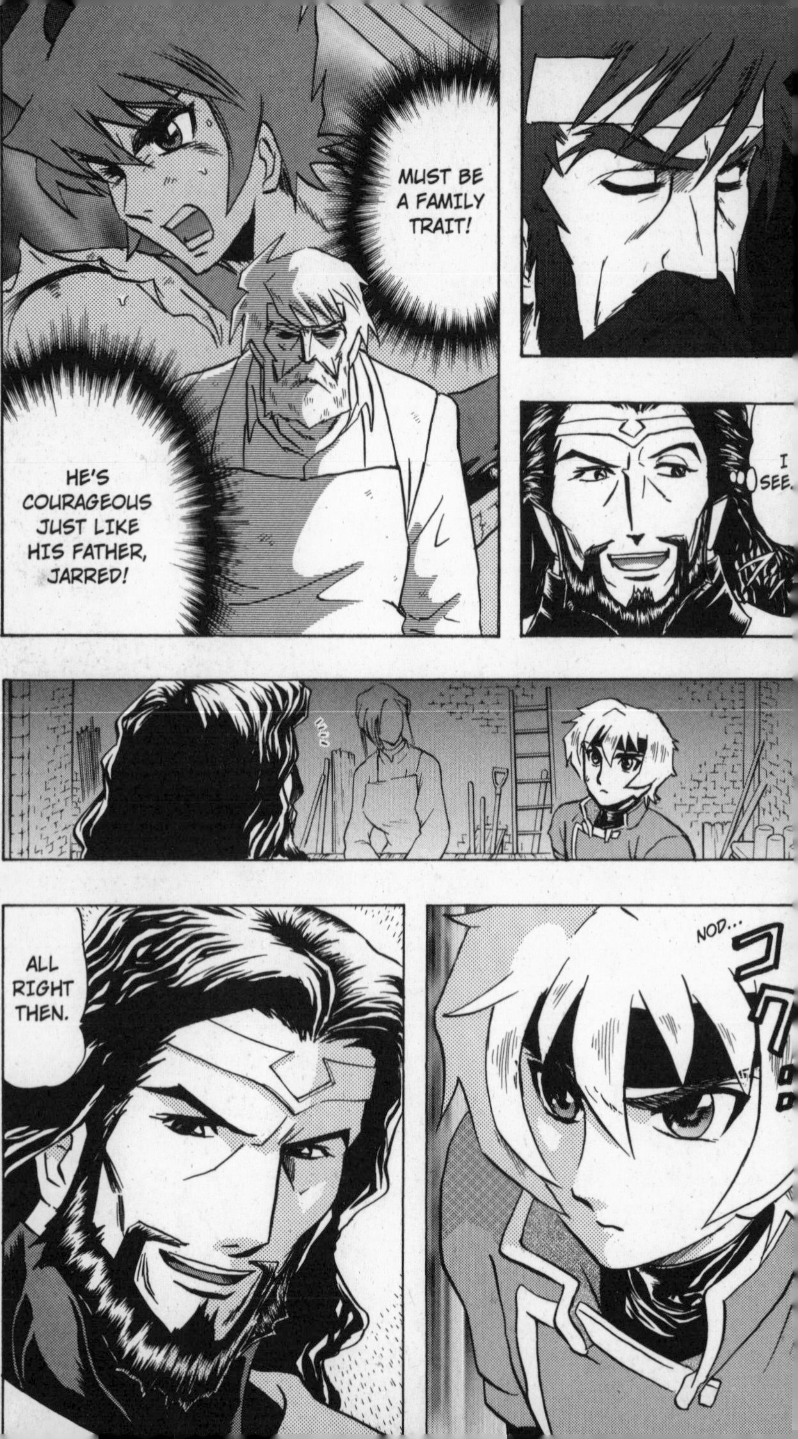
I SEE.
MUST BE A FAMILY TRAIT!
HE'S COURAGEOUS JUST LIKE HIS FATHER, JARRED!
NOD...
ALL RIGHT THEN.

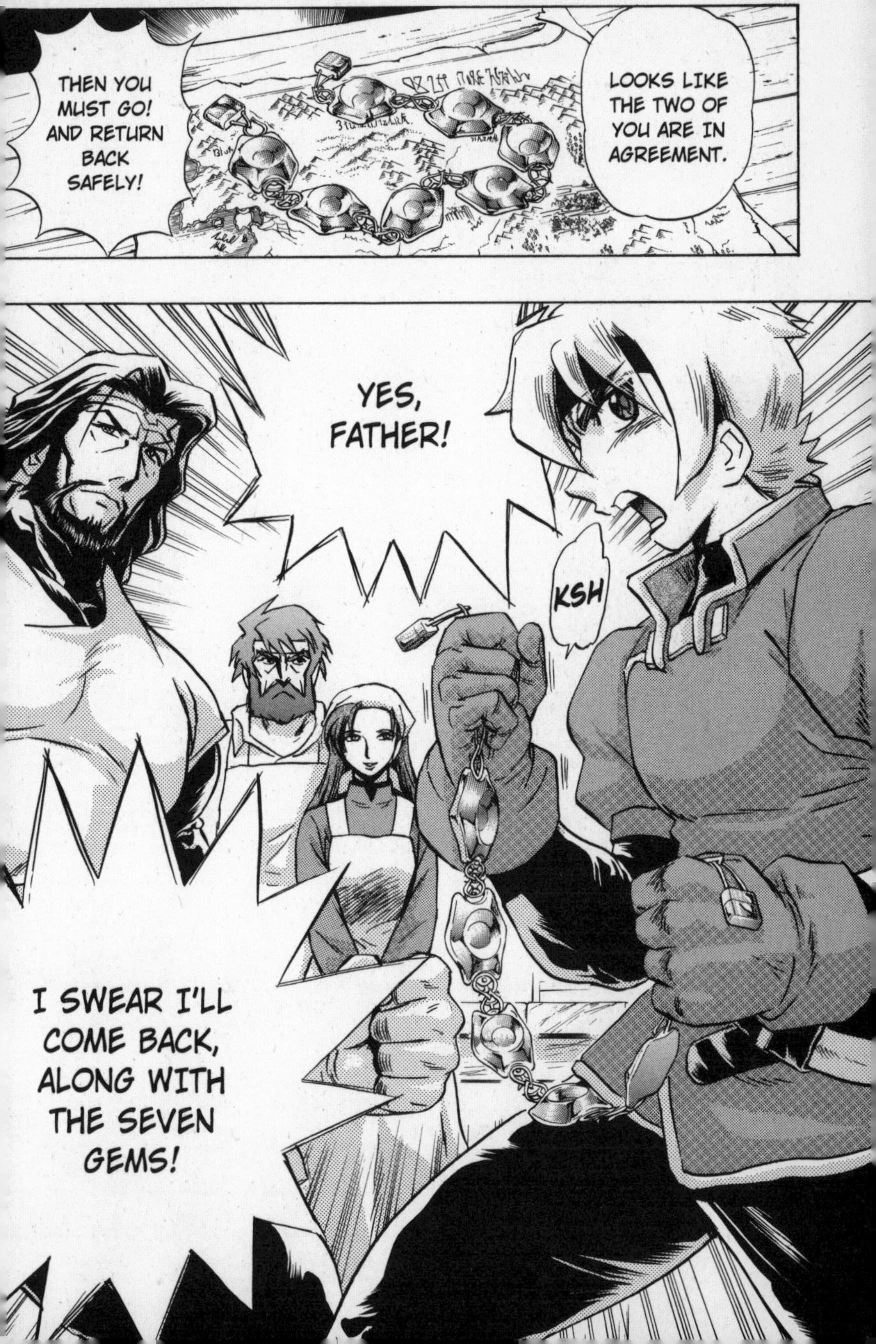
LOOKS LIKE THE TWO OF YOU ARE IN AGREEMENT.
THEN YOU MUST GO! AND RETURN BACK SAFELY!
YES, FATHER!
KSH
I SWEAR I'LL COME BACK, ALONG WITH THE SEVEN GEMS!

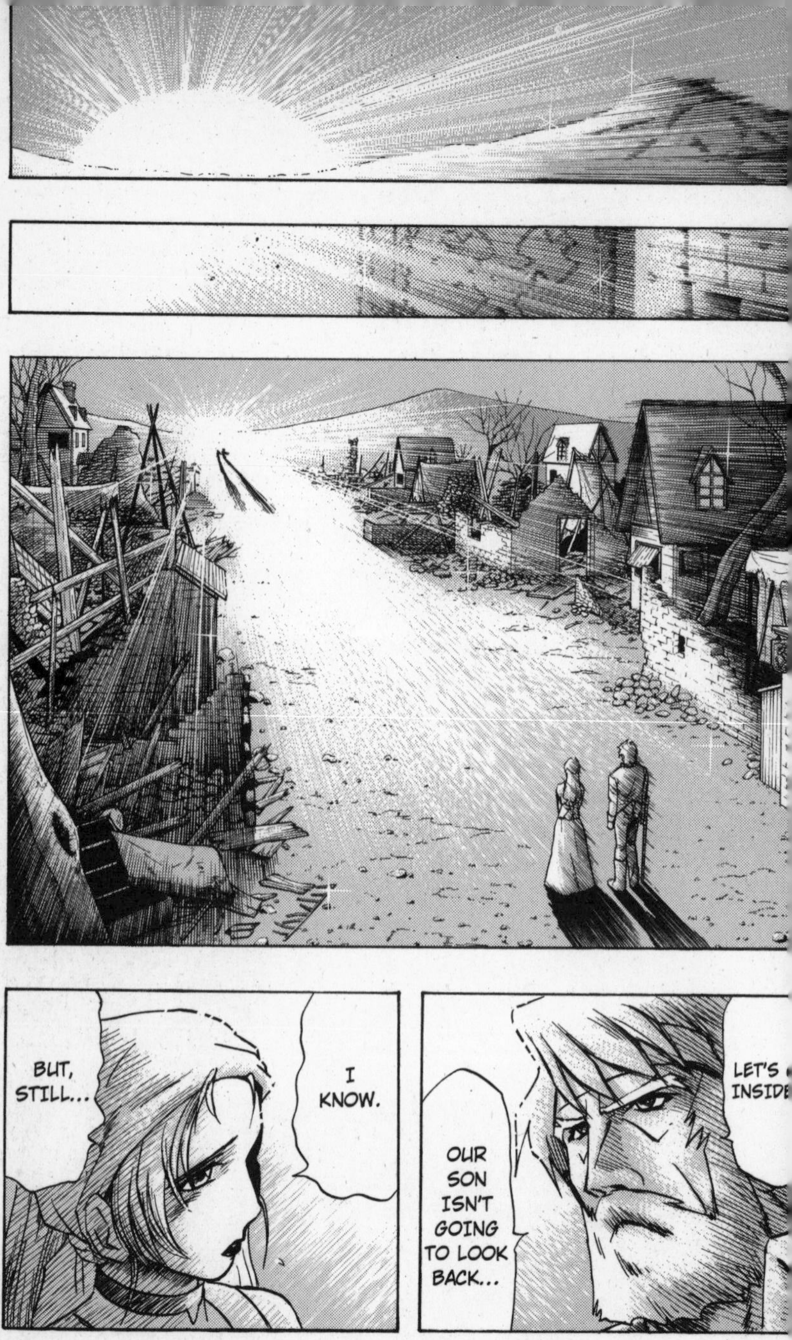
LET'S INSIDE
OUR SON ISN'T GOING TO LOOK BACK...
I KNOW.
BUT, STILL...

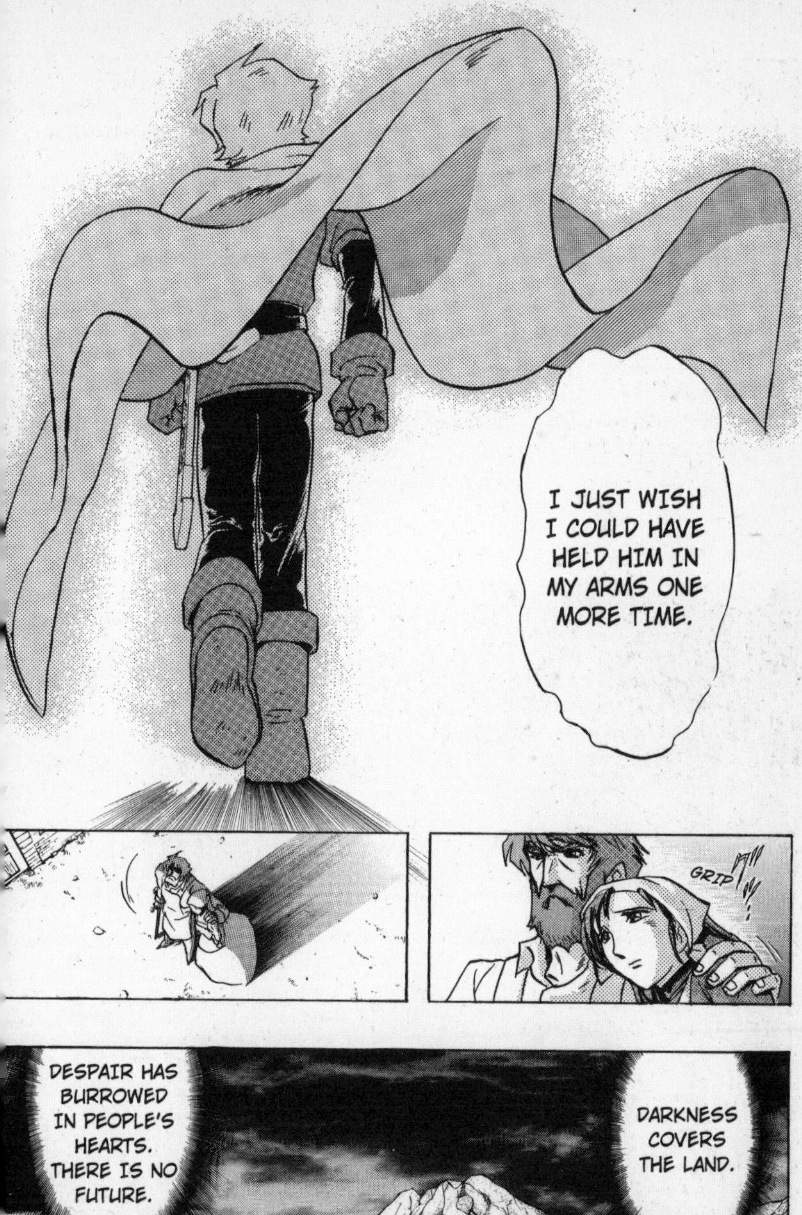
I JUST WISH I COULD HAVE HELD HIM IN MY ARMS ONE MORE TIME.
GRIP
DARKNESS COVERS THE LAND.
DESPAIR HAS BURROWED IN PEOPLE'S HEARTS. THERE IS NO FUTURE.

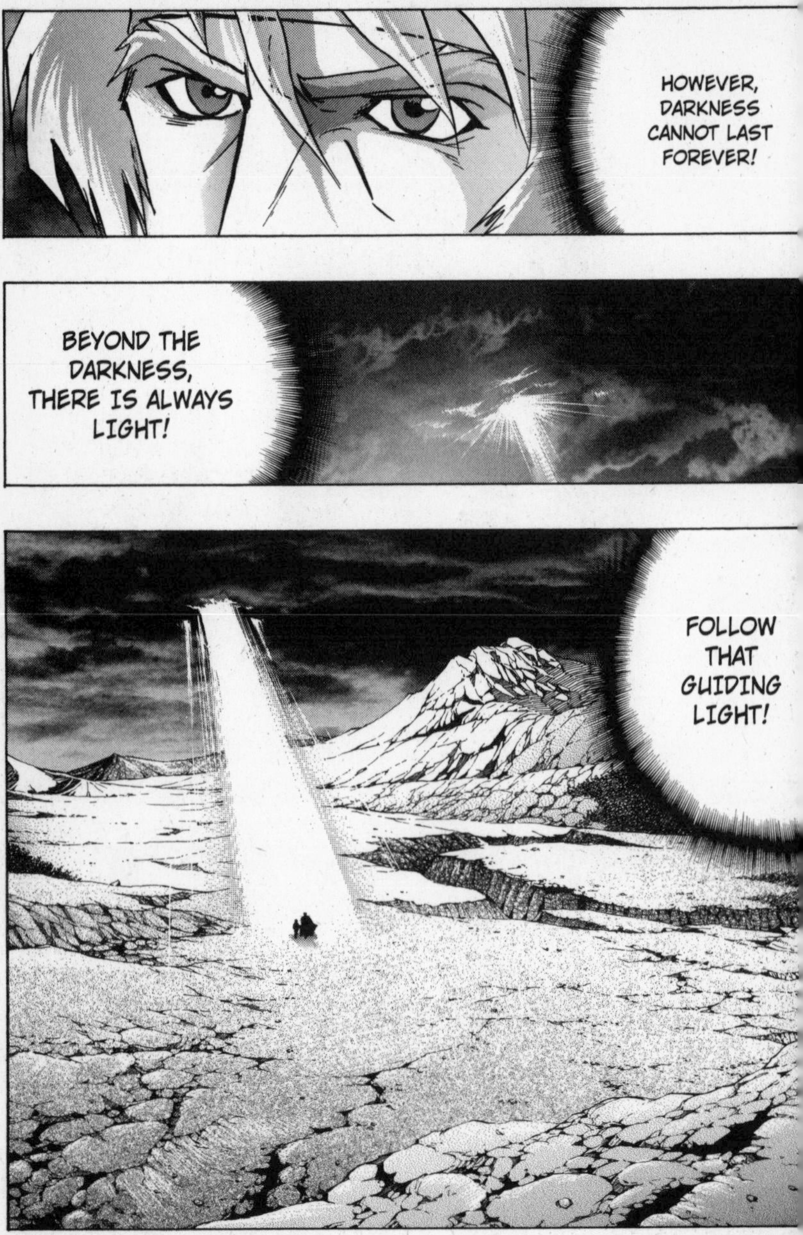
HOWEVER, DARKNESS CANNOT LAST FOREVER!
BEYOND THE DARKNESS, THERE IS ALWAYS LIGHT!
FOLLOW THAT GUIDING LIGHT!

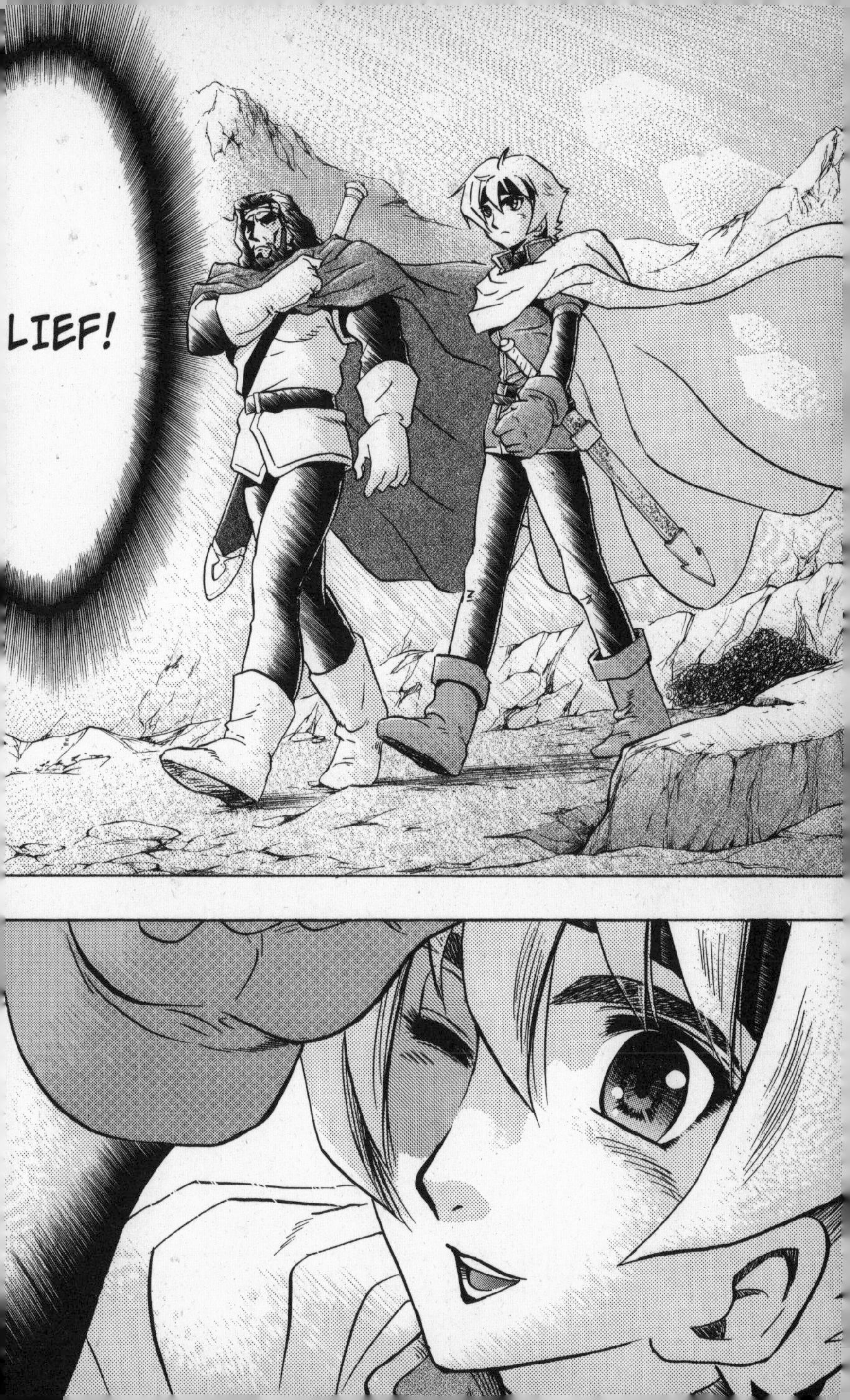
LIEF!

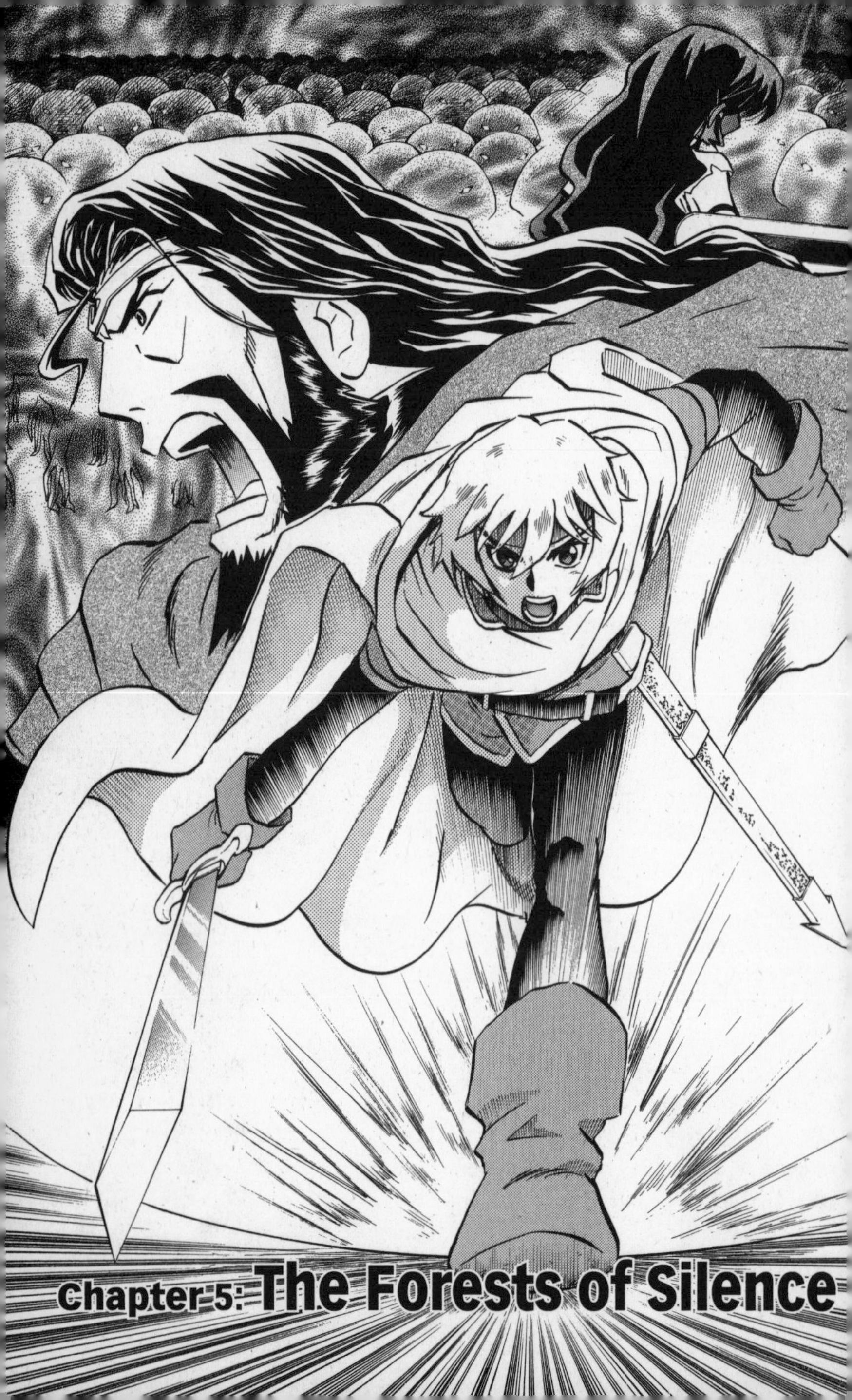
Chapter 5: The Forests of Silence

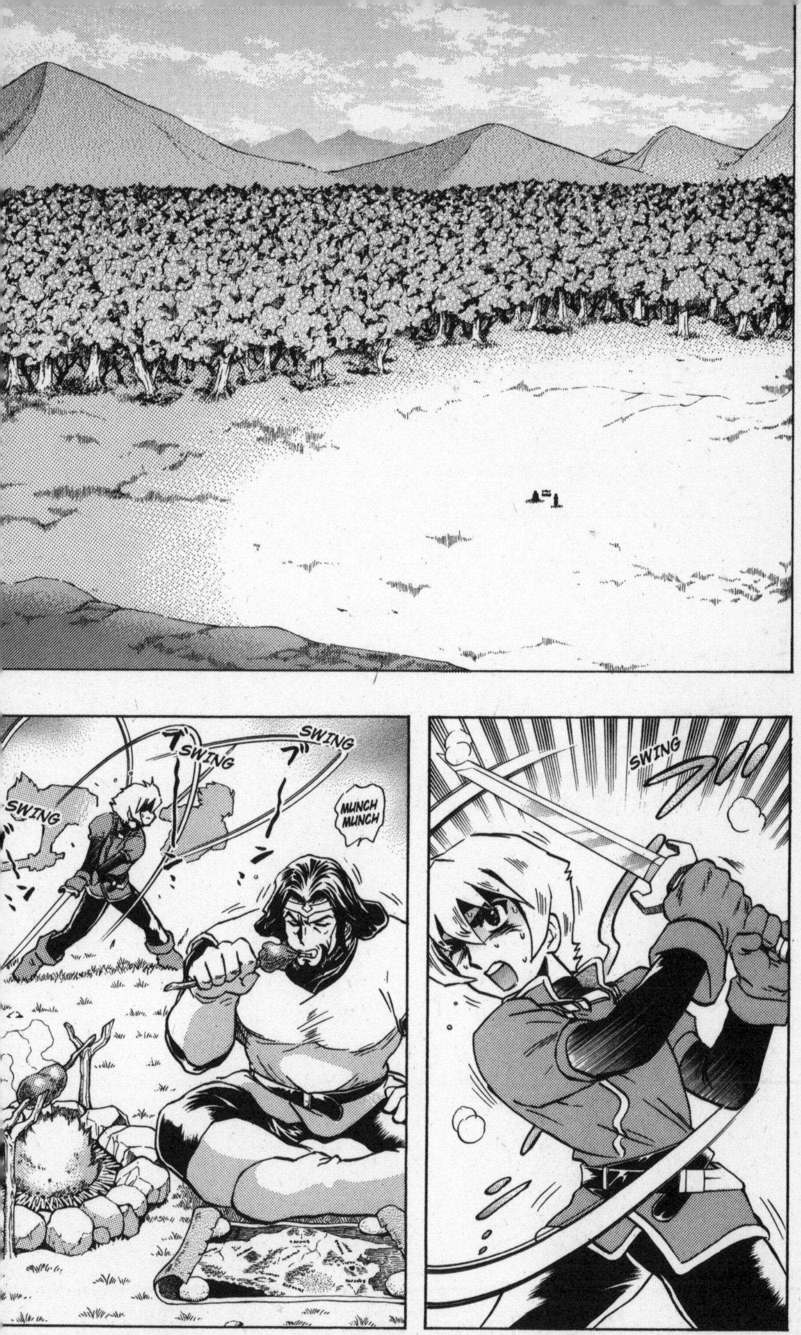
SWING
SWING
SWING
MUNCH MUNCH
SWING

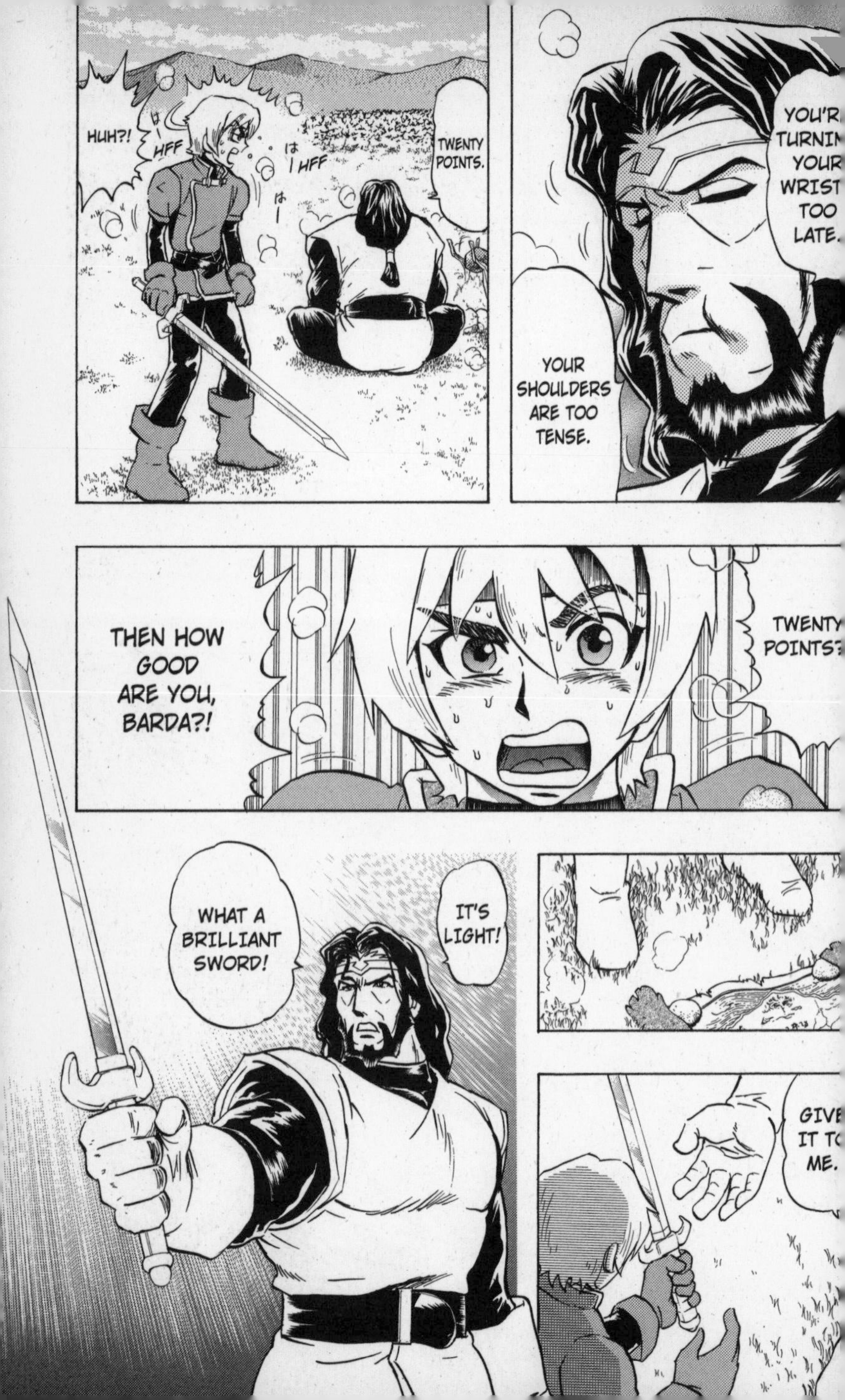

YOU'R TURNIN YOUR WRIST TOO LATE.
YOUR SHOULDERS ARE TOO TENSE.
TWENTY POINTS.
は HFF
HUH?!
は HFF
は
TWENTY POINTS?
THEN HOW GOOD ARE YOU, BARDA?!
GIVE IT TO ME.
IT'S LIGHT!
WHAT A BRILLIANT SWORD!

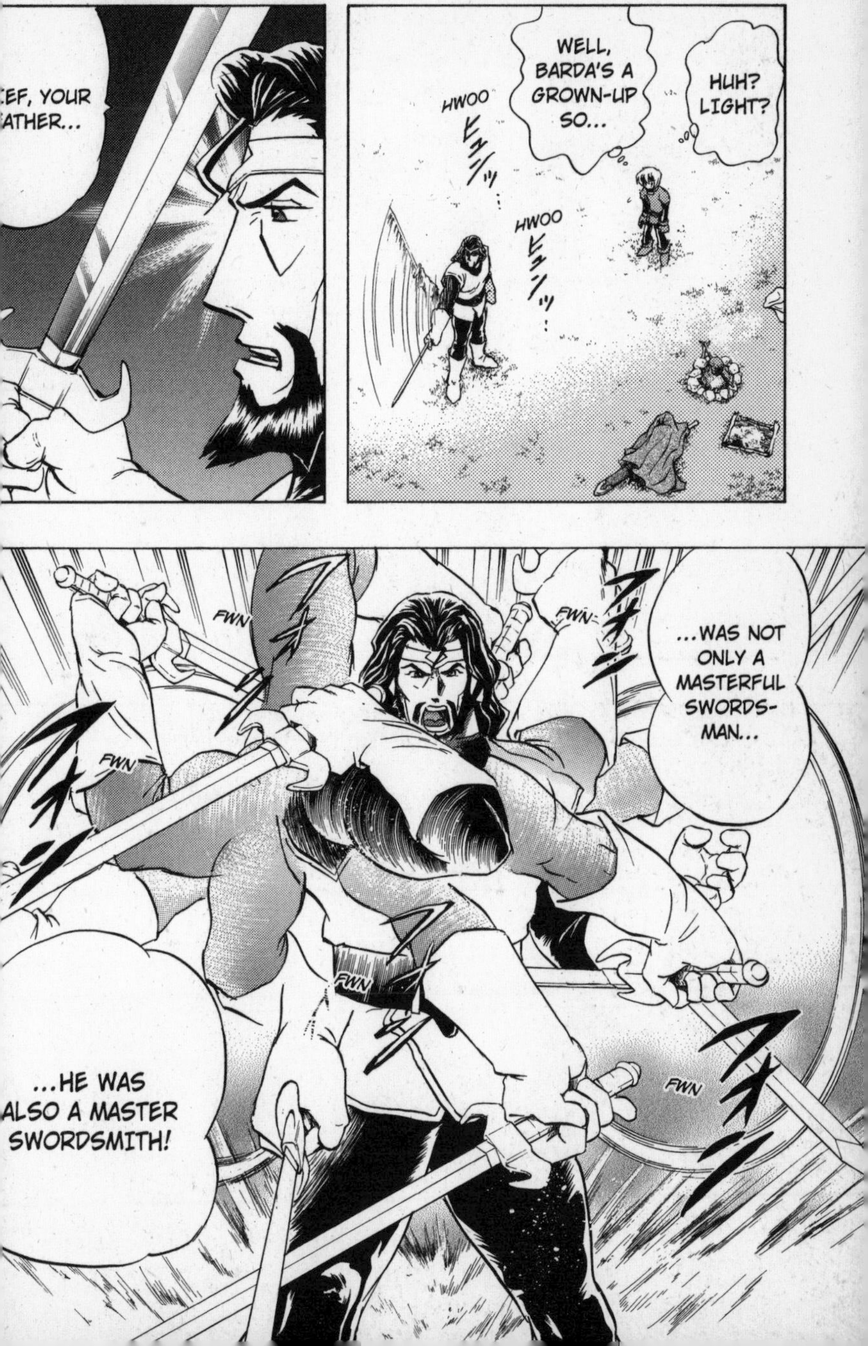
HUH? LIGHT?
WELL, BARDA'S A GROWN-UP SO...
HWOO
HWOO
EF, YOUR ATHER...
...WAS NOT ONLY A MASTERFUL SWORDS-MAN...
FWN
FWN
FWN
FWN
FWN
...HE WAS ALSO A MASTER SWORDSMITH!

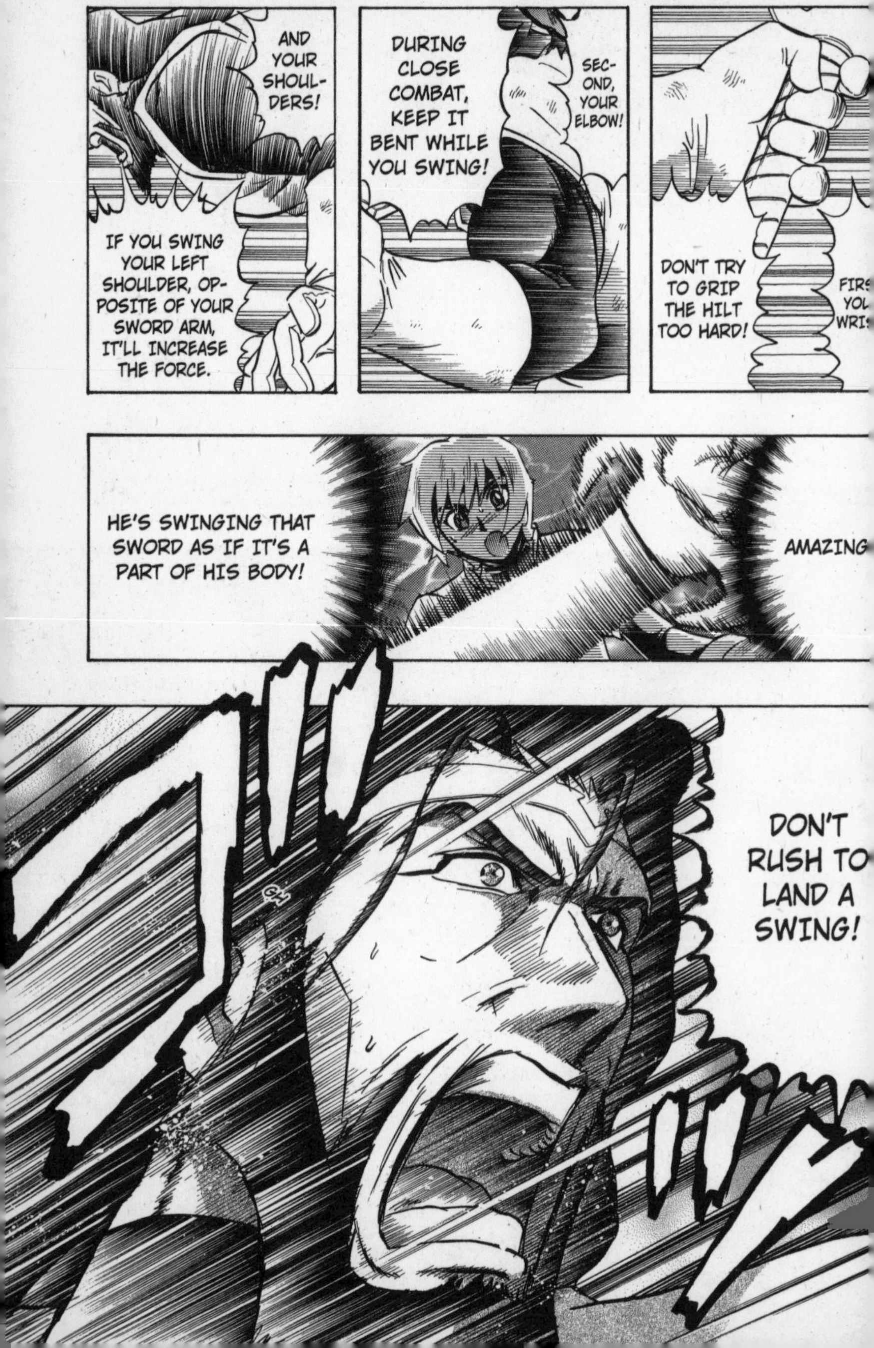
DON'T TRY TO GRIP THE HILT TOO HARD!
SEC-OND, YOUR ELBOW!
DURING CLOSE COMBAT, KEEP IT BENT WHILE YOU SWING!
AND YOUR SHOUL-DERS!
IF YOU SWING YOUR LEFT SHOULDER, OP-POSITE OF YOUR SWORD ARM, IT'LL INCREASE THE FORCE.
AMAZING
HE'S SWINGING THAT SWORD AS IF IT'S A PART OF HIS BODY!
DON'T RUSH TO LAND A SWING!

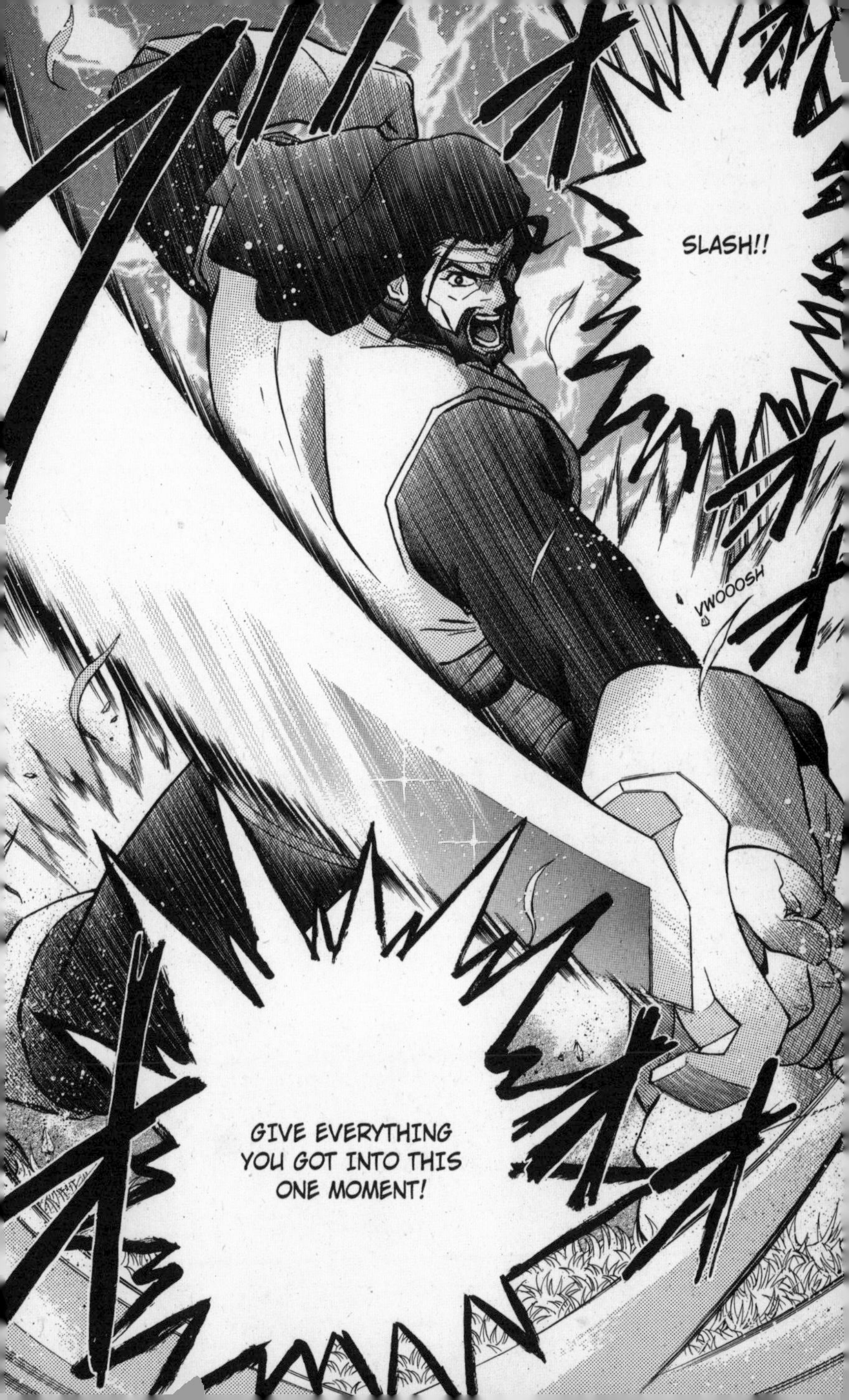
SLASH!!
VWOOOSH
GIVE EVERYTHING YOU GOT INTO THIS ONE MOMENT!

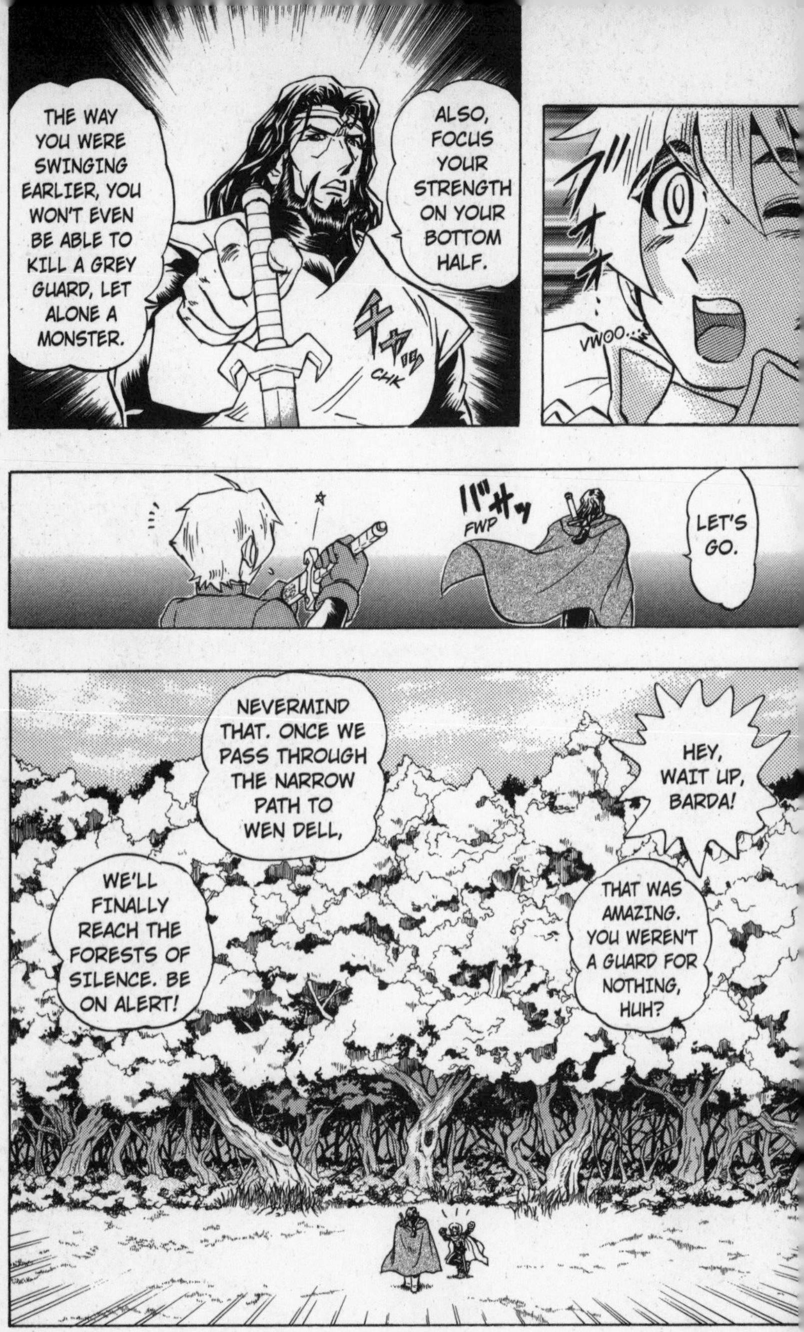
VWOO...
THE WAY YOU WERE SWINGING EARLIER, YOU WON'T EVEN BE ABLE TO KILL A GREY GUARD, LET ALONE A MONSTER.
ALSO, FOCUS YOUR STRENGTH ON YOUR BOTTOM HALF.
CHK
LET'S GO.
FWP
HEY, WAIT UP, BARDA!
THAT WAS AMAZING. YOU WEREN'T A GUARD FOR NOTHING, HUH?
NEVERMIND THAT. ONCE WE PASS THROUGH THE NARROW PATH TO WEN DELL,
WE'LL FINALLY REACH THE FORESTS OF SILENCE. BE ON ALERT!

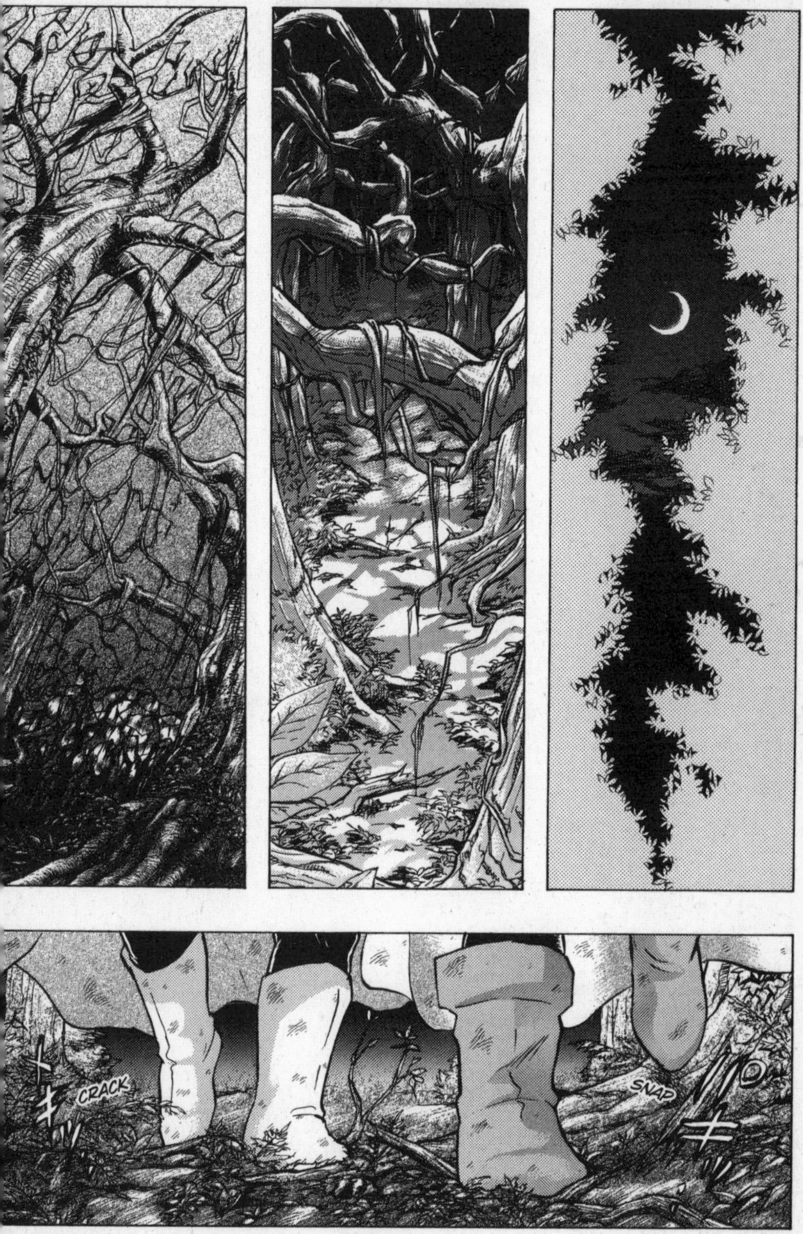
SNAP
CRACK

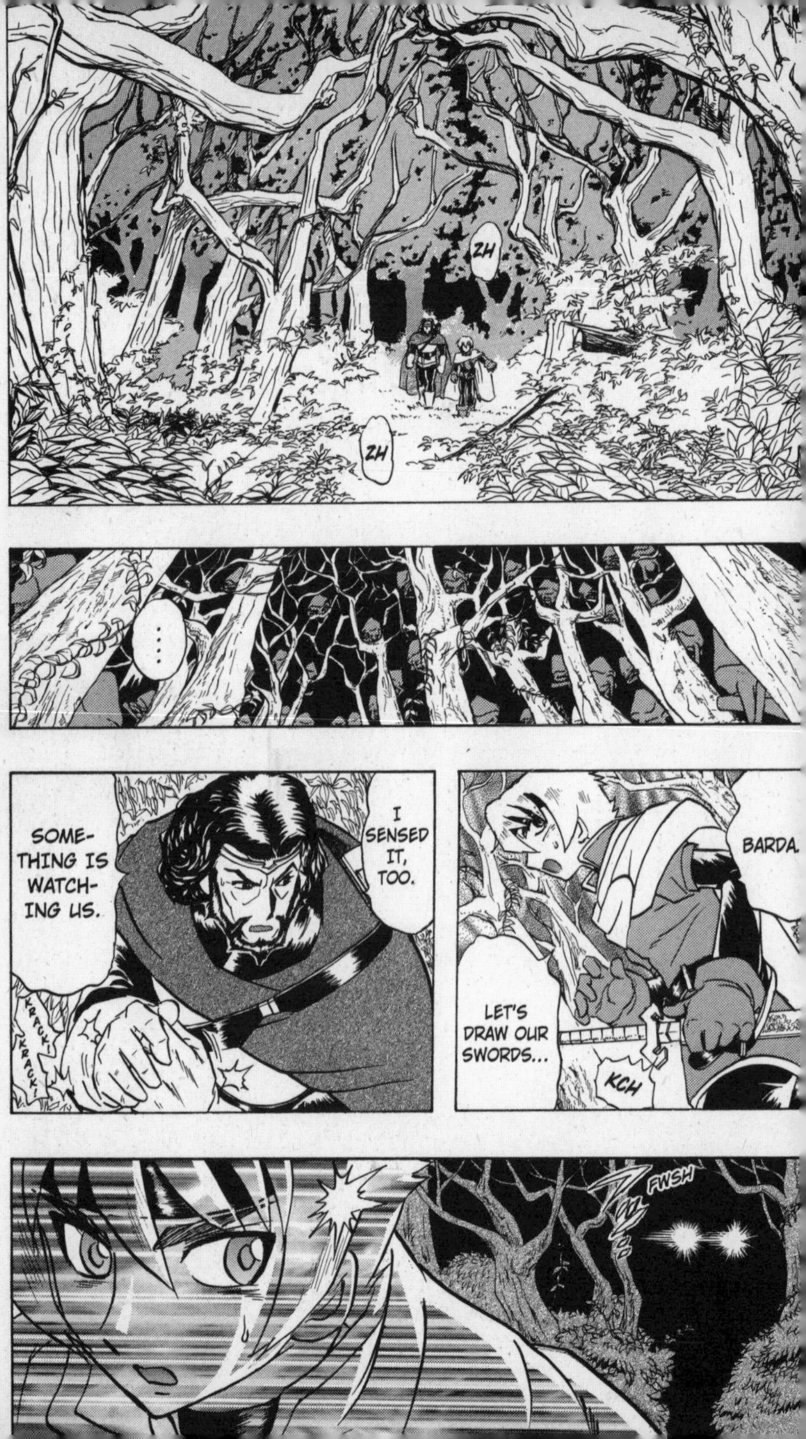
ZH
ZH
.....
BARDA.
LET'S DRAW OUR SWORDS...
KCH
I SENSED IT, TOO.
SOME-THING IS WATCH-ING US.
KRACK! KRACK!
FWSH

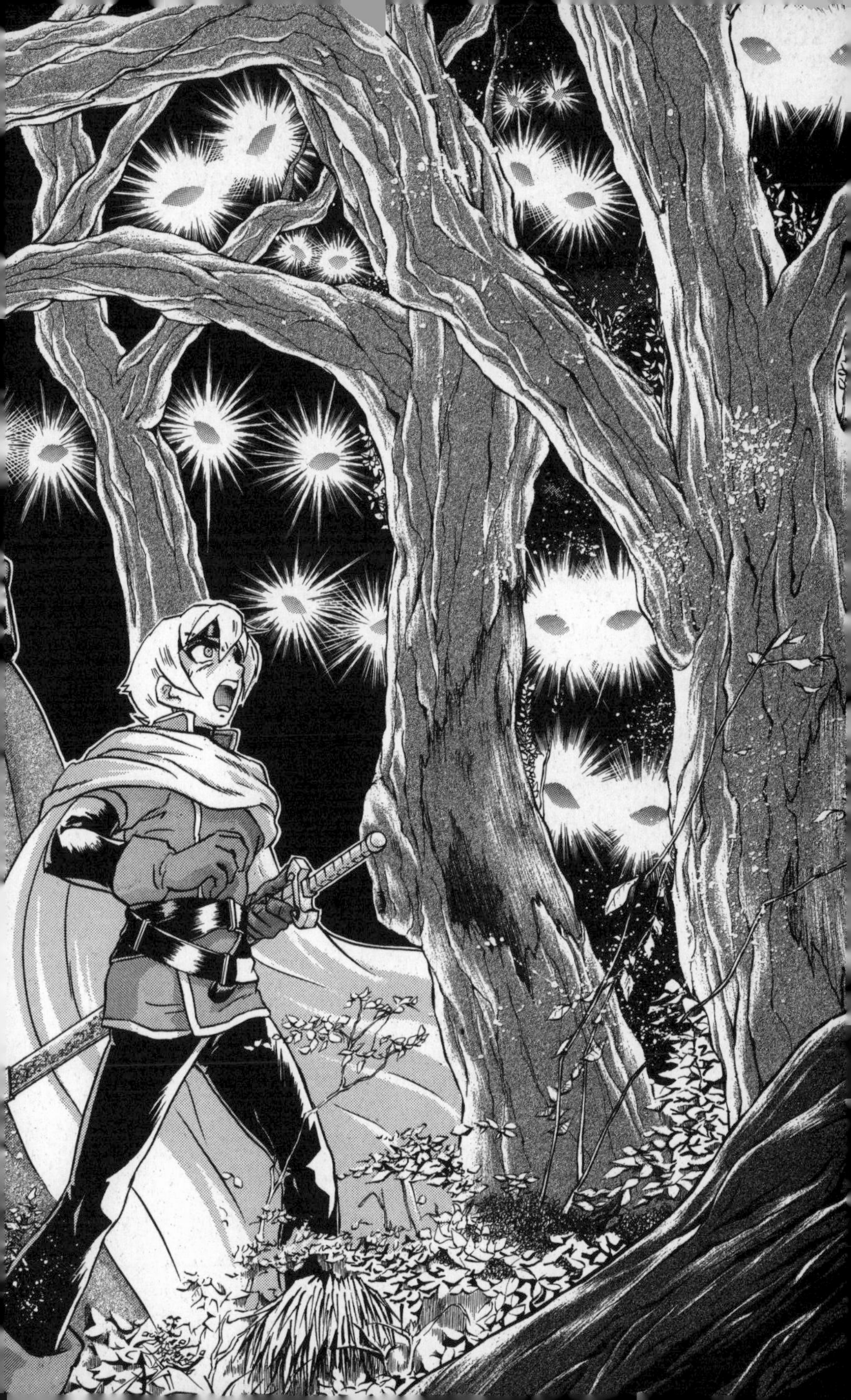

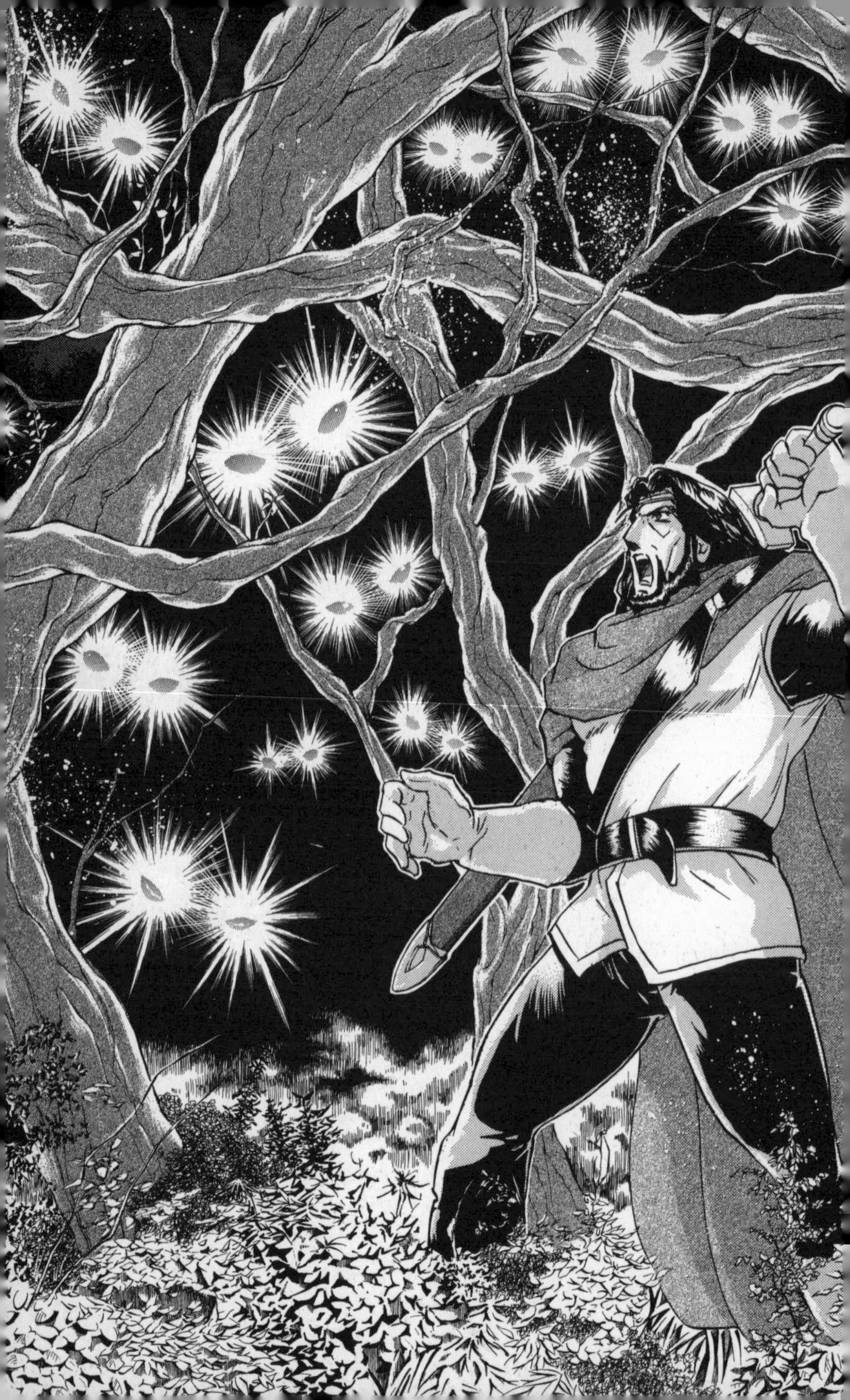

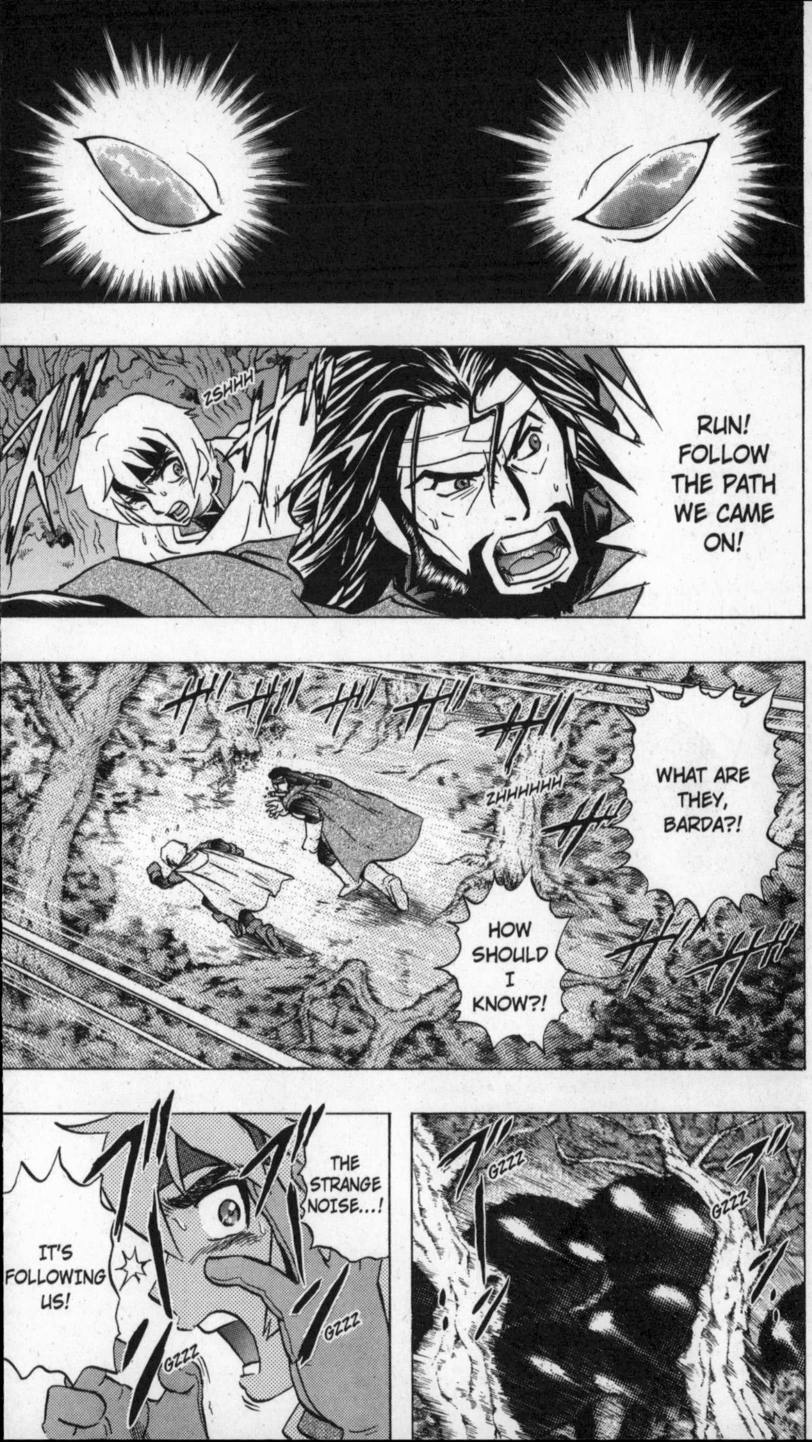
ZSHHH
RUN! FOLLOW THE PATH WE CAME ON!
WHAT ARE THEY, BARDA?!
ZHHHHHH
HOW SHOULD I KNOW?!
GZZZ
GZZZ
THE STRANGE NOISE...!
IT'S FOLLOWING US!
GZZZ
GZZZ

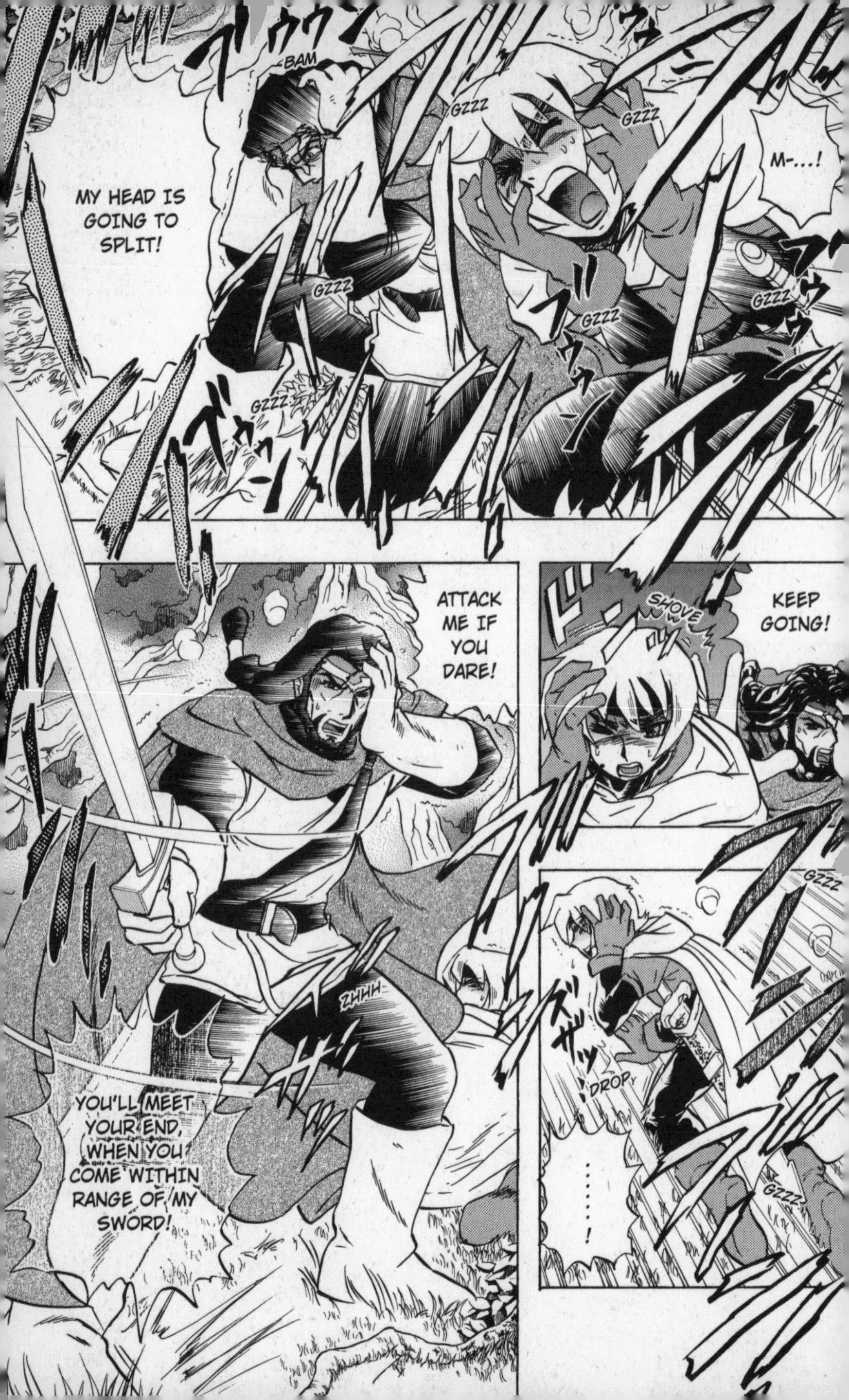
M-...!
GZZZ
BAM
GZZZ
MY HEAD IS GOING TO SPLIT!
GZZZ
GZZZ
GZZZ
GZZZ
KEEP GOING!
SHOVE
GZZZ
DROP
GZZZ
ATTACK ME IF YOU DARE!
ZHHH
YOU'LL MEET YOUR END, WHEN YOU COME WITHIN RANGE OF MY SWORD!

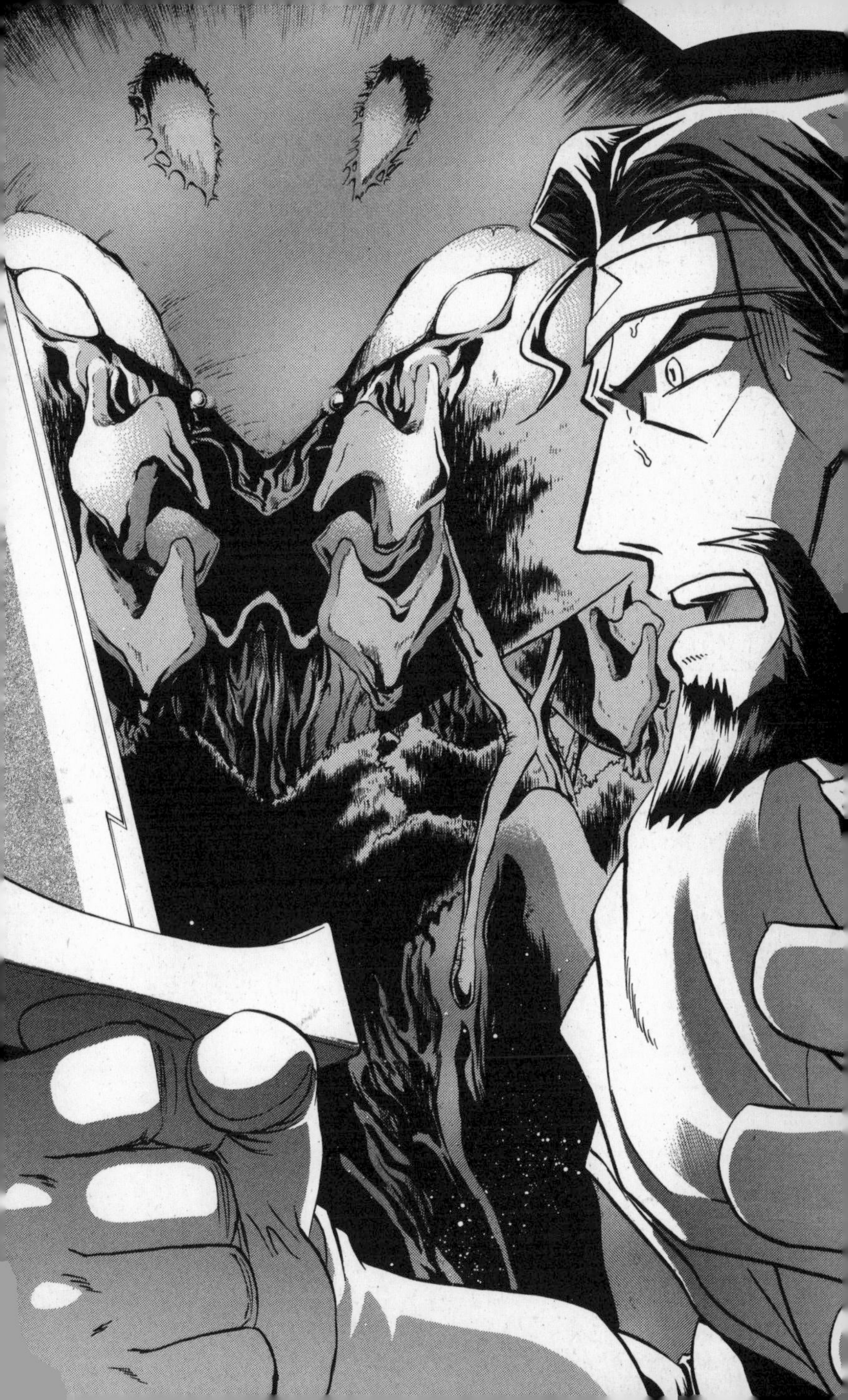

STAB

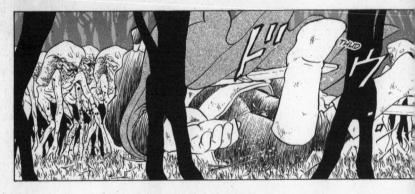

THUD

BARDA...?!

B-.....!

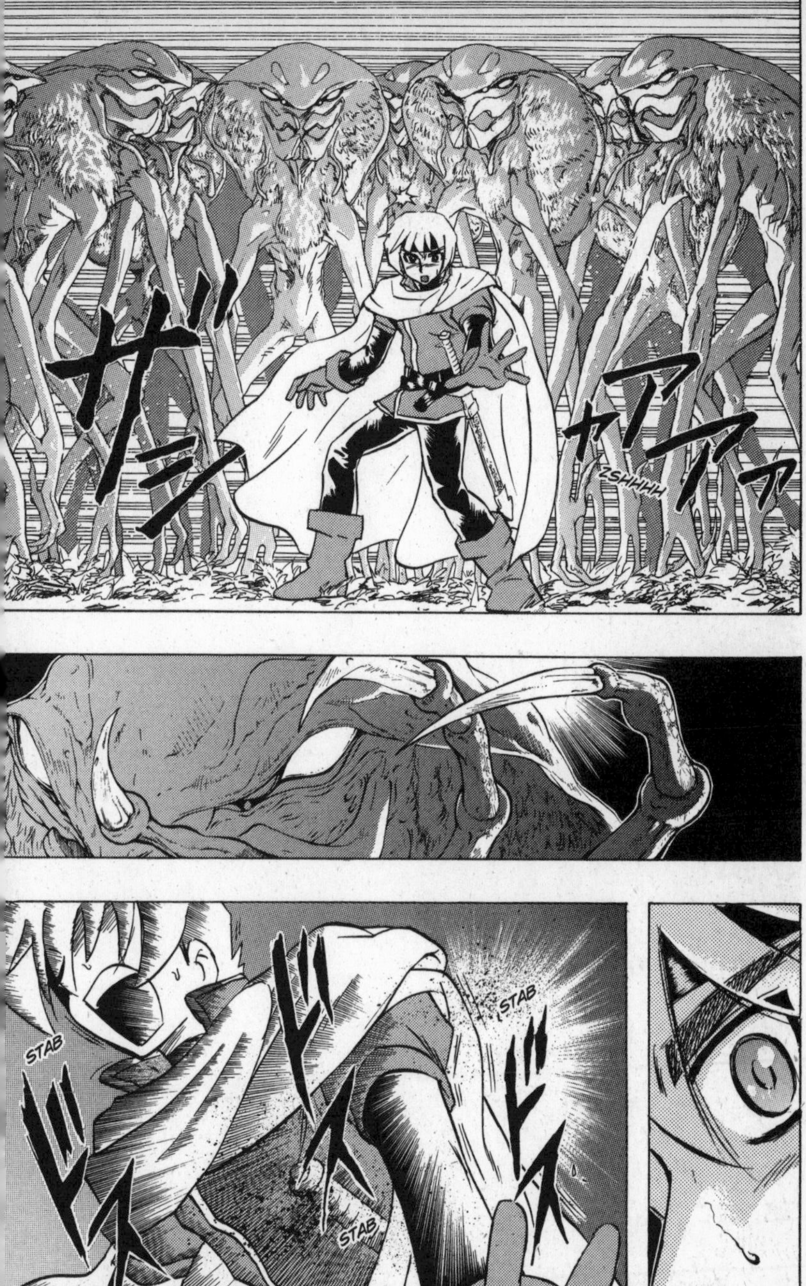
ZSHHHH
STAB
STAB
STAB

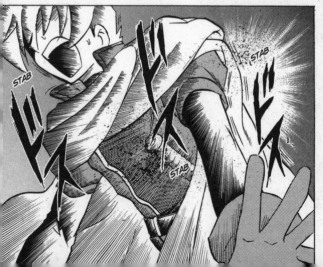

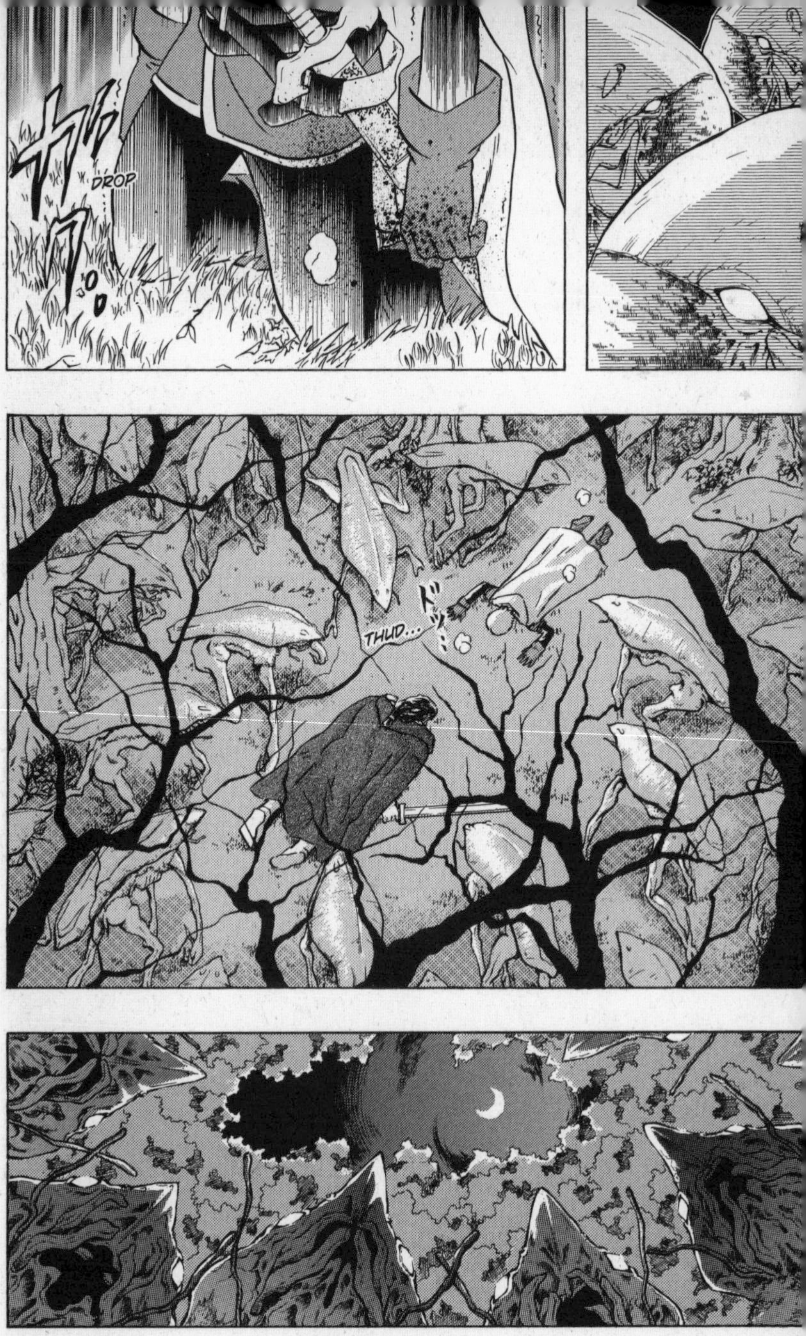
DROP
THUD...

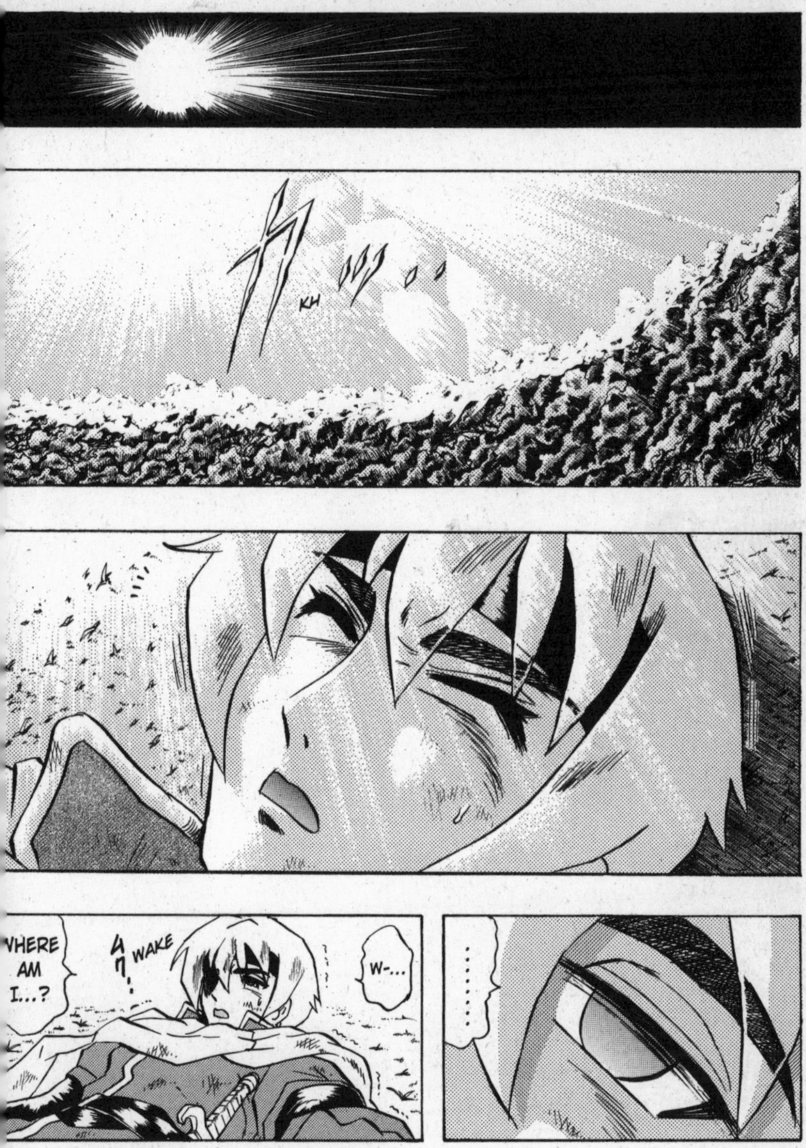
KH
......
W-...
WAKE
WHERE AM I...?

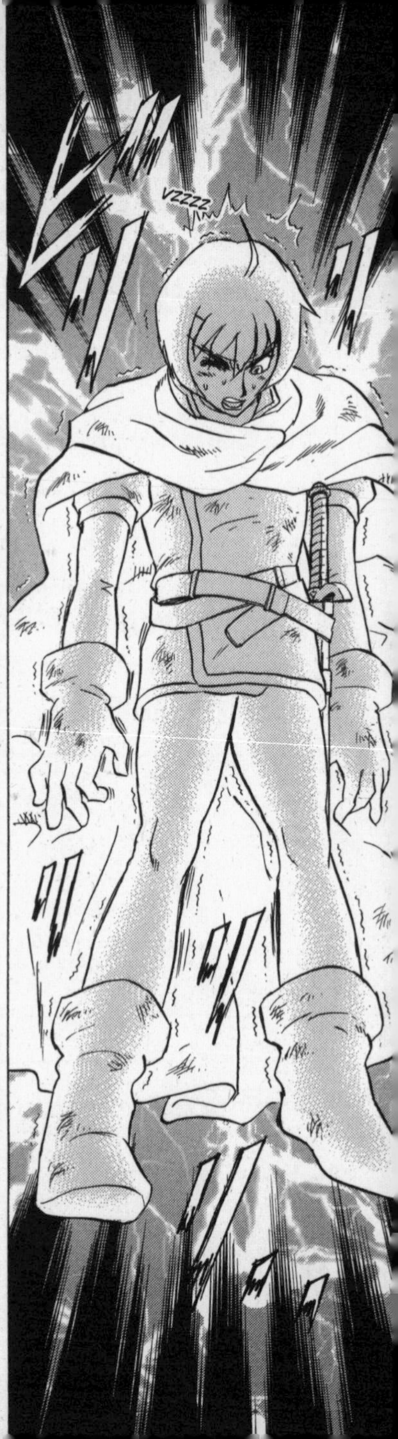
VZZZZ

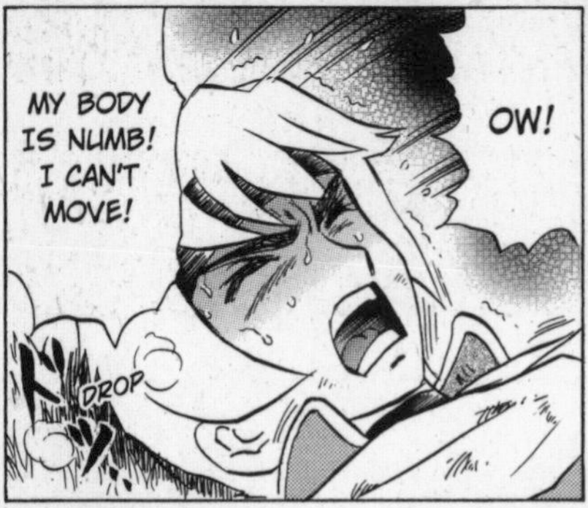
OW!
MY BODY IS NUMB! I CAN'T MOVE!
DROP

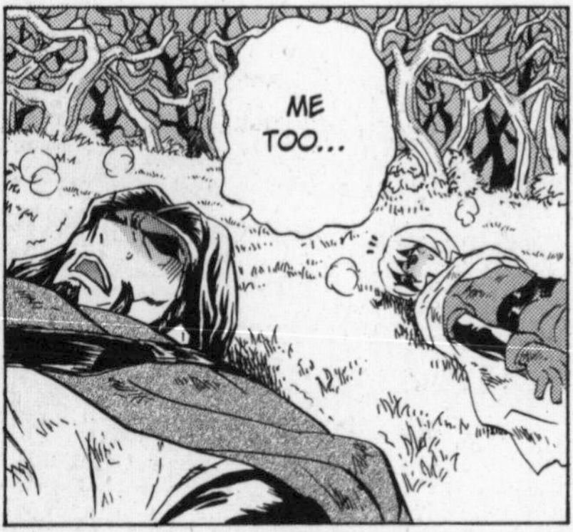
ME TOO...

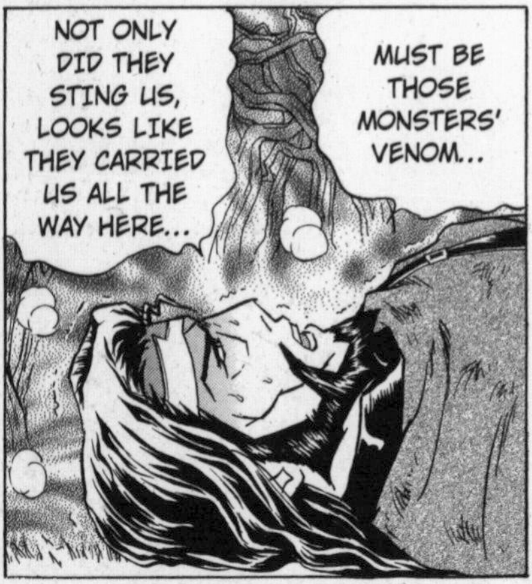
MUST BE THOSE MONSTERS' VENOM...
NOT ONLY DID THEY STING US, LOOKS LIKE THEY CARRIED US ALL THE WAY HERE...

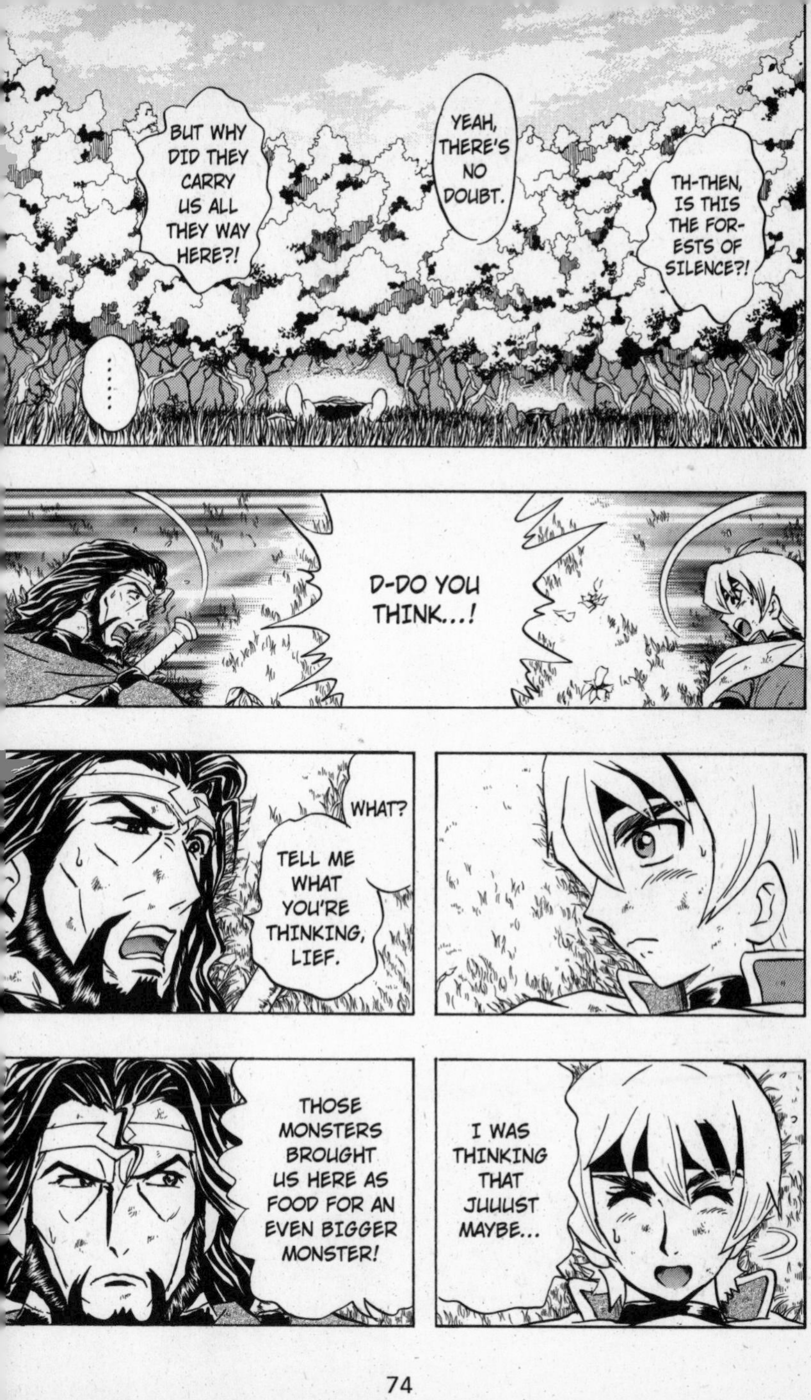
TH-THEN, IS THIS THE FOR-ESTS OF SILENCE?!
YEAH, THERE'S NO DOUBT.
BUT WHY DID THEY CARRY US ALL THEY WAY HERE?!
......
D-DO YOU THINK...!
WHAT?
TELL ME WHAT YOU'RE THINKING, LIEF.
I WAS THINKING THAT JUUUST MAYBE...
THOSE MONSTERS BROUGHT US HERE AS FOOD FOR AN EVEN BIGGER MONSTER!

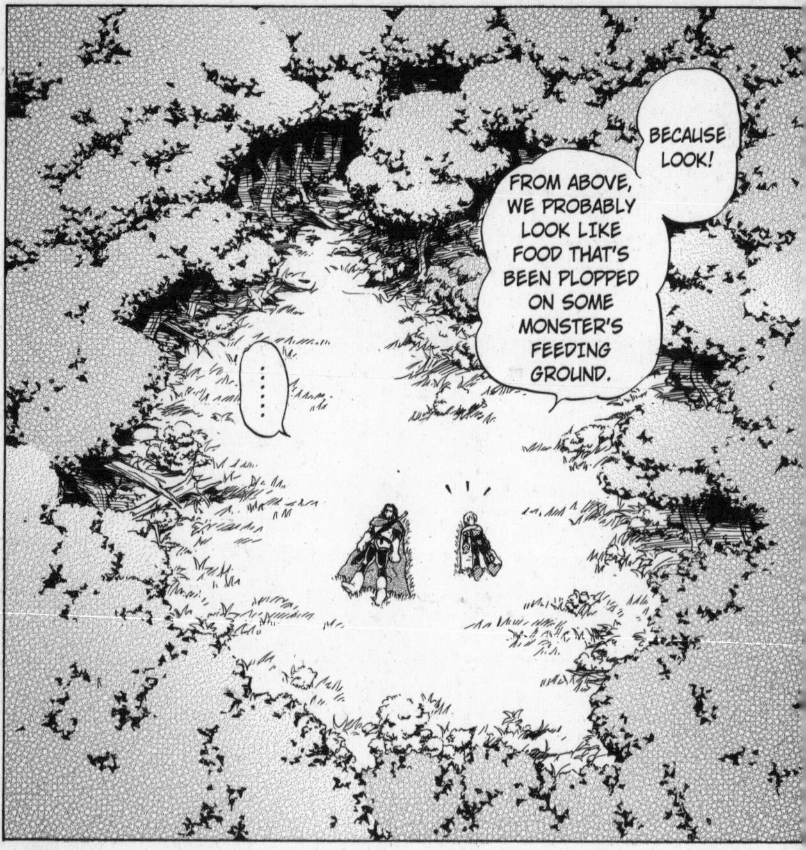
BECAUSE LOOK!
FROM ABOVE, WE PROBABLY LOOK LIKE FOOD THAT'S BEEN PLOPPED ON SOME MONSTER'S FEEDING GROUND.
......

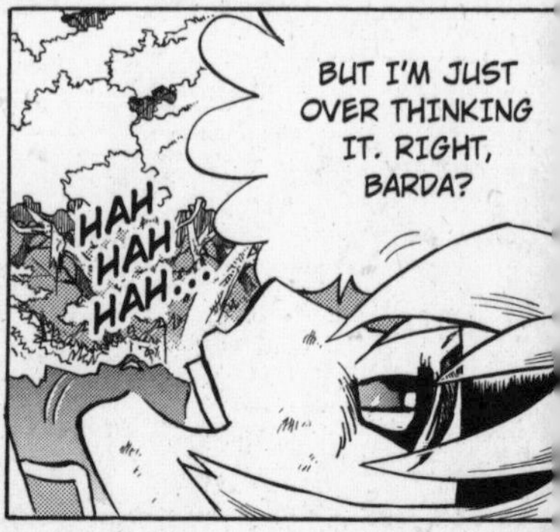
BUT I'M JUST OVER THINKING IT. RIGHT, BARDA?
HAH HAH HAH...

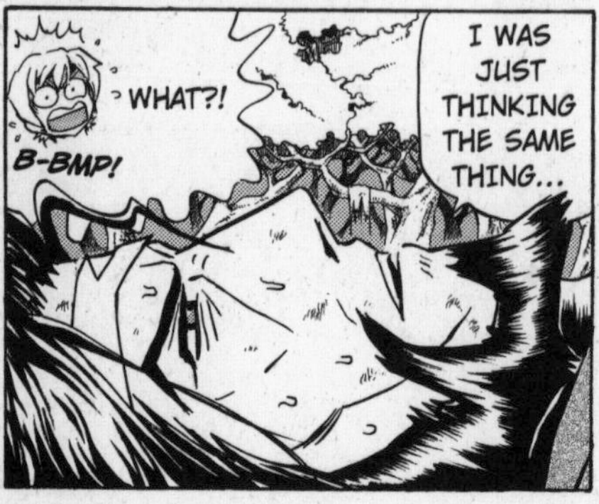
I WAS JUST THINKING THE SAME THING...
WHAT?!
B-BMP!

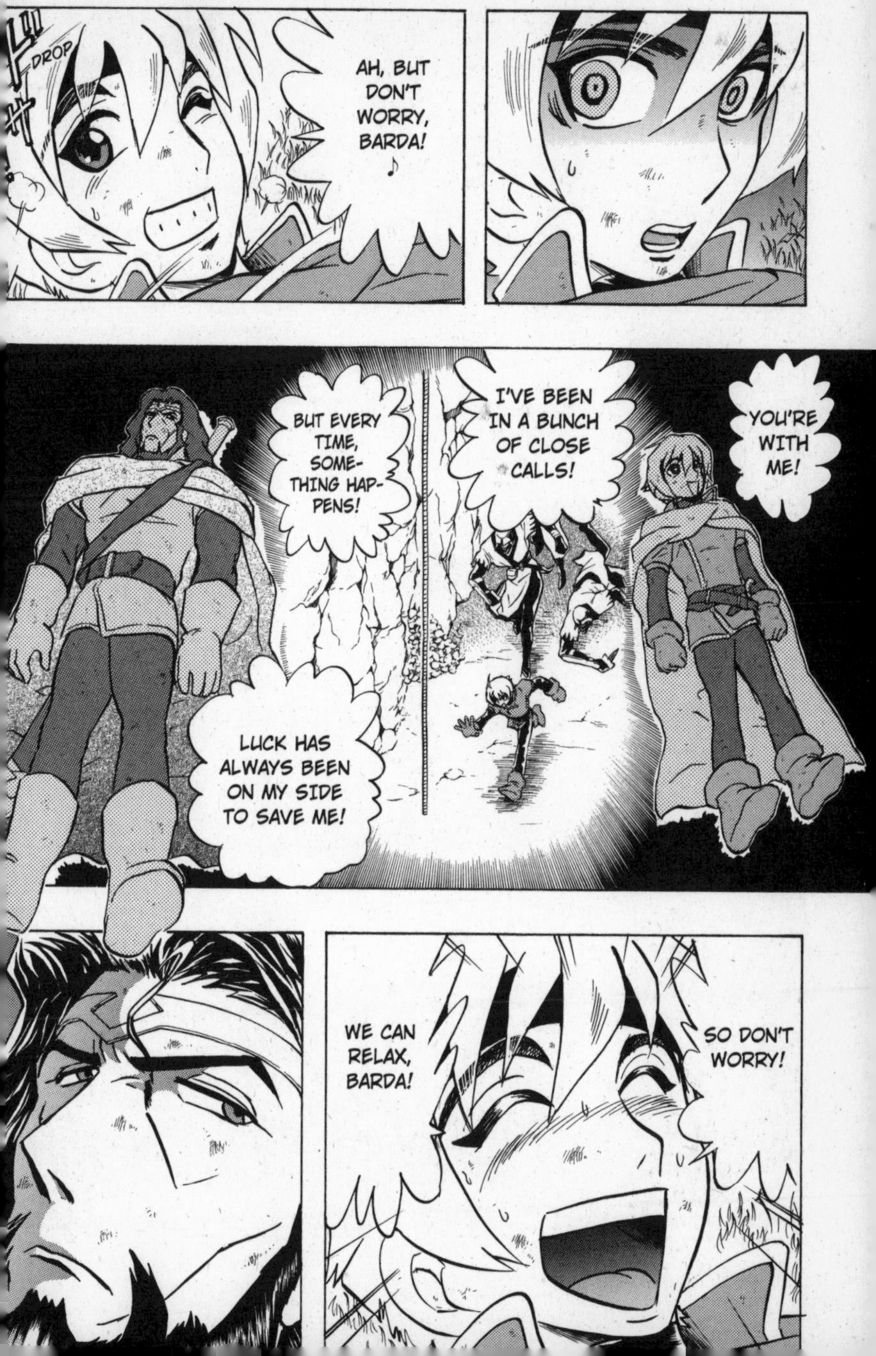
AH, BUT DON'T WORRY, BARDA! ♪
DROP
YOU'RE WITH ME!
I'VE BEEN IN A BUNCH OF CLOSE CALLS!
BUT EVERY TIME, SOME-THING HAP-PENS!
LUCK HAS ALWAYS BEEN ON MY SIDE TO SAVE ME!
SO DON'T WORRY!
WE CAN RELAX, BARDA!

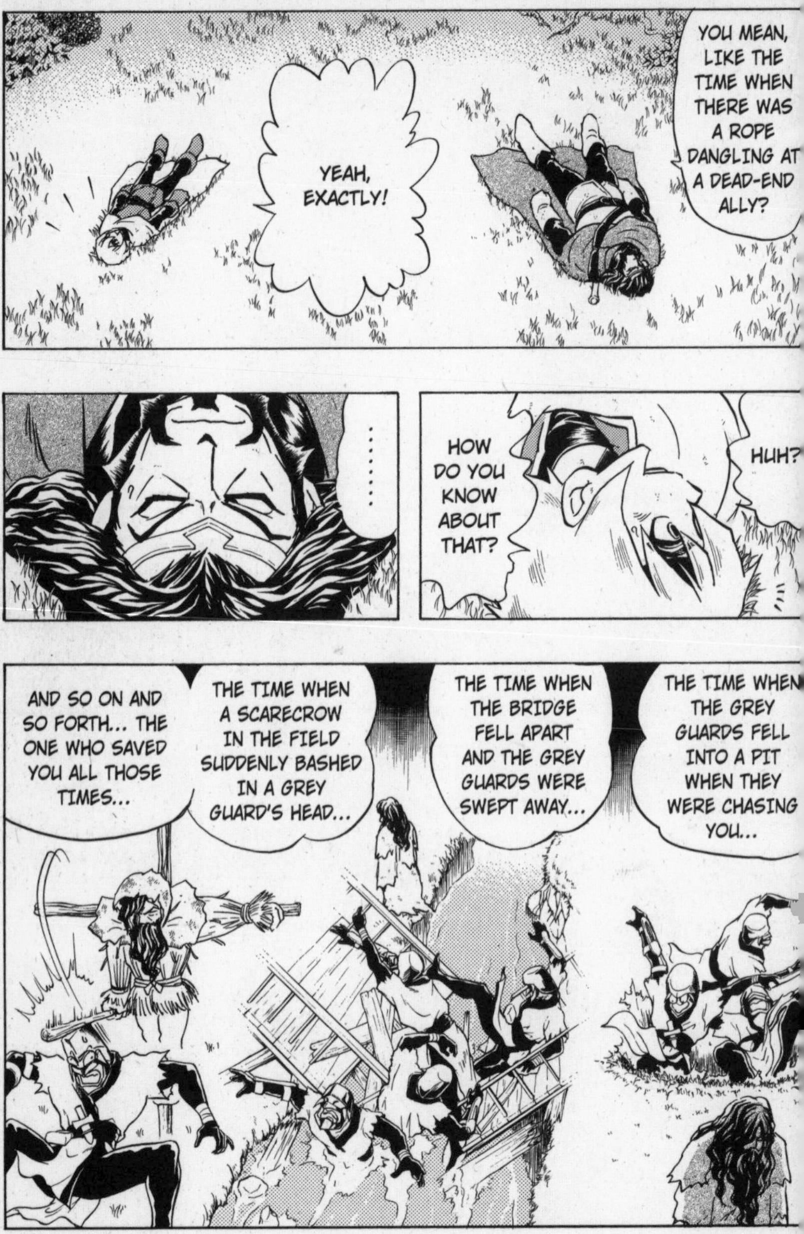
YOU MEAN, LIKE THE TIME WHEN THERE WAS A ROPE DANGLING AT A DEAD-END ALLY?
YEAH, EXACTLY!
HUH?
HOW DO YOU KNOW ABOUT THAT?
......
THE TIME WHEN THE GREY GUARDS FELL INTO A PIT WHEN THEY WERE CHASING YOU...
THE TIME WHEN THE BRIDGE FELL APART AND THE GREY GUARDS WERE SWEPT AWAY...
THE TIME WHEN A SCARECROW IN THE FIELD SUDDENLY BASHED IN A GREY GUARD'S HEAD...
AND SO ON AND SO FORTH... THE ONE WHO SAVED YOU ALL THOSE TIMES...

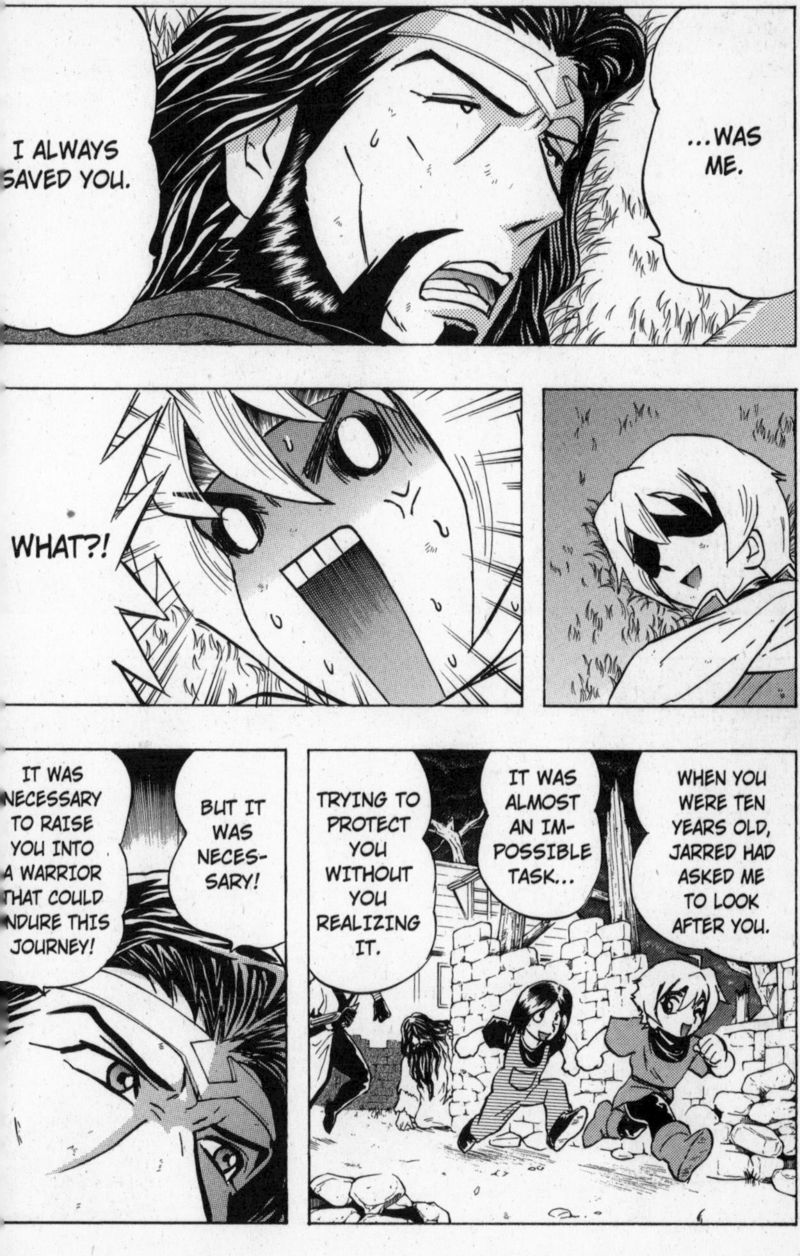

...WAS ME.
I ALWAYS SAVED YOU.
WHAT?!
WHEN YOU WERE TEN YEARS OLD, JARRED HAD ASKED ME TO LOOK AFTER YOU.
IT WAS ALMOST AN IM-POSSIBLE TASK...
TRYING TO PROTECT YOU WITHOUT YOU REALIZING IT.
BUT IT WAS NECES-SARY!
IT WAS NECESSARY TO RAISE YOU INTO A WARRIOR THAT COULD NDURE THIS JOURNEY!

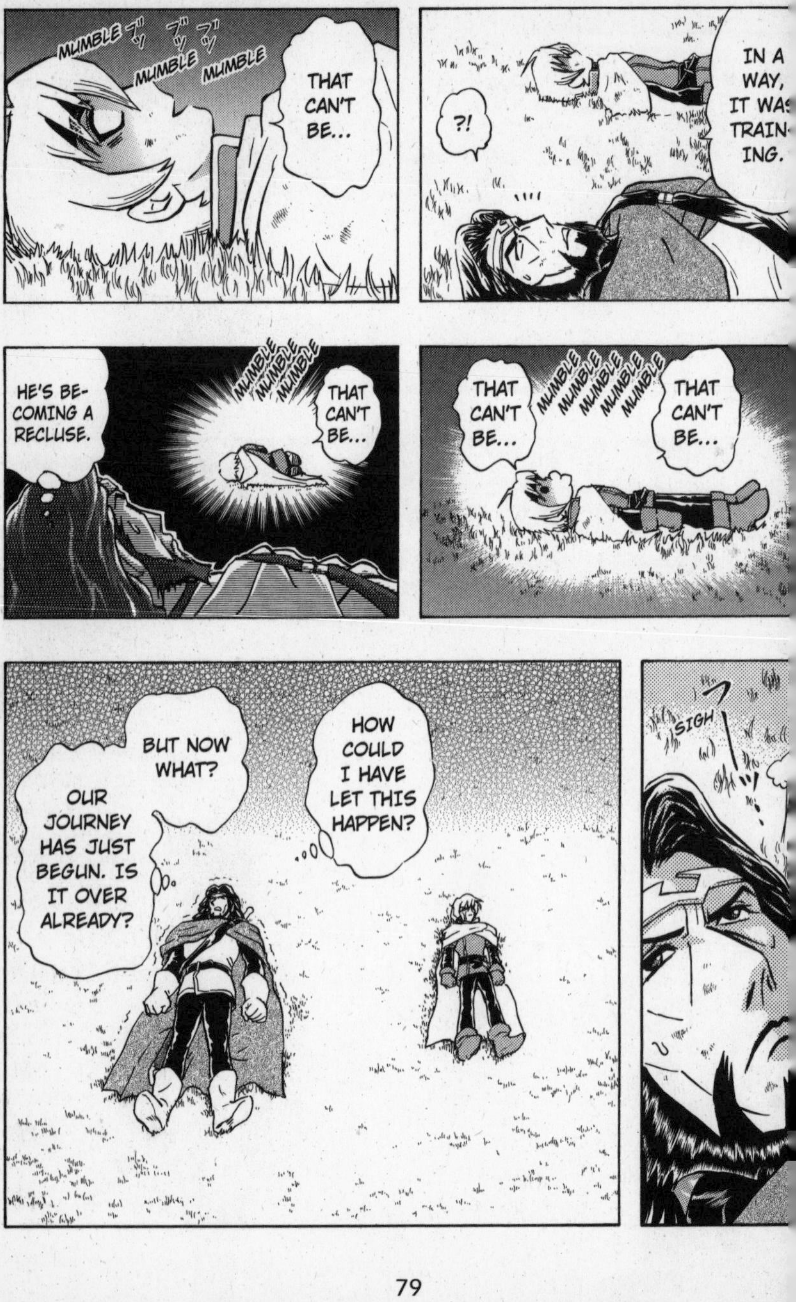

IN A WAY, IT WAS TRAIN-ING.
?!
MUMBLE MUMBLE MUMBLE
ブツ ブツ ブツ
THAT CAN'T BE...
THAT CAN'T BE...
MUMBLE MUMBLE MUMBLE MUMBLE MUMBLE
THAT CAN'T BE...
THAT CAN'T BE...
MUMBLE MUMBLE MUMBLE
HE'S BE-COMING A RECLUSE.
SIGH
HOW COULD I HAVE LET THIS HAPPEN?
BUT NOW WHAT?
OUR JOURNEY HAS JUST BEGUN. IS IT OVER ALREADY?

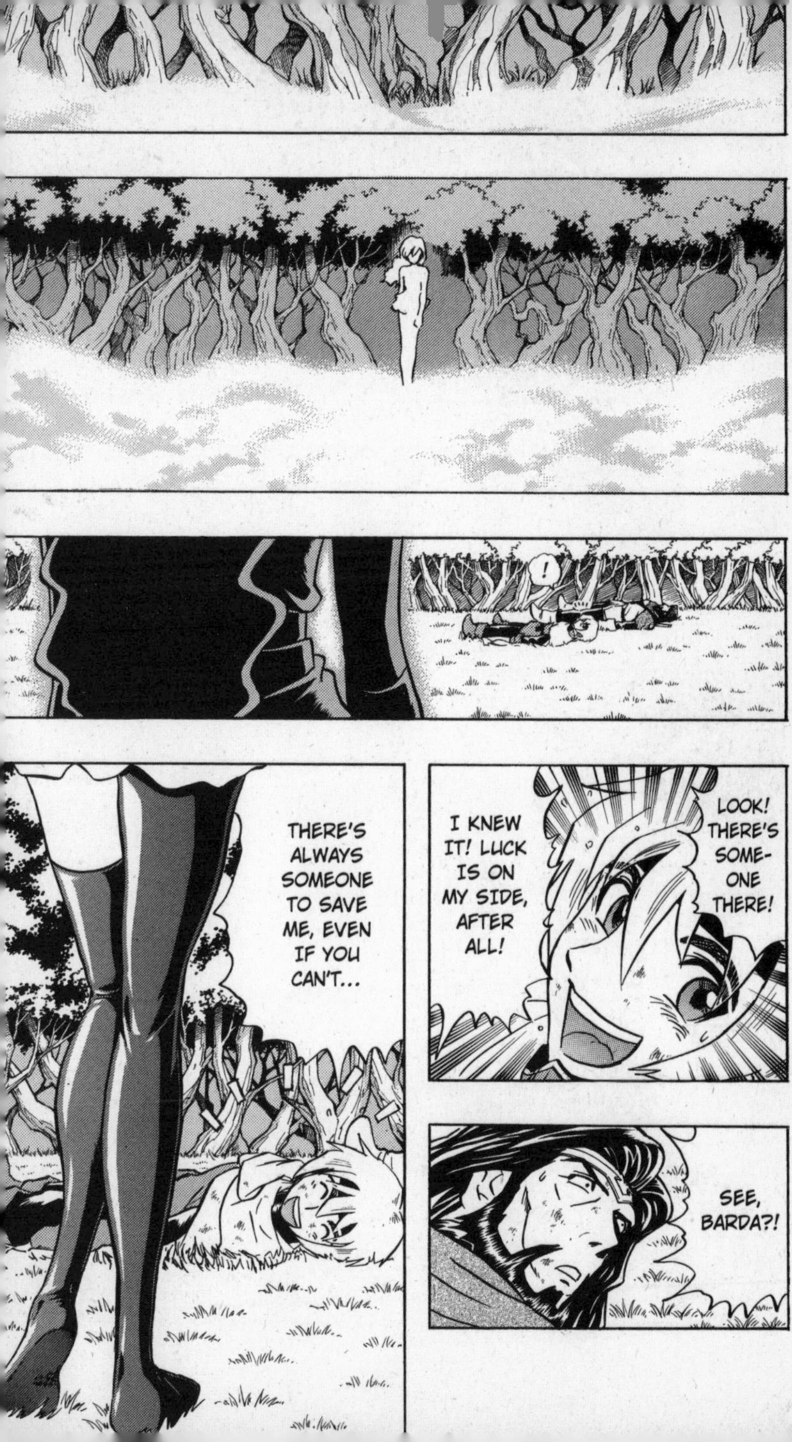
!
LOOK! THERE'S SOME-ONE THERE!
I KNEW IT! LUCK IS ON MY SIDE, AFTER ALL!
SEE, BARDA?!
THERE'S ALWAYS SOMEONE TO SAVE ME, EVEN IF YOU CAN'T...

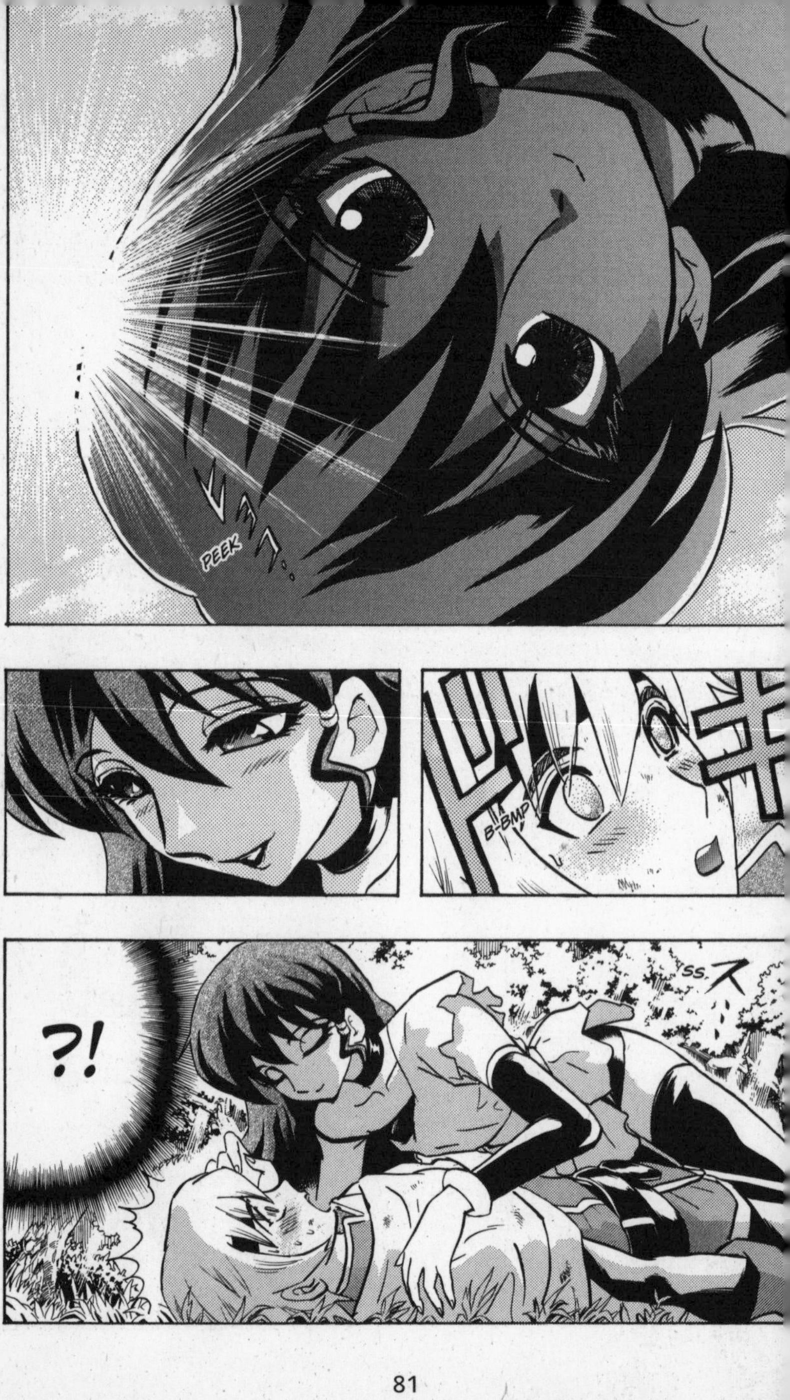
PEEK
B-BMP
SS
?!

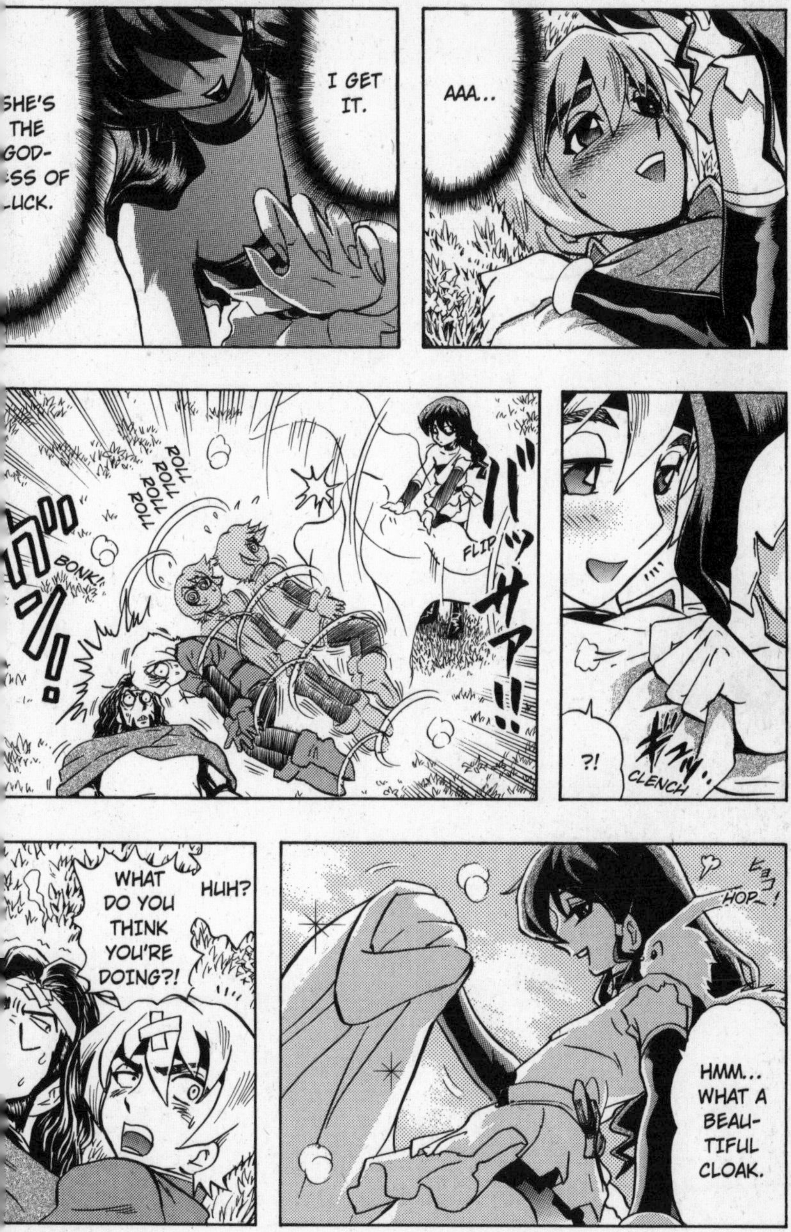
AAA...
I GET IT.
SHE'S THE GODDESS OF LUCK.
?!
CLENCH
FLIP
バッサァ!!
ROLL ROLL ROLL ROLL
BONK!
HOP!
HMM... WHAT A BEAUTIFUL CLOAK.
HUH?
WHAT DO YOU THINK YOU'RE DOING?!

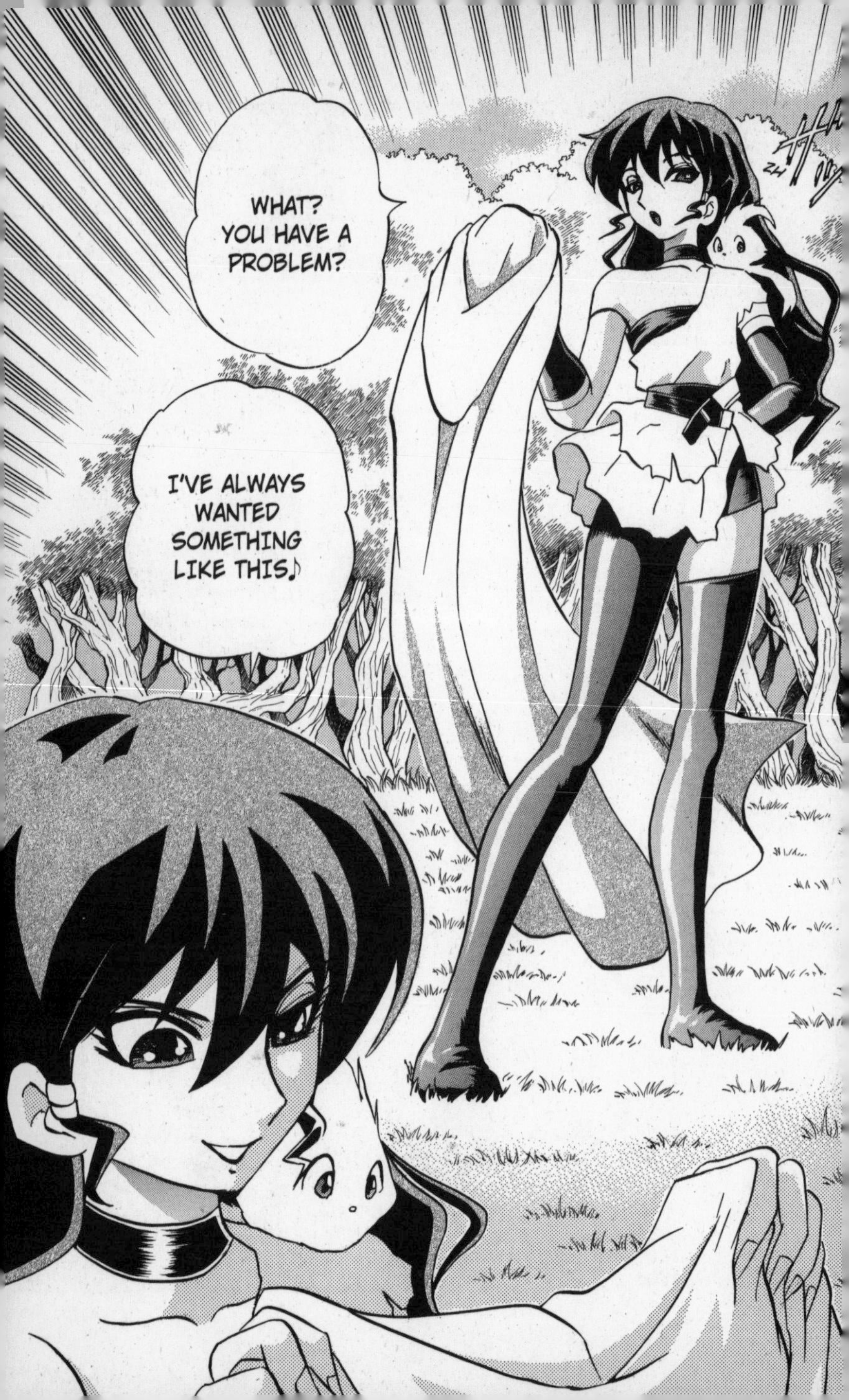
WHAT? YOU HAVE A PROBLEM?
I'VE ALWAYS WANTED SOMETHING LIKE THIS♪

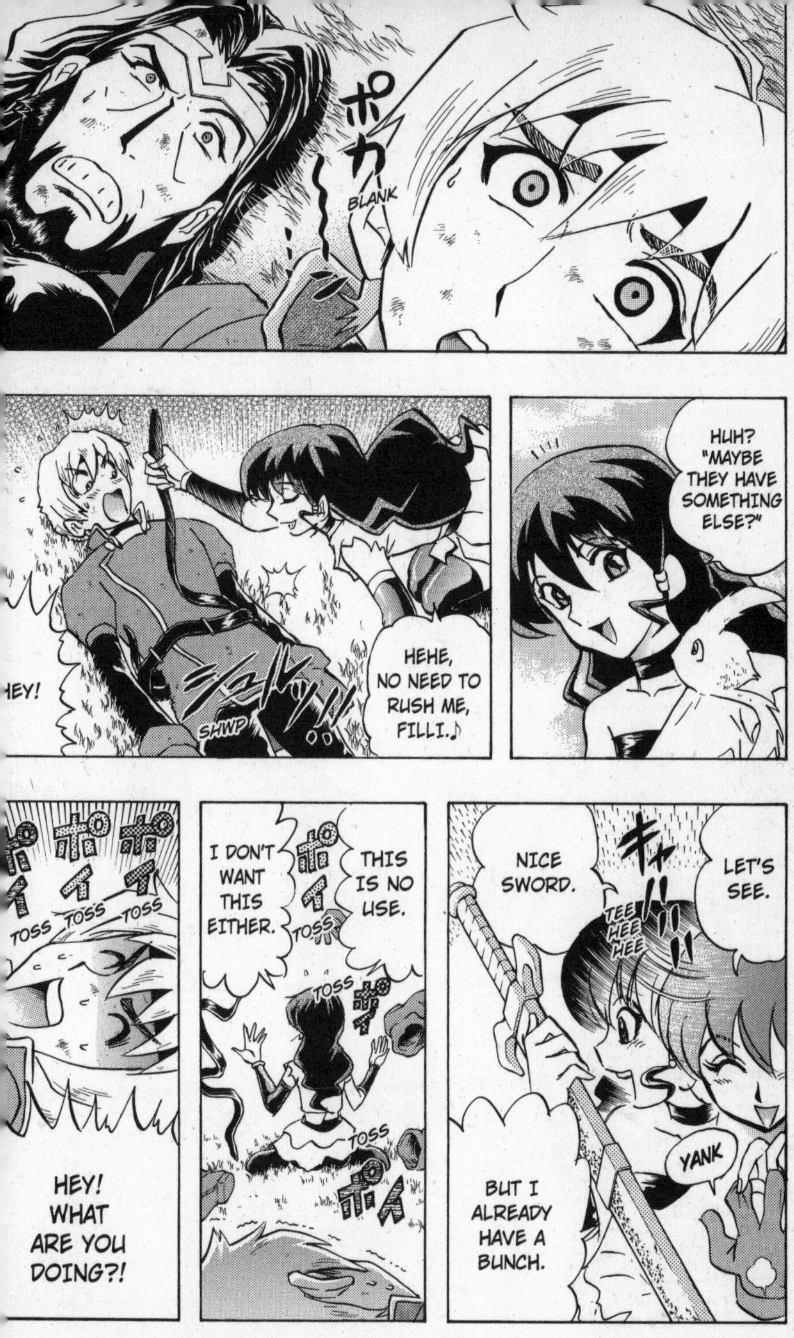

ポカ
BLANK
HUH? "MAYBE THEY HAVE SOMETHING ELSE?"
HEHE, NO NEED TO RUSH ME, FILLI.♪
シュルッ
SHWP
HEY!
LET'S SEE.
キャ
TEE HEE HEE
NICE SWORD.
YANK
BUT I ALREADY HAVE A BUNCH.
THIS IS NO USE.
ポイ
TOSS
I DON'T WANT THIS EITHER.
TOSS
ポイ
TOSS
ポイ
ポイポイポイ
TOSS TOSS TOSS
HEY! WHAT ARE YOU DOING?!

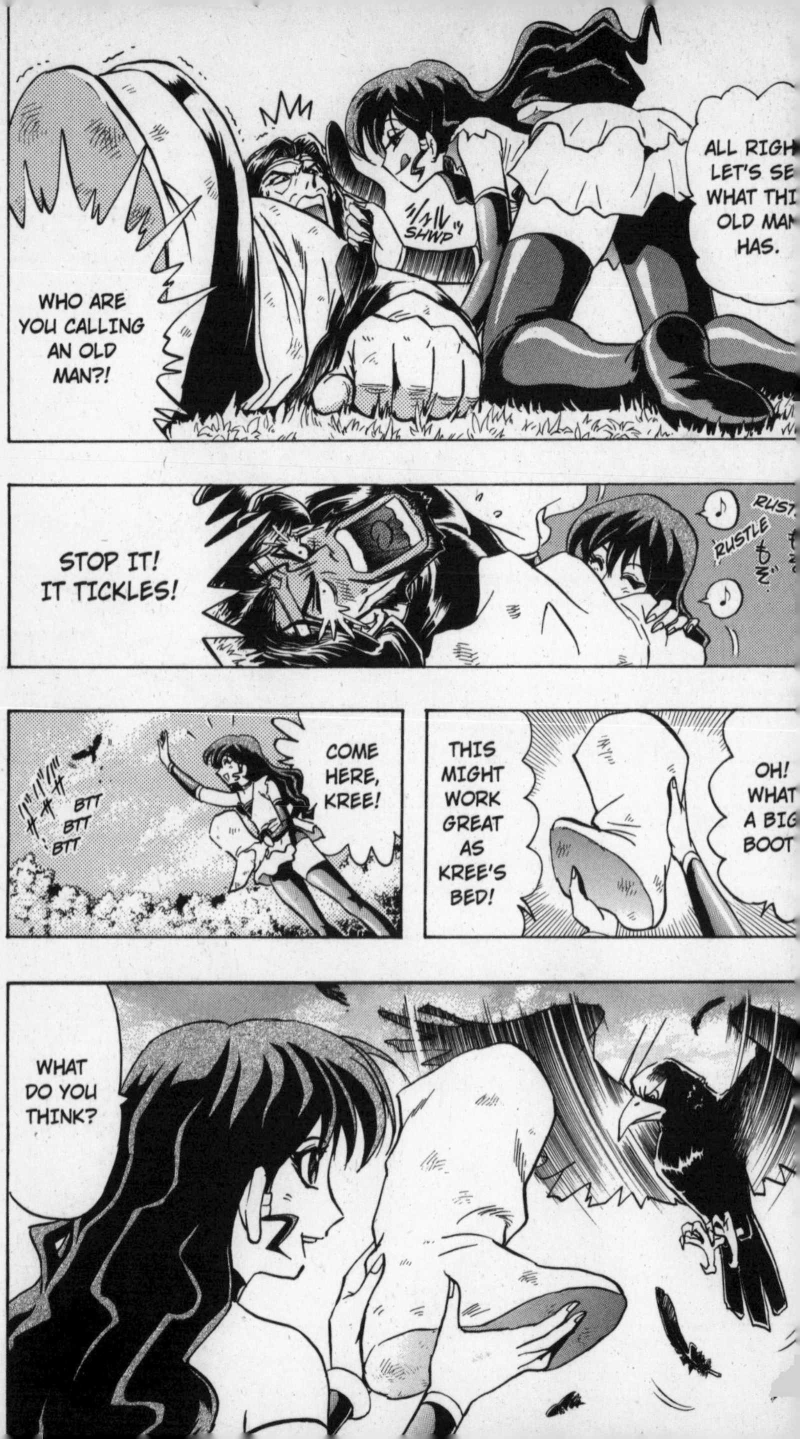
ALL RIGH
LET'S SE
WHAT THI
OLD MA
HAS.
SHWP
WHO ARE YOU CALLING AN OLD MAN?!
RUST
RUSTLE
STOP IT! IT TICKLES!
OH! WHAT A BIG BOOT
THIS MIGHT WORK GREAT AS KREE'S BED!
COME HERE, KREE!
BTT BTT BTT
WHAT DO YOU THINK?

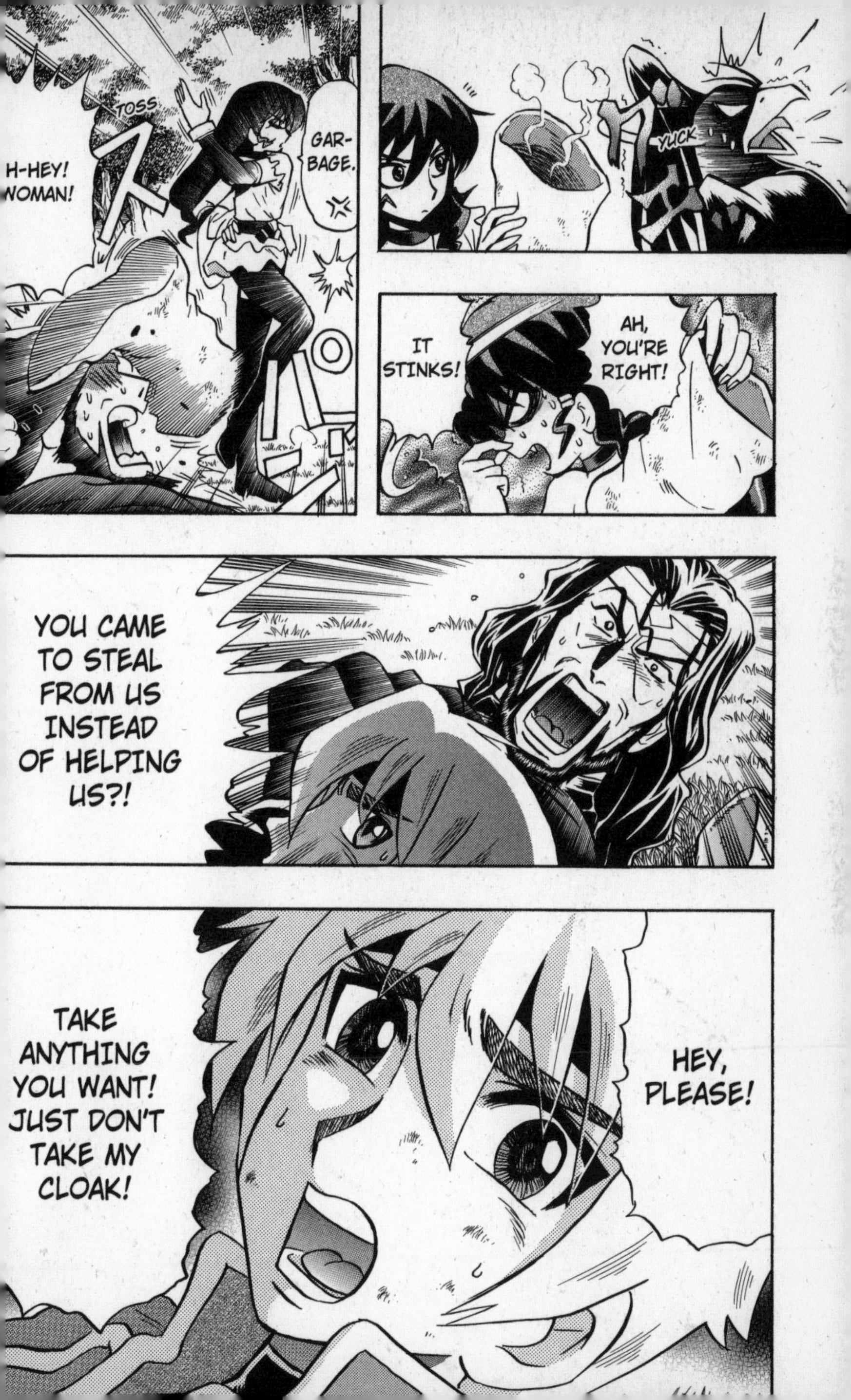
YUCK
AH, YOU'RE RIGHT!
IT STINKS!
GAR-BAGE.
TOSS
H-HEY! WOMAN!
YOU CAME TO STEAL FROM US INSTEAD OF HELPING US?!
HEY, PLEASE!
TAKE ANYTHING YOU WANT! JUST DON'T TAKE MY CLOAK!

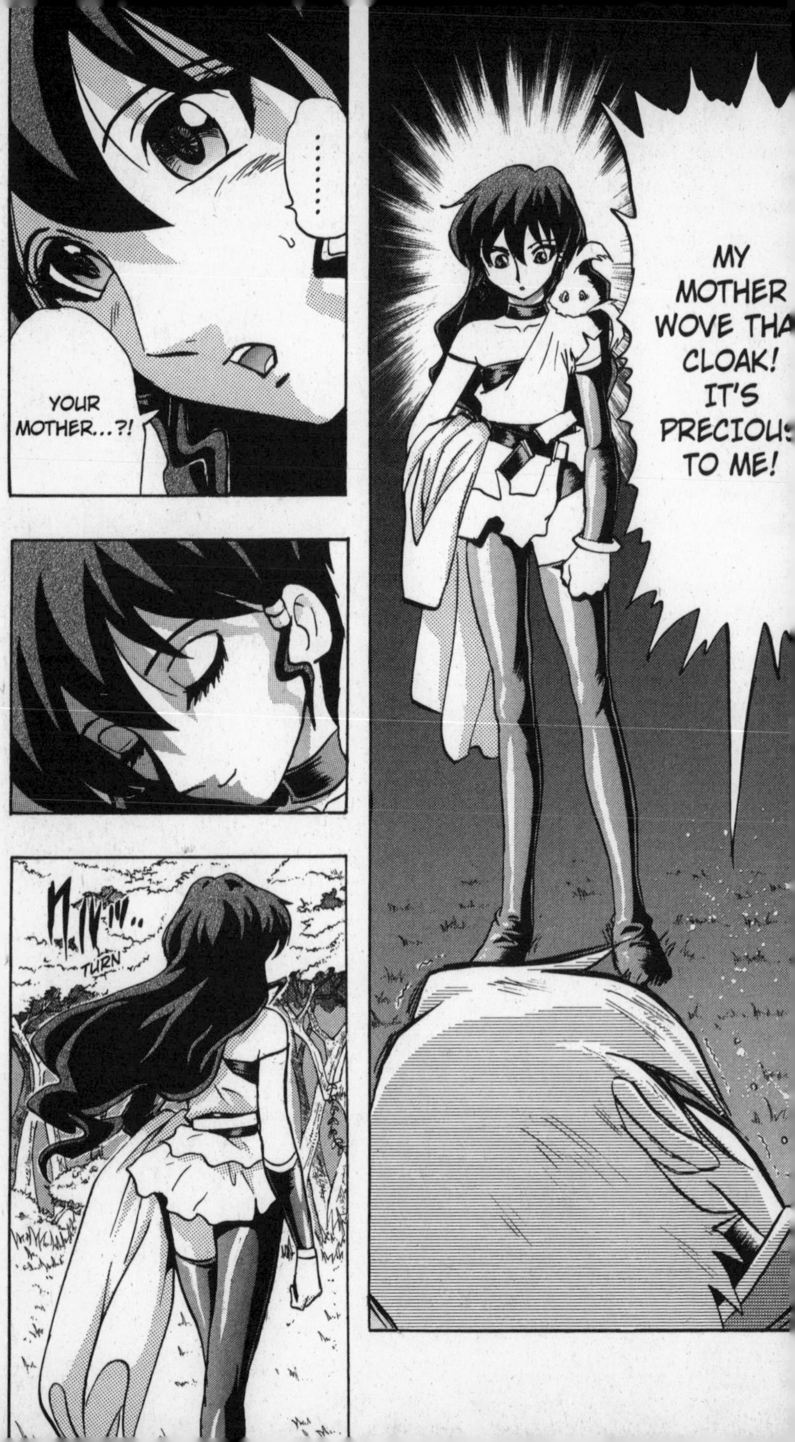
MY MOTHER WOVE THA CLOAK! IT'S PRECIOU TO ME!
......
YOUR MOTHER...?!
TURN

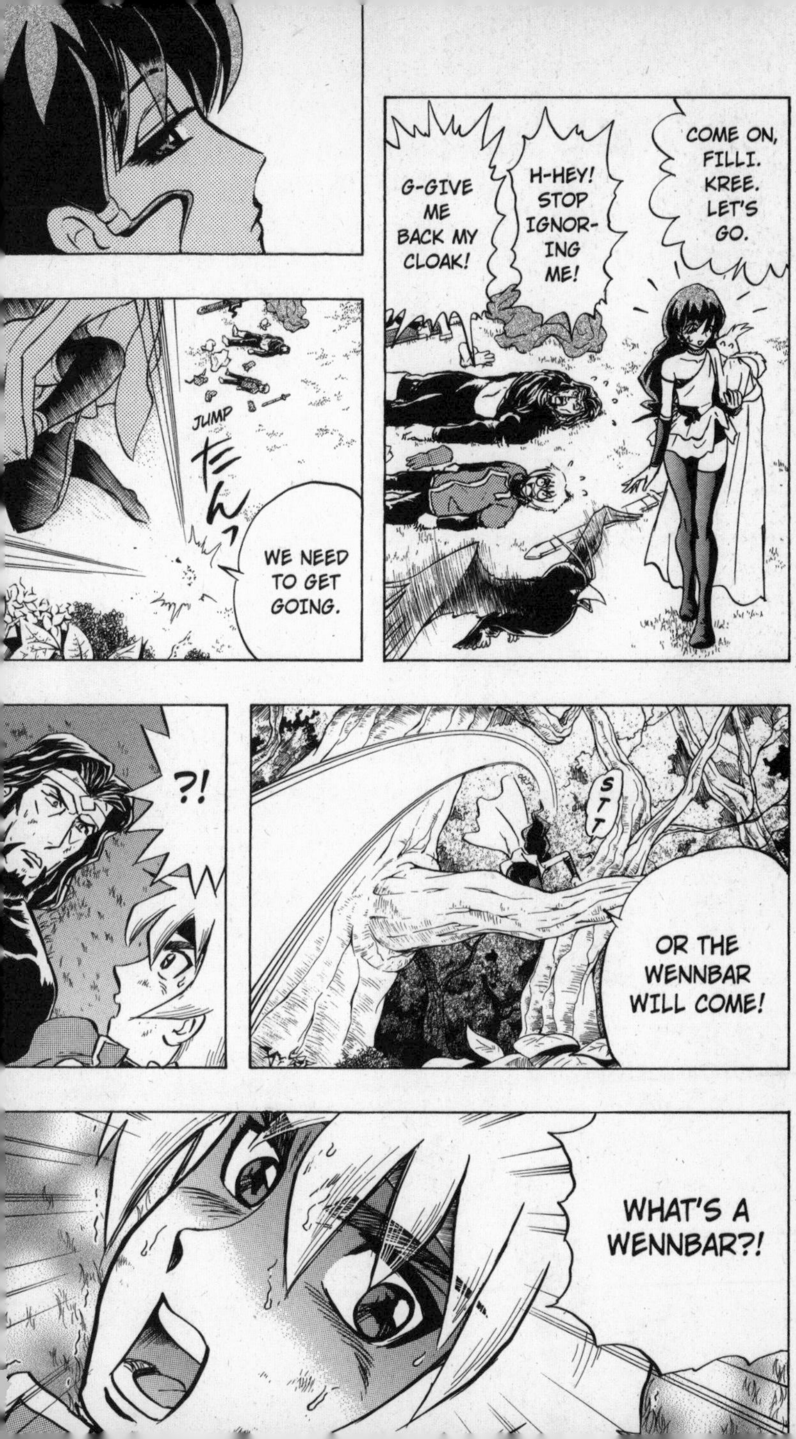
COME ON, FILLI. KREE. LET'S GO.
H-HEY! STOP IGNOR-ING ME!
G-GIVE ME BACK MY CLOAK!
JUMP
たんっ
WE NEED TO GET GOING.
STT
OR THE WENNBAR WILL COME!
?!
WHAT'S A WENNBAR?!

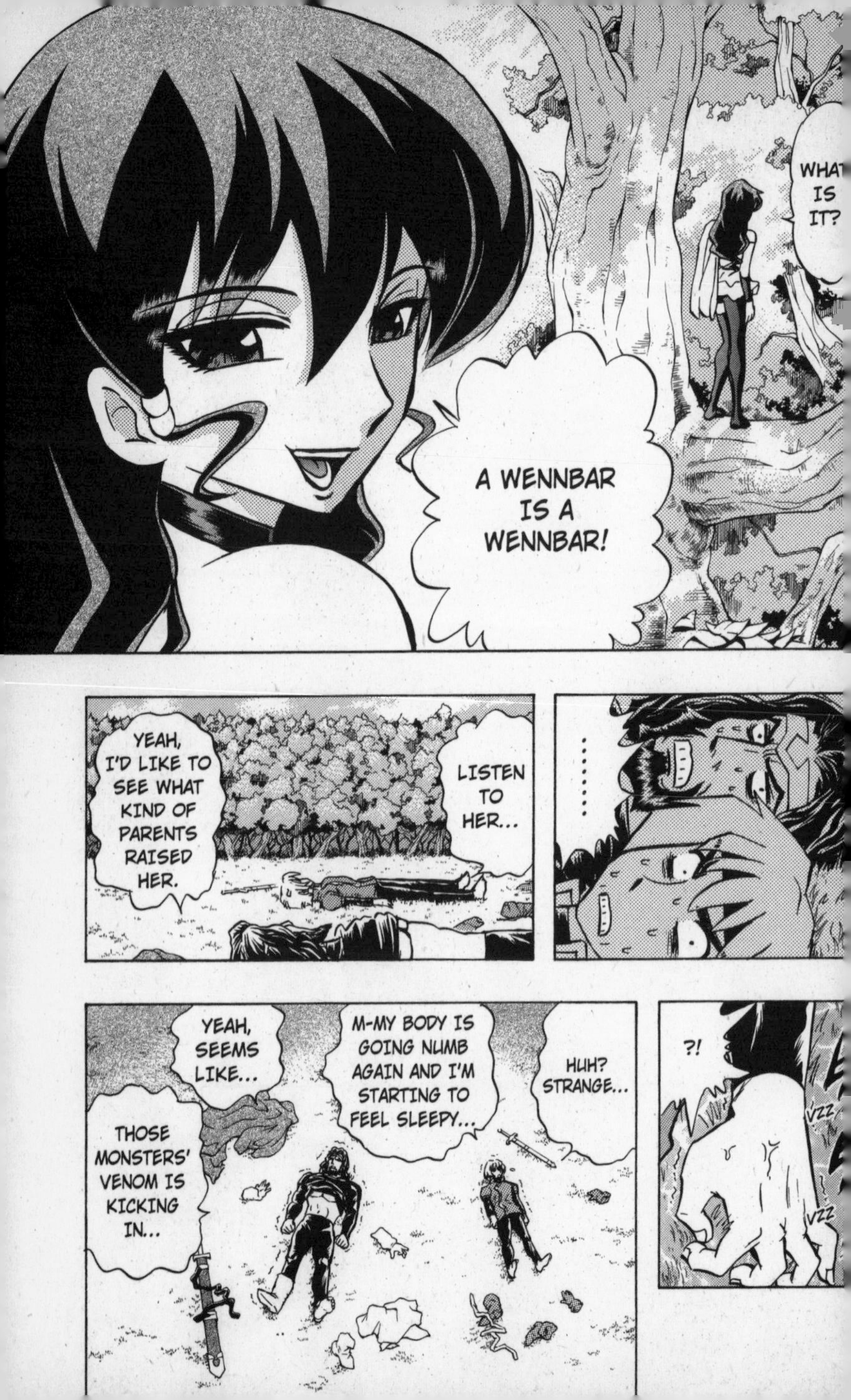
WHAT IS IT?
A WENNBAR IS A WENNBAR!
......
LISTEN TO HER...
YEAH, I'D LIKE TO SEE WHAT KIND OF PARENTS RAISED HER.
?!
VZZ
VZZ
HUH? STRANGE...
M-MY BODY IS GOING NUMB AGAIN AND I'M STARTING TO FEEL SLEEPY...
YEAH, SEEMS LIKE...
THOSE MONSTERS' VENOM IS KICKING IN...

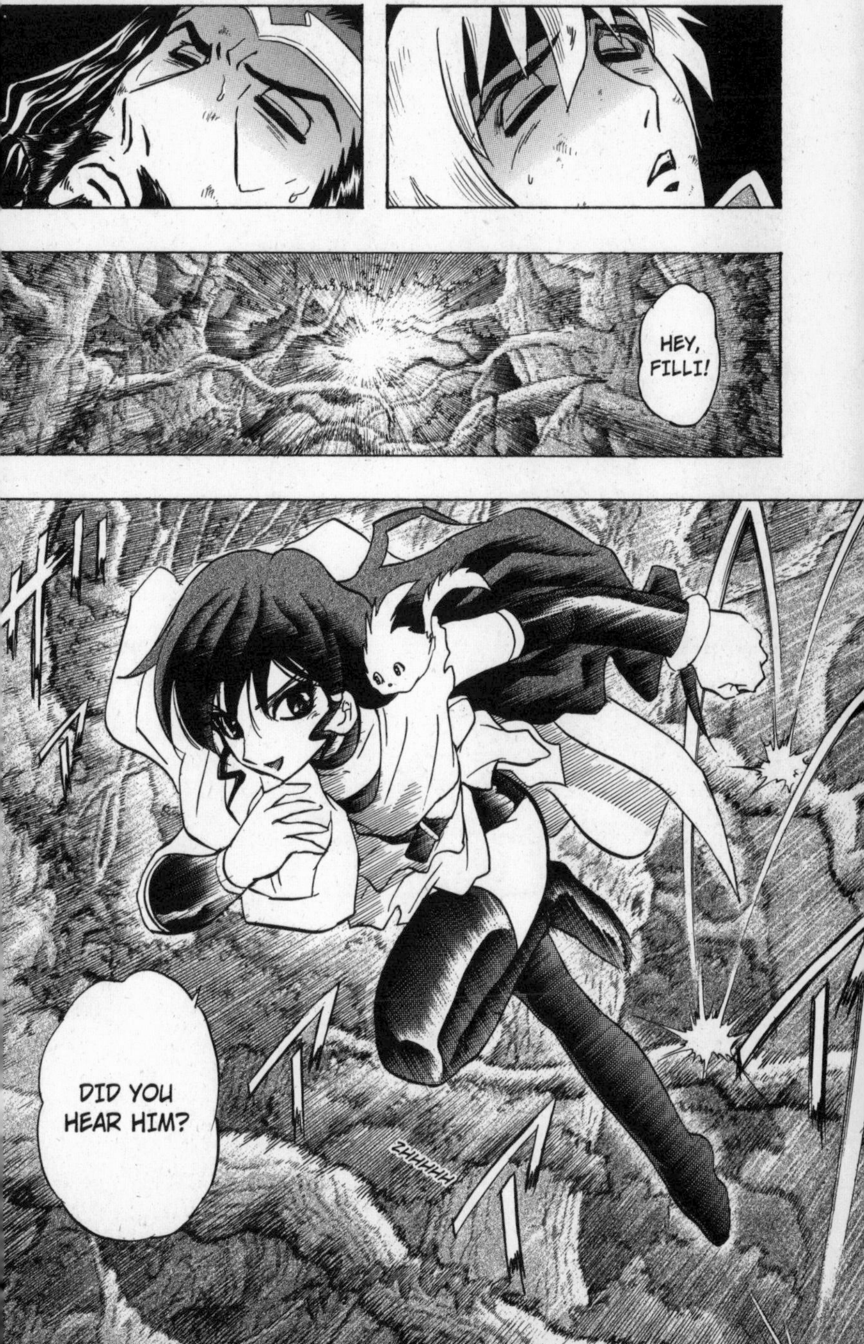
HEY, FILLI!
DID YOU HEAR HIM?
ZHHHHH

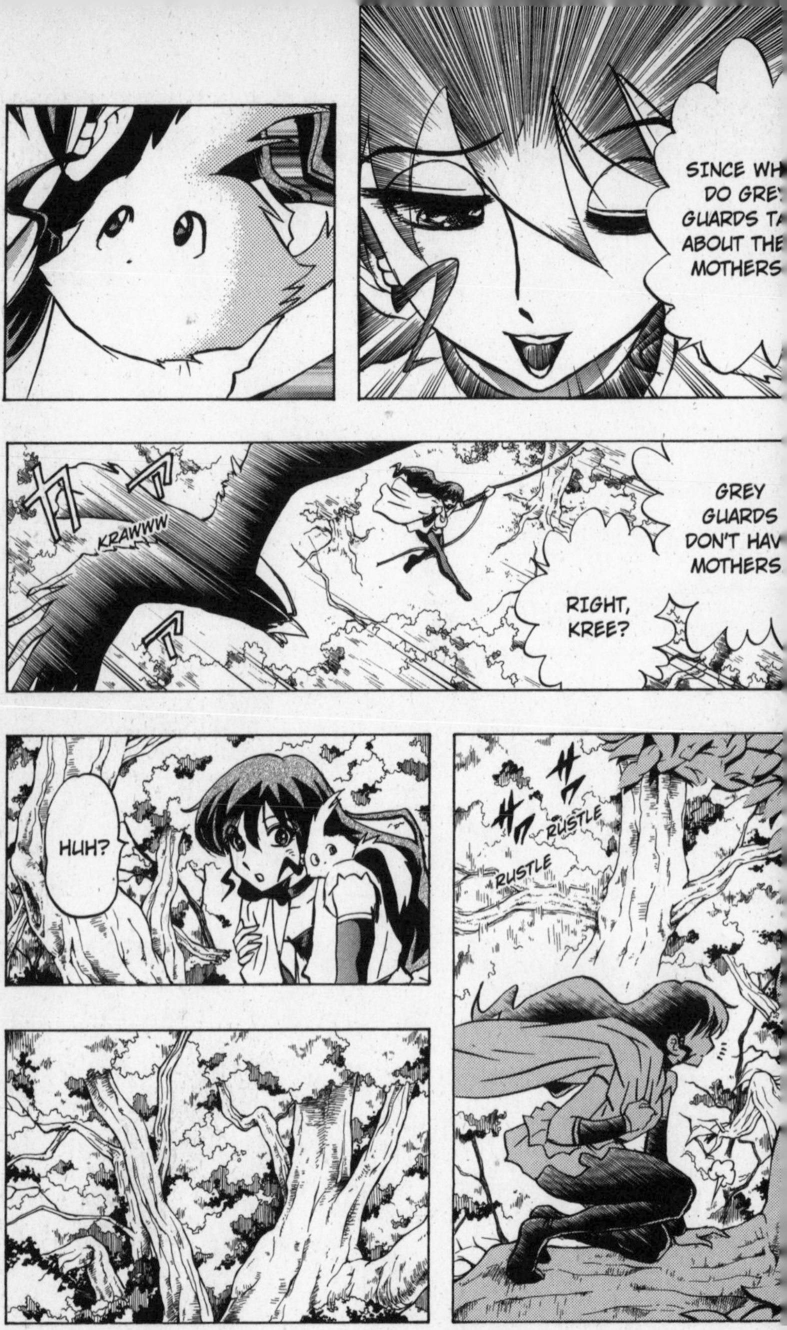
SINCE WH DO GREY GUARDS TA ABOUT THE MOTHERS
GREY GUARDS DON'T HAV MOTHERS
RIGHT, KREE?
KRAWWW
RUSTLE
RUSTLE
HUH?

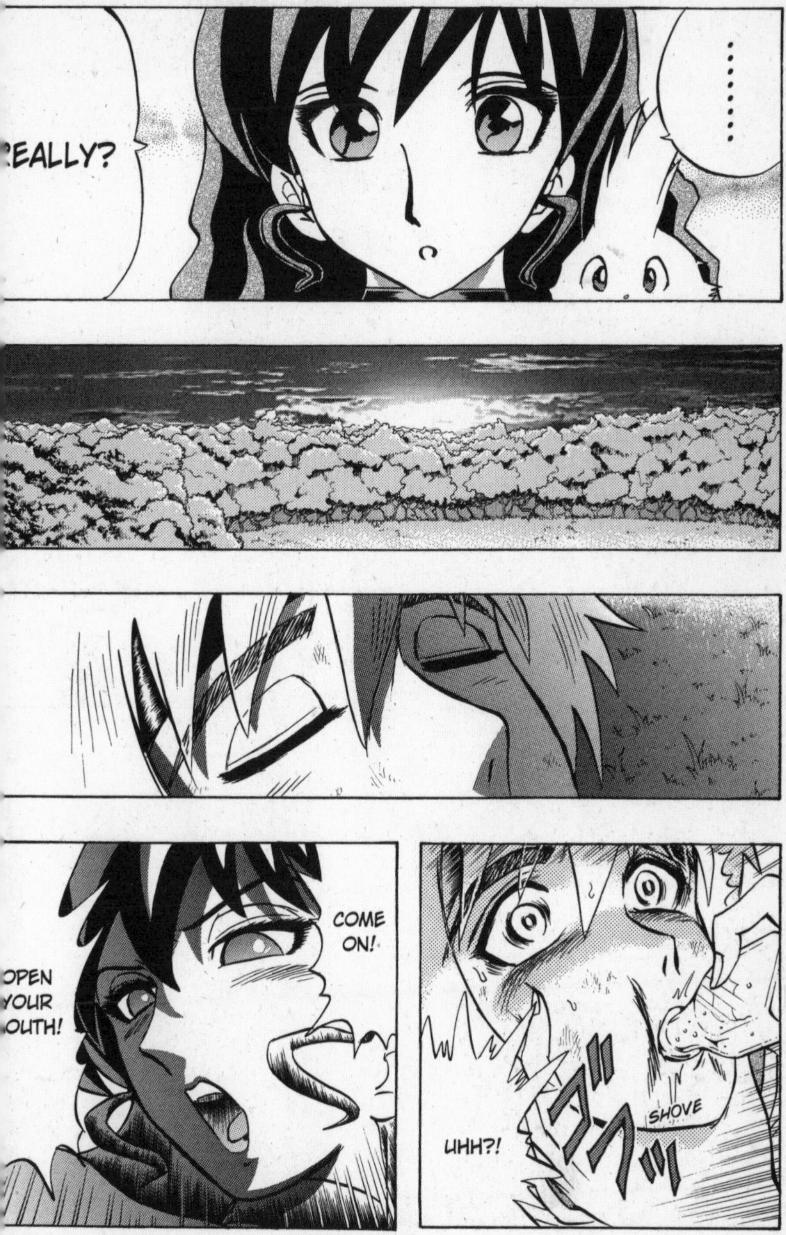
......
REALLY?
SHOVE
UHH?!
COME ON!
OPEN YOUR MOUTH!

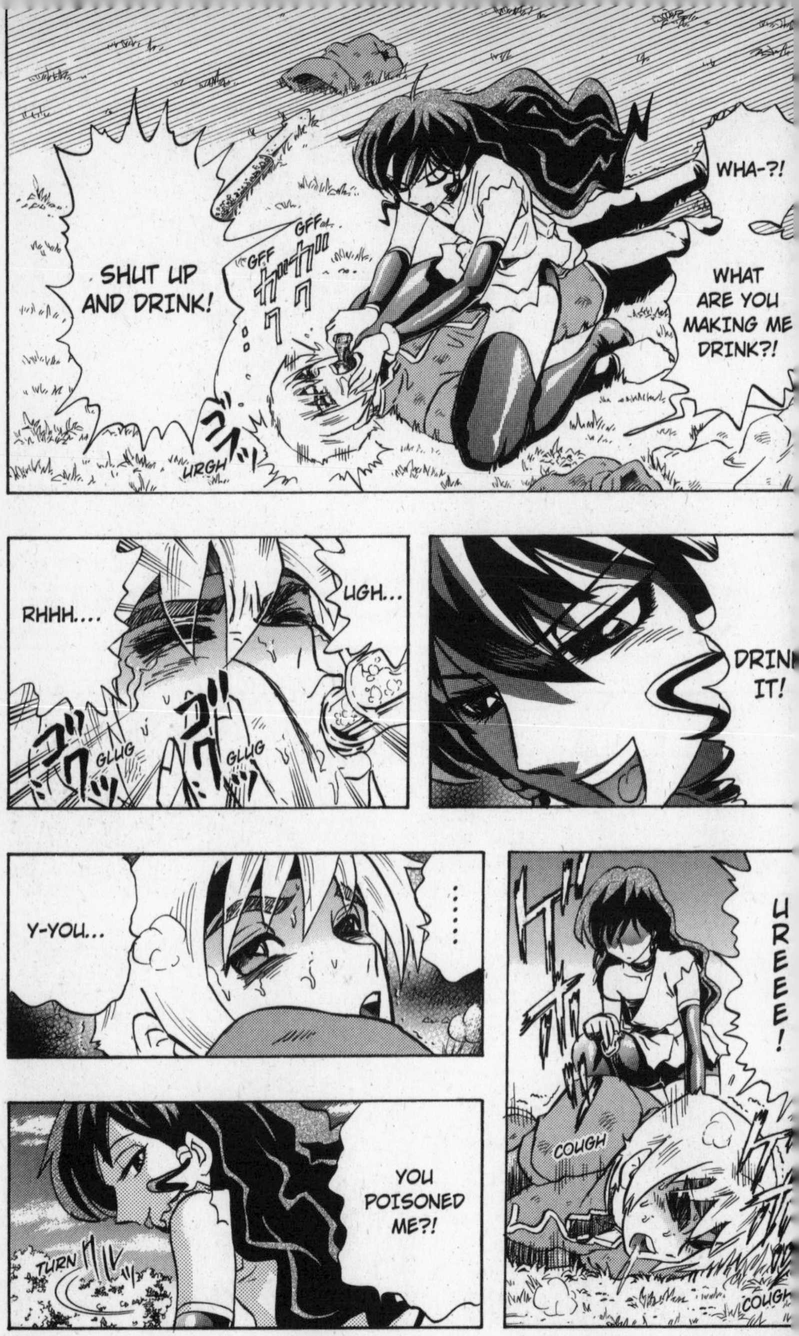

WHA-?!
WHAT ARE YOU MAKING ME DRINK?!
GFF
GFF
SHUT UP AND DRINK!
URGH
DRINK IT!
UGH...
RHHH....
GLUG
GLUG
UREEEE!
COUGH
COUGH
......
Y-YOU...
YOU POISONED ME?!
TURN

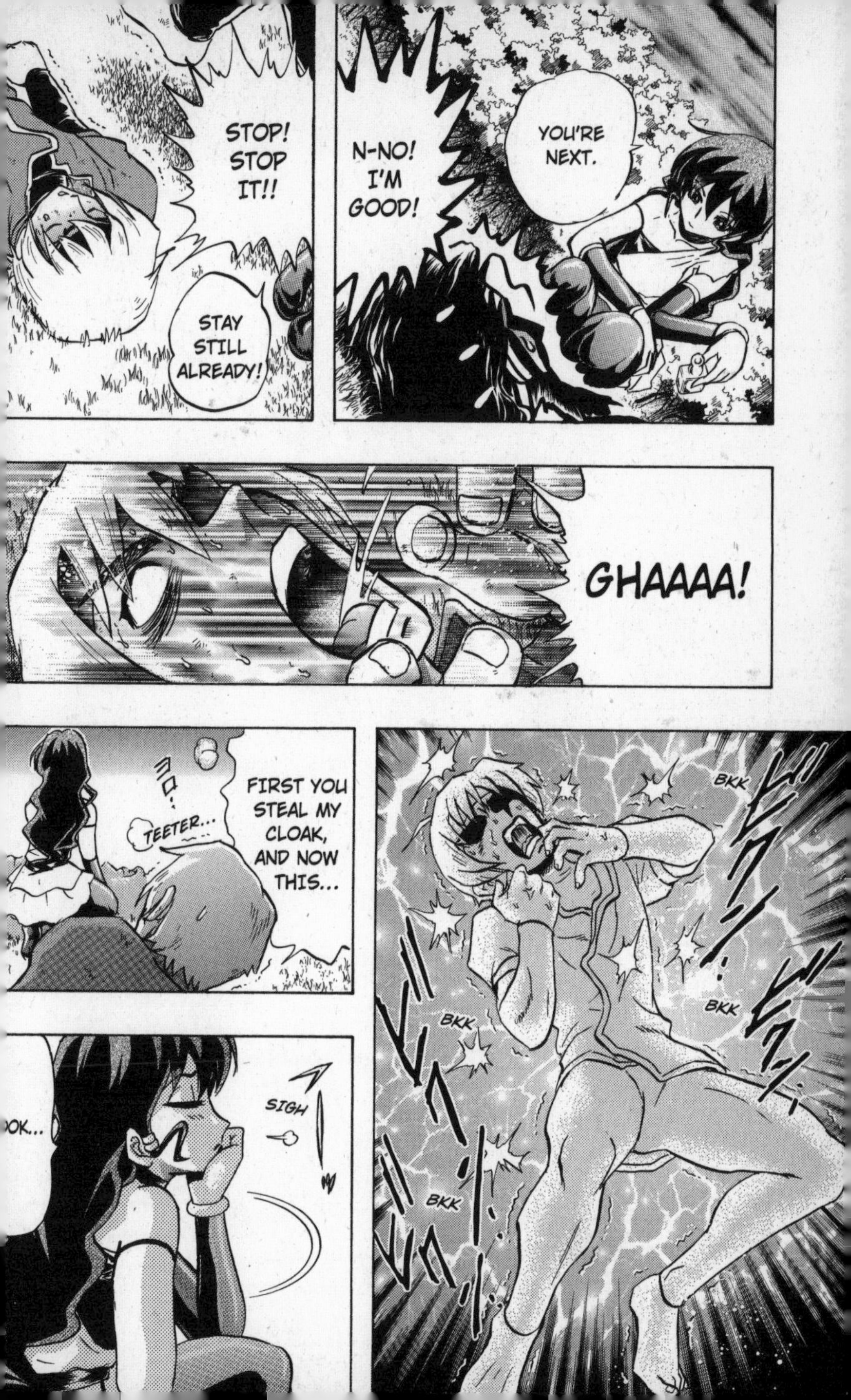
YOU'RE NEXT.
N-NO! I'M GOOD!
STOP! STOP IT!!
STAY STILL ALREADY!
GHAAAA!
BKK
BKK
BKK
BKK
FIRST YOU STEAL MY CLOAK, AND NOW THIS...
TEETER...
SIGH

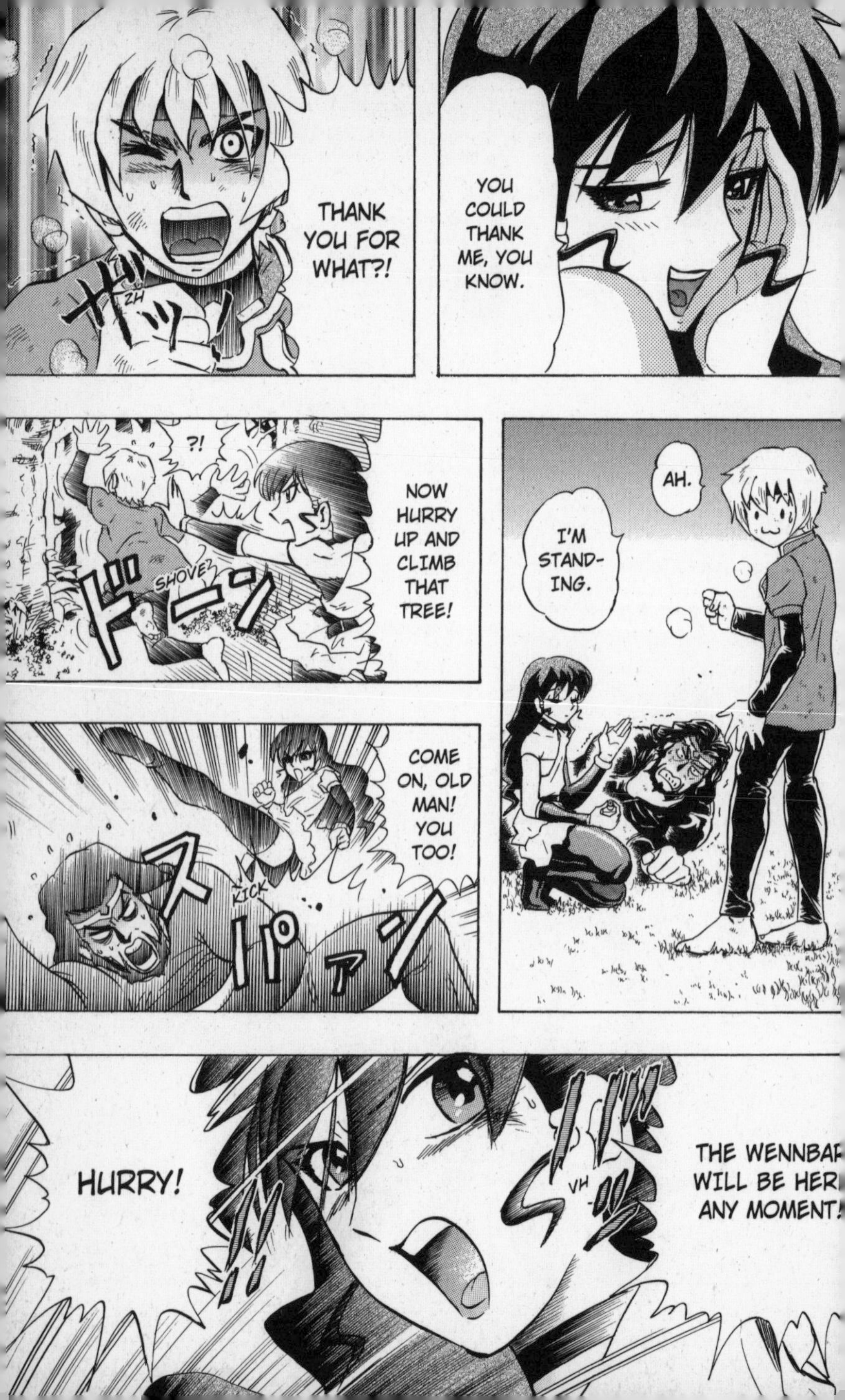
YOU COULD THANK ME, YOU KNOW.
THANK YOU FOR WHAT?!
ZH
AH.
I'M STAND-ING.
NOW HURRY UP AND CLIMB THAT TREE!
SHOVE
COME ON, OLD MAN! YOU TOO!
KICK
THE WENNBAR WILL BE HER ANY MOMENT!
VH
HURRY!

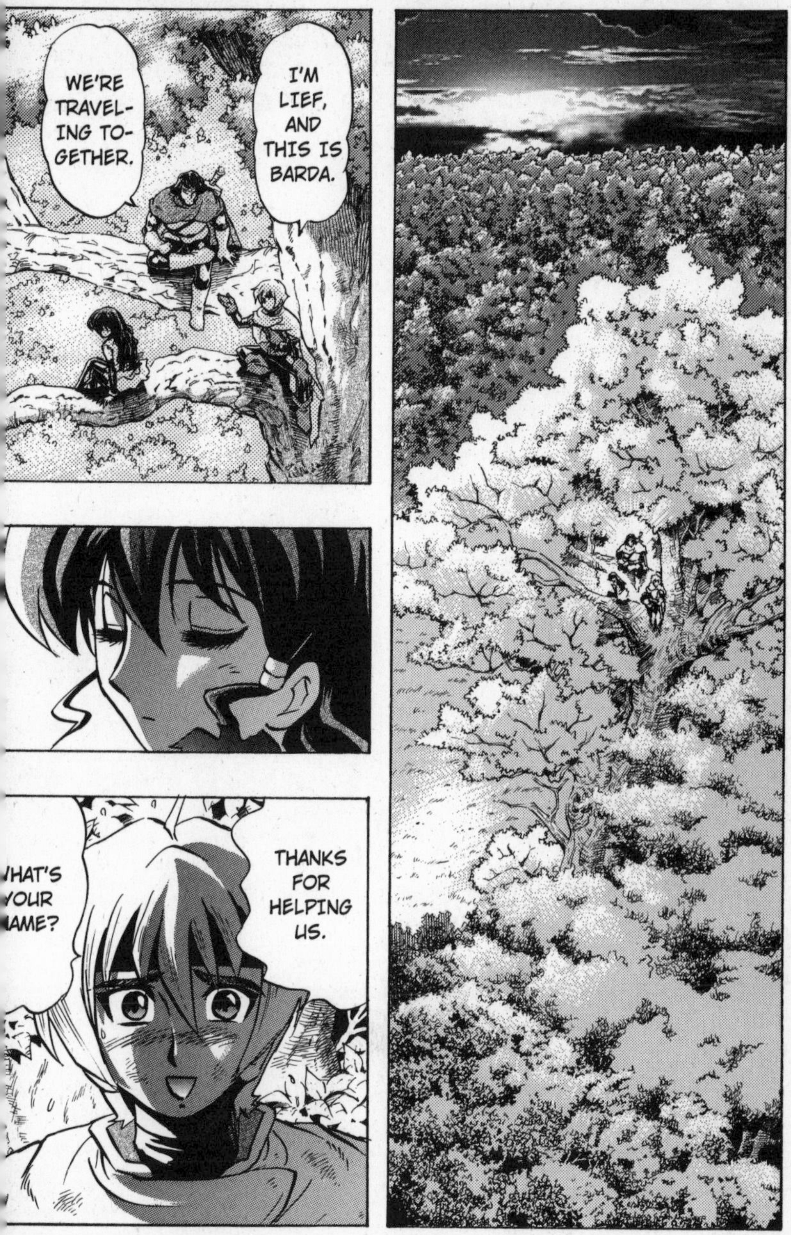
I'M LIEF, AND THIS IS BARDA.
WE'RE TRAVEL-ING TO-GETHER.
THANKS FOR HELPING US.
HAT'S YOUR AME?

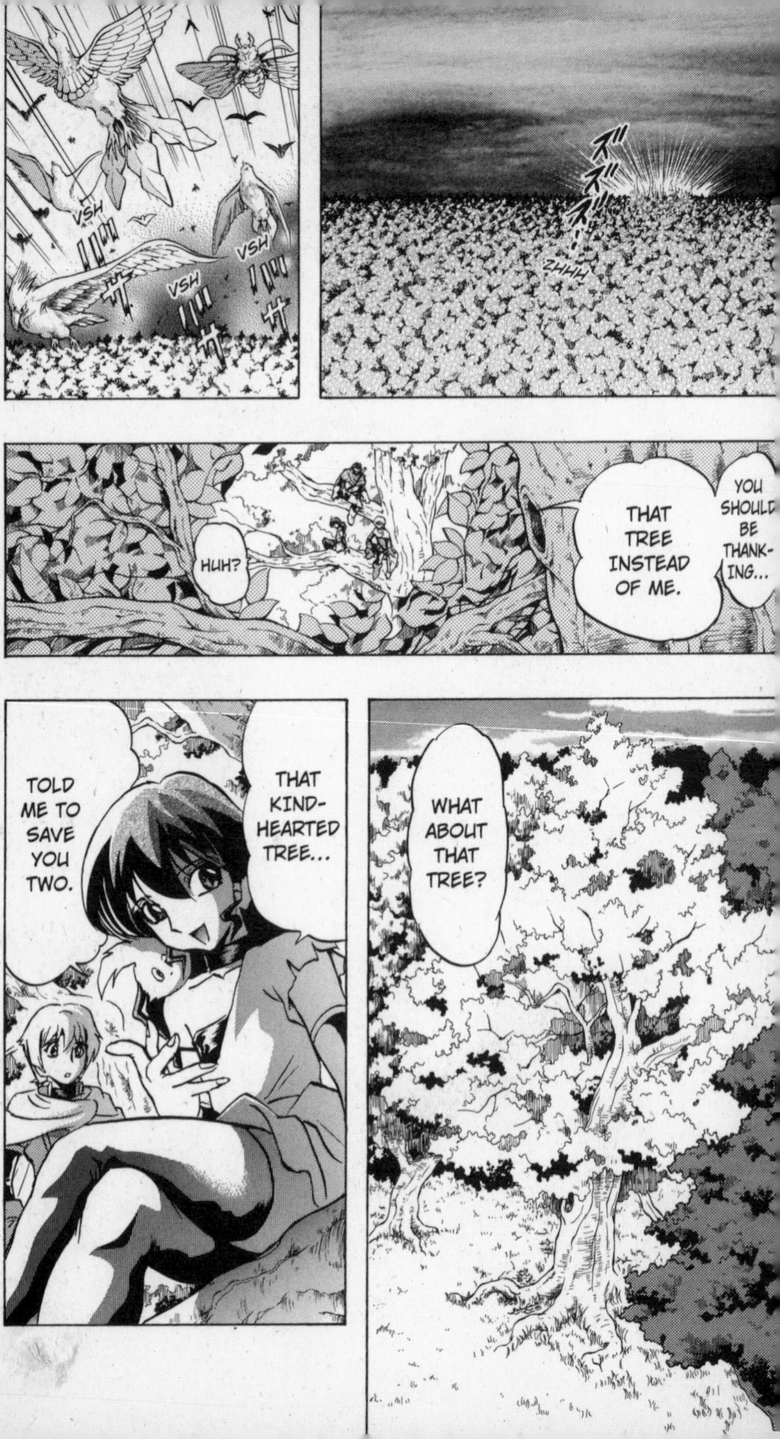
ZHHH
VSH
VSH
VSH
YOU SHOULD BE THANKING...
THAT TREE INSTEAD OF ME.
HUH?
WHAT ABOUT THAT TREE?
THAT KIND-HEARTED TREE...
TOLD ME TO SAVE YOU TWO.

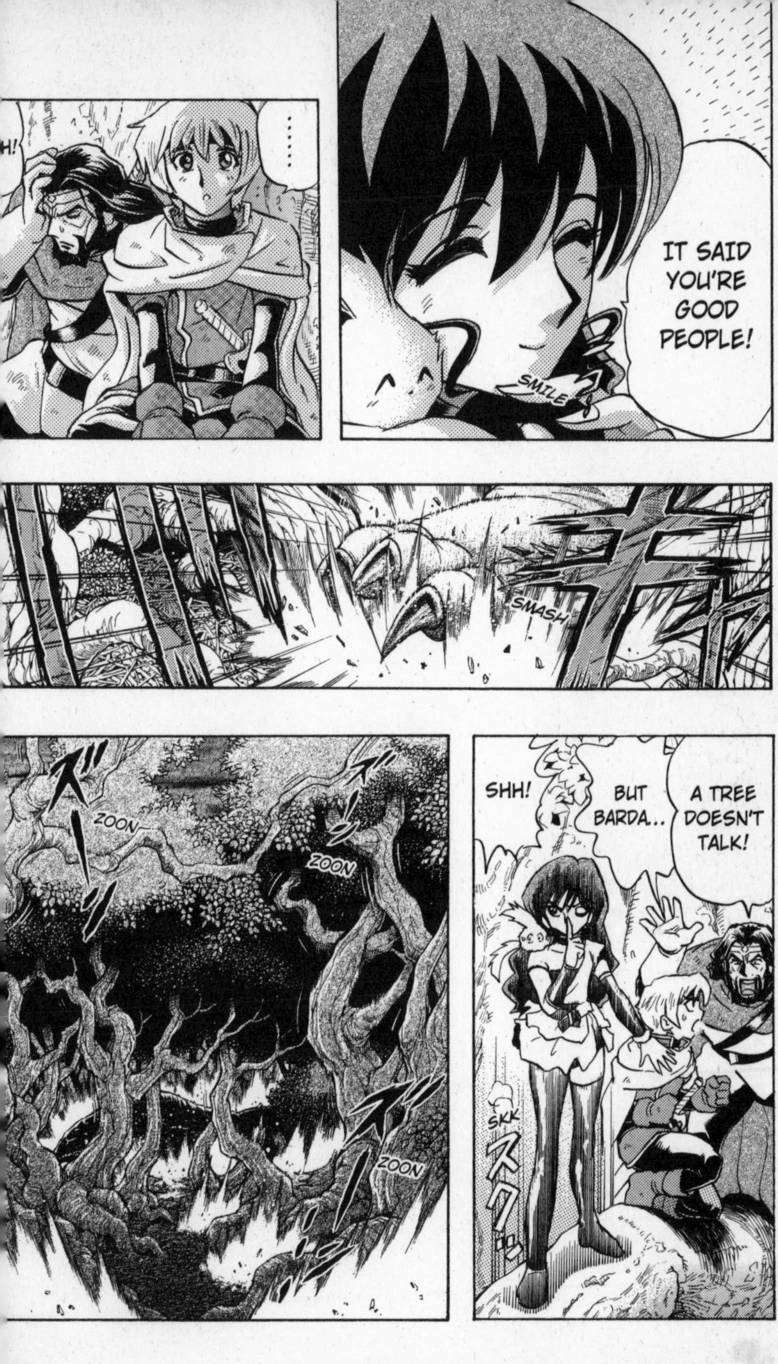
IT SAID YOU'RE GOOD PEOPLE!
SMILE
SMASH
A TREE DOESN'T TALK!
BUT BARDA...
SHH!
SKK
ZOON
ZOON
ZOON

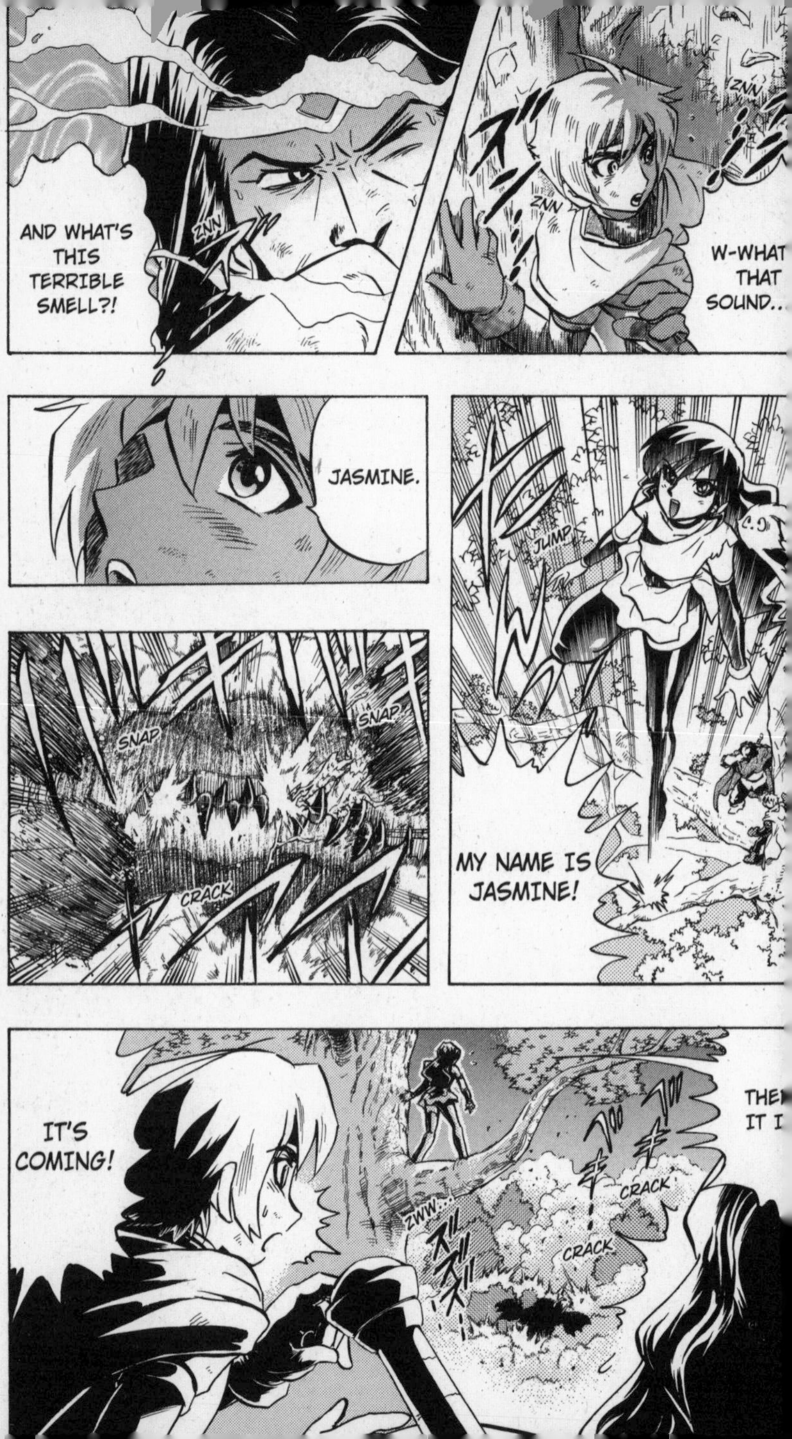
ZNN
ZNN
W-WHAT THAT SOUND..
ZNN
AND WHAT'S THIS TERRIBLE SMELL?!
JUMP
MY NAME IS JASMINE!
JASMINE.
SNAP
SNAP
CRACK
CRACK
CRACK
ZWW...
IT'S COMING!

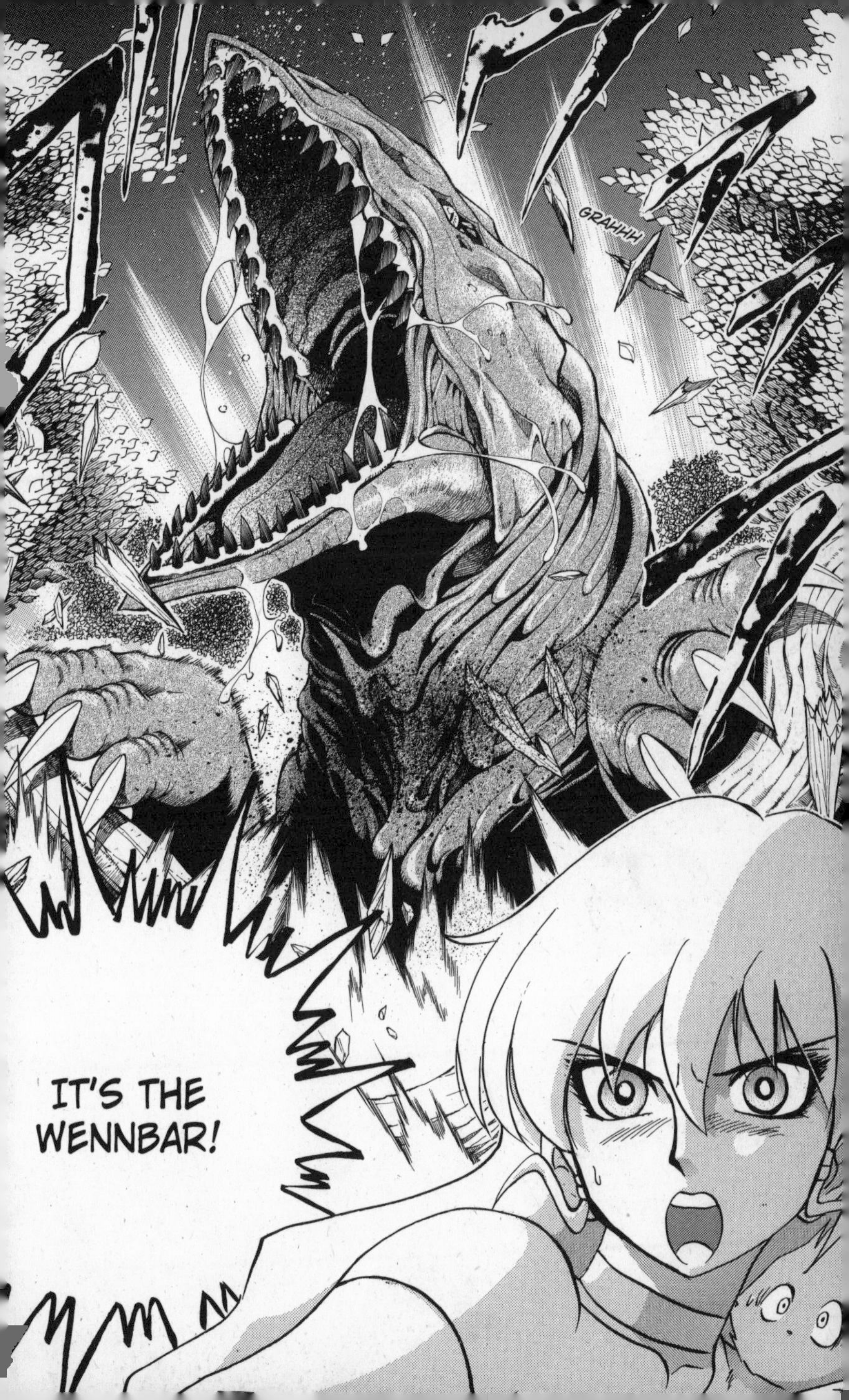
GRAHHH
IT'S THE WENNBAR!

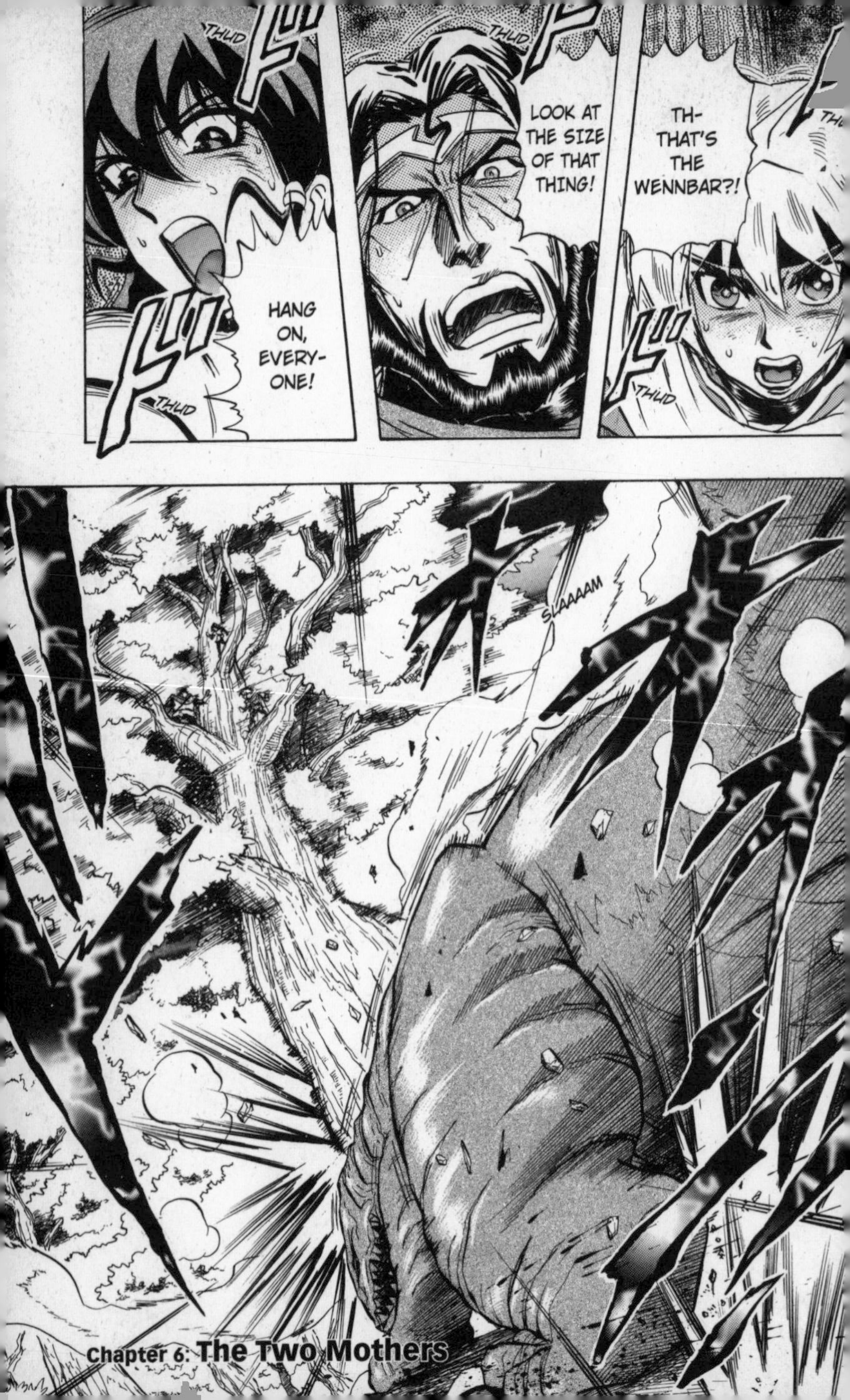
THUD
TH-
THAT'S
THE
WENNBAR?!
THUD
THUD
LOOK AT
THE SIZE
OF THAT
THING!
THUD
HANG
ON,
EVERY-
ONE!
THUD
SLAAAAM

Chapter 6: The Two Mothers

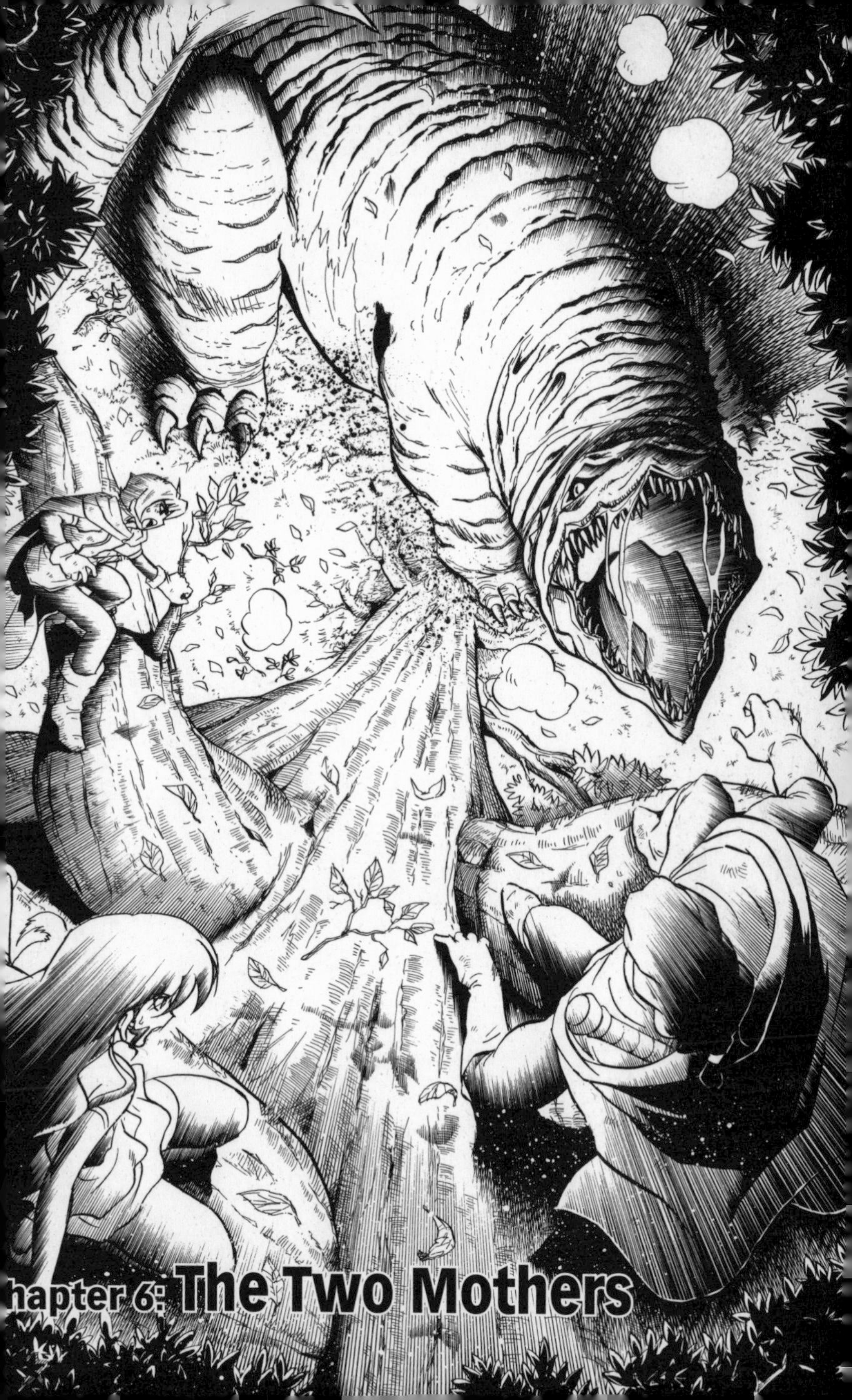
hapter 6: The Two Mothers

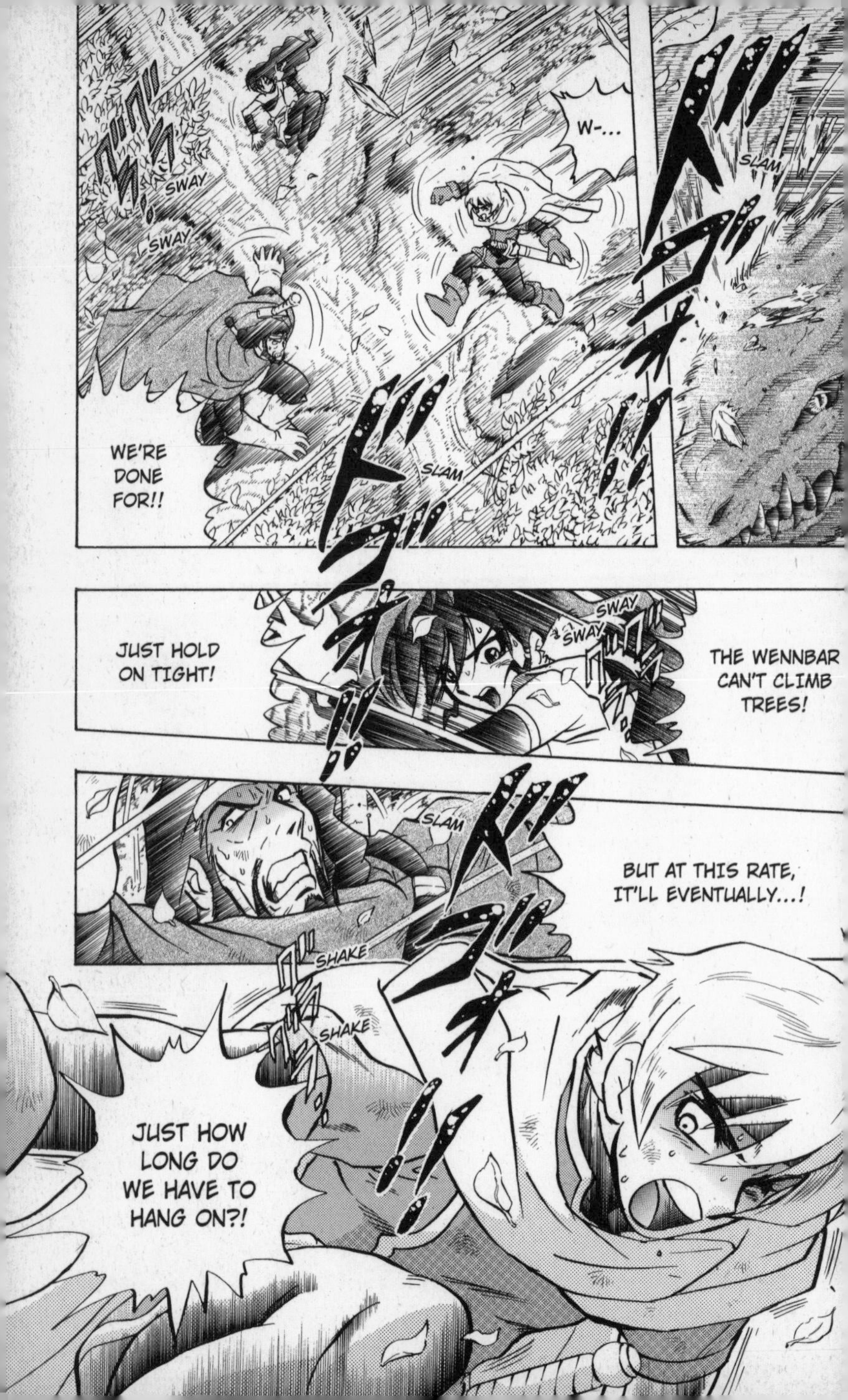
SLAM
W-...
SWAY
SWAY
SLAM
WE'RE DONE FOR!!
THE WENNBAR CAN'T CLIMB TREES!
SWAY
SWAY
JUST HOLD ON TIGHT!
BUT AT THIS RATE, IT'LL EVENTUALLY...!
SLAM
SHAKE
SHAKE
JUST HOW LONG DO WE HAVE TO HANG ON?!

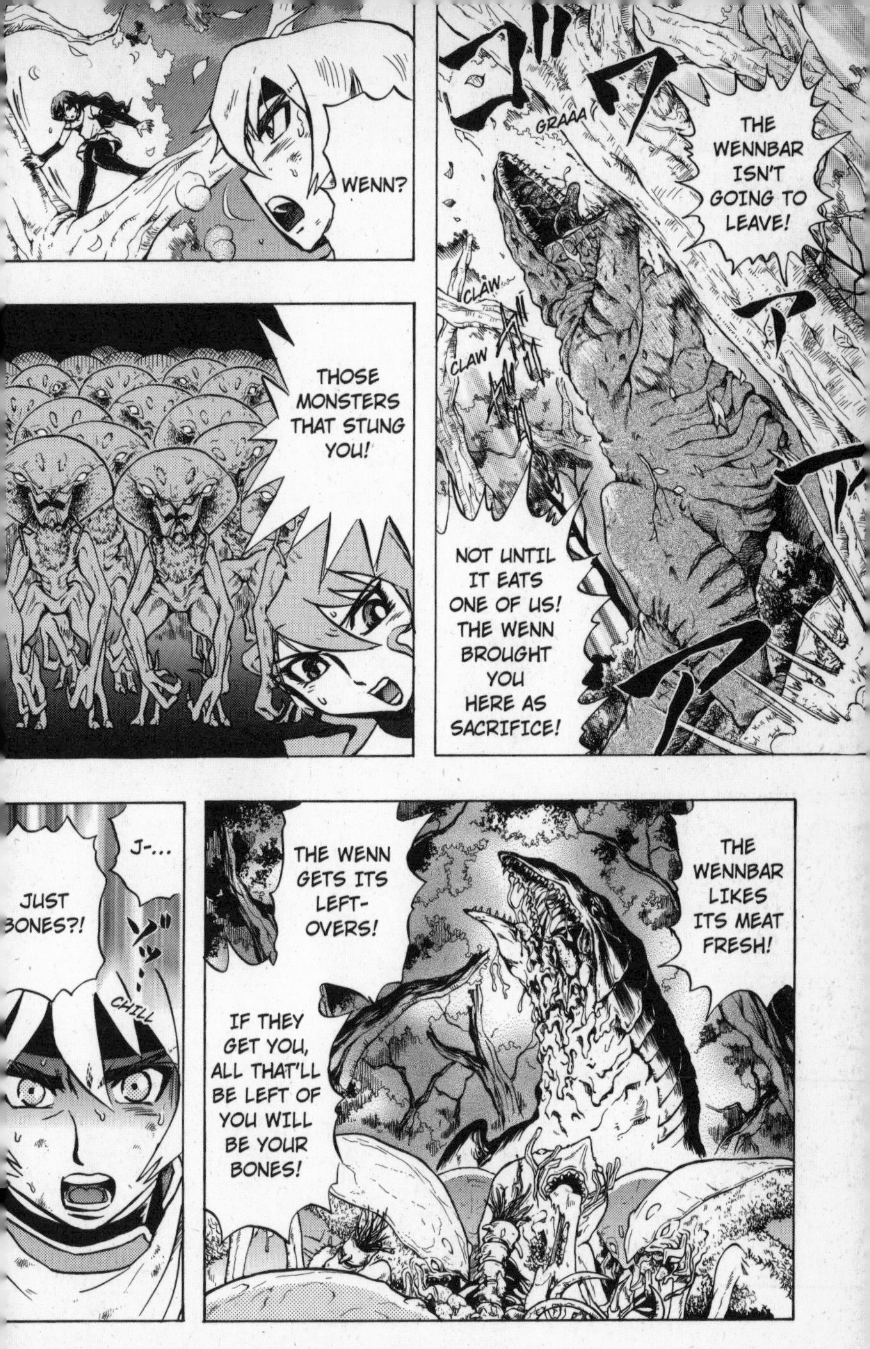
GRAAA
THE WENNBAR ISN'T GOING TO LEAVE!
CLAW
CLAW
NOT UNTIL IT EATS ONE OF US! THE WENN BROUGHT YOU HERE AS SACRIFICE!
WENN?
THOSE MONSTERS THAT STUNG YOU!
THE WENNBAR LIKES ITS MEAT FRESH!
THE WENN GETS ITS LEFT-OVERS!
IF THEY GET YOU, ALL THAT'LL BE LEFT OF YOU WILL BE YOUR BONES!
J-...
JUST BONES?!
CHILL

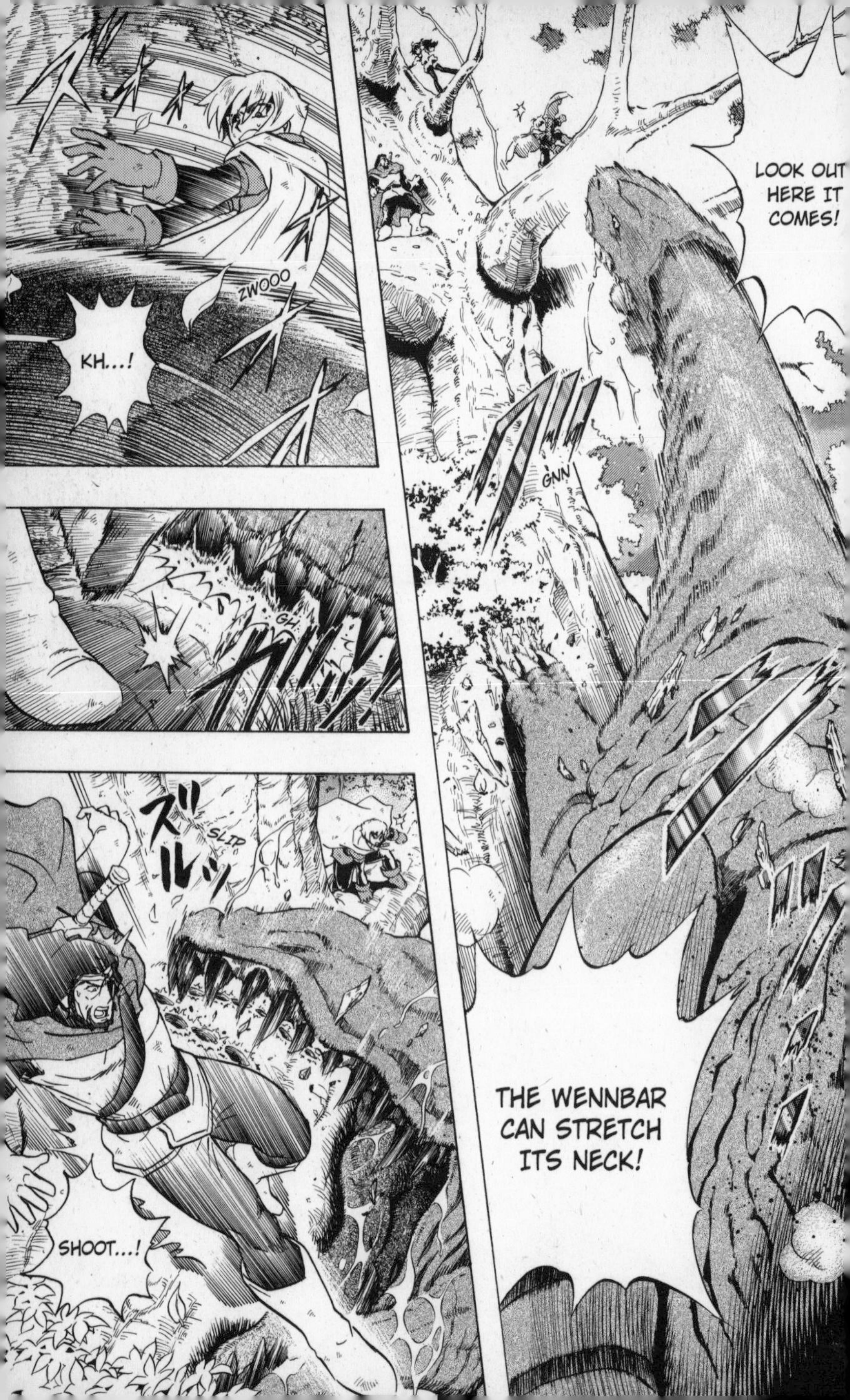
LOOK OUT HERE IT COMES!
GNN
THE WENNBAR CAN STRETCH ITS NECK!
ZWOOO
KH...!
GH
ズリルッ
SLIP
SHOOT...!

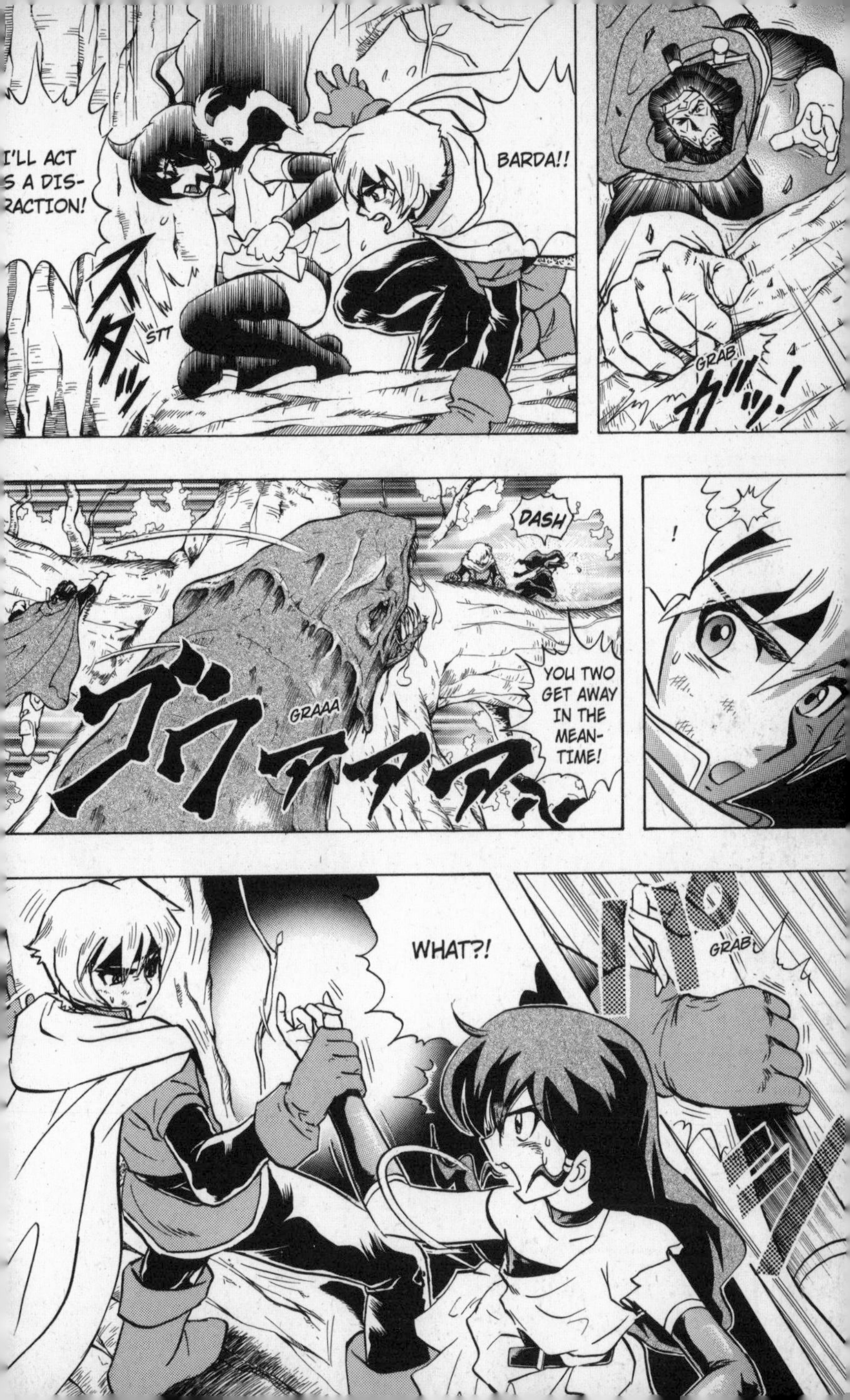
GRAB
BARDA!!
I'LL ACT
S A DIS-
RACTION!
STT
!
DASH
YOU TWO GET AWAY IN THE MEAN-TIME!
GRAAA
GRAB
WHAT?!

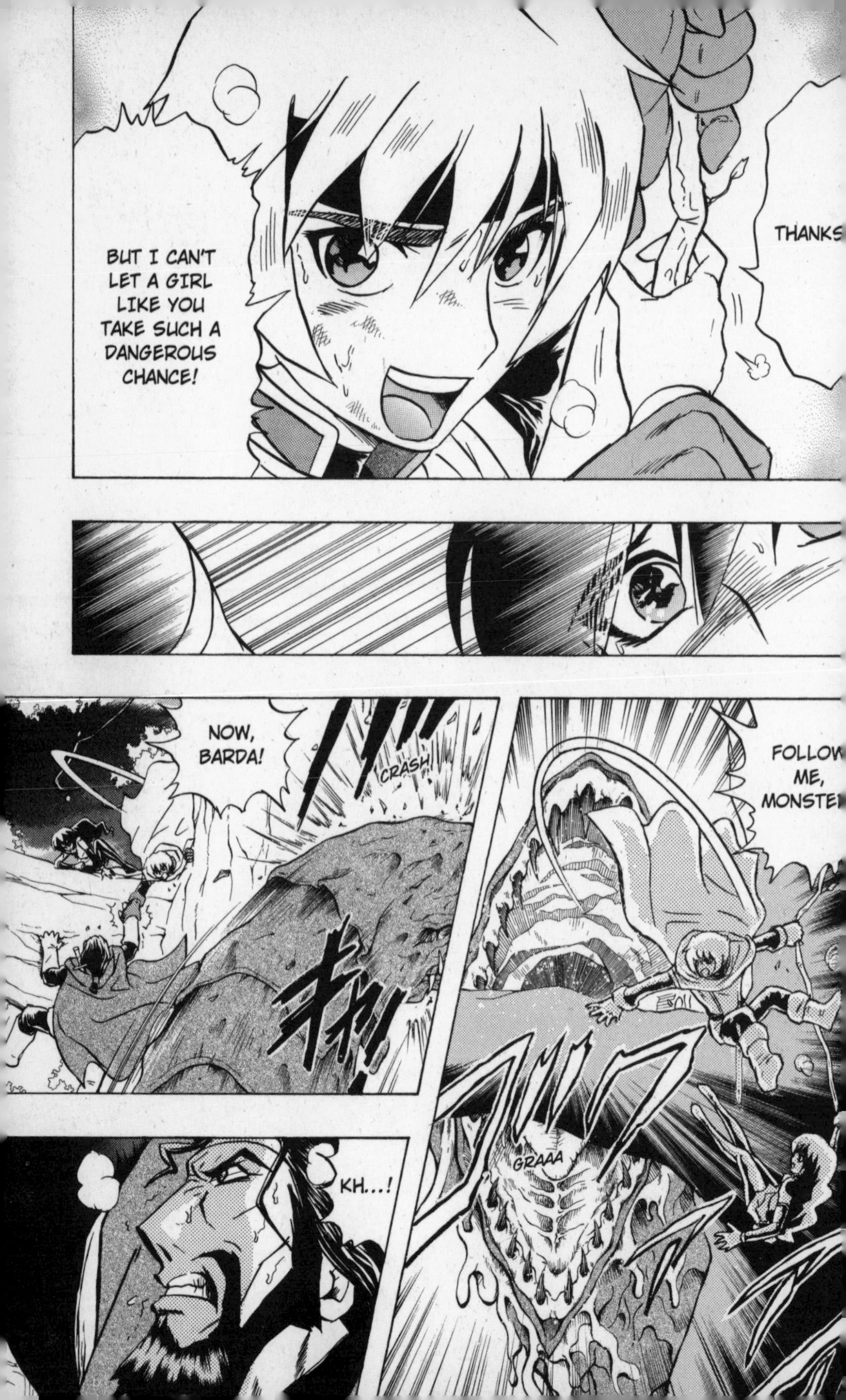
THANKS
BUT I CAN'T LET A GIRL LIKE YOU TAKE SUCH A DANGEROUS CHANCE!
FOLLOW ME, MONSTE
GRAAA
NOW, BARDA!
CRASH
KH...!

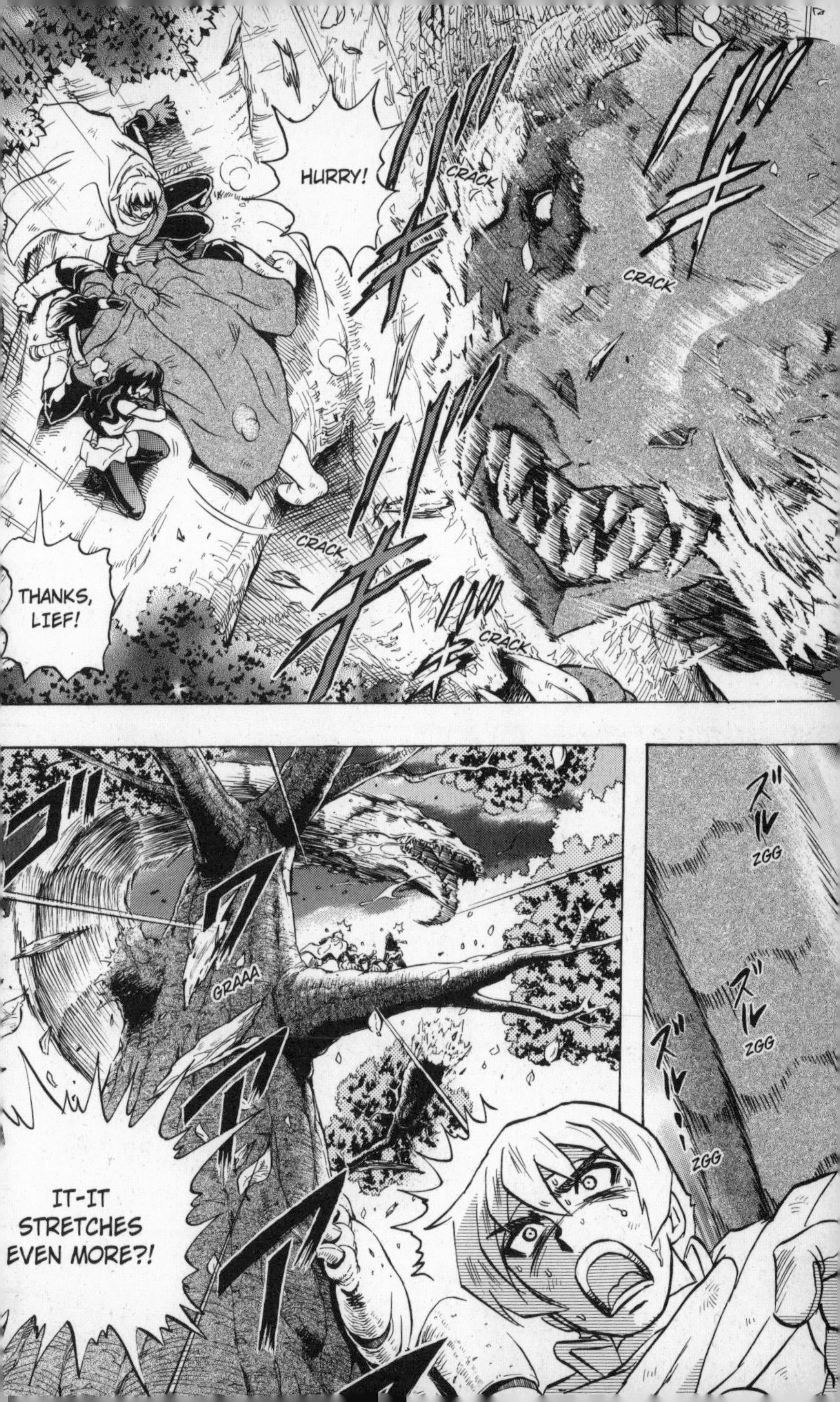
CRACK
CRACK
HURRY!
CRACK
CRACK
THANKS, LIEF!
ZGG
ZGG
ZGG
GRAAA
IT-IT STRETCHES EVEN MORE?!

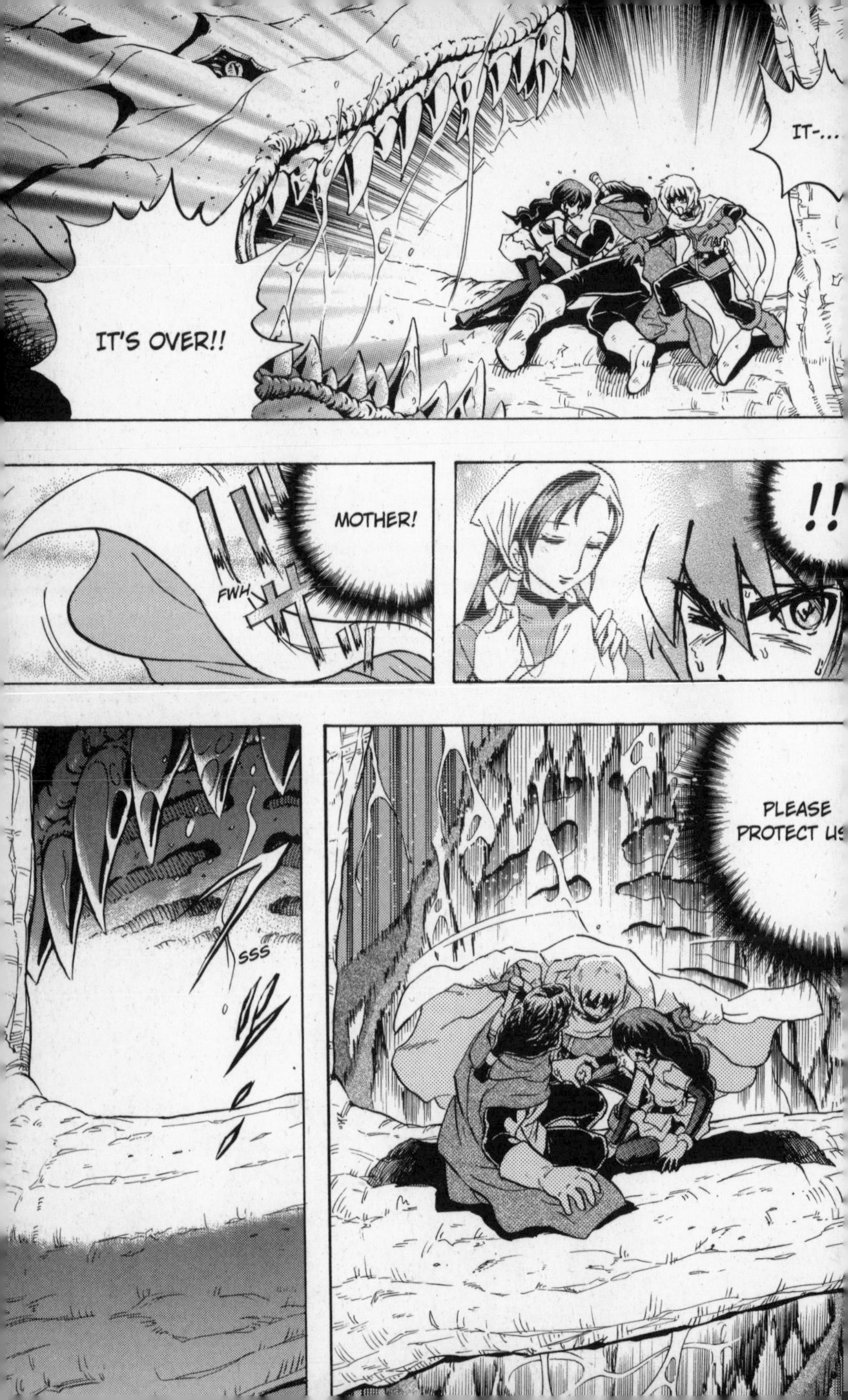
IT-...
IT'S OVER!!
!!
MOTHER!
FWH
PLEASE PROTECT US
SSS

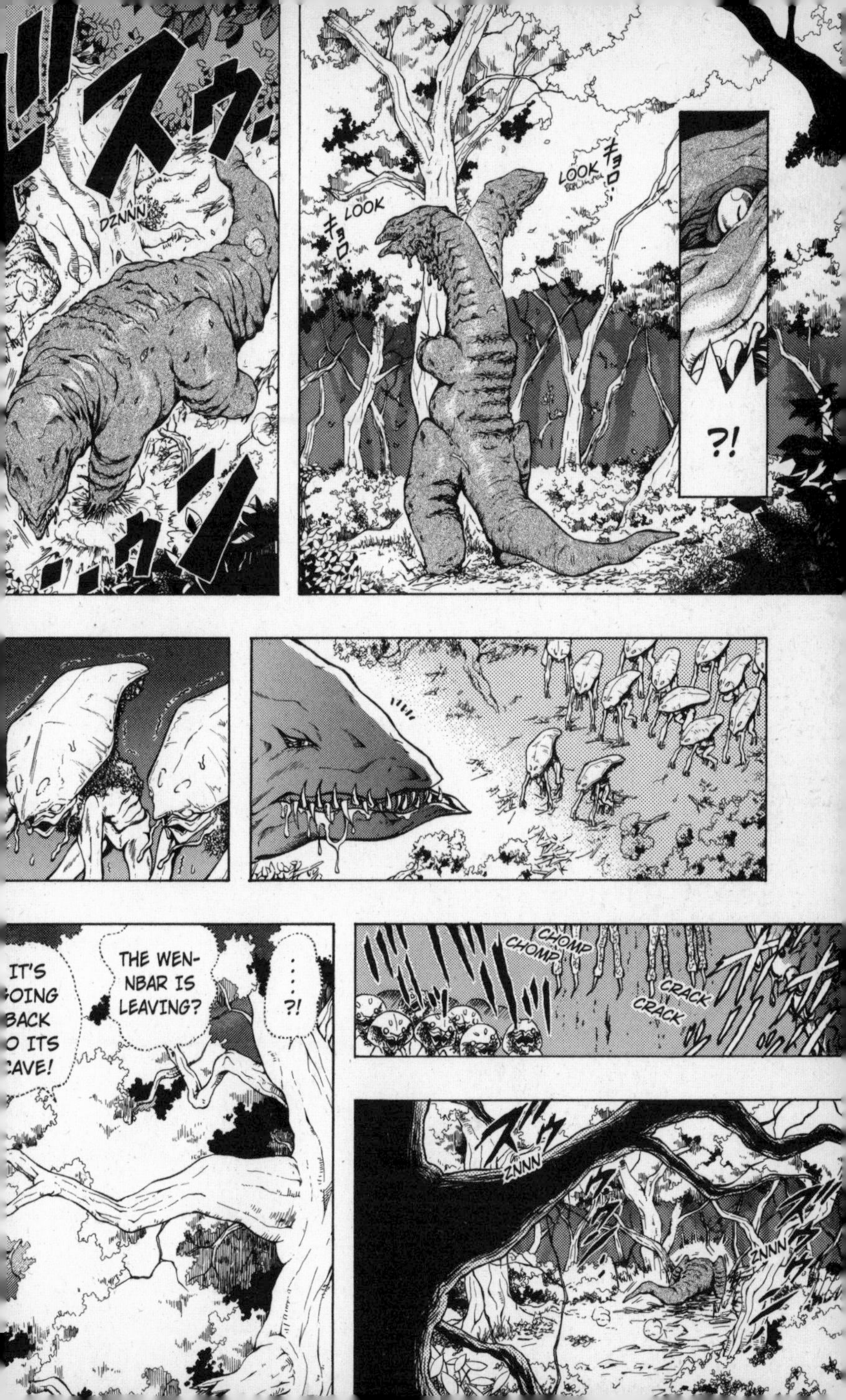

LOOK
LOOK
?!
DZNNN
CHOMP
CHOMP
CRACK
CRACK
ZNNN
ZNNN
. . . ?!
THE WEN-NBAR IS LEAVING?
IT'S OING BACK O ITS CAVE!

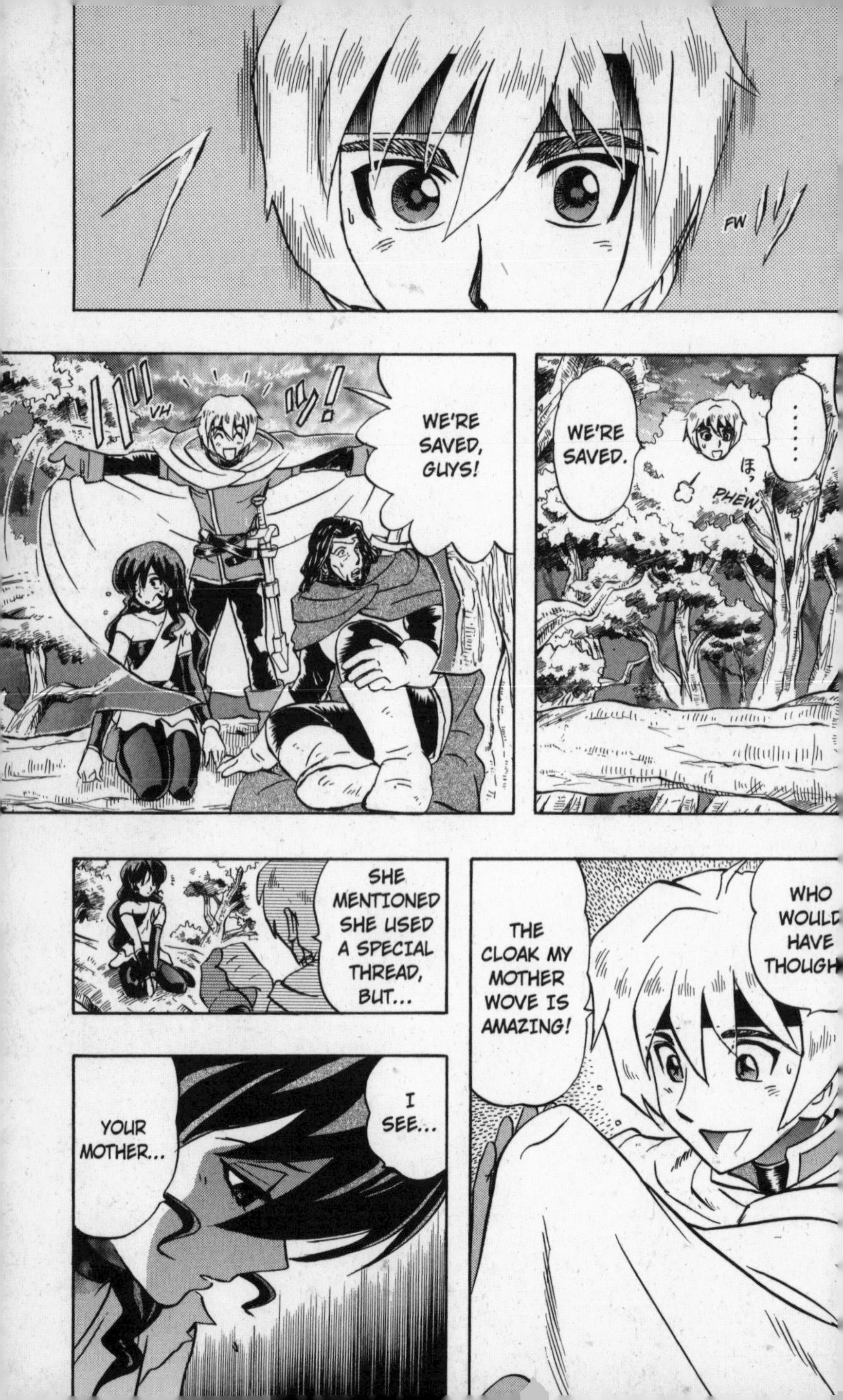
FW
......
WE'RE SAVED.
PHEW
VH
WE'RE SAVED, GUYS!
WHO WOULD HAVE THOUGH
THE CLOAK MY MOTHER WOVE IS AMAZING!
SHE MENTIONED SHE USED A SPECIAL THREAD, BUT...
I SEE...
YOUR MOTHER...

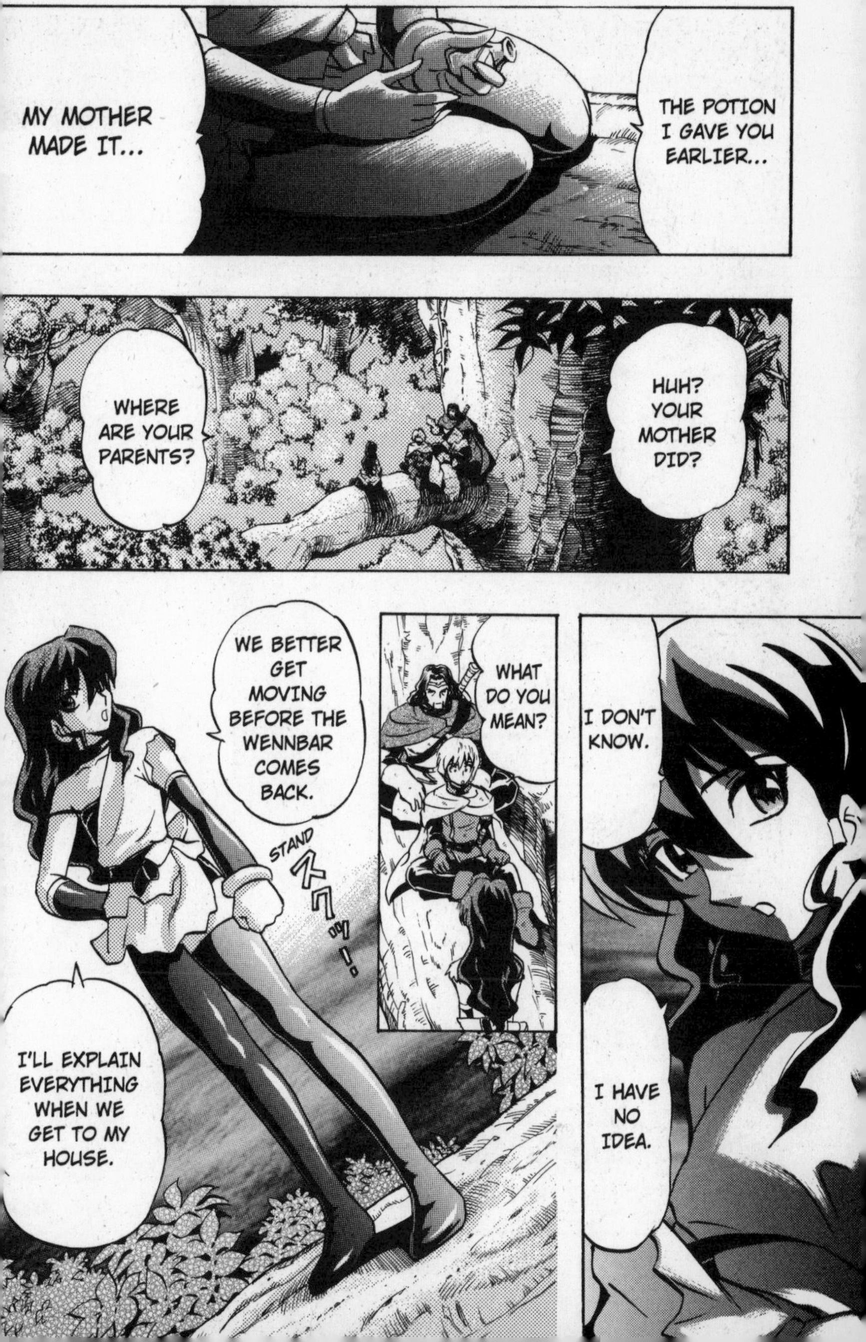
THE POTION I GAVE YOU EARLIER...
MY MOTHER MADE IT...
HUH? YOUR MOTHER DID?
WHERE ARE YOUR PARENTS?
I DON'T KNOW.
I HAVE NO IDEA.
WHAT DO YOU MEAN?
WE BETTER GET MOVING BEFORE THE WENNBAR COMES BACK.
STAND
I'LL EXPLAIN EVERYTHING WHEN WE GET TO MY HOUSE.

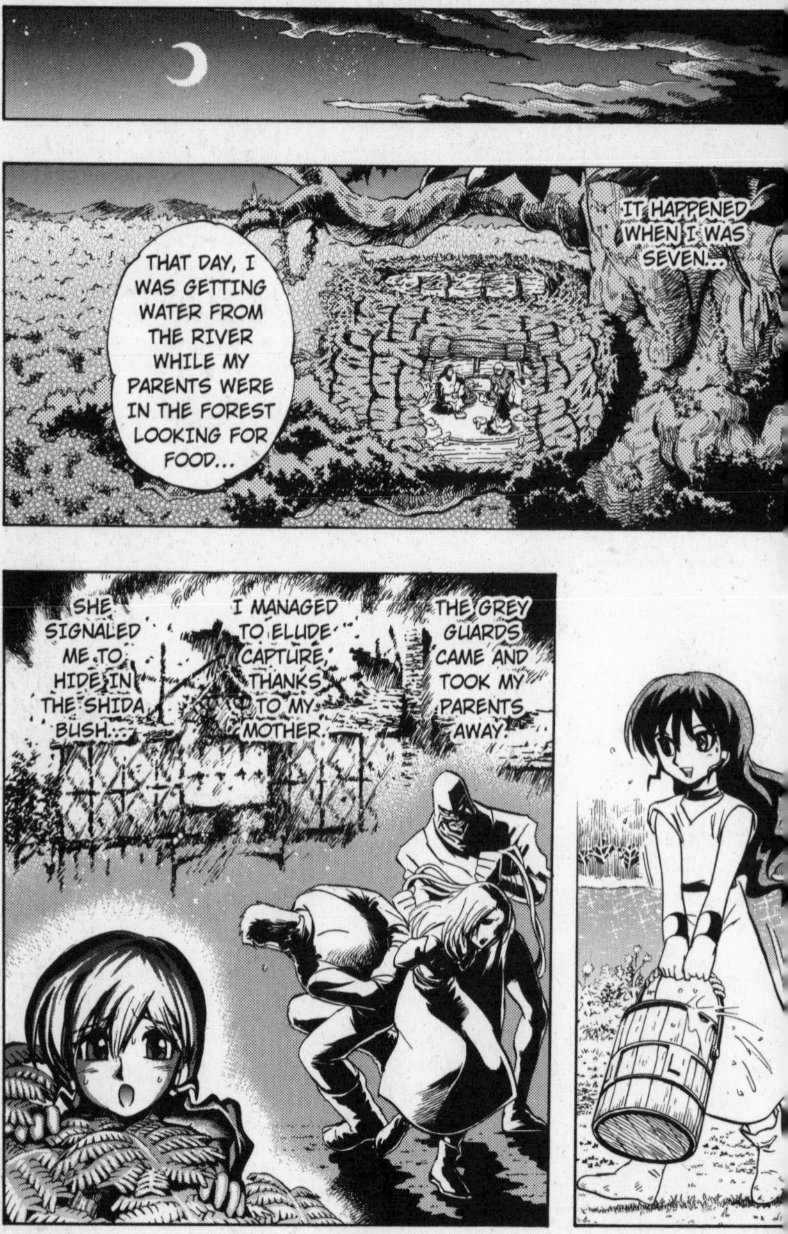
IT HAPPENED WHEN I WAS SEVEN...
THAT DAY, I WAS GETTING WATER FROM THE RIVER WHILE MY PARENTS WERE IN THE FOREST LOOKING FOR FOOD...
THE GREY GUARDS CAME AND TOOK MY PARENTS AWAY.
I MANAGED TO ELUDE CAPTURE, THANKS TO MY MOTHER.
SHE SIGNALED ME TO HIDE IN THE SHIDA BUSH...

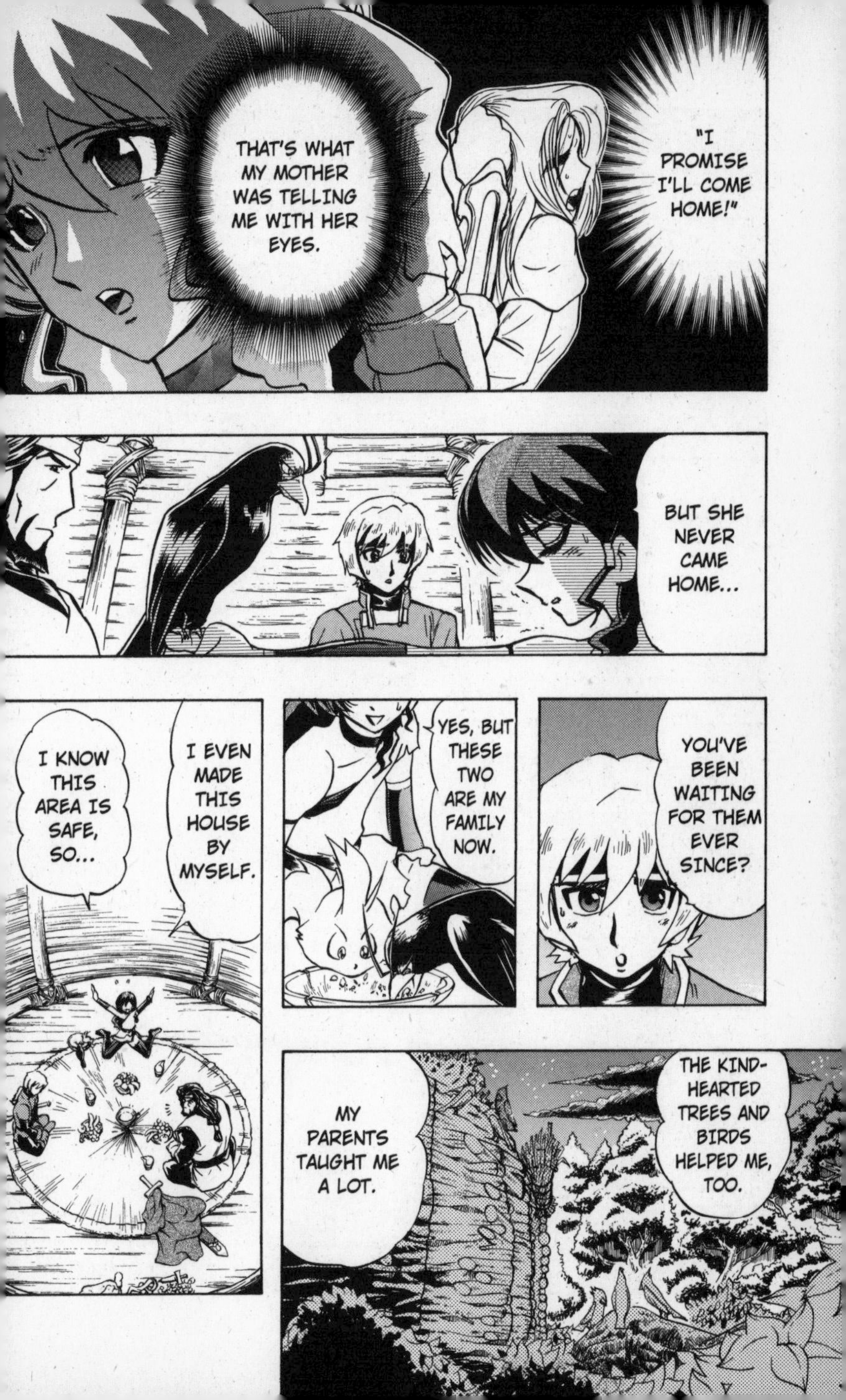
"I PROMISE I'LL COME HOME!"
THAT'S WHAT MY MOTHER WAS TELLING ME WITH HER EYES.
BUT SHE NEVER CAME HOME...
YOU'VE BEEN WAITING FOR THEM EVER SINCE?
YES, BUT THESE TWO ARE MY FAMILY NOW.
THE KIND-HEARTED TREES AND BIRDS HELPED ME, TOO.
MY PARENTS TAUGHT ME A LOT.
I EVEN MADE THIS HOUSE BY MYSELF.
I KNOW THIS AREA IS SAFE, SO...

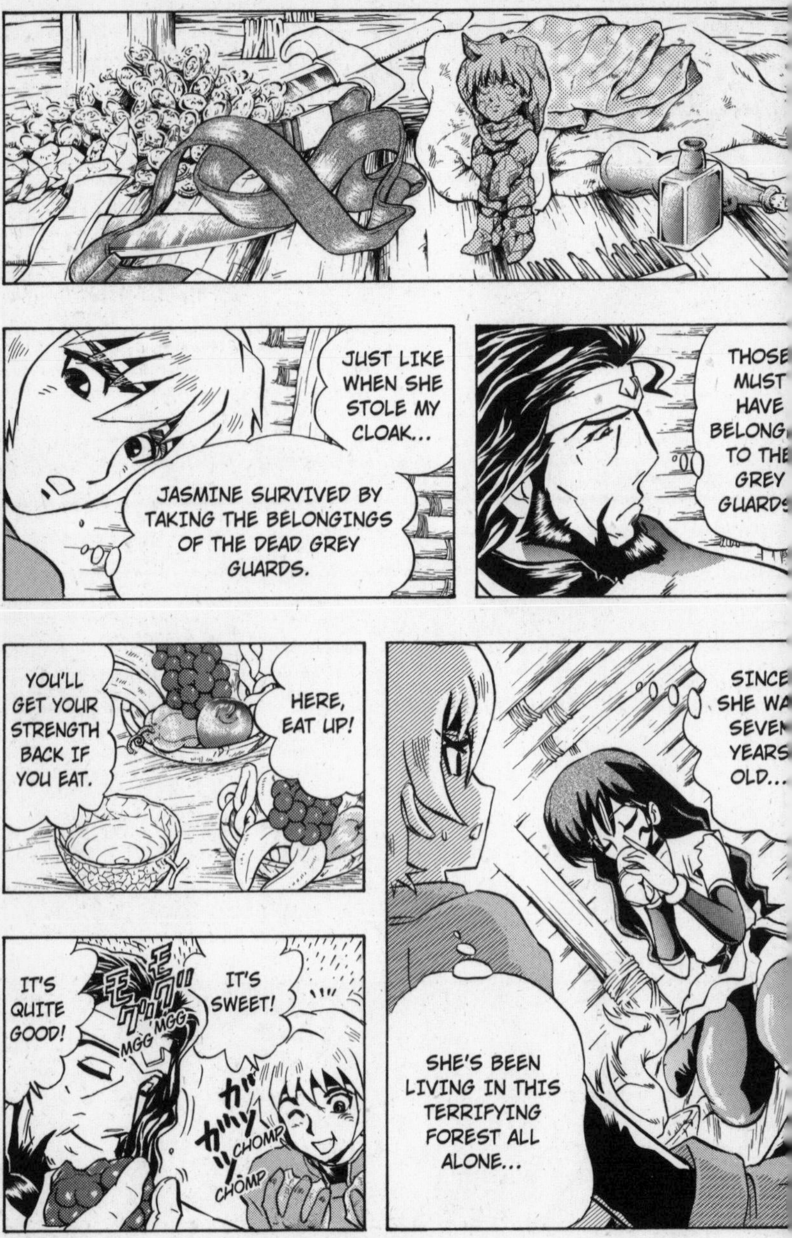
THOSE MUST HAVE BELONG TO THE GREY GUARDS
JUST LIKE WHEN SHE STOLE MY CLOAK...
JASMINE SURVIVED BY TAKING THE BELONGINGS OF THE DEAD GREY GUARDS.
SINCE SHE WA SEVEN YEARS OLD...
SHE'S BEEN LIVING IN THIS TERRIFYING FOREST ALL ALONE...
HERE, EAT UP!
YOU'LL GET YOUR STRENGTH BACK IF YOU EAT.
IT'S SWEET!
モグ モグ
MGG MGG
IT'S QUITE GOOD!
ガツ ガツ
CHOMP
CHOMP

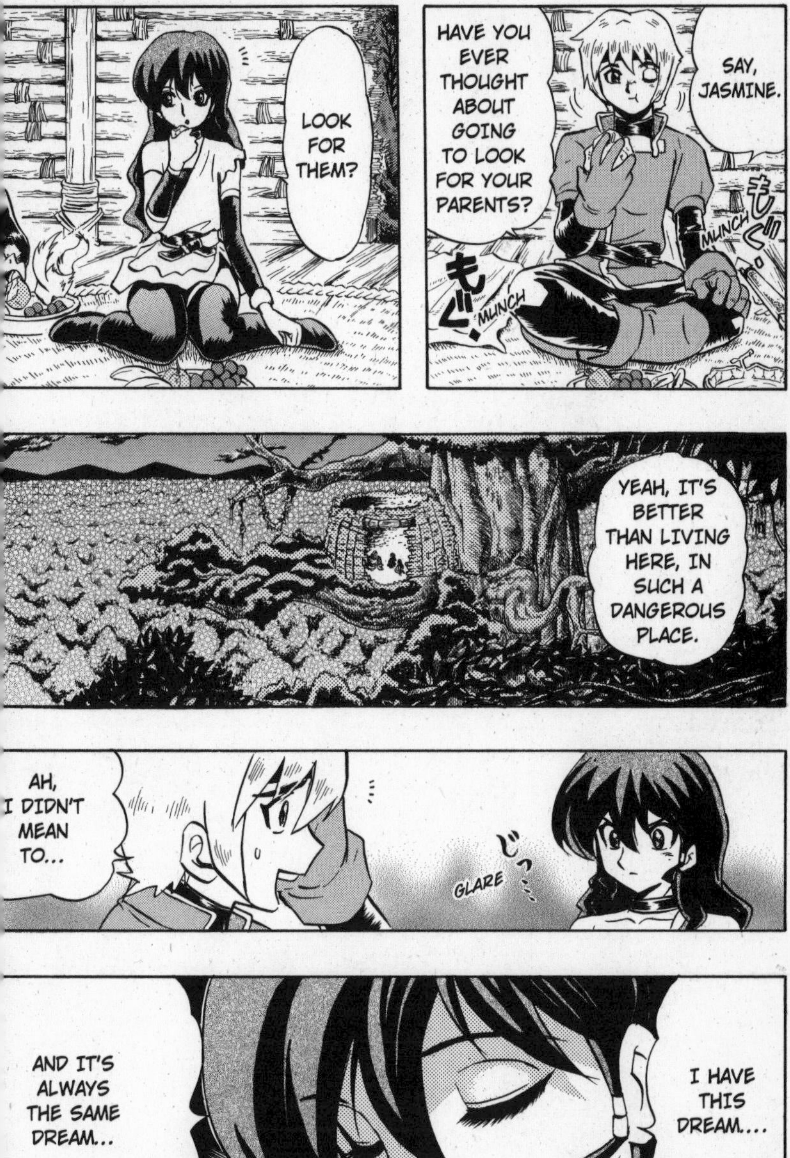
SAY, JASMINE.
HAVE YOU EVER THOUGHT ABOUT GOING TO LOOK FOR YOUR PARENTS?
もぐ MUNCH
もぐ MUNCH
LOOK FOR THEM?
YEAH, IT'S BETTER THAN LIVING HERE, IN SUCH A DANGEROUS PLACE.
じっ... GLARE
AH, I DIDN'T MEAN TO...
I HAVE THIS DREAM....
AND IT'S ALWAYS THE SAME DREAM...

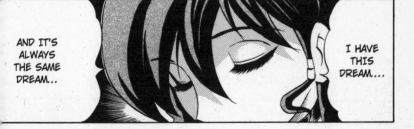

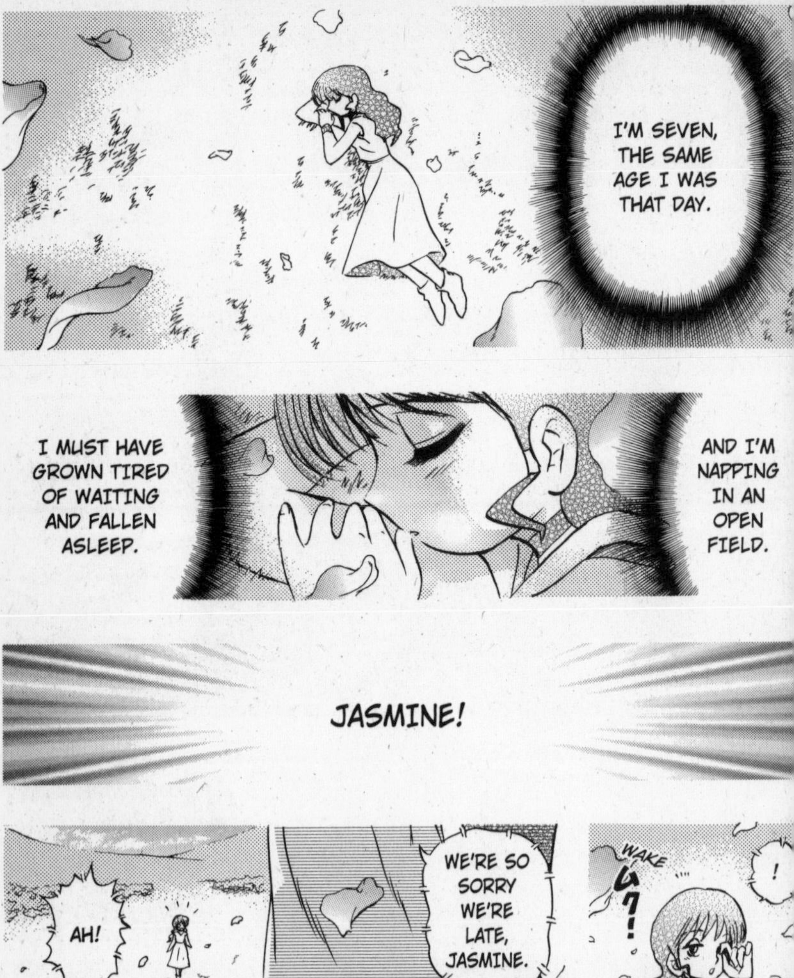
I'M SEVEN, THE SAME AGE I WAS THAT DAY.
AND I'M NAPPING IN AN OPEN FIELD.
I MUST HAVE GROWN TIRED OF WAITING AND FALLEN ASLEEP.
JASMINE!
WAKE
....
!
WE'RE SO SORRY WE'RE LATE, JASMINE.
AH!

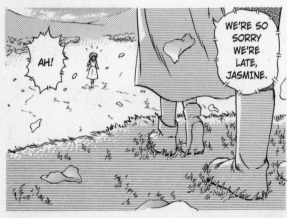

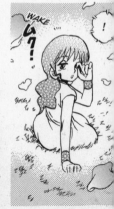

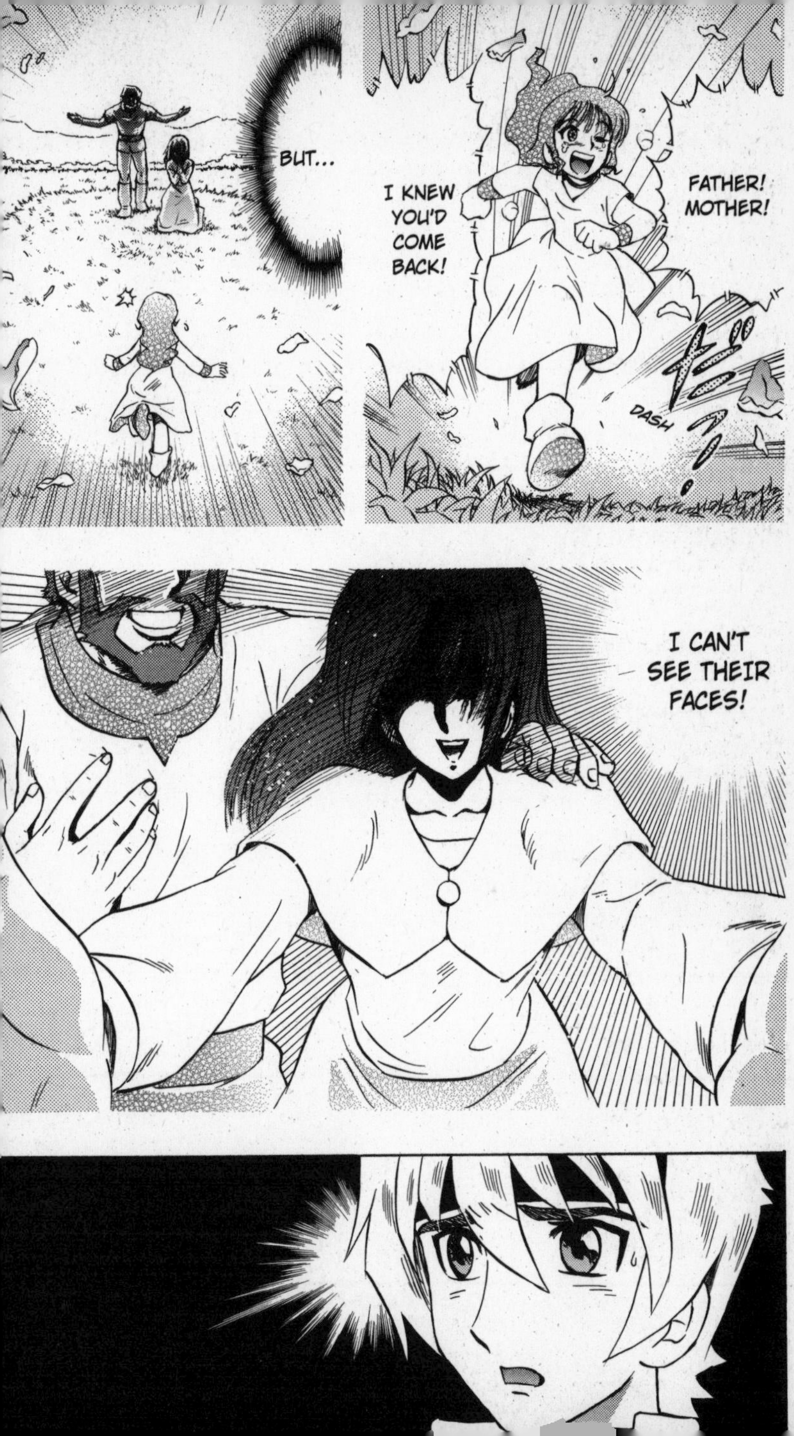
FATHER! MOTHER!
I KNEW YOU'D COME BACK!
DASH
BUT...
I CAN'T SEE THEIR FACES!

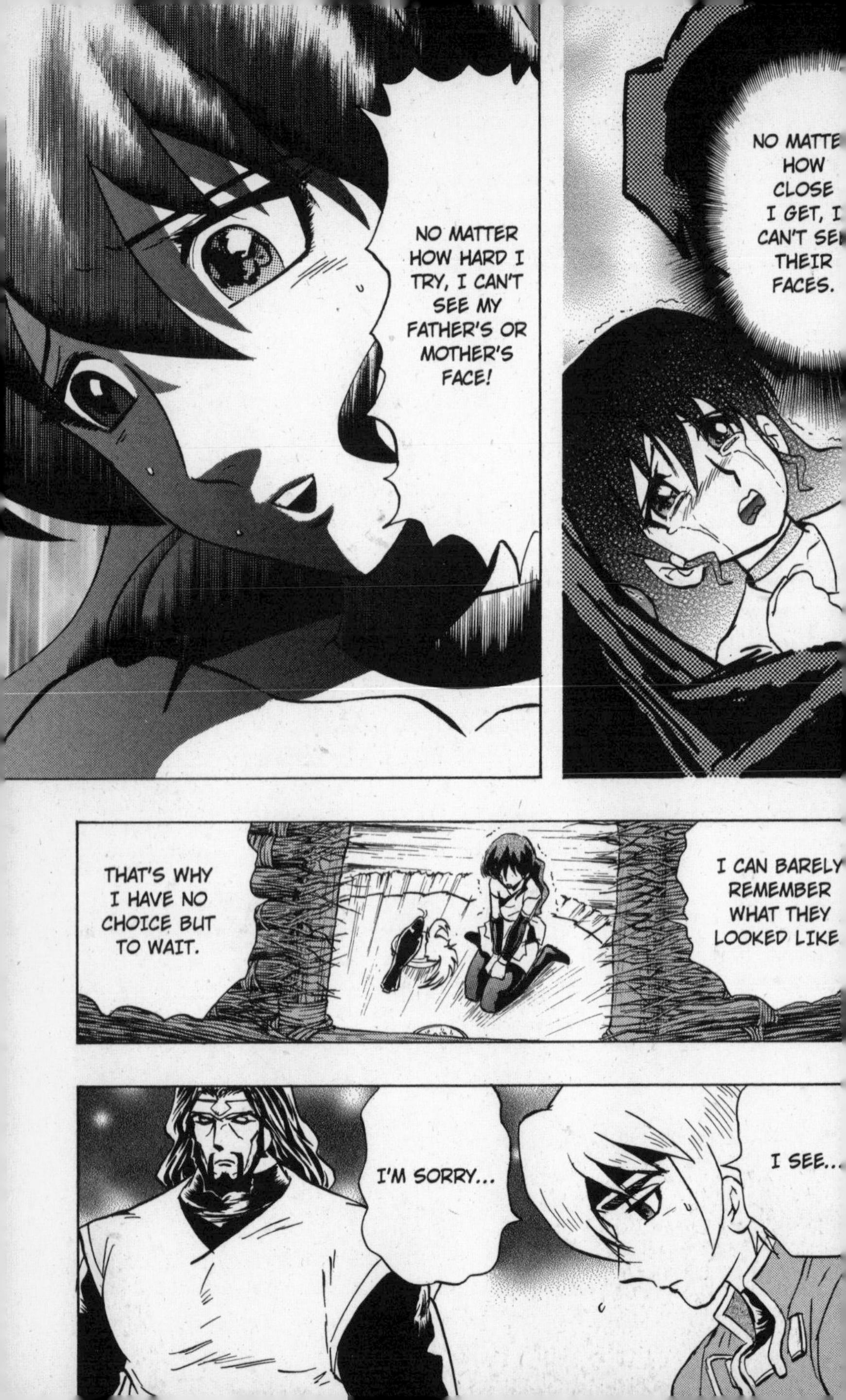
NO MATTE HOW CLOSE I GET, I CAN'T SE THEIR FACES.
NO MATTER HOW HARD I TRY, I CAN'T SEE MY FATHER'S OR MOTHER'S FACE!
I CAN BARELY REMEMBER WHAT THEY LOOKED LIKE
THAT'S WHY I HAVE NO CHOICE BUT TO WAIT.
I SEE...
I'M SORRY...

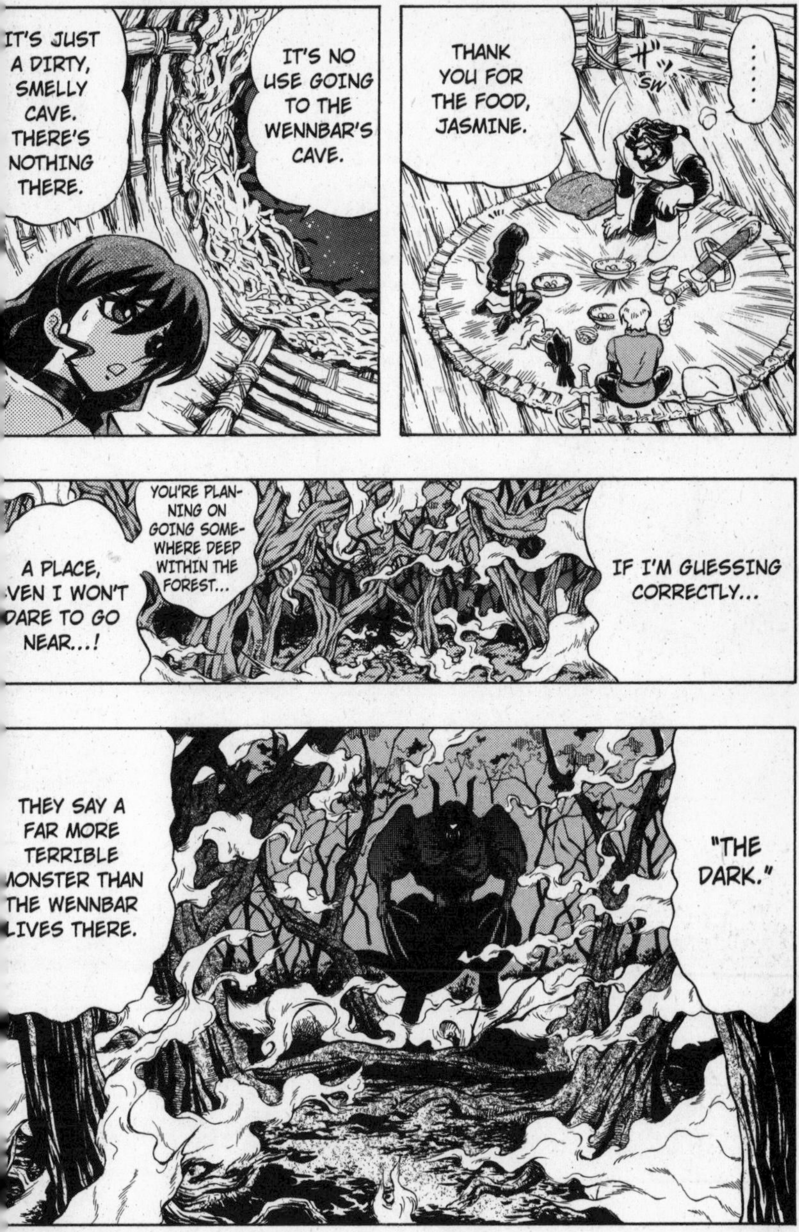

THANK YOU FOR THE FOOD, JASMINE.
......
ザッ
SW
IT'S NO USE GOING TO THE WENNBAR'S CAVE.
IT'S JUST A DIRTY, SMELLY CAVE. THERE'S NOTHING THERE.
IF I'M GUESSING CORRECTLY...
YOU'RE PLANNING ON GOING SOMEWHERE DEEP WITHIN THE FOREST...
A PLACE, VEN I WON'T DARE TO GO NEAR...!
"THE DARK."
THEY SAY A FAR MORE TERRIBLE MONSTER THAN THE WENNBAR LIVES THERE.

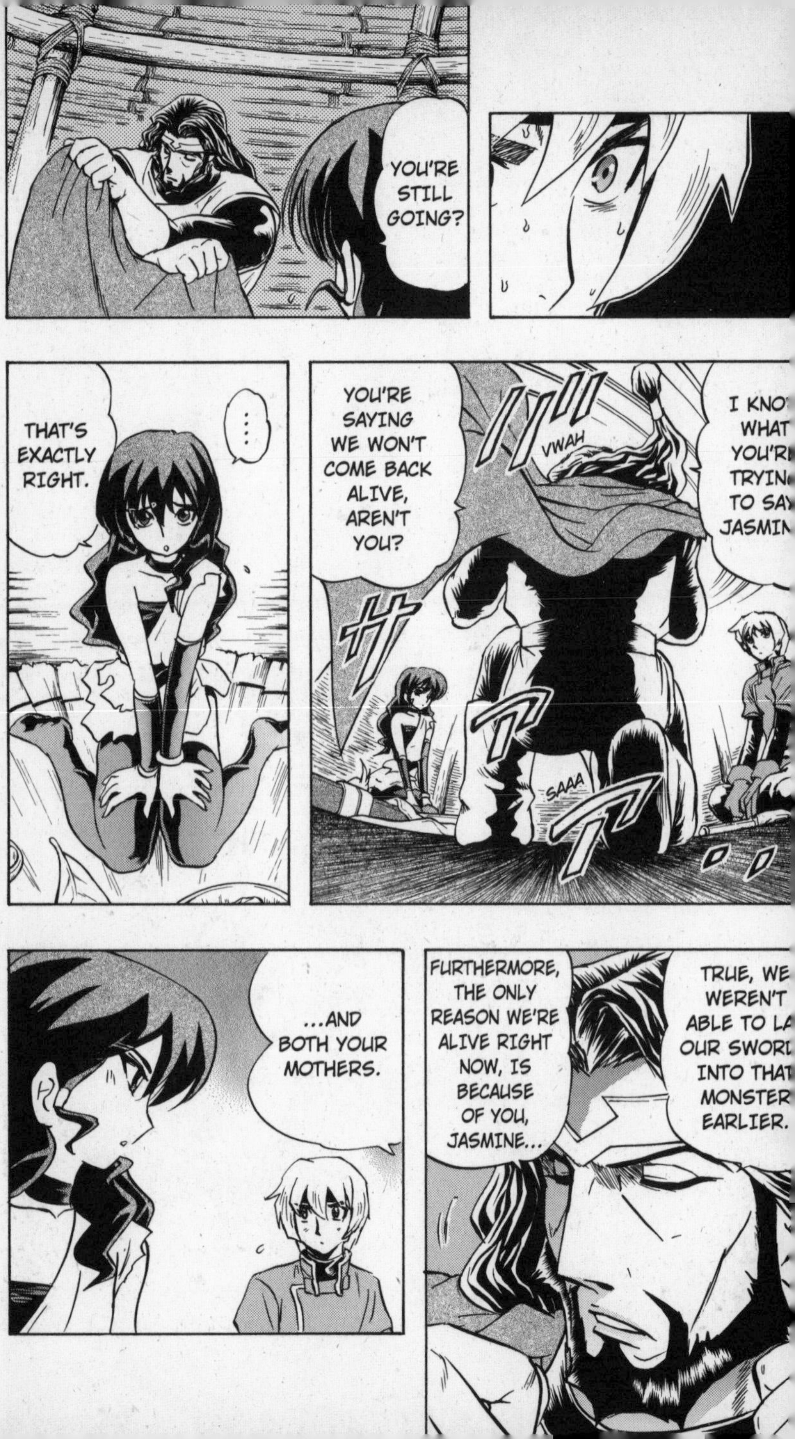
YOU'RE STILL GOING?
I KNO WHAT YOU'R TRYIN TO SA JASMIN
VWAH
SAAA
YOU'RE SAYING WE WON'T COME BACK ALIVE, AREN'T YOU?
......
THAT'S EXACTLY RIGHT.
TRUE, WE WEREN'T ABLE TO LA OUR SWORD INTO THAT MONSTER EARLIER.
FURTHERMORE, THE ONLY REASON WE'RE ALIVE RIGHT NOW, IS BECAUSE OF YOU, JASMINE...
...AND BOTH YOUR MOTHERS.

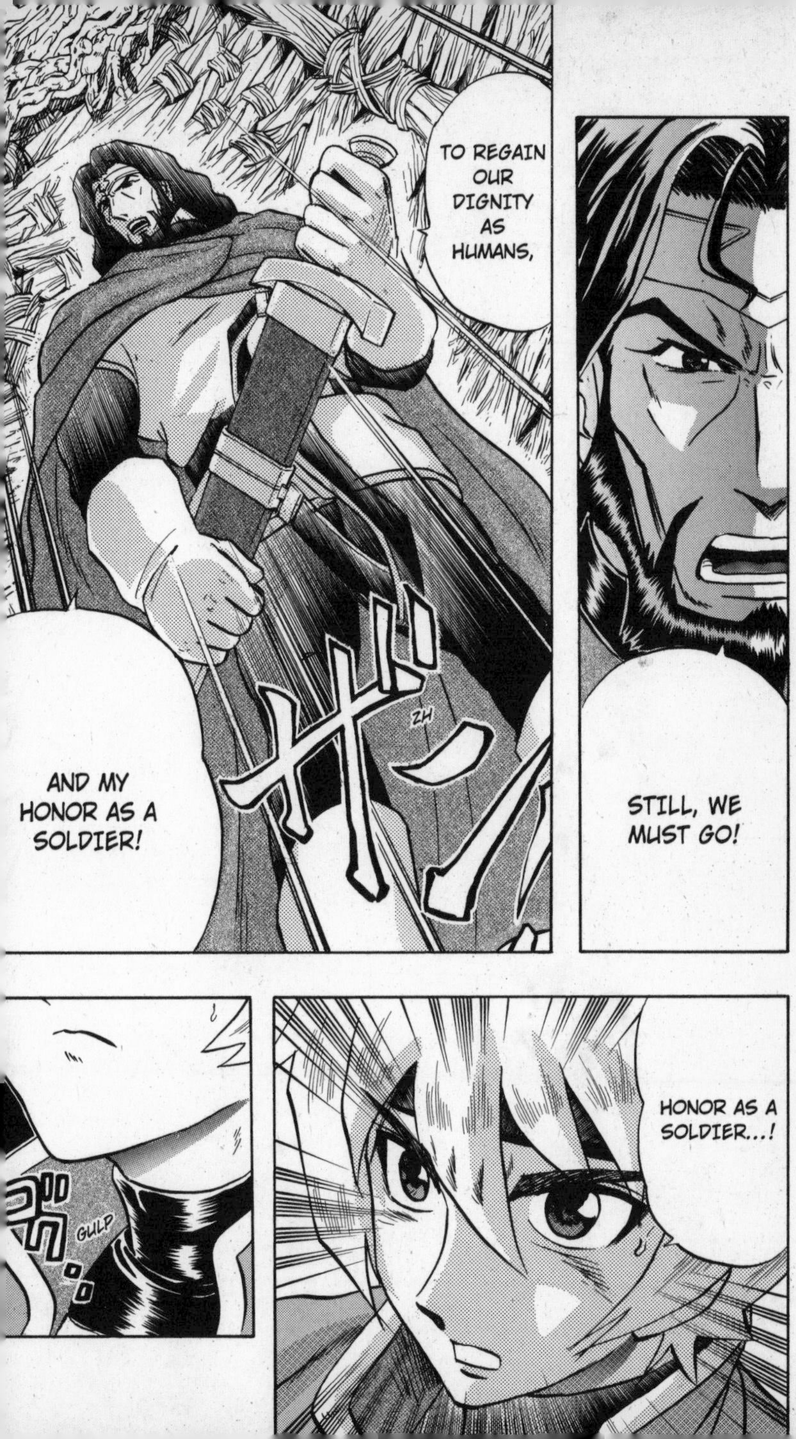
STILL, WE MUST GO!
TO REGAIN OUR DIGNITY AS HUMANS,
AND MY HONOR AS A SOLDIER!
ZH
HONOR AS A SOLDIER...!
GULP

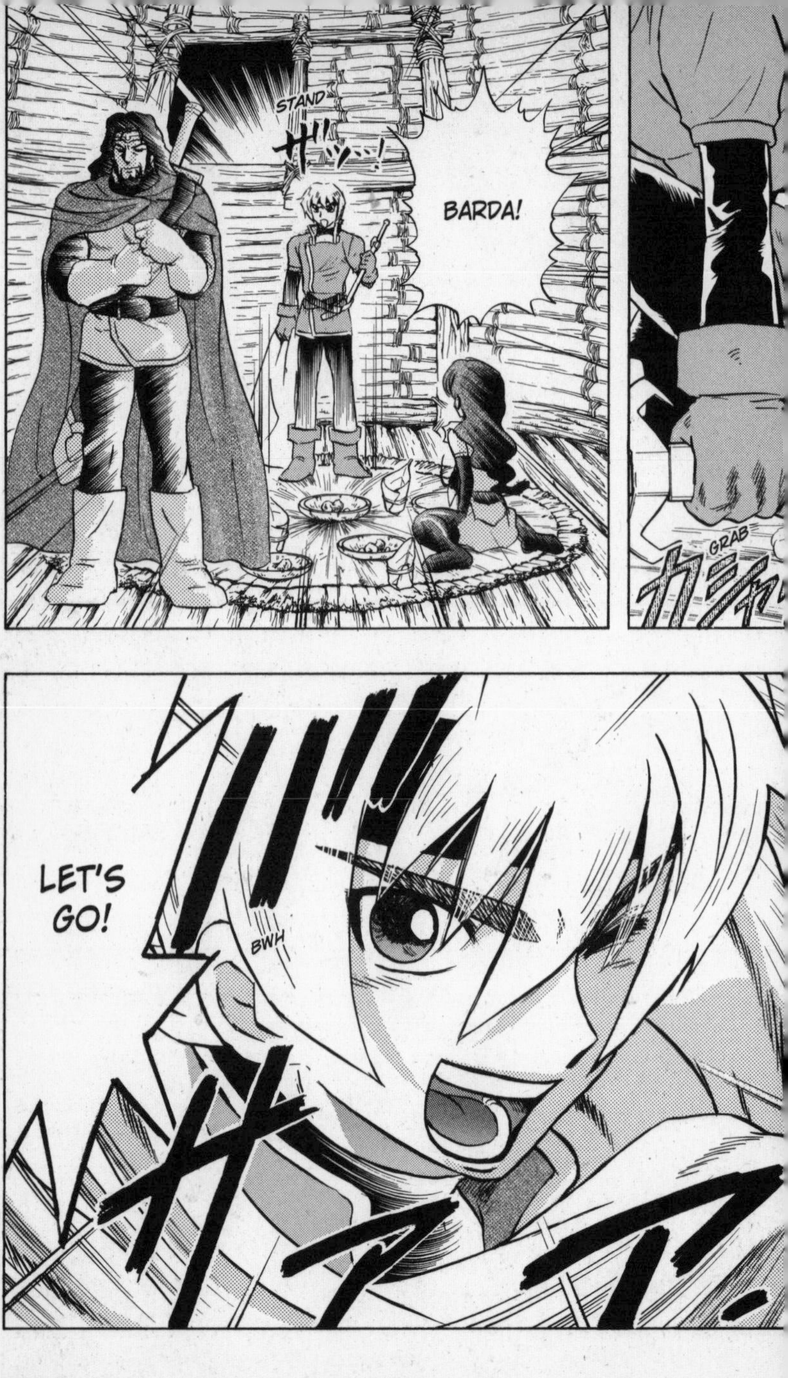
GRAB
STAND
BARDA!
BWH
LET'S GO!

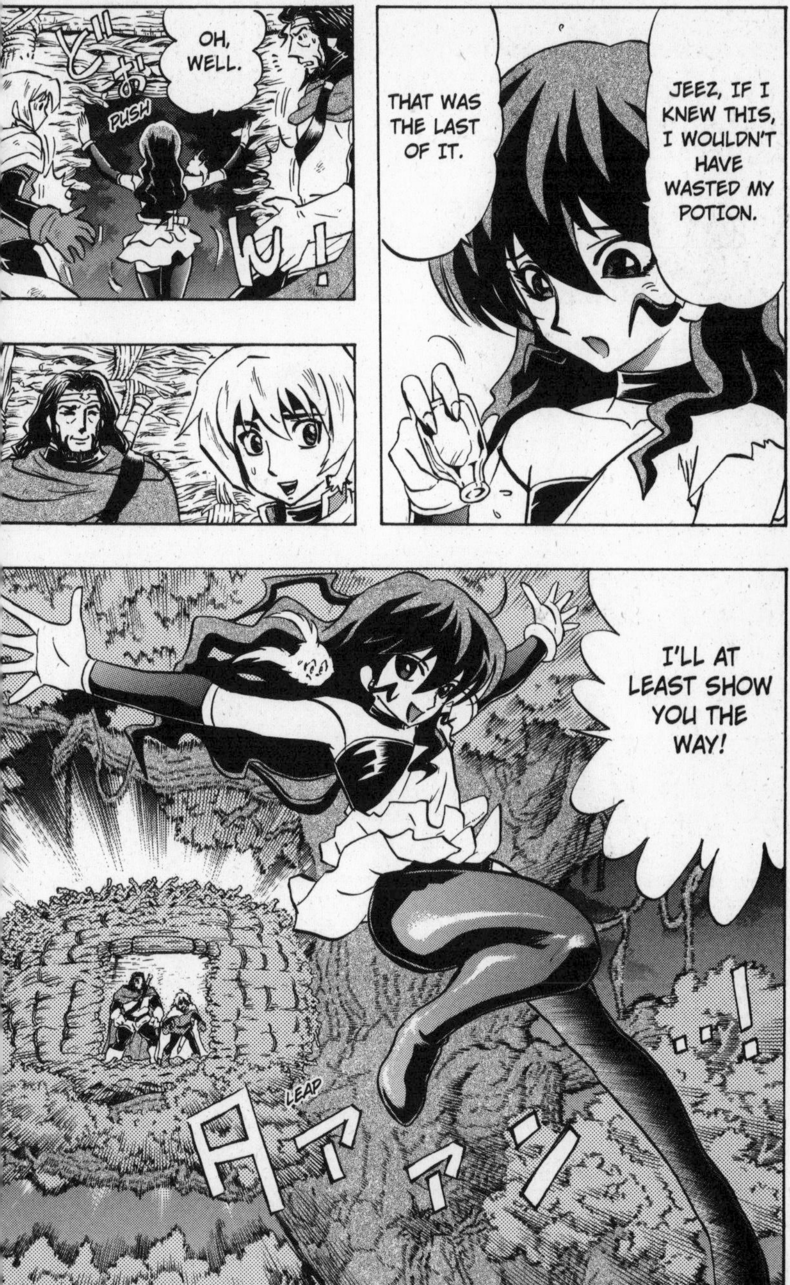
JEEZ, IF I KNEW THIS, I WOULDN'T HAVE WASTED MY POTION.
THAT WAS THE LAST OF IT.
OH, WELL.
PUSH
I'LL AT LEAST SHOW YOU THE WAY!
LEAP

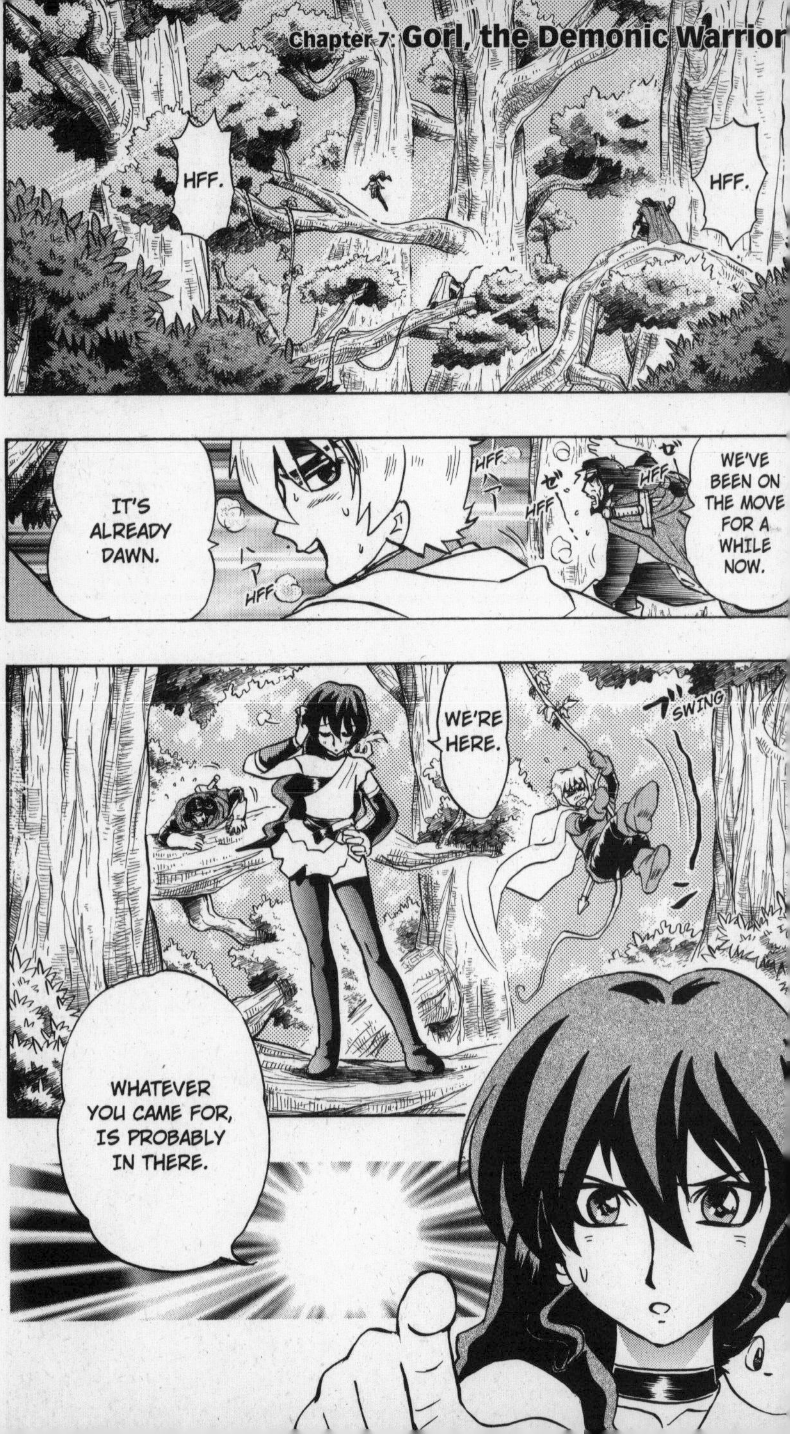
Chapter 7: Gorl, the Demonic Warrior
HFF.
HFF.
WE'VE BEEN ON THE MOVE FOR A WHILE NOW.
HFF
HFF
HFF
IT'S ALREADY DAWN.
HFF
SWING
WE'RE HERE.
WHATEVER YOU CAME FOR, IS PROBABLY IN THERE.

Chapter 7: Gorl, the Demonic Warrior

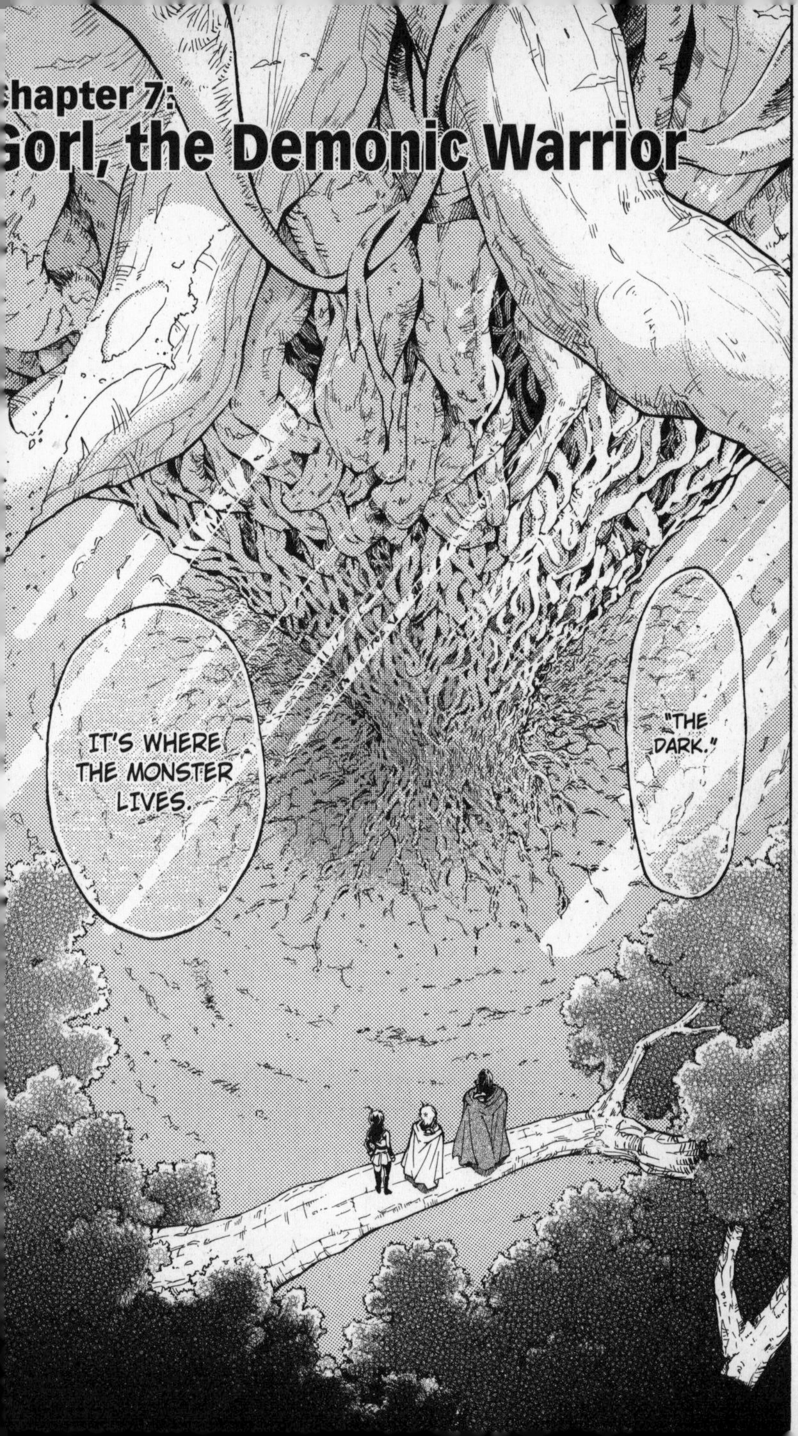
"THE DARK."
IT'S WHERE THE MONSTER LIVES.

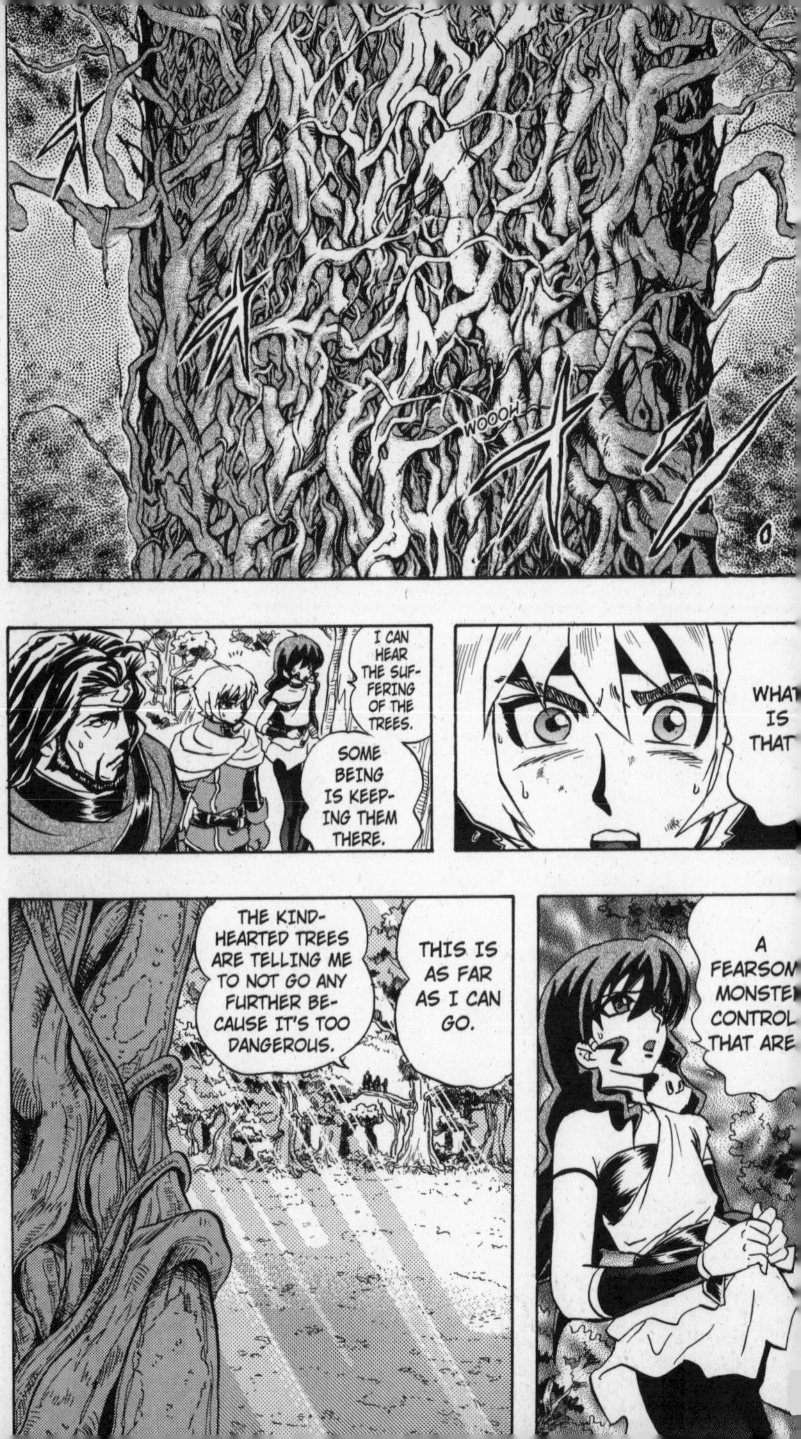
WOOOH
WHAT IS THAT
I CAN HEAR THE SUFFERING OF THE TREES.
SOME BEING IS KEEPING THEM THERE.
A FEARSOM MONSTE CONTROL THAT ARE
THIS IS AS FAR AS I CAN GO.
THE KIND-HEARTED TREES ARE TELLING ME TO NOT GO ANY FURTHER BECAUSE IT'S TOO DANGEROUS.

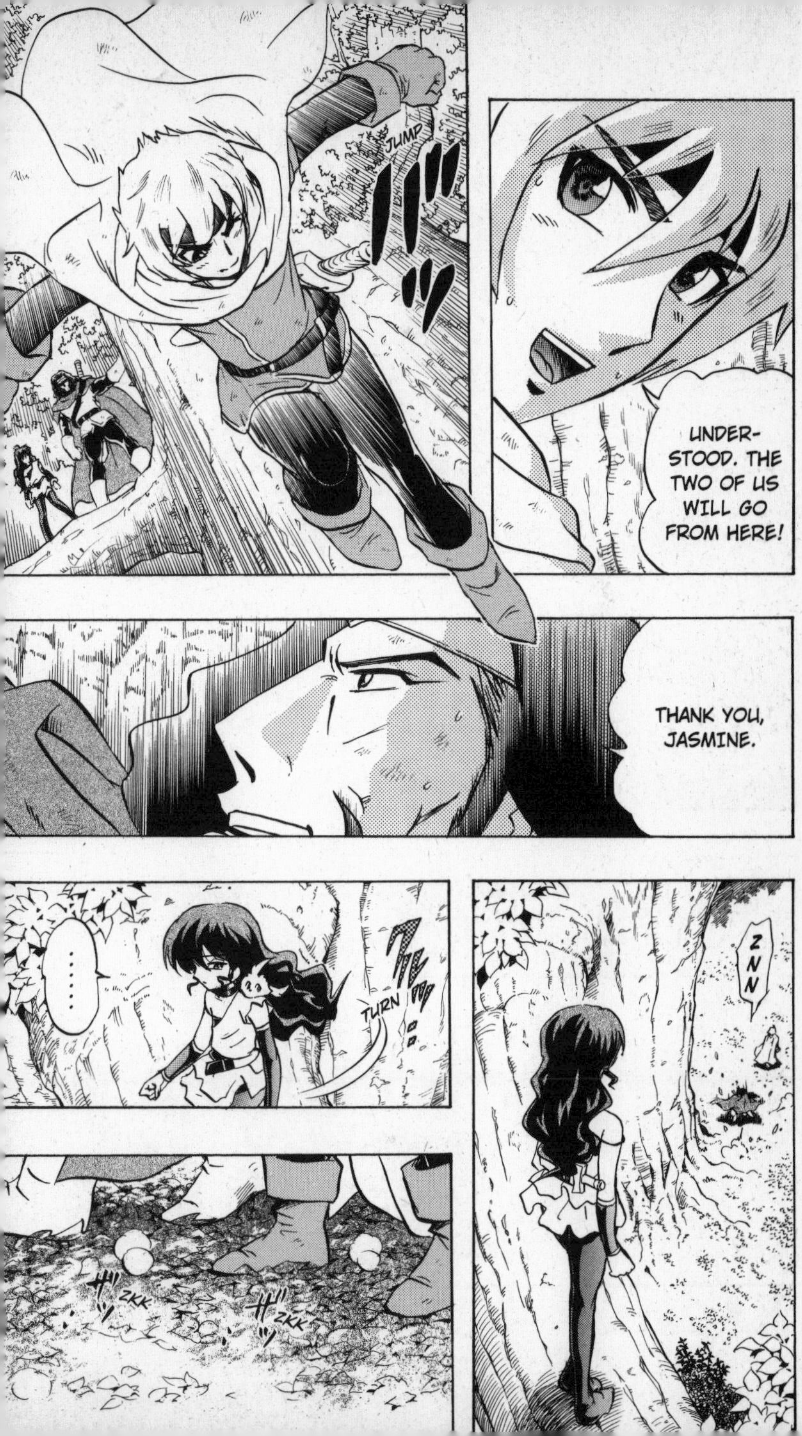
UNDER-STOOD. THE TWO OF US WILL GO FROM HERE!
JUMP
THANK YOU, JASMINE.
ZNN
......
TURN
ZKK
ZKK

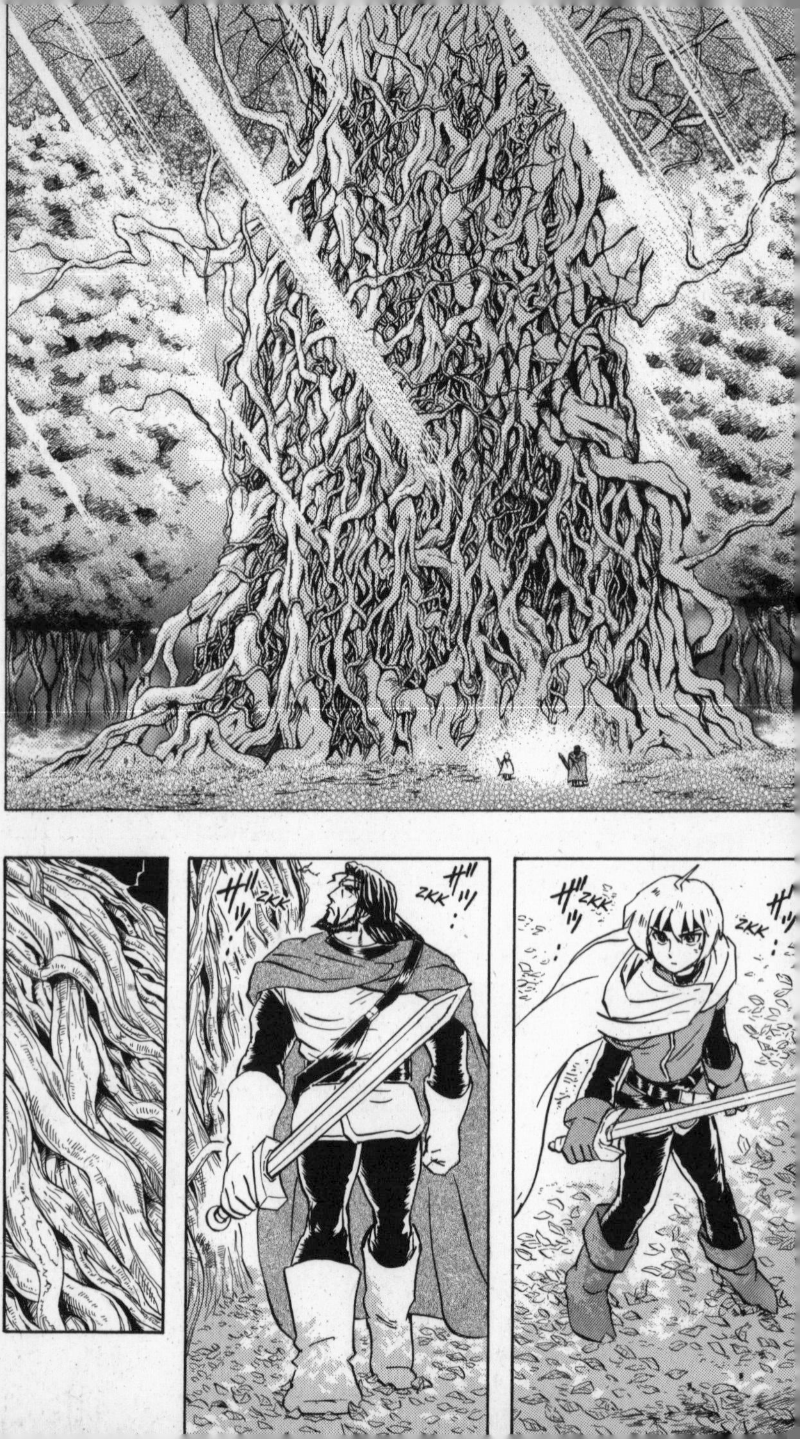
ZKK
ZKK
ZKK
ZKK

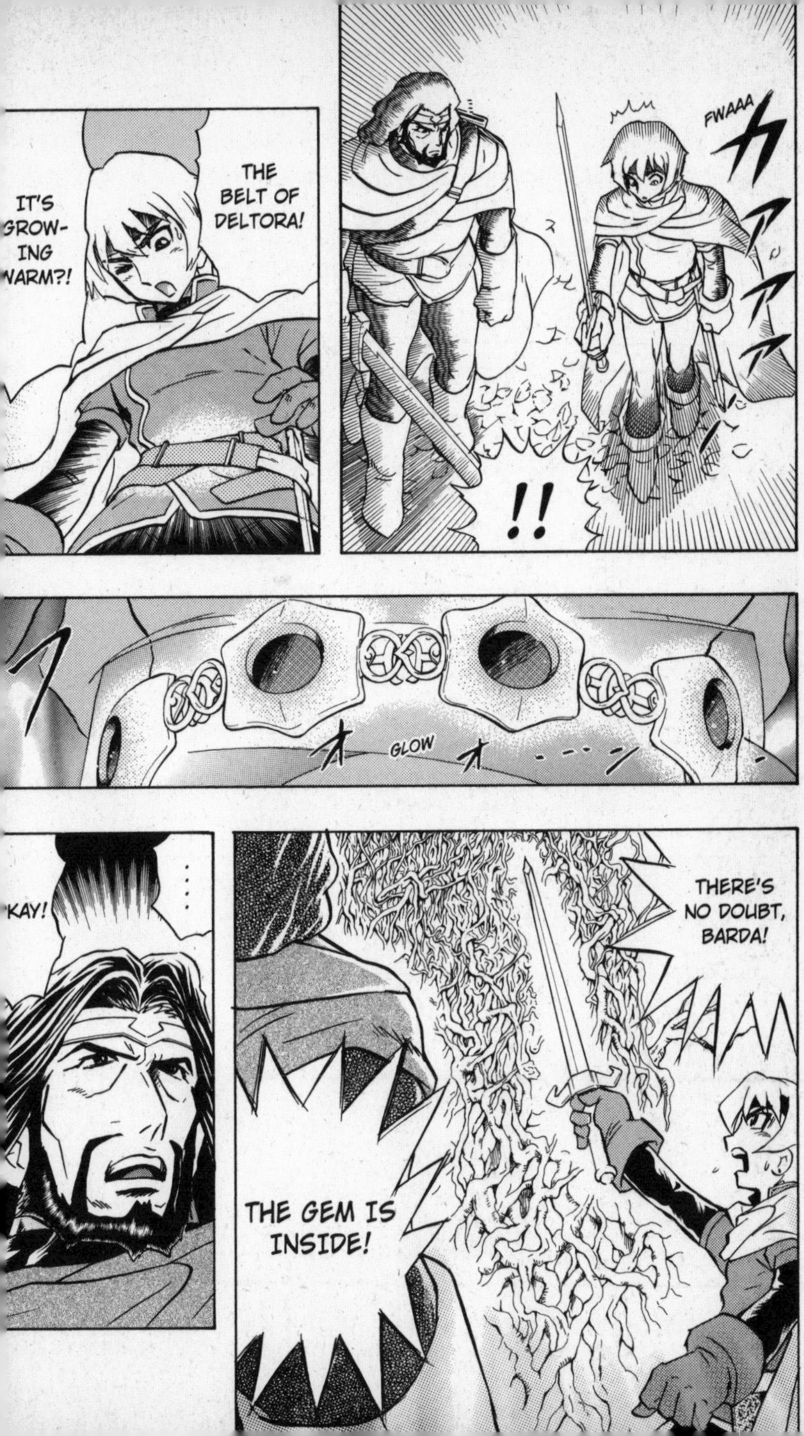
FWAAA
!!
THE BELT OF DELTORA!
IT'S GROWING WARM?!
GLOW
THERE'S NO DOUBT, BARDA!
THE GEM IS INSIDE!
....
KAY!

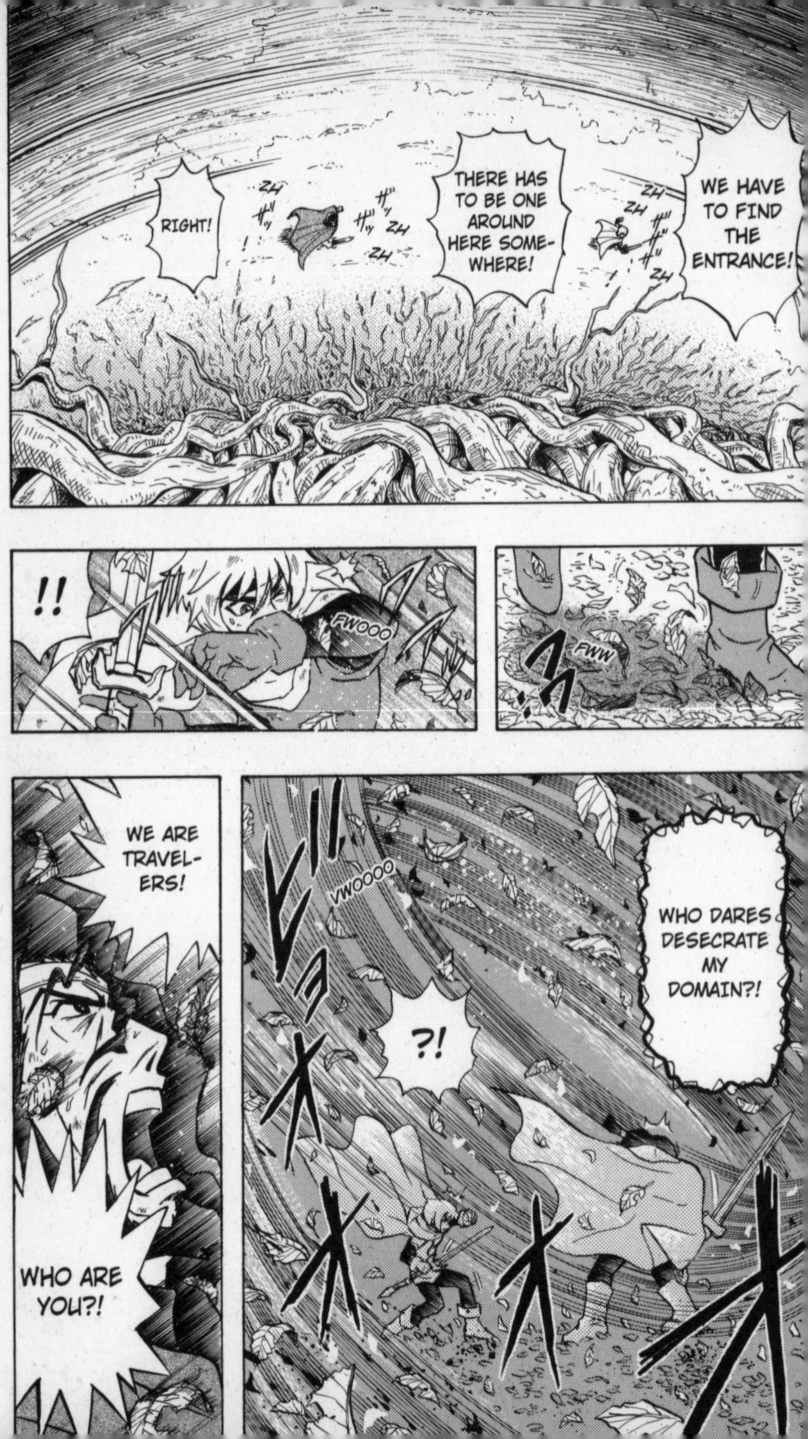
WE HAVE TO FIND THE ENTRANCE!
ZH
ZH
ZH
THERE HAS TO BE ONE AROUND HERE SOME-WHERE!
ZH
ZH
ZH
RIGHT!
FWW
!!
FWOOO
WHO DARES DESECRATE MY DOMAIN?!
VWOOOO
?!
WE ARE TRAVEL-ERS!
WHO ARE YOU?!

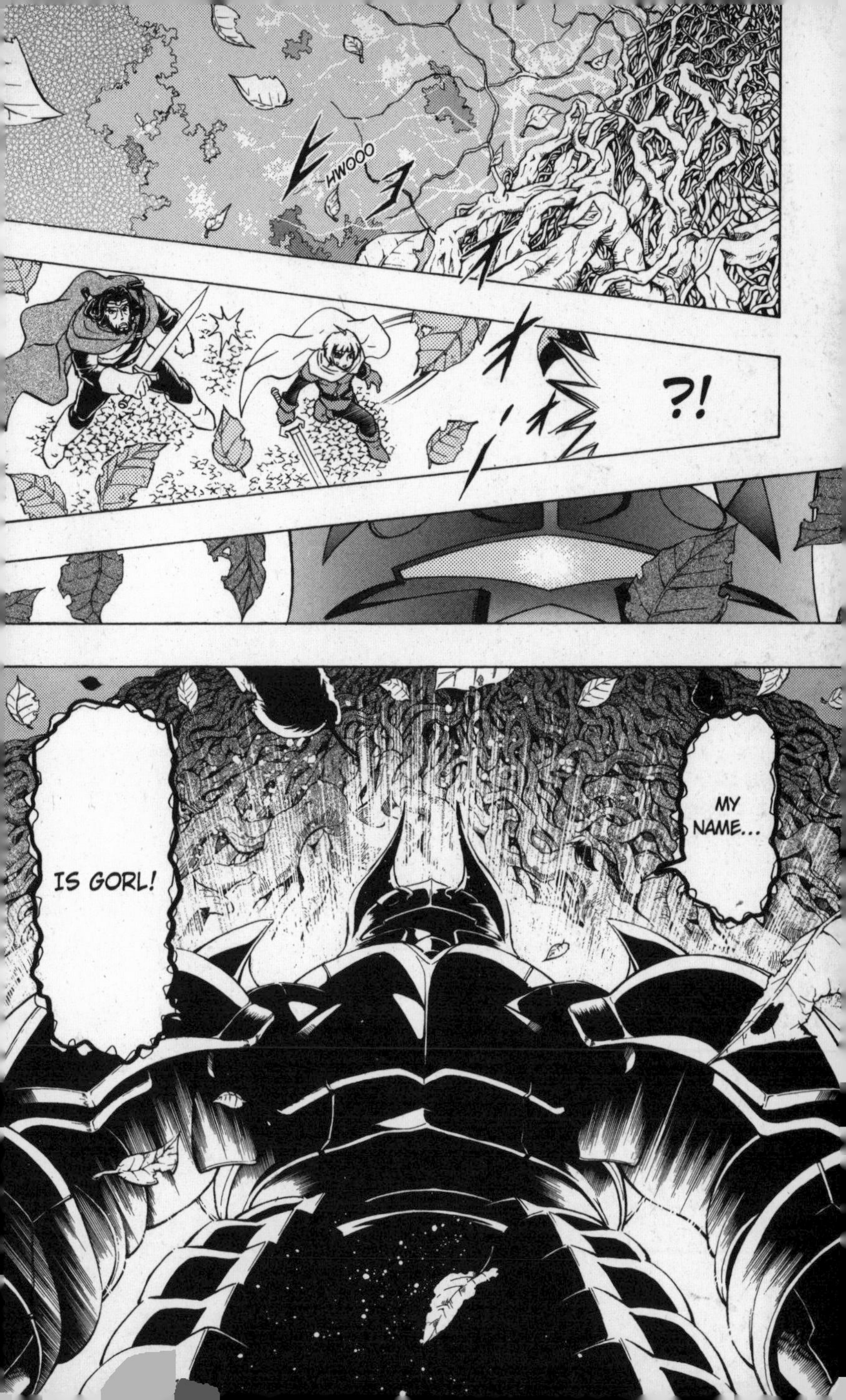
HWOOO
?!
MY NAME...
IS GORL!

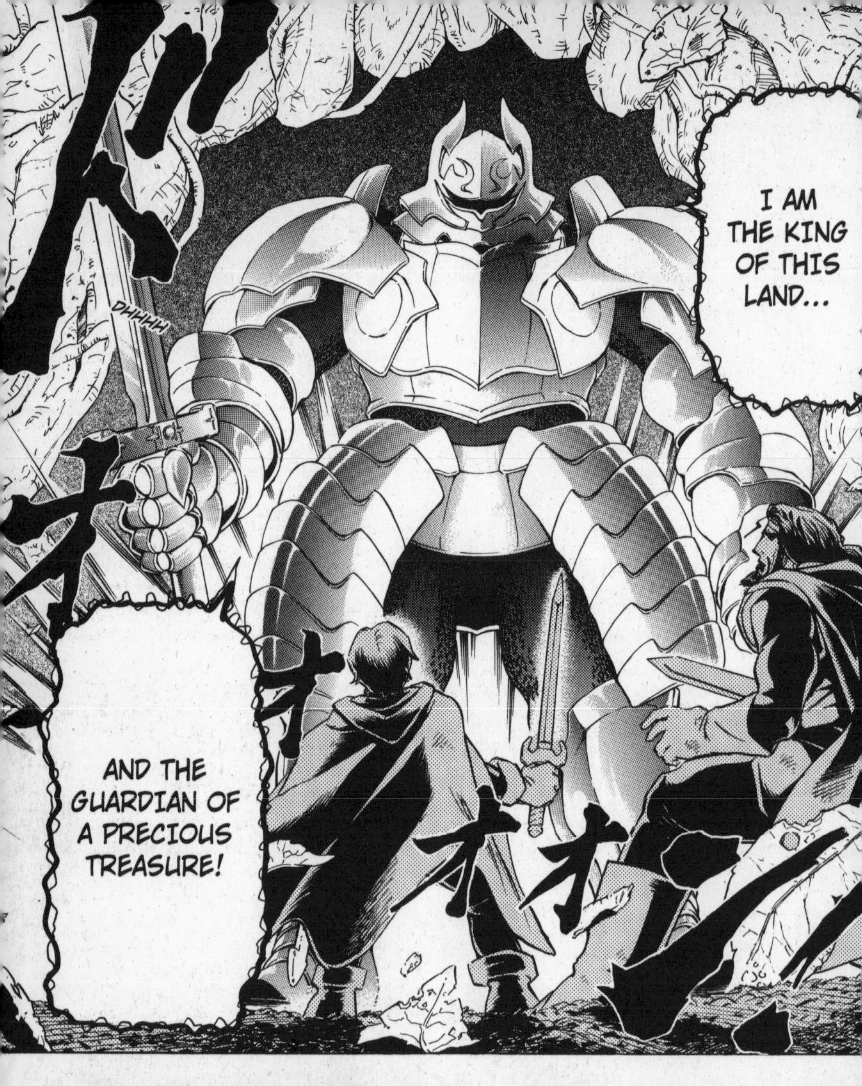
I AM THE KING OF THIS LAND...
DHHHHH
AND THE GUARDIAN OF A PRECIOUS TREASURE!

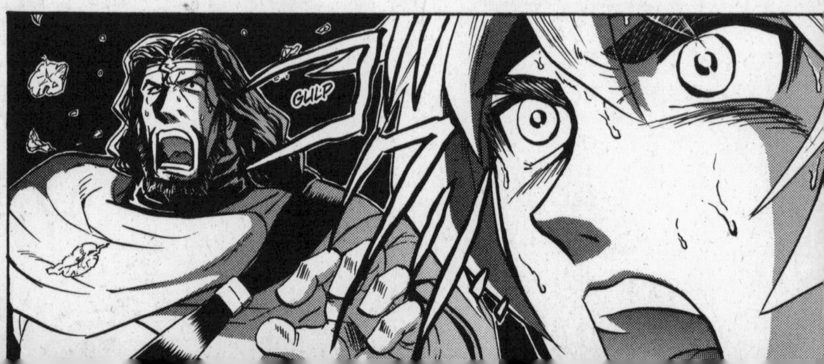
GULP

LOOKS
LIKE...

!!

AH!

IT'S THE
TOPAZ!

BUT
HOW...?!

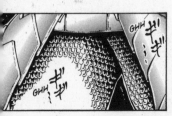

BARDA...!

WE HAVE
NO CHOICE,
BUT TO
TAKE IT BY
FORCE.

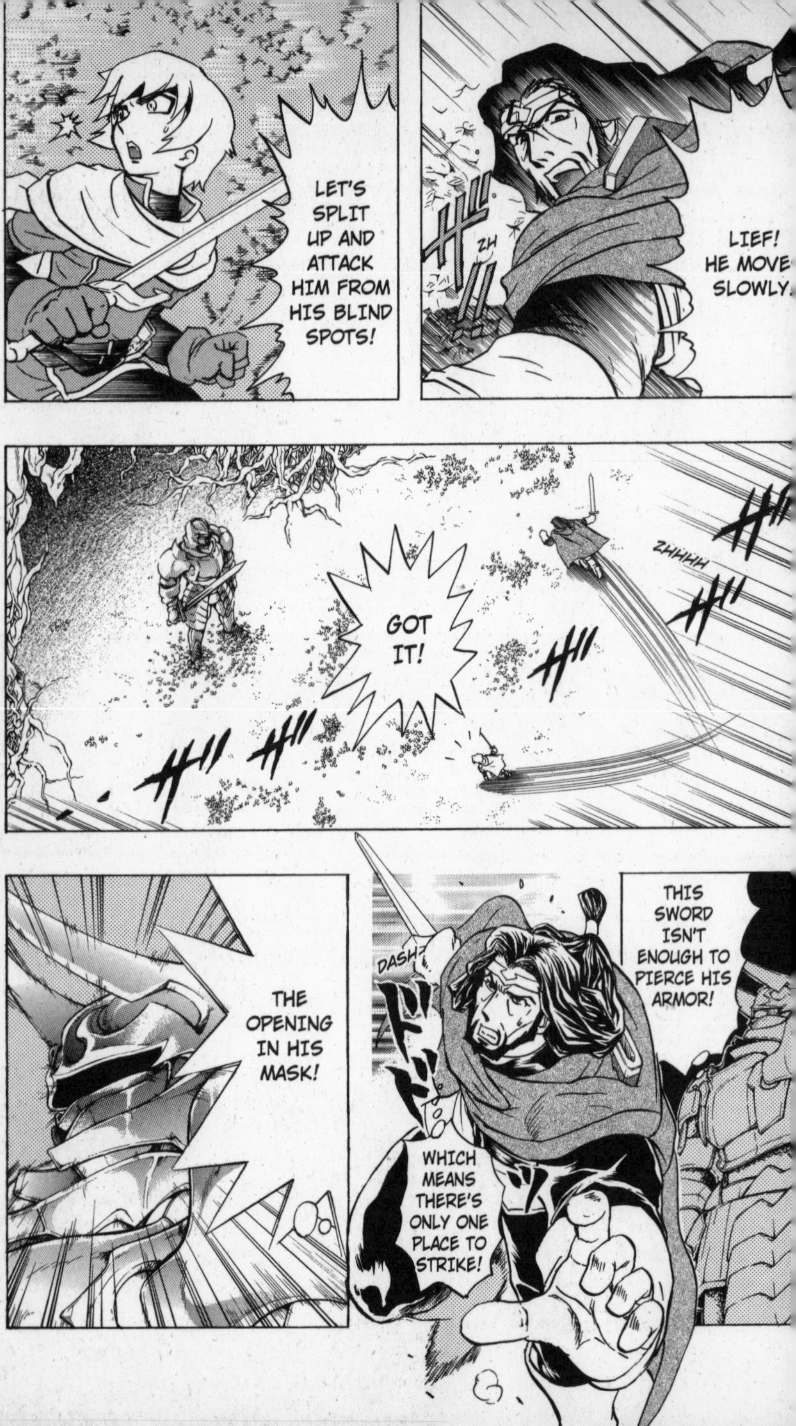

LIEF! HE MOVE SLOWLY
ZH
LET'S SPLIT UP AND ATTACK HIM FROM HIS BLIND SPOTS!
ZHHHHZ
GOT IT!
THIS SWORD ISN'T ENOUGH TO PIERCE HIS ARMOR!
DASH
WHICH MEANS THERE'S ONLY ONE PLACE TO STRIKE!
THE OPENING IN HIS MASK!

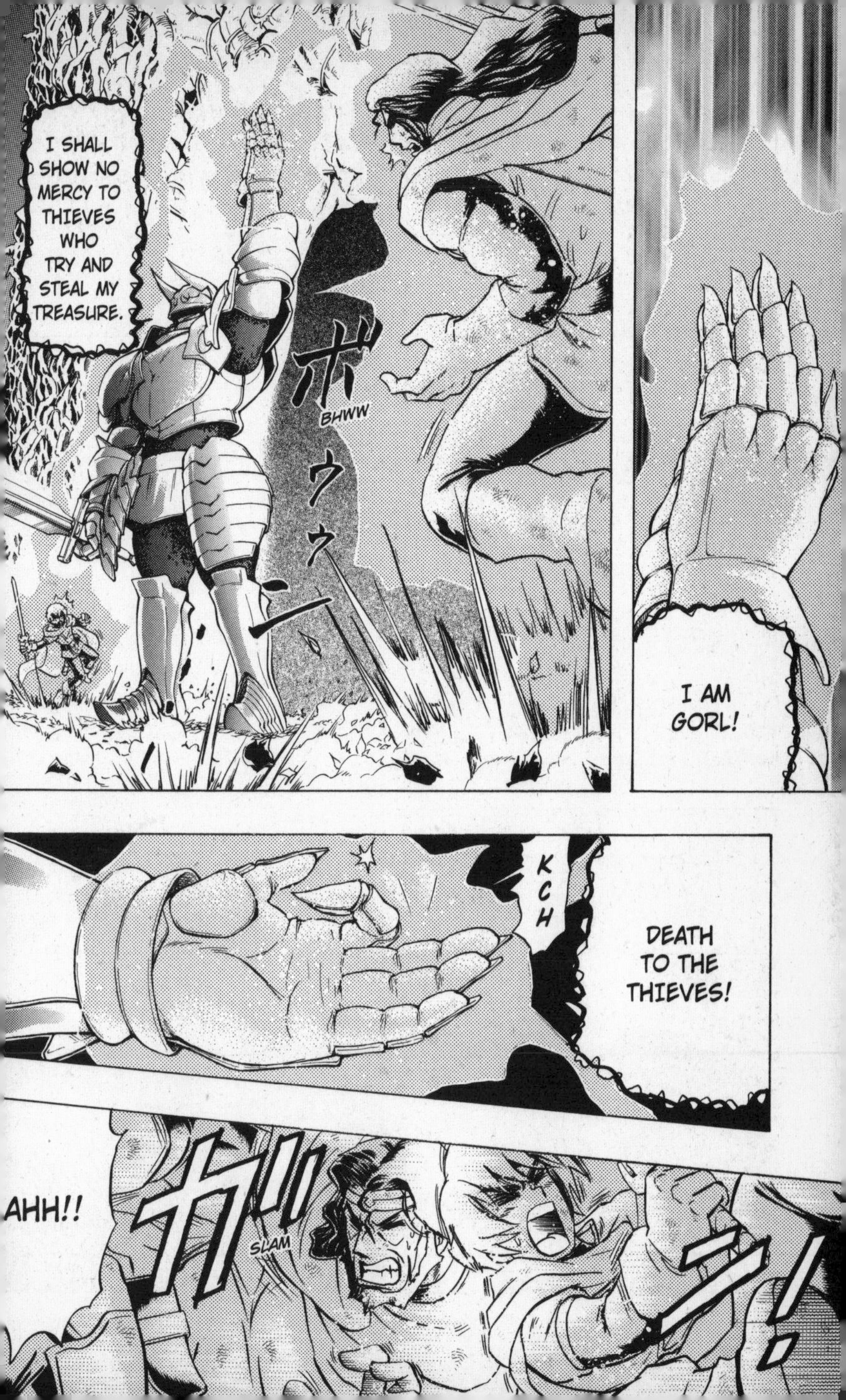
I AM GORL!
I SHALL SHOW NO MERCY TO THIEVES WHO TRY AND STEAL MY TREASURE.
BHWW
KCH
DEATH TO THE THIEVES!
AHH!!
SLAM

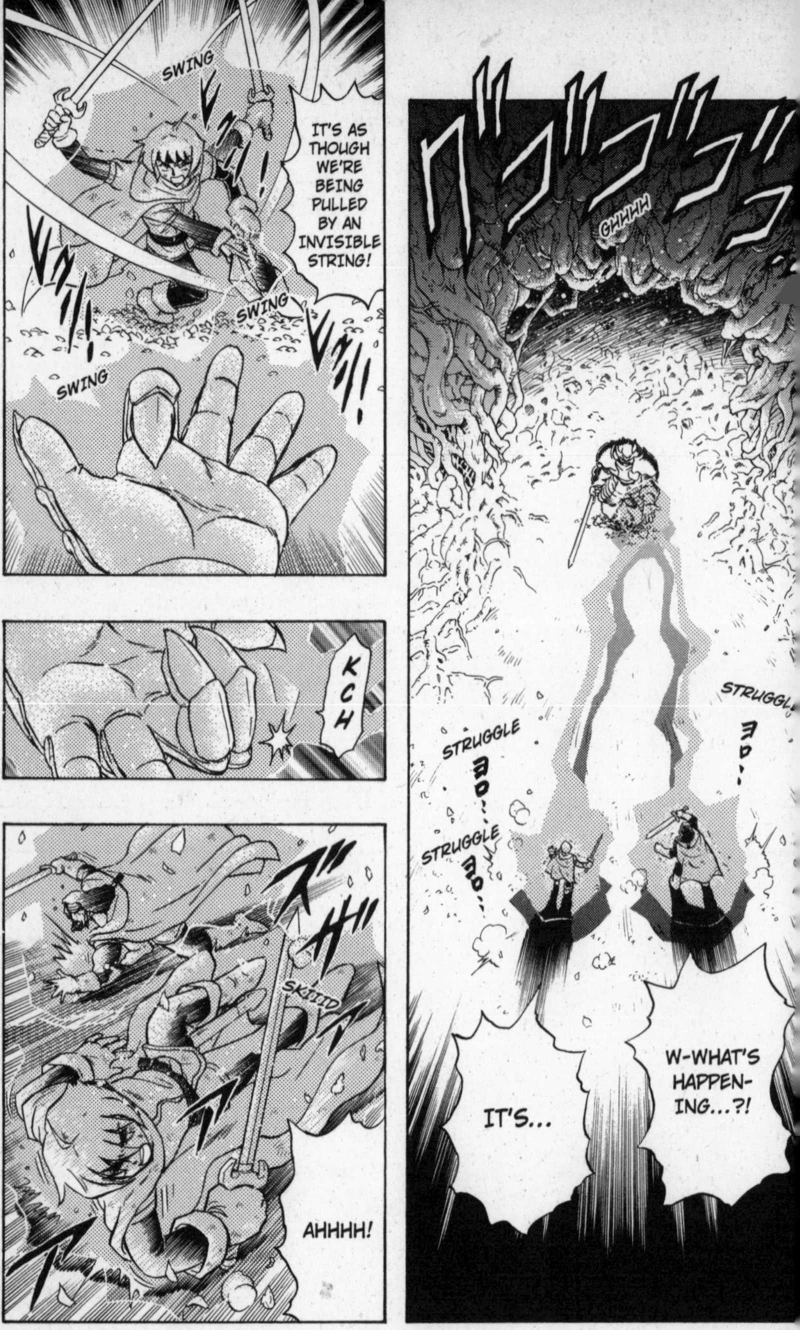
GHHHH
STRUGGL
ヨロ・・
STRUGGLE
ヨロ・・・
STRUGGLE
ヨロ・・・
W-WHAT'S HAPPEN-ING...?!
IT'S...
SWING
IT'S AS THOUGH WE'RE BEING PULLED BY AN INVISIBLE STRING!
SWING
SWING
KCH
SKIIID
AHHHH!

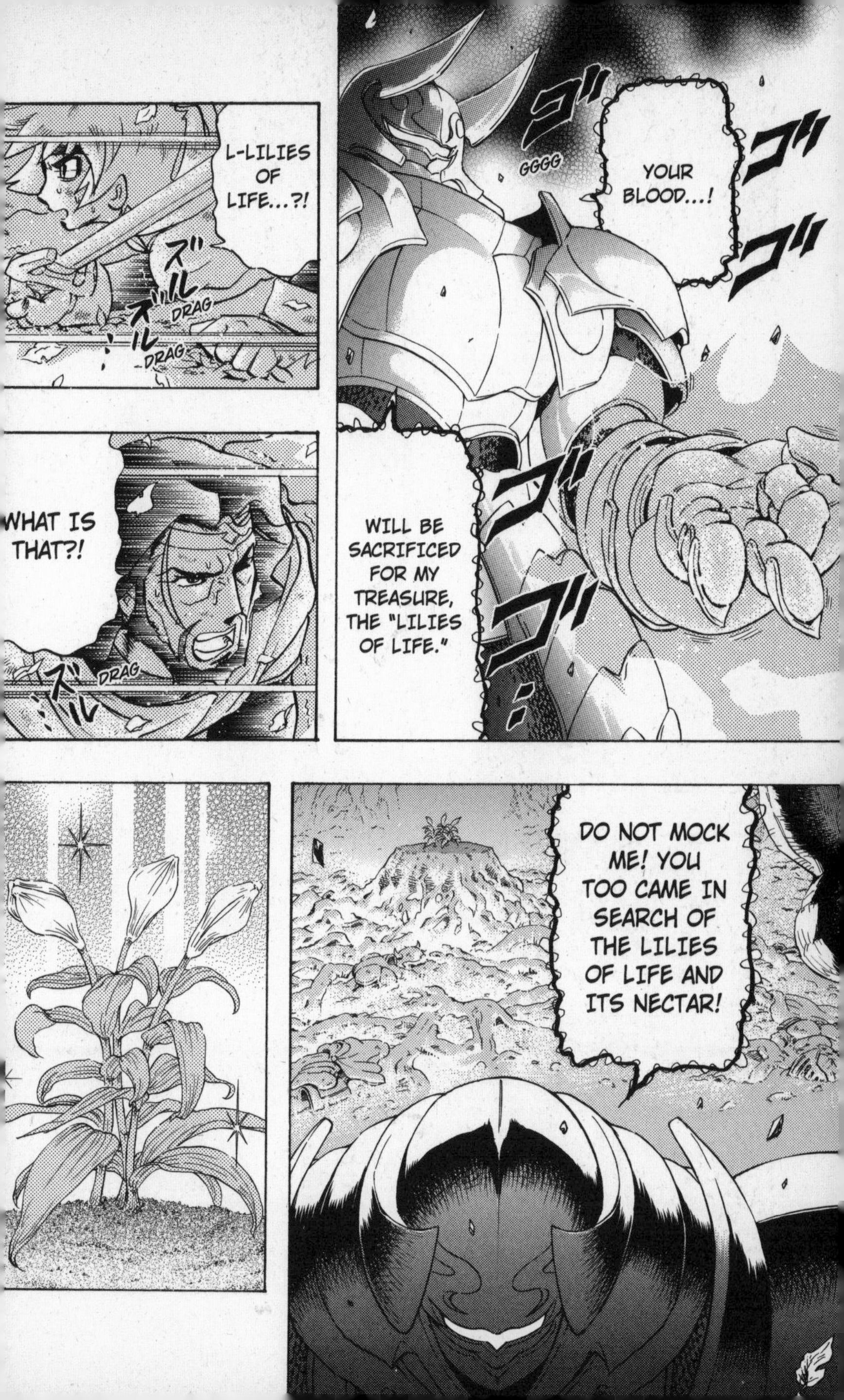

ゴ
GGGG
YOUR BLOOD...!
ゴゴ
ゴゴ
WILL BE SACRIFICED FOR MY TREASURE, THE "LILIES OF LIFE."
L-LILIES OF LIFE...?!
ズル
DRAG
ズル
DRAG
WHAT IS THAT?!
ズル
DRAG
DO NOT MOCK ME! YOU TOO CAME IN SEARCH OF THE LILIES OF LIFE AND ITS NECTAR!

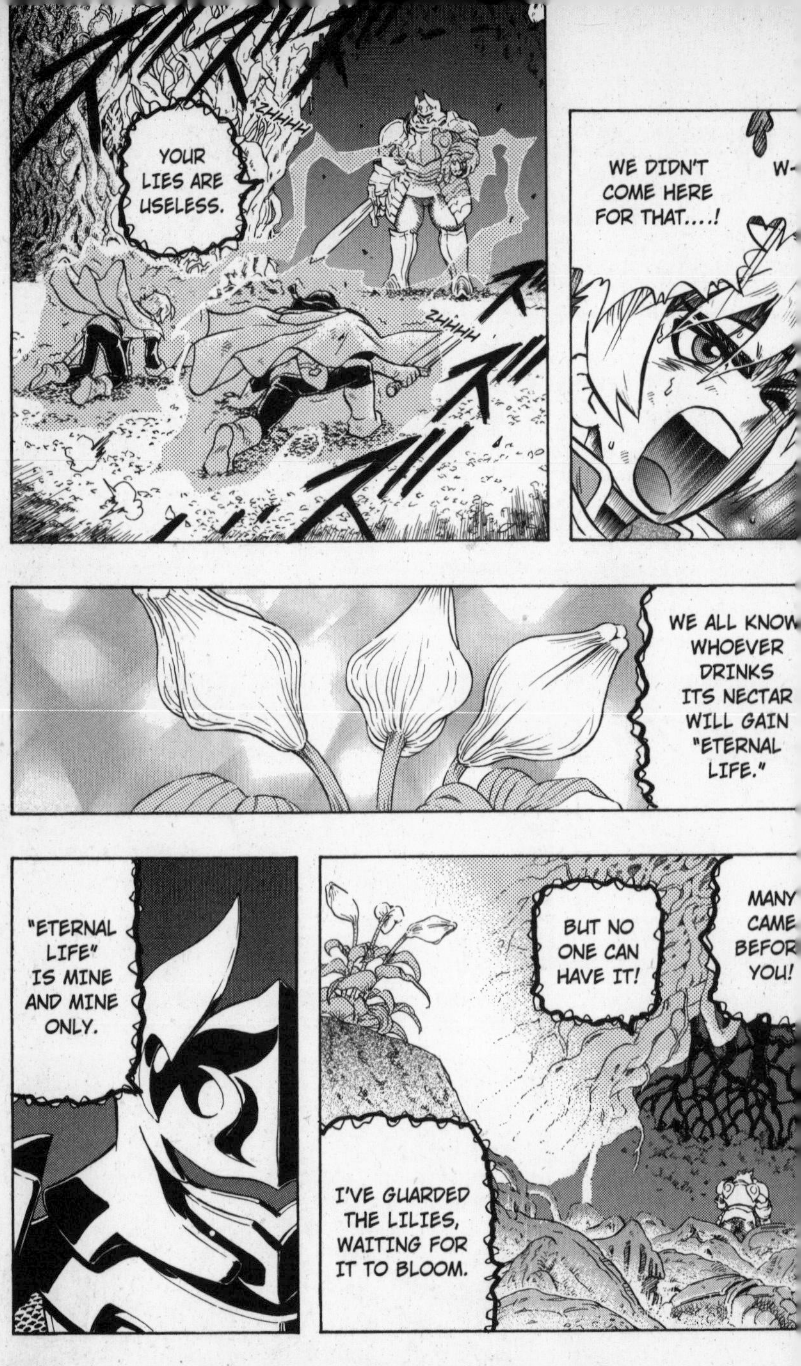
W-
WE DIDN'T COME HERE FOR THAT....!
YOUR LIES ARE USELESS.
ZHHHH
ZHHHH
WE ALL KNOW WHOEVER DRINKS ITS NECTAR WILL GAIN "ETERNAL LIFE."
MANY CAME BEFOR YOU!
BUT NO ONE CAN HAVE IT!
I'VE GUARDED THE LILIES, WAITING FOR IT TO BLOOM.
"ETERNAL LIFE" IS MINE AND MINE ONLY.

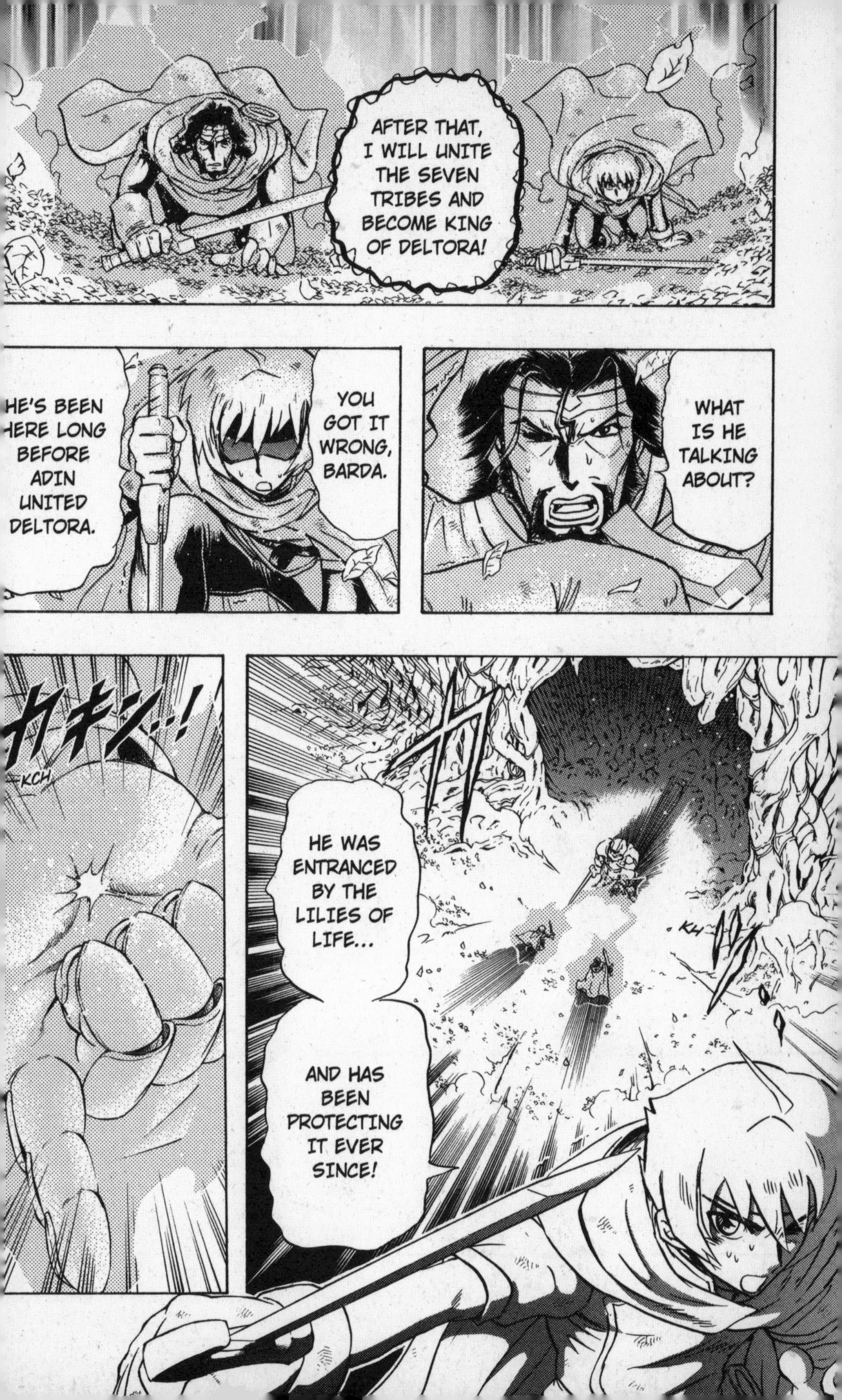
AFTER THAT, I WILL UNITE THE SEVEN TRIBES AND BECOME KING OF DELTORA!
WHAT IS HE TALKING ABOUT?
YOU GOT IT WRONG, BARDA.
HE'S BEEN HERE LONG BEFORE ADIN UNITED DELTORA.
HE WAS ENTRANCED BY THE LILIES OF LIFE...
AND HAS BEEN PROTECTING IT EVER SINCE!
KH
カキン…!
KCH

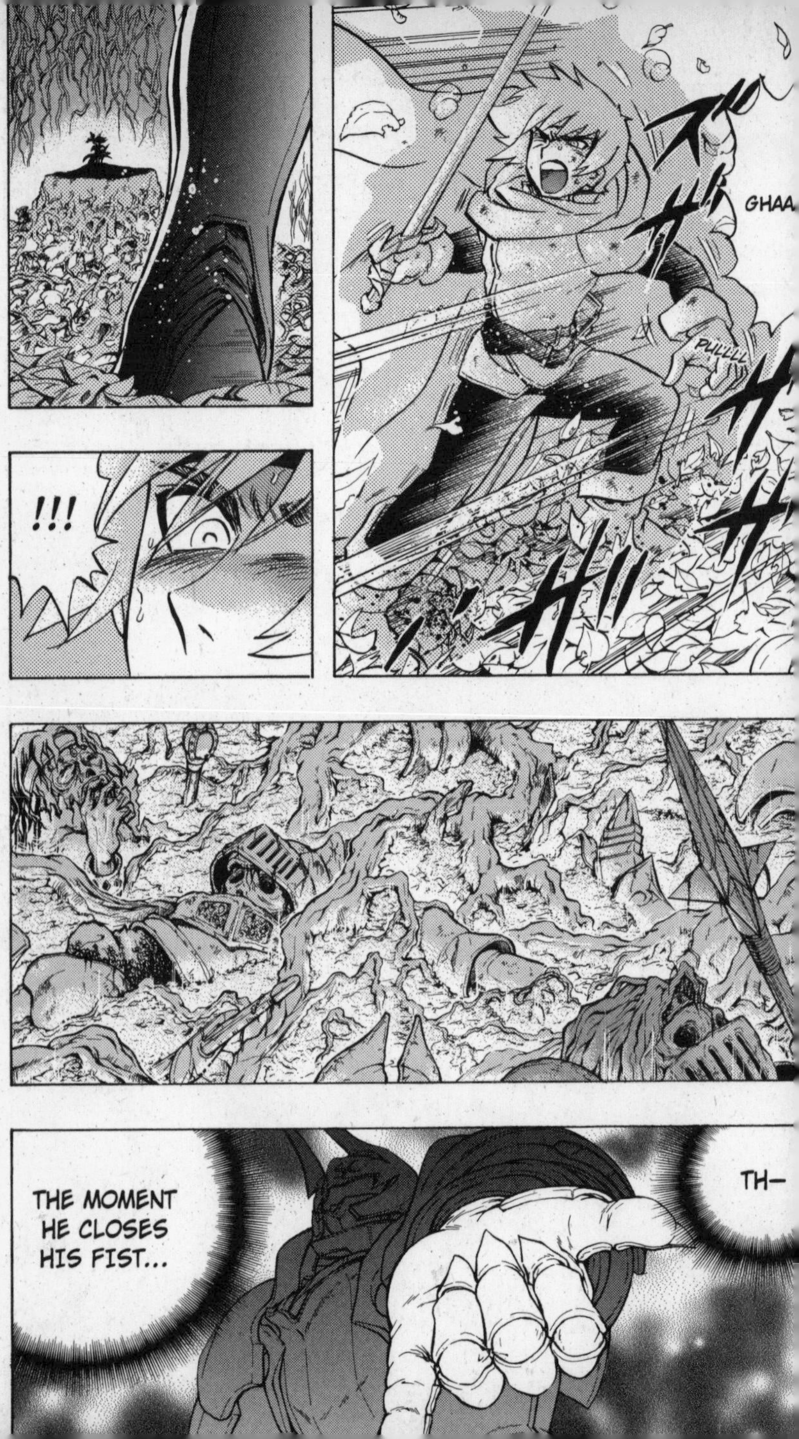
GHAA
PULLLL
!!!
TH—
THE MOMENT HE CLOSES HIS FIST...

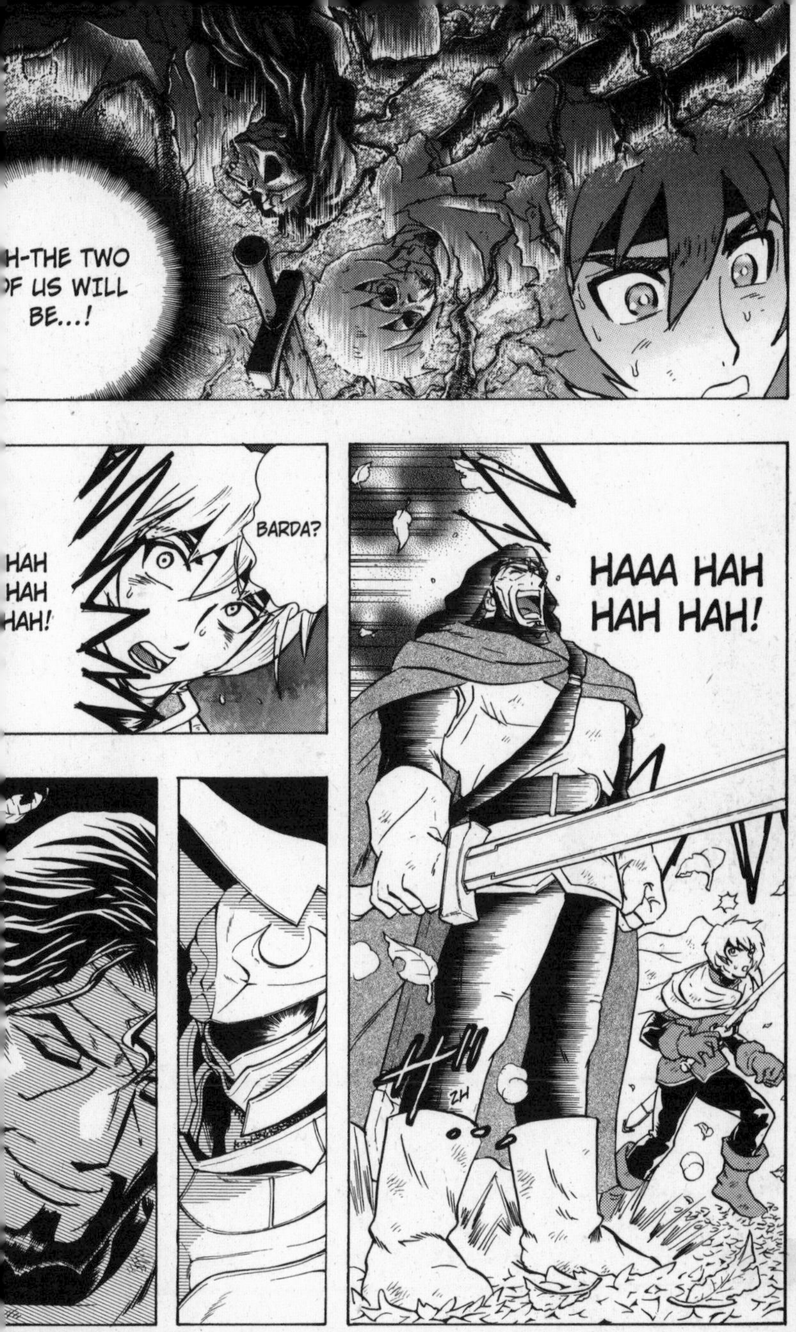
H-THE TWO OF US WILL BE...!
HAAA HAH HAH HAH!
BARDA?
HAH HAH HAH!

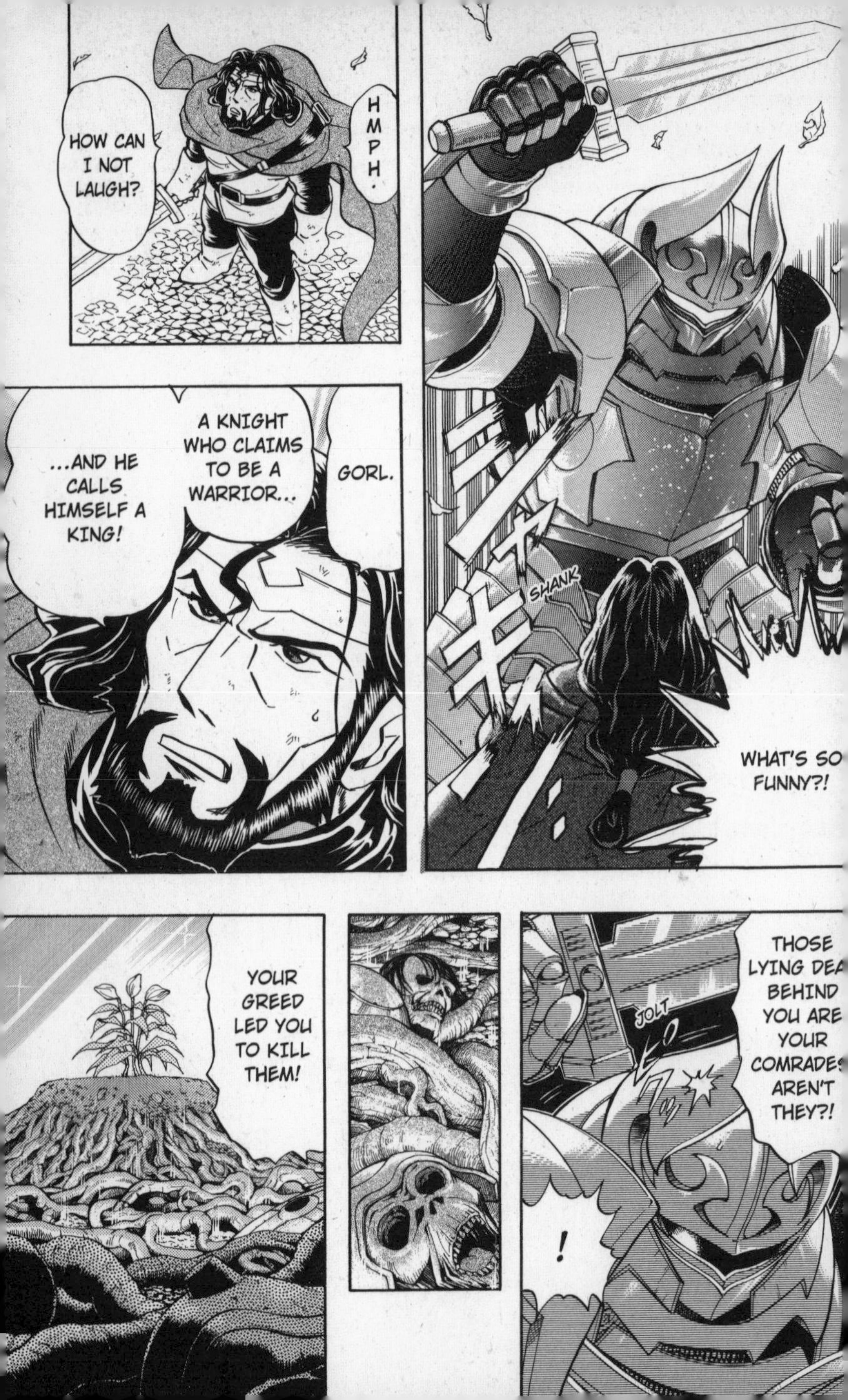
SHANK
WHAT'S SO FUNNY?!
HMPH.
HOW CAN I NOT LAUGH?
GORL.
A KNIGHT WHO CLAIMS TO BE A WARRIOR...
...AND HE CALLS HIMSELF A KING!
THOSE LYING DEA BEHIND YOU ARE YOUR COMRADES AREN'T THEY?!
JOLT
!
YOUR GREED LED YOU TO KILL THEM!

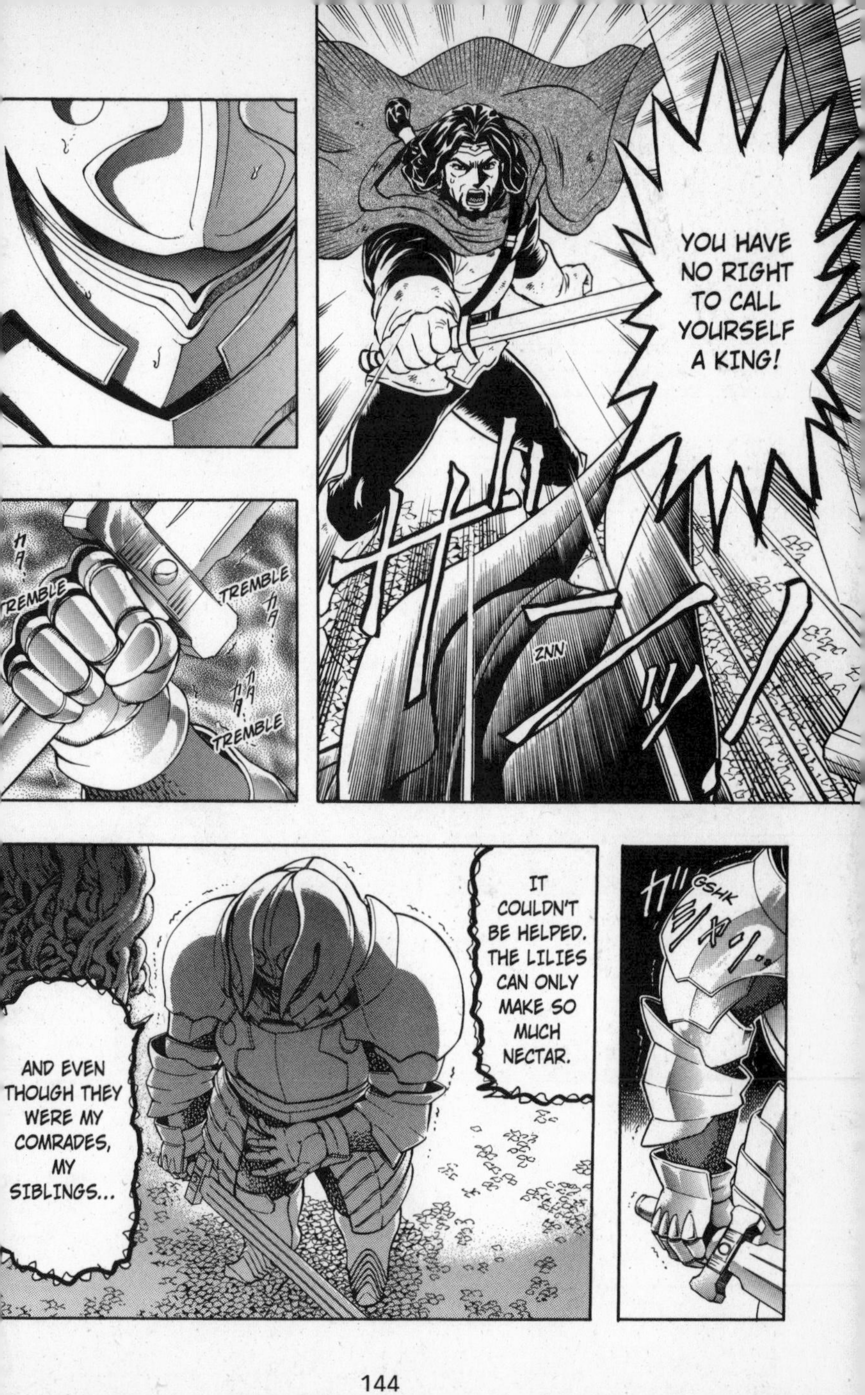
YOU HAVE NO RIGHT TO CALL YOURSELF A KING!
ZNN
TREMBLE
TREMBLE
TREMBLE
GSHK
IT COULDN'T BE HELPED. THE LILIES CAN ONLY MAKE SO MUCH NECTAR.
AND EVEN THOUGH THEY WERE MY COMRADES, MY SIBLINGS...

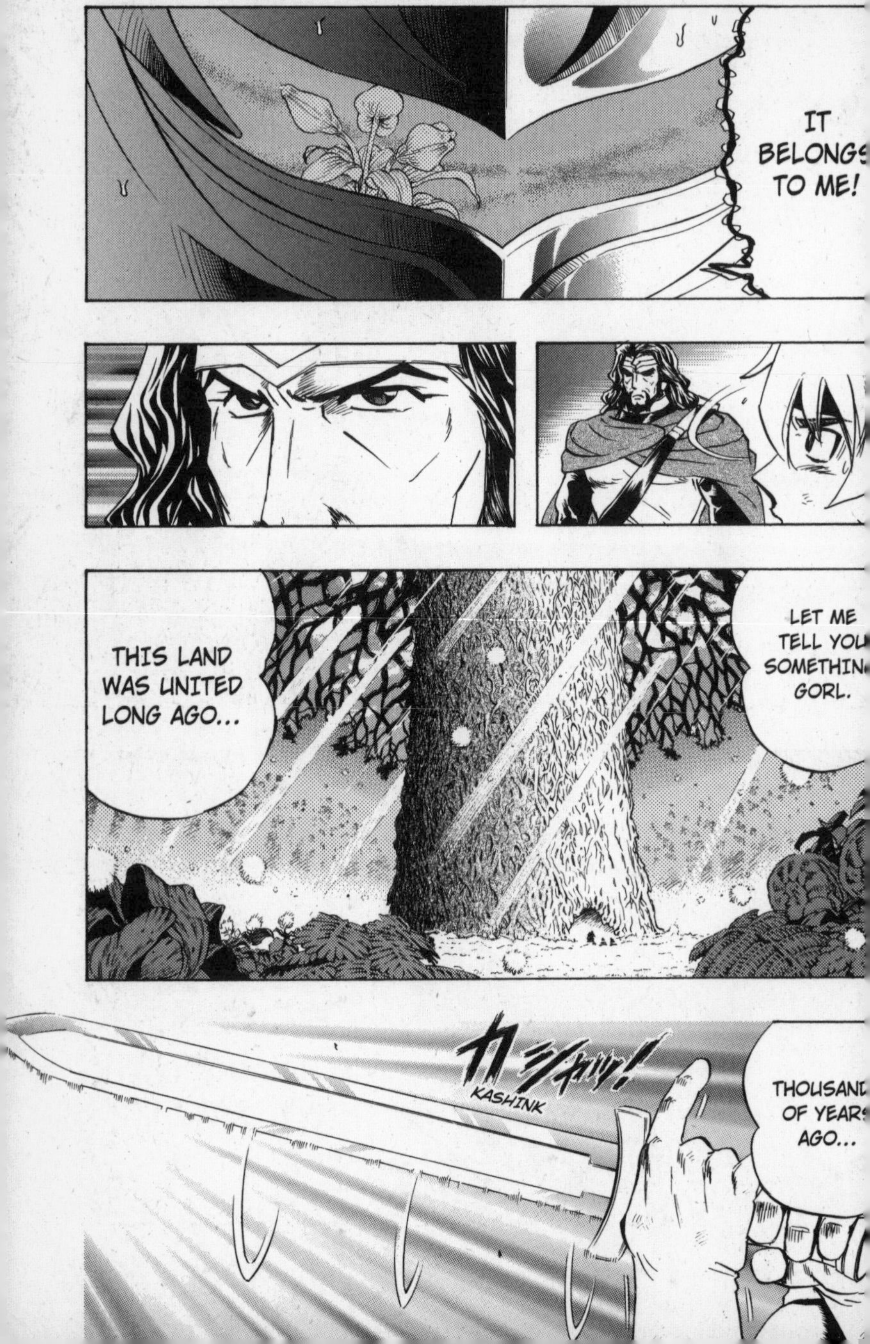
IT BELONGS TO ME!
LET ME TELL YOU SOMETHIN GORL.
THIS LAND WAS UNITED LONG AGO...
THOUSAND OF YEARS AGO...
KASHINK

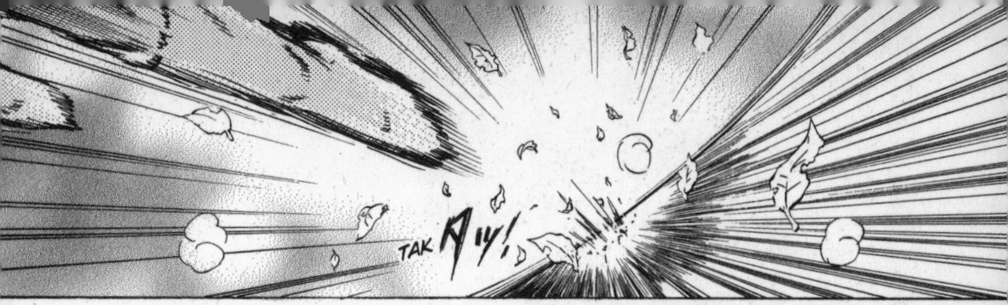
TAK

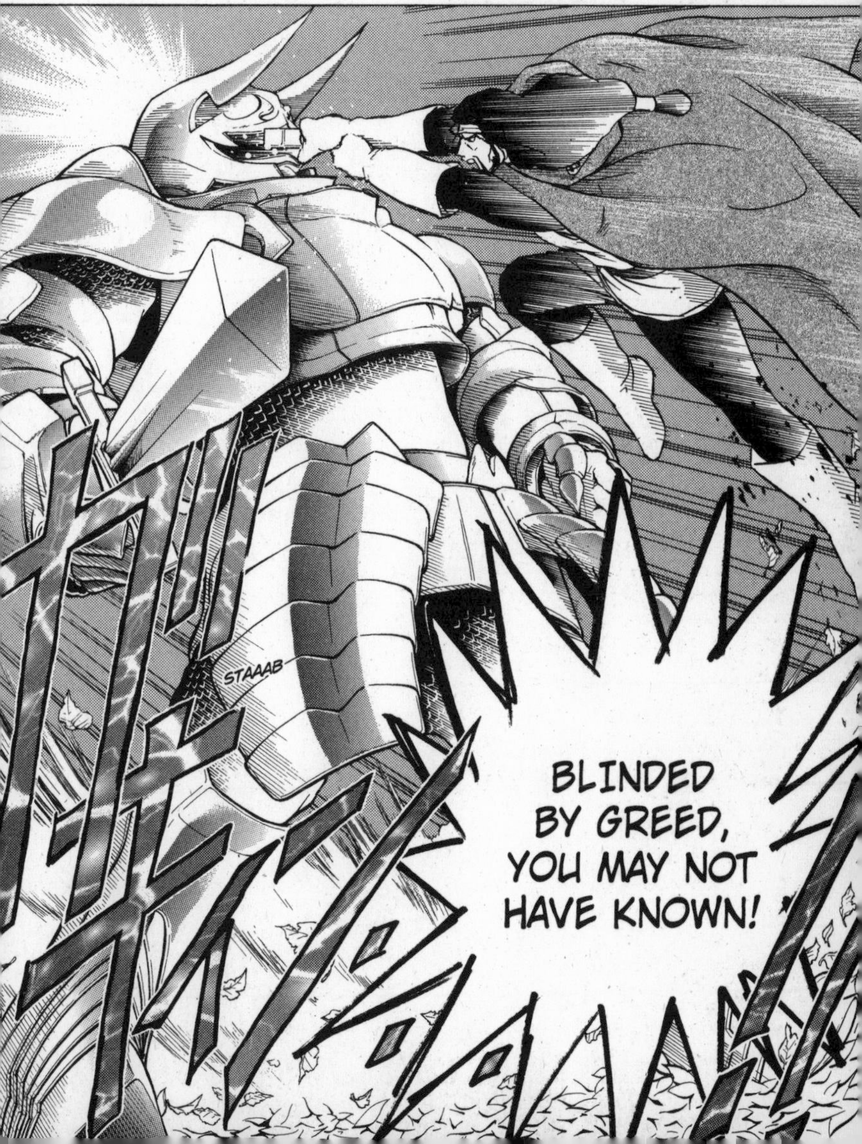
STAAAB
BLINDED BY GREED, YOU MAY NOT HAVE KNOWN!

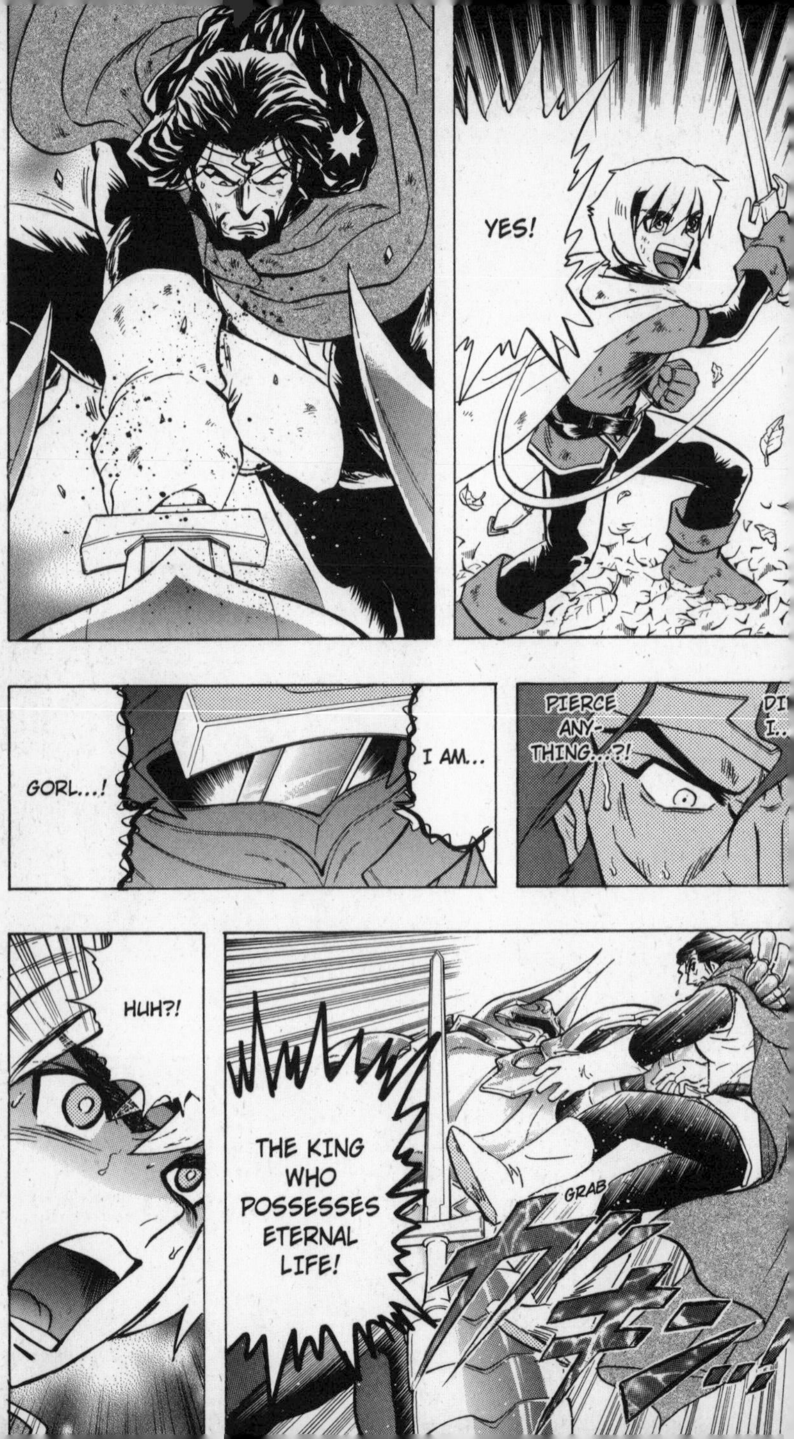
YES!
DI
I...
PIERCE ANY-THING...?!
I AM...
GORL...!
THE KING WHO POSSESSES ETERNAL LIFE!
GRAB
HUH?!

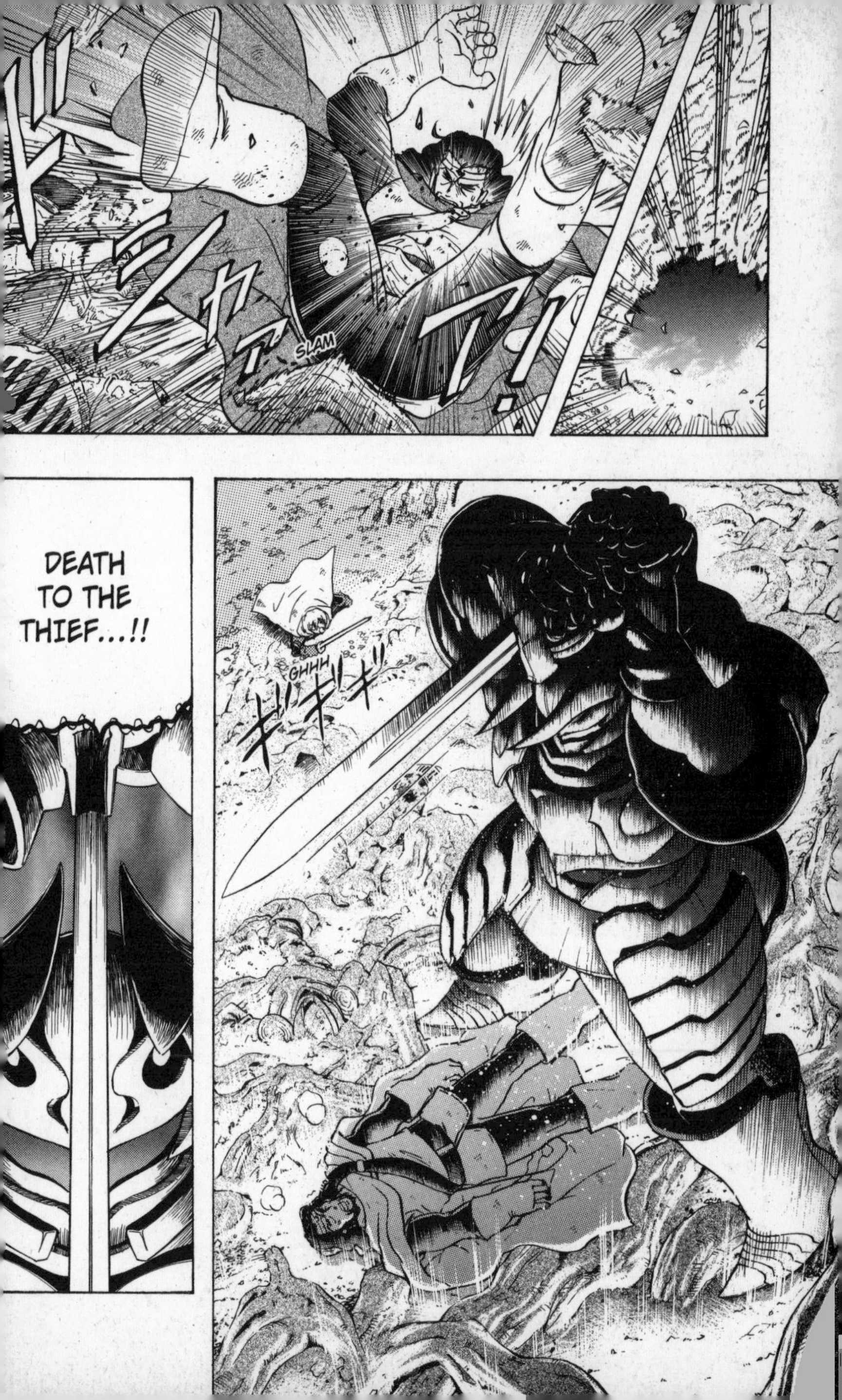
ドシャァア!!
SLAM
GHHH
ギギギ
DEATH TO THE THIEF...!!

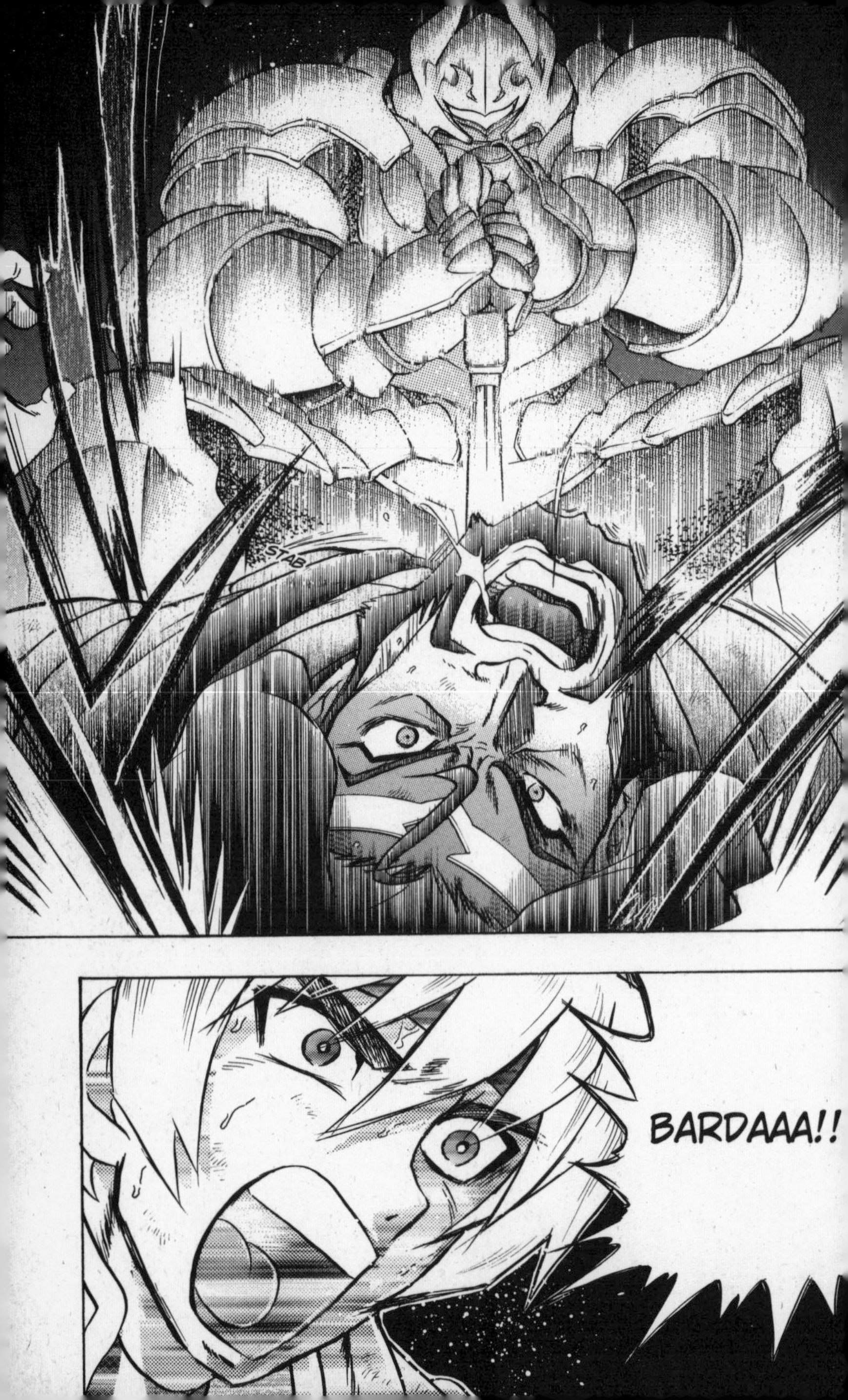
STAB!
BARDAAA!!

Chapter 8: Barda's Death

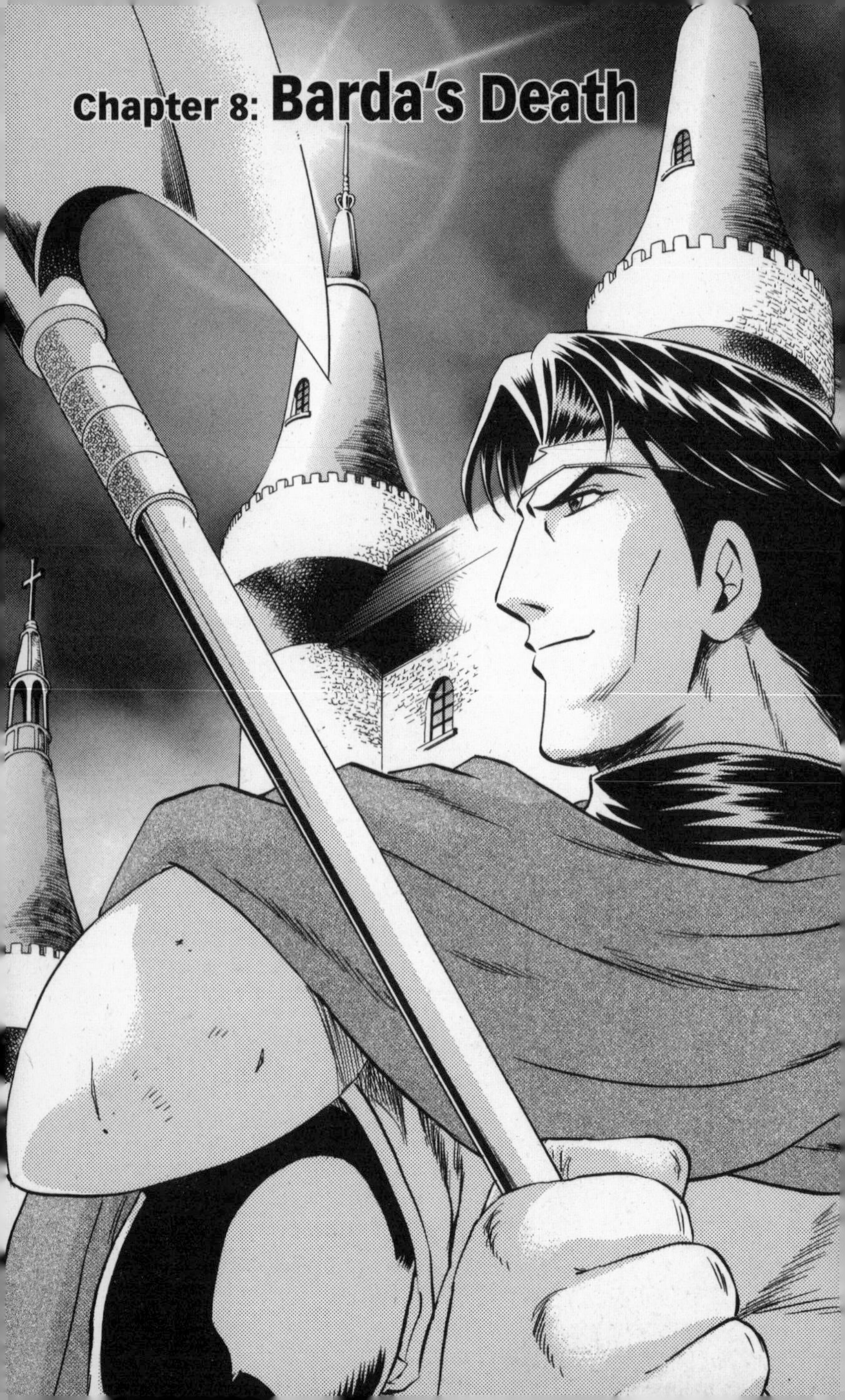

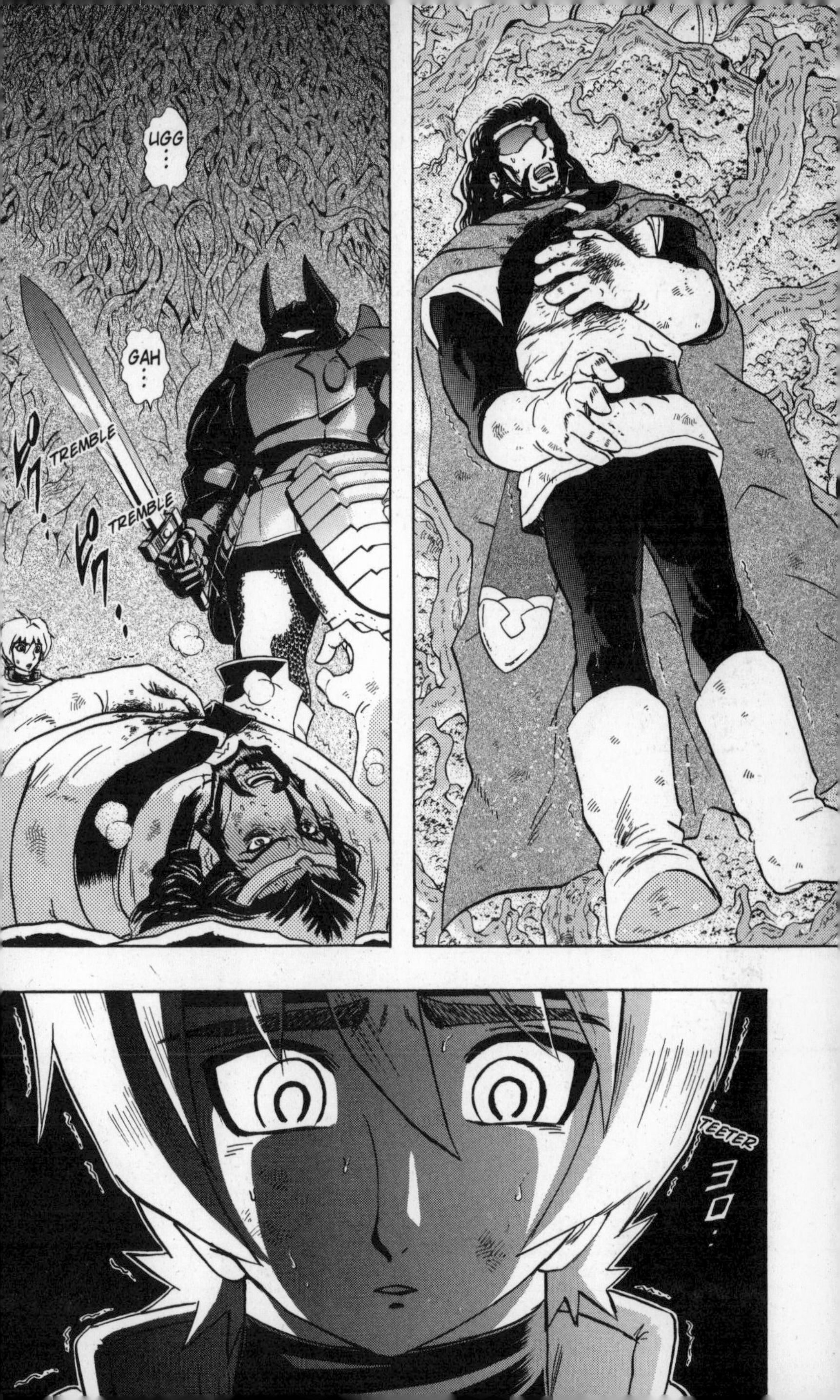
UGG...
GAH...
TREMBLE
TREMBLE
TEETER
ヨロ‥

SWISH

I AM GORL...!

DRIP

THE THIEF HAS BEEN PUNISHED WITH DEATH!

SPLISH

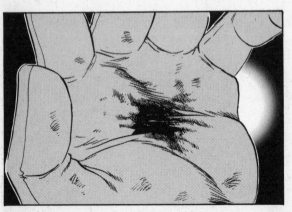

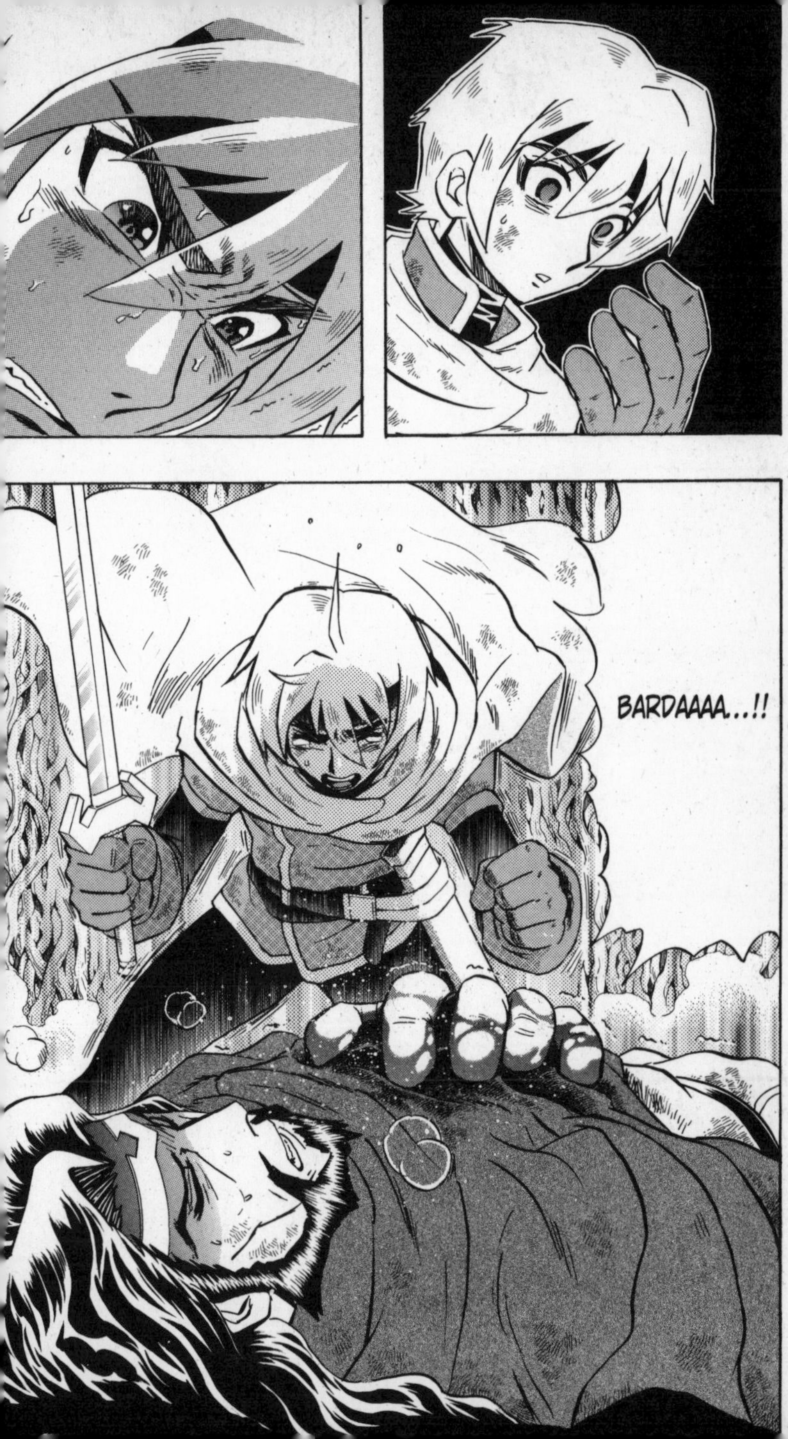
BARDAAAA...!!

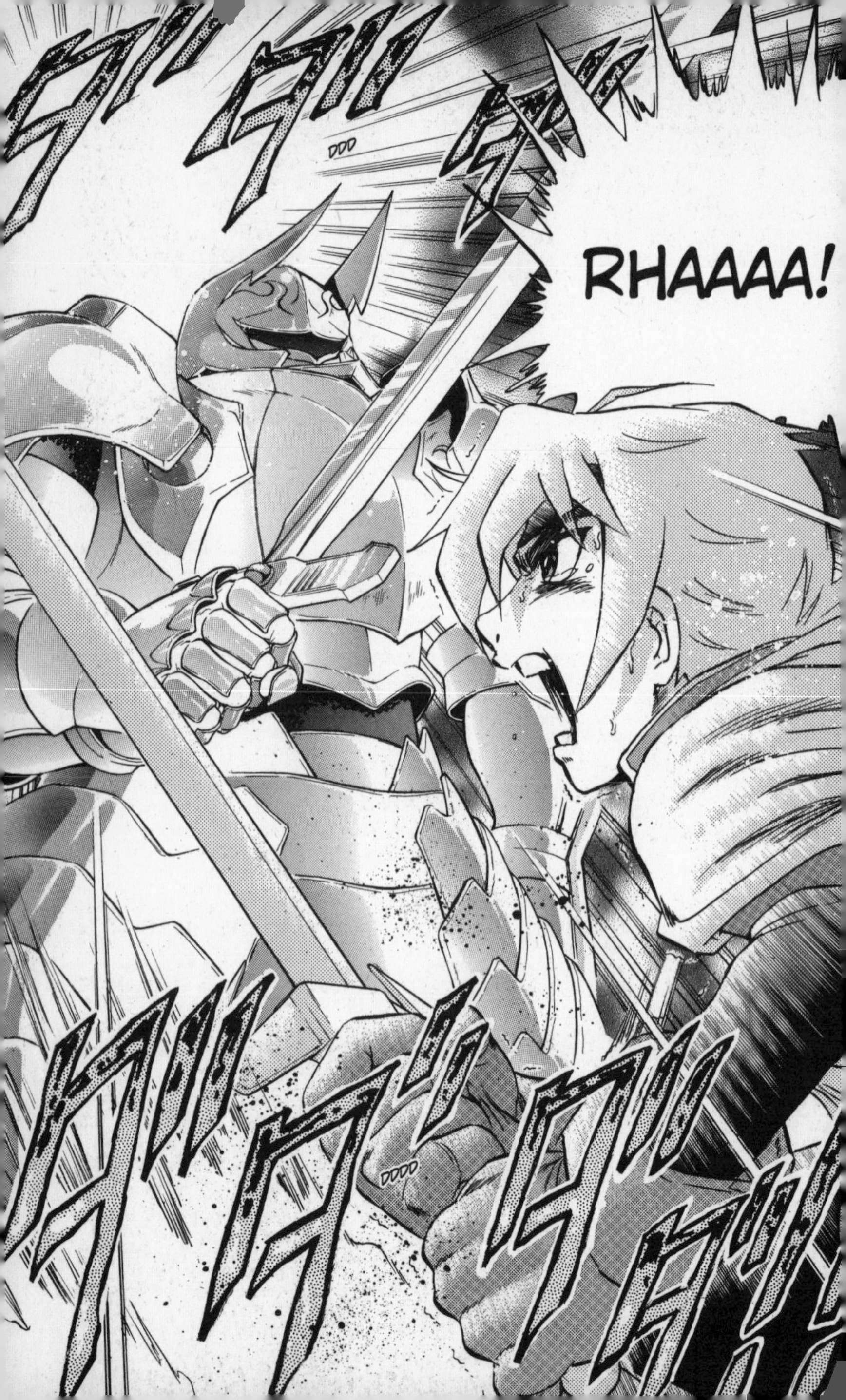
DDD
RHAAAA!
DDDD

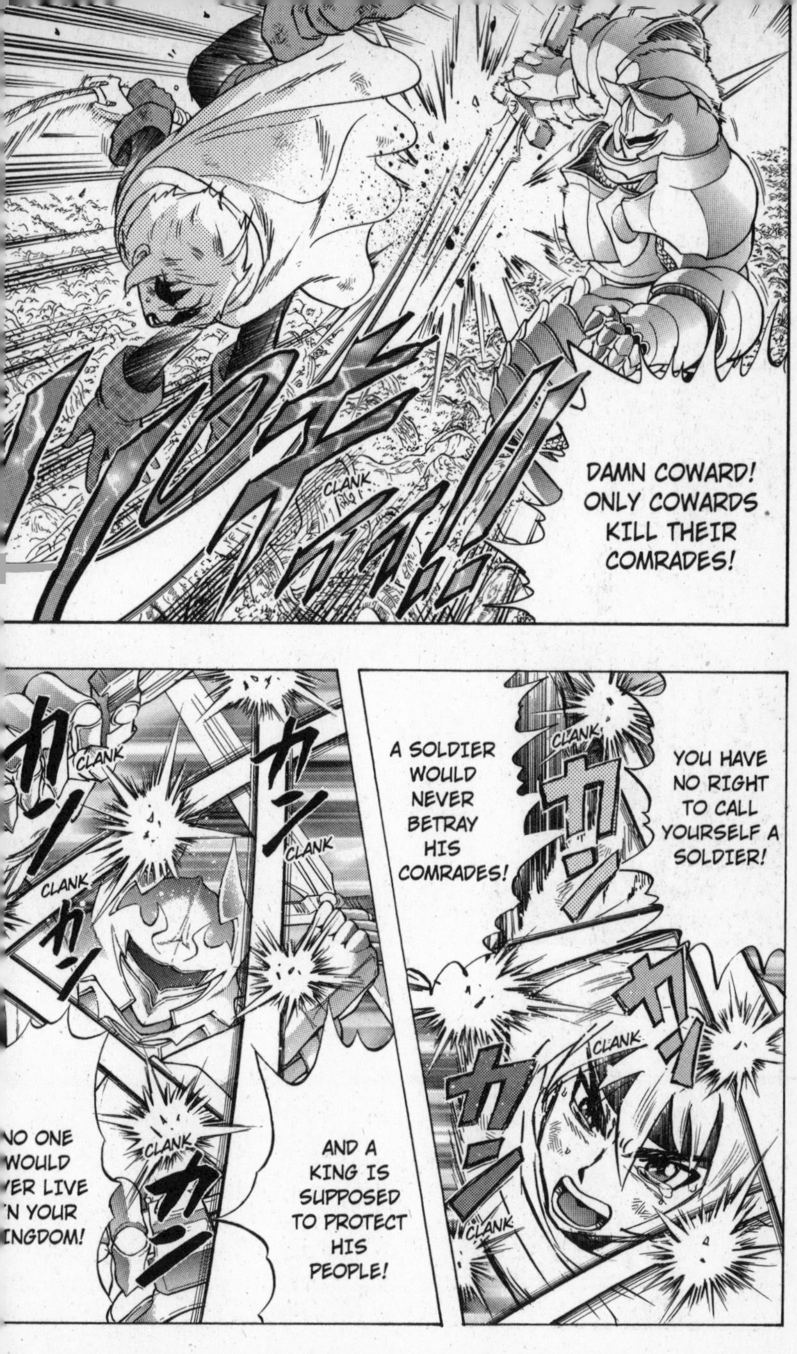
CLANK
DAMN COWARD! ONLY COWARDS KILL THEIR COMRADES!
CLANK
YOU HAVE NO RIGHT TO CALL YOURSELF A SOLDIER!
A SOLDIER WOULD NEVER BETRAY HIS COMRADES!
CLANK
CLANK
CLANK
CLANK
CLANK
AND A KING IS SUPPOSED TO PROTECT HIS PEOPLE!
CLANK
NO ONE WOULD
ER LIVE
N YOUR
INGDOM!

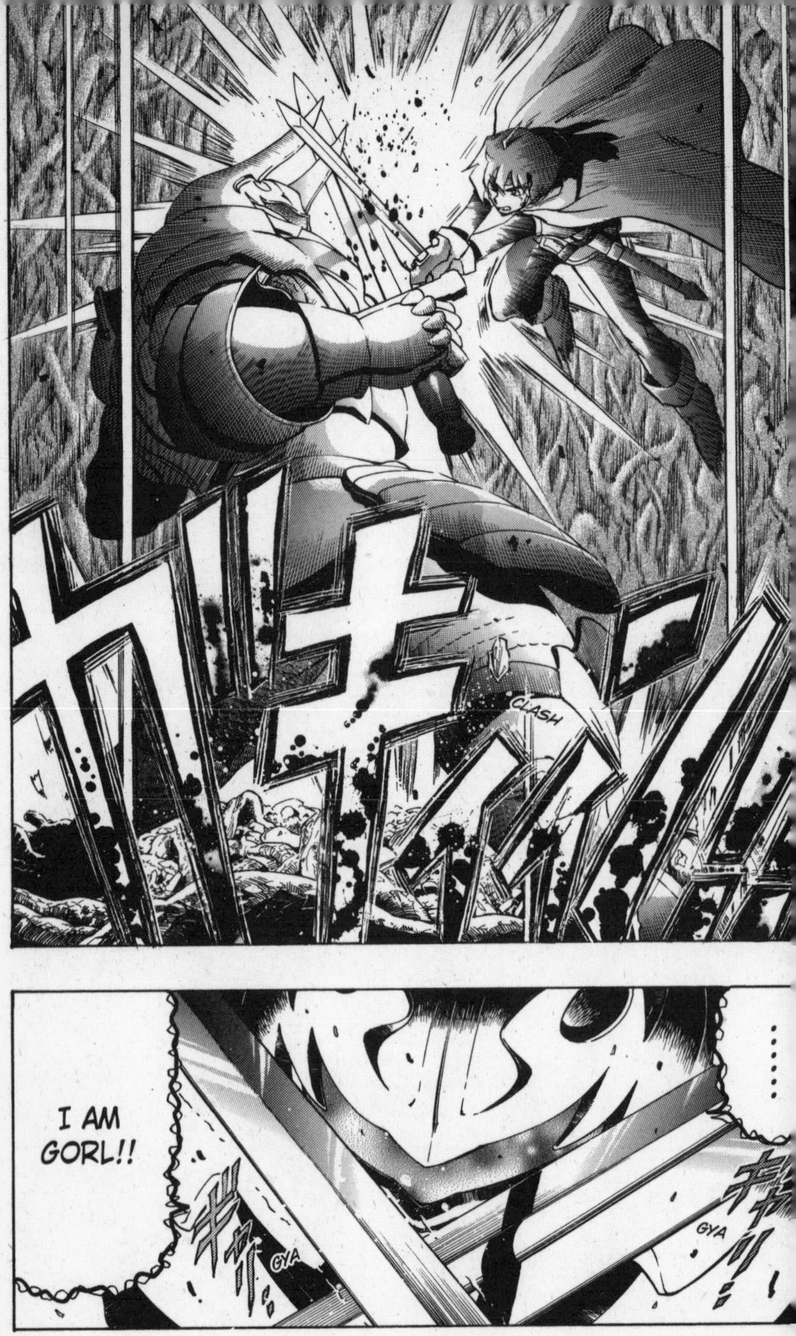
CLASH
.....
GYA
I AM GORL!!
GYA

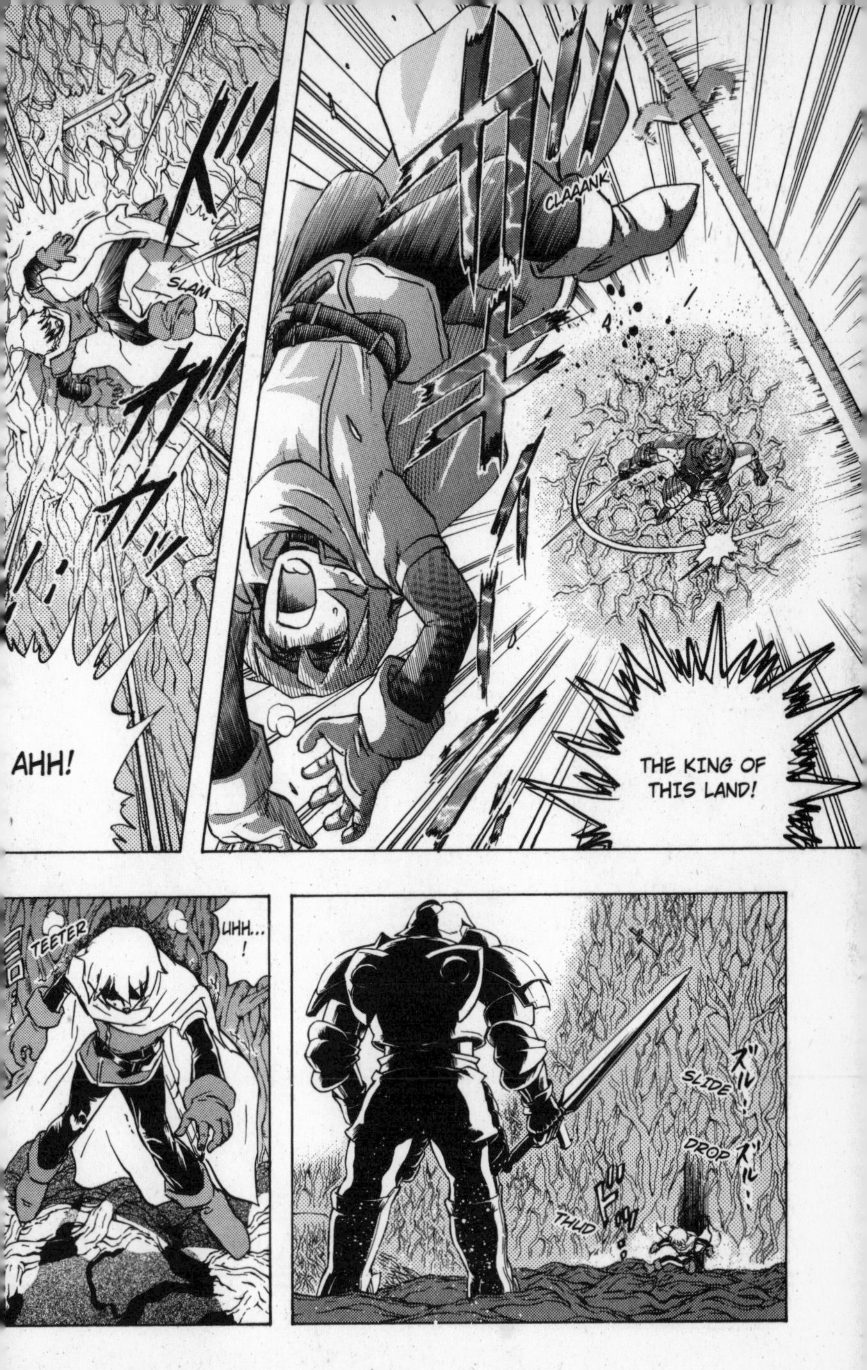
CLAAANK
SLAM
THE KING OF THIS LAND!
AHH!
SLIDE
DROP
THUD
UHH... !
TEETER

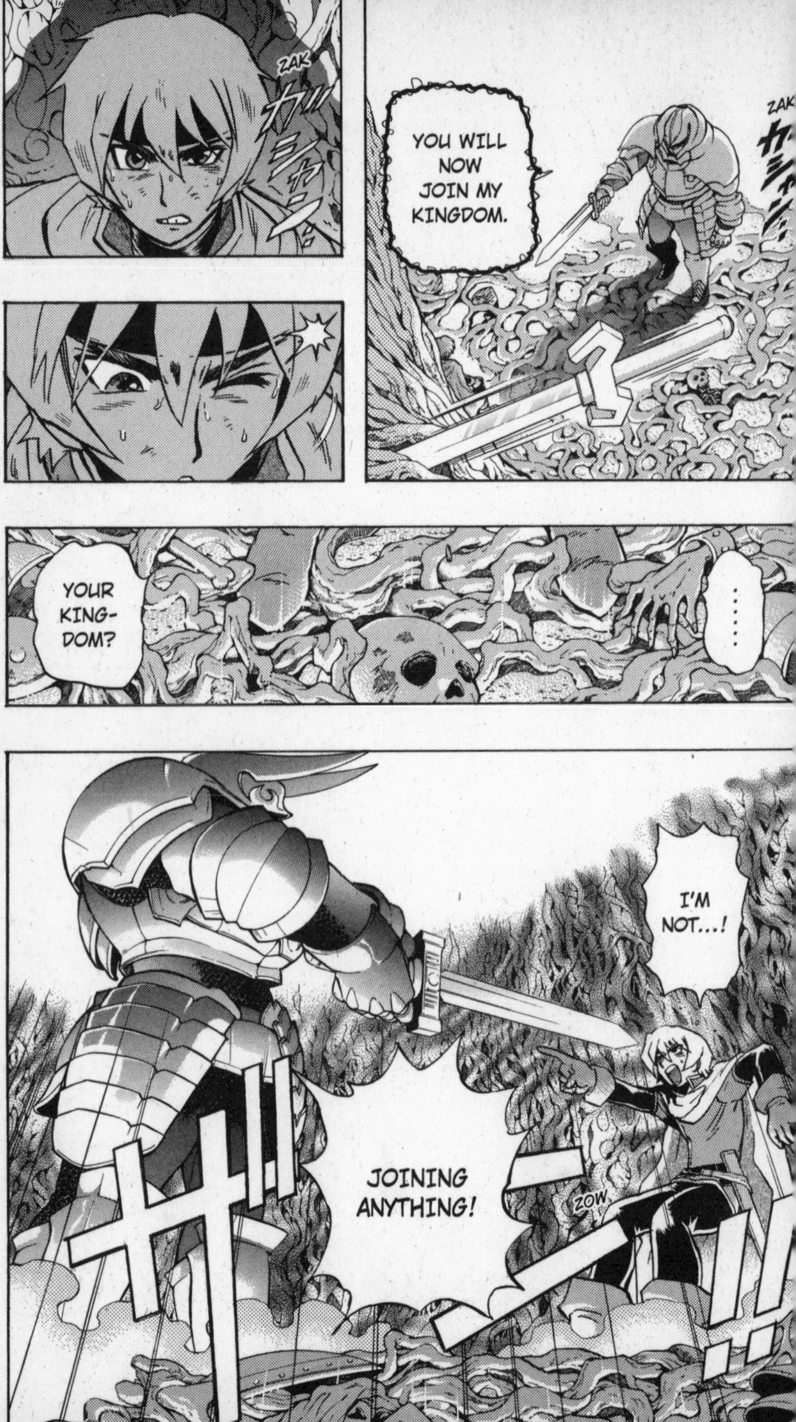
ZAK
YOU WILL NOW JOIN MY KINGDOM.
ZAK
......
YOUR KING-DOM?
I'M NOT...!
ZOW
JOINING ANYTHING!

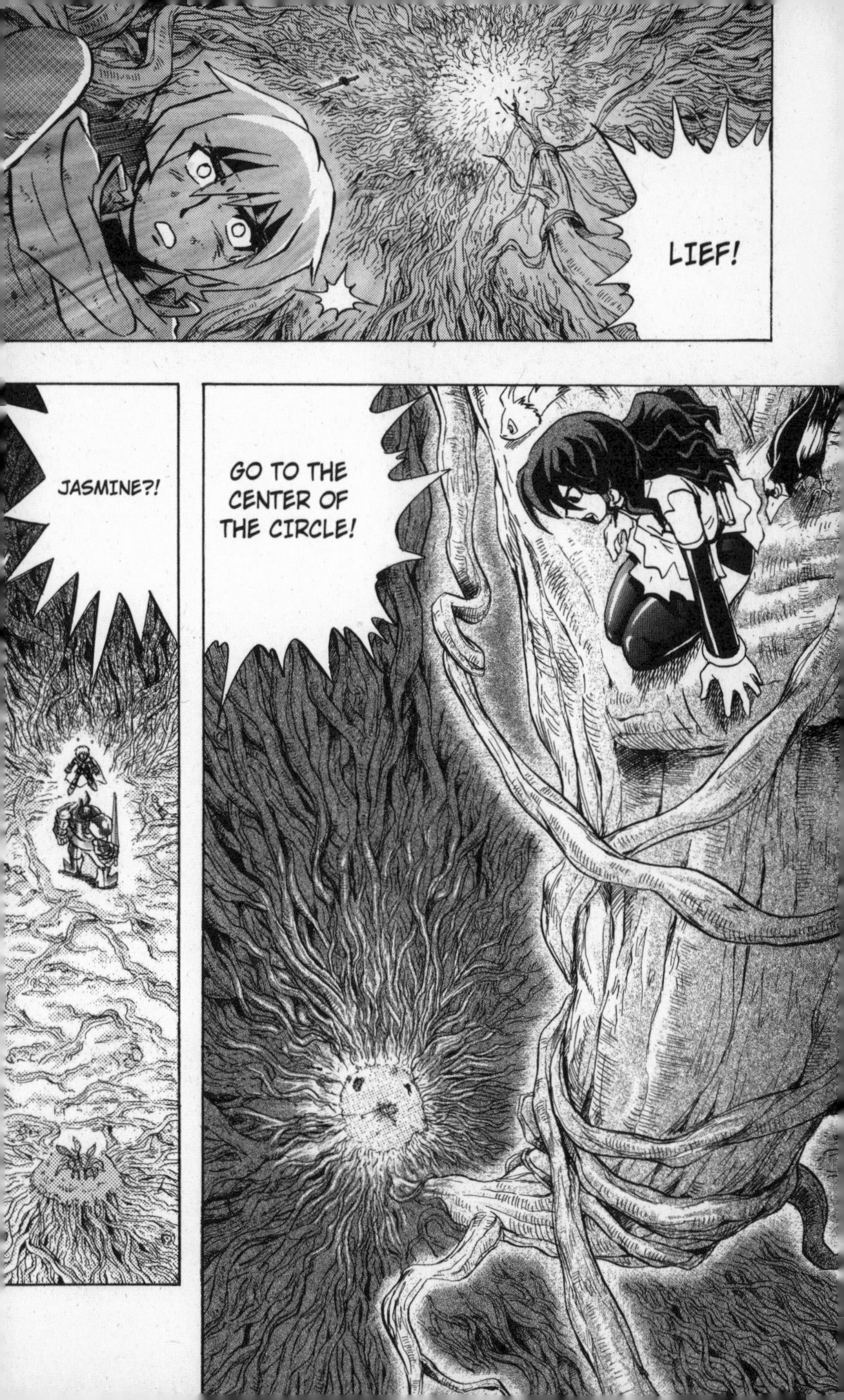
LIEF!
GO TO THE CENTER OF THE CIRCLE!
JASMINE?!

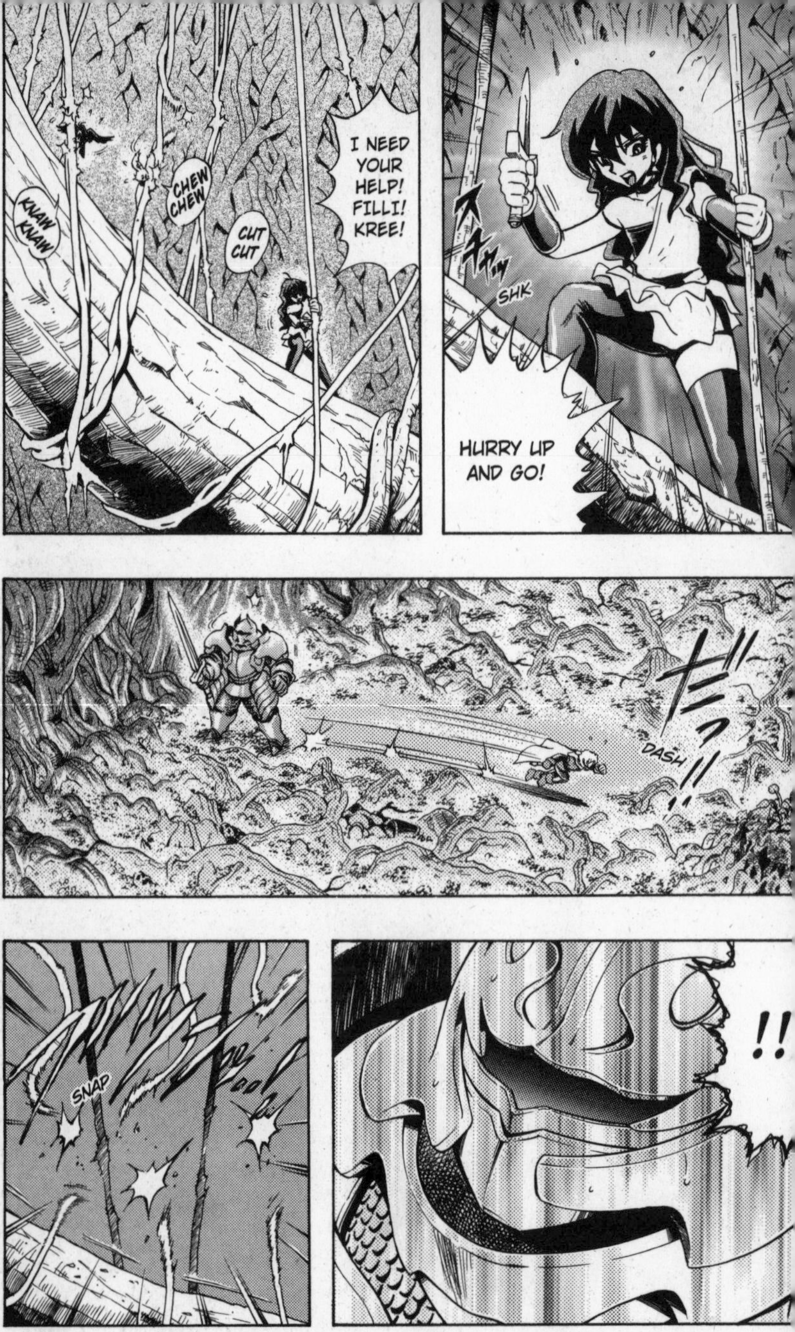
SHK
HURRY UP AND GO!
I NEED YOUR HELP! FILLI! KREE!
CHEW CHEW
CUT CUT
KNAW KNAW
DASH
!!
SNAP

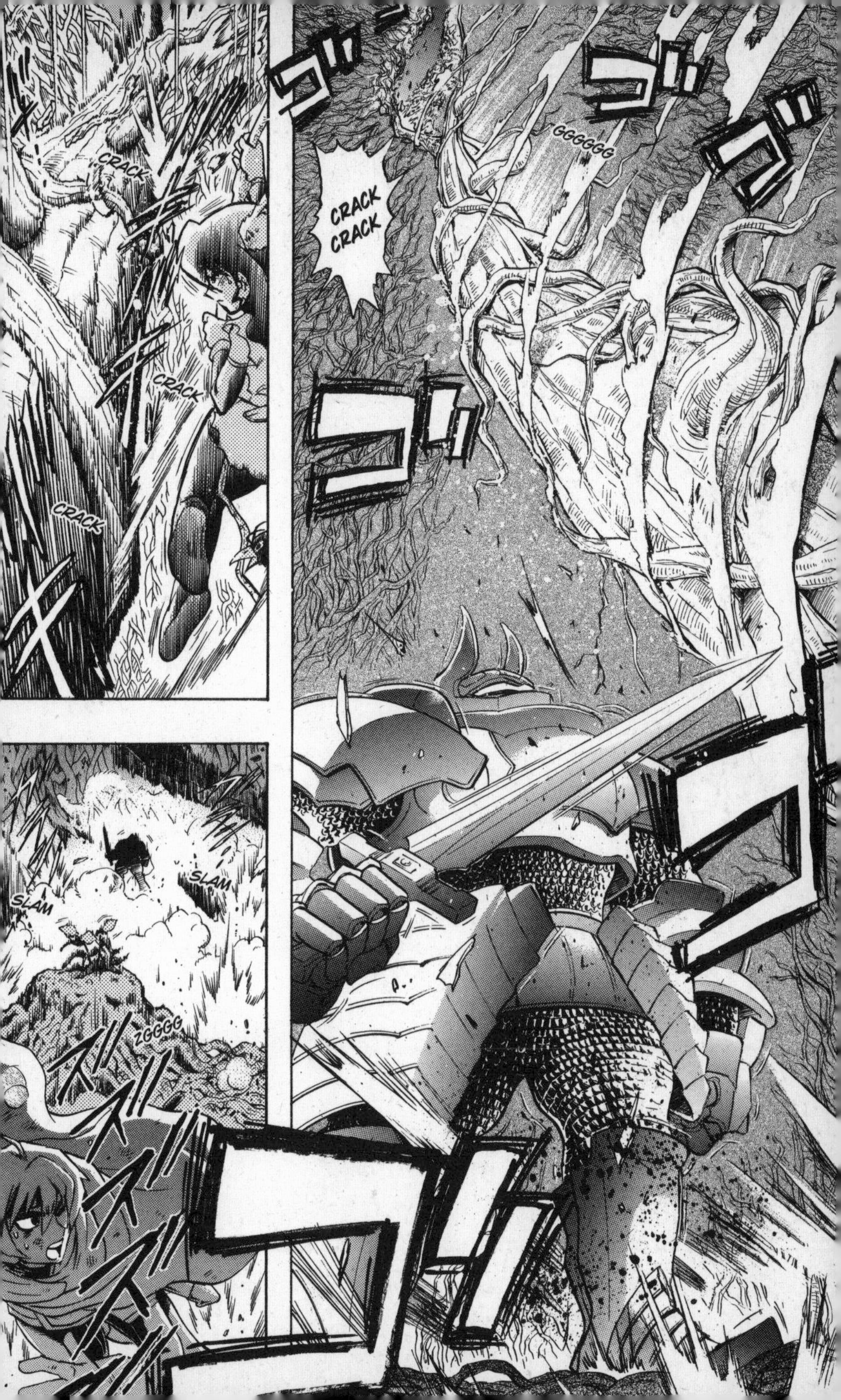
GGGGGG
CRACK CRACK
CRACK
CRACK
CRACK
SLAM
SLAM
ZGGGG

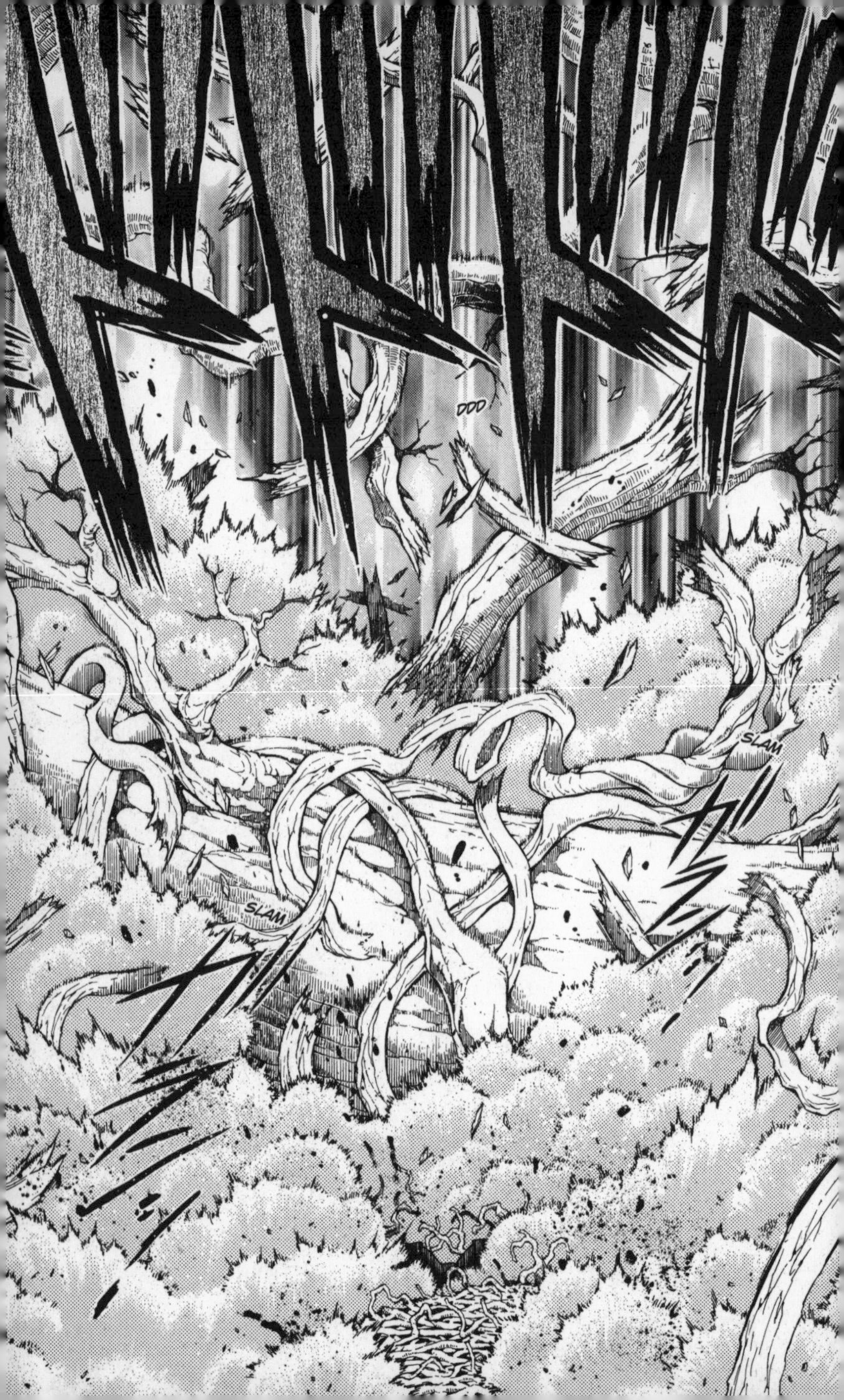
SLAM
DDD
SLAM

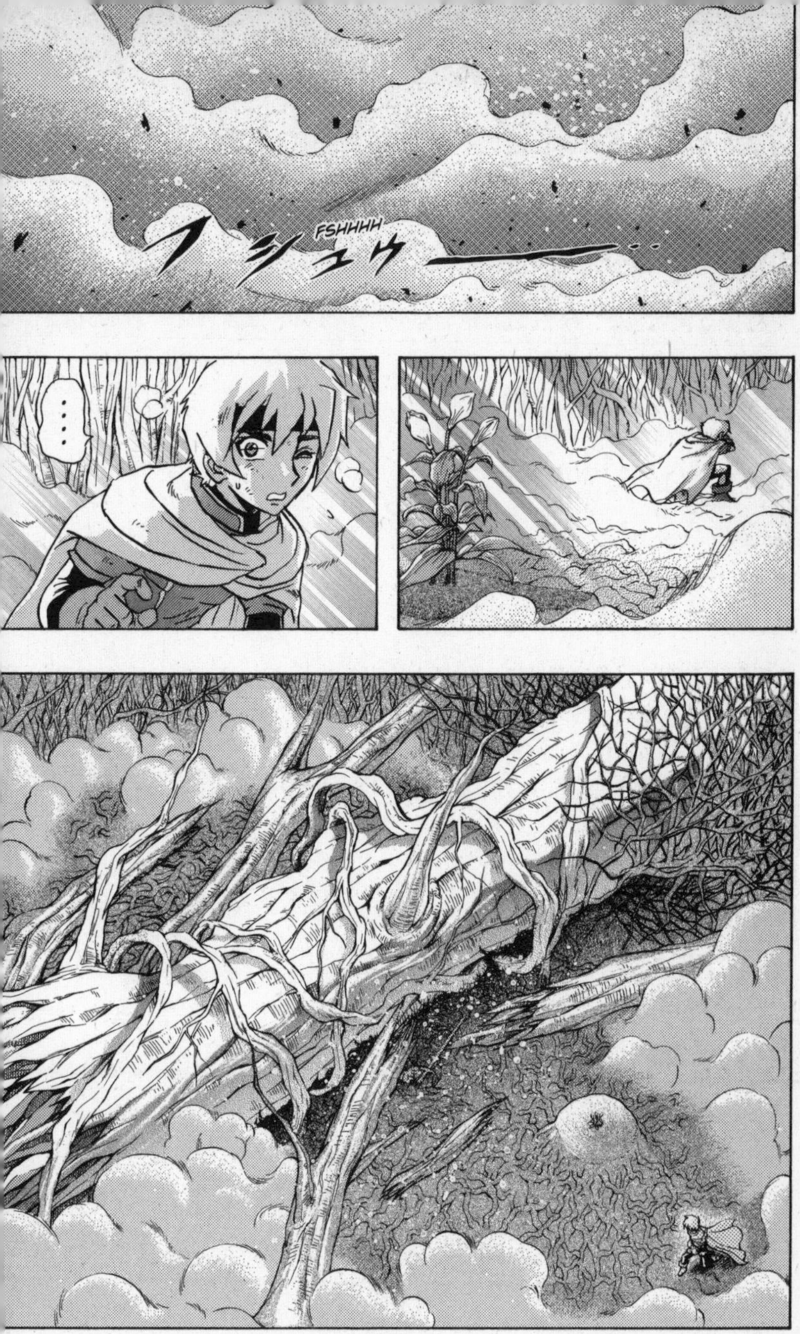
FSHHHH
フシュウ
....

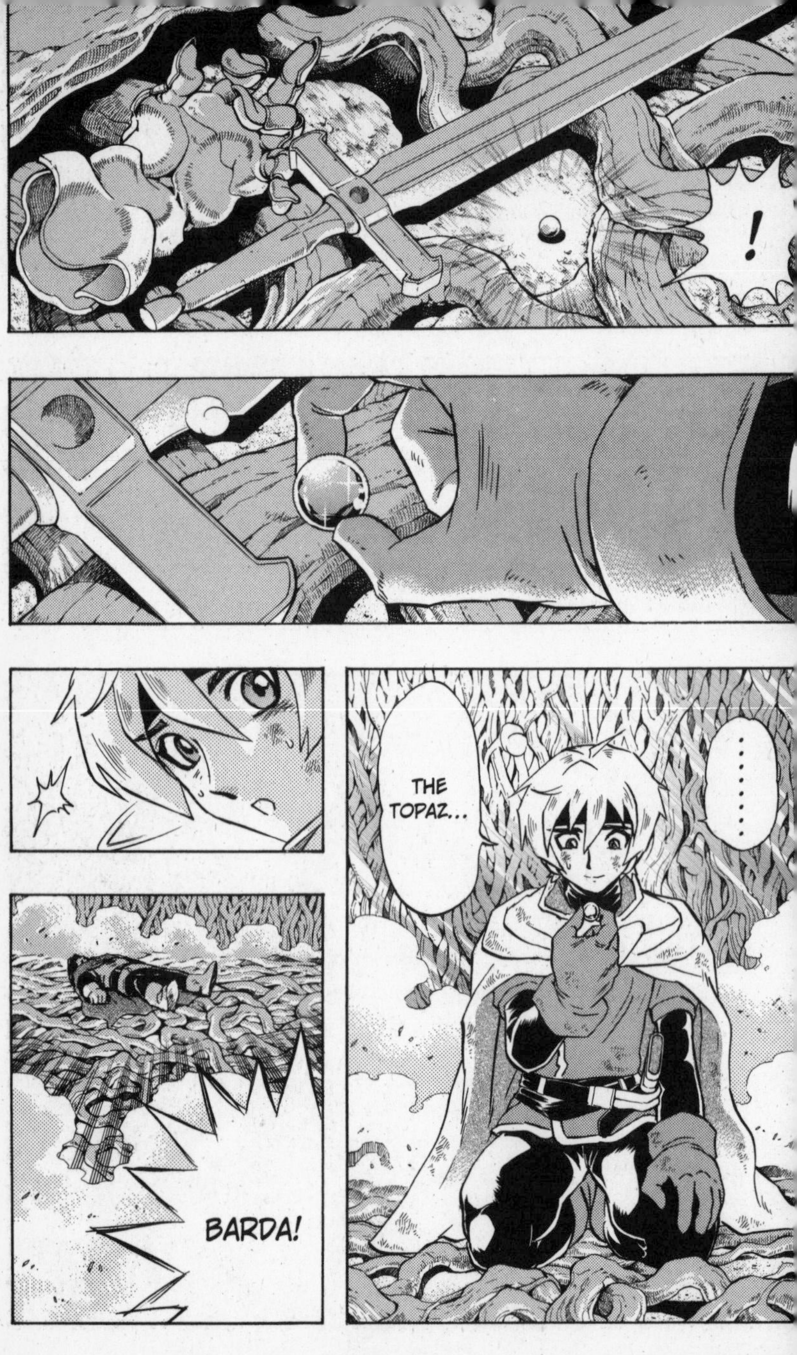
!
......
THE TOPAZ...
BARDA!

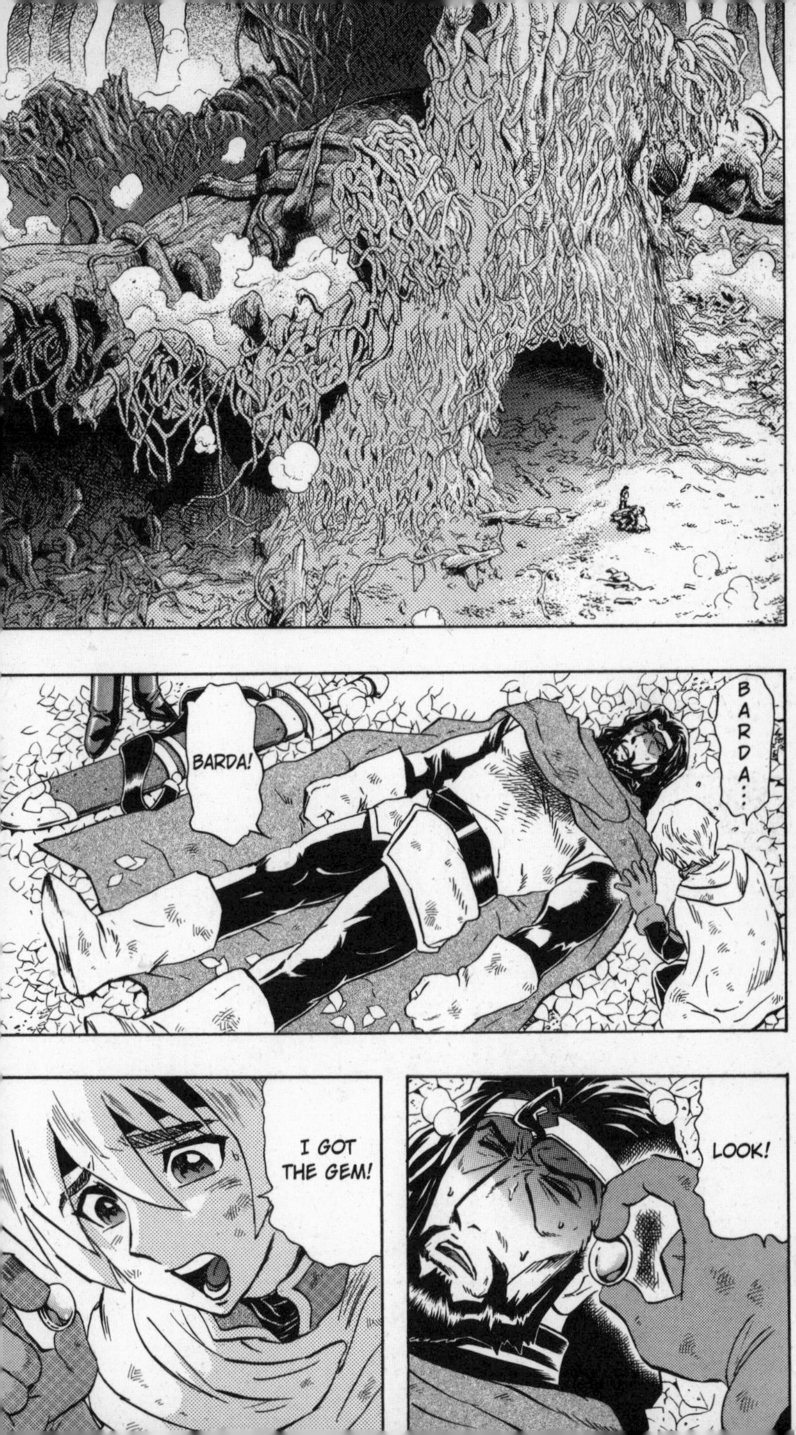

BARDA...
BARDA!
LOOK!
I GOT THE GEM!

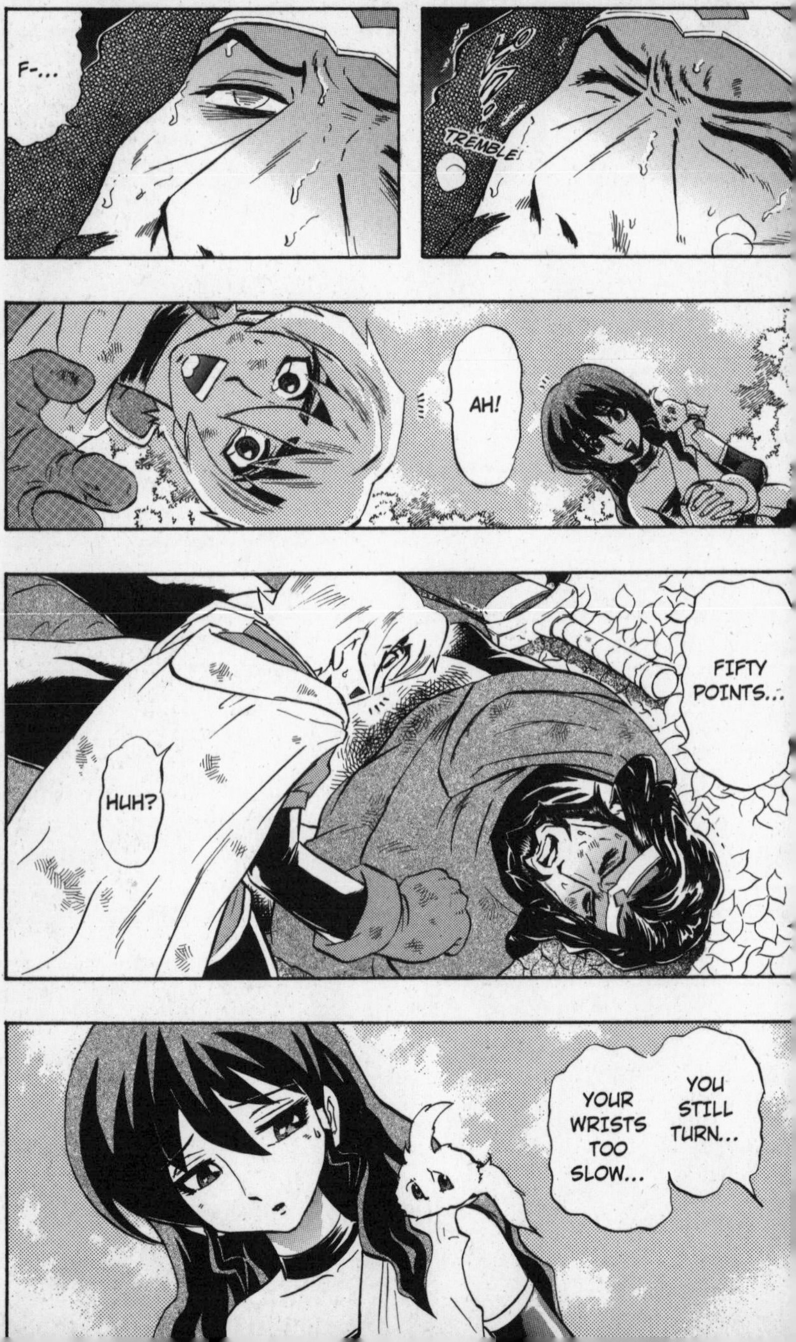
TREMBLE
F-...
AH!
FIFTY POINTS...
HUH?
YOU STILL TURN...
YOUR WRISTS TOO SLOW...

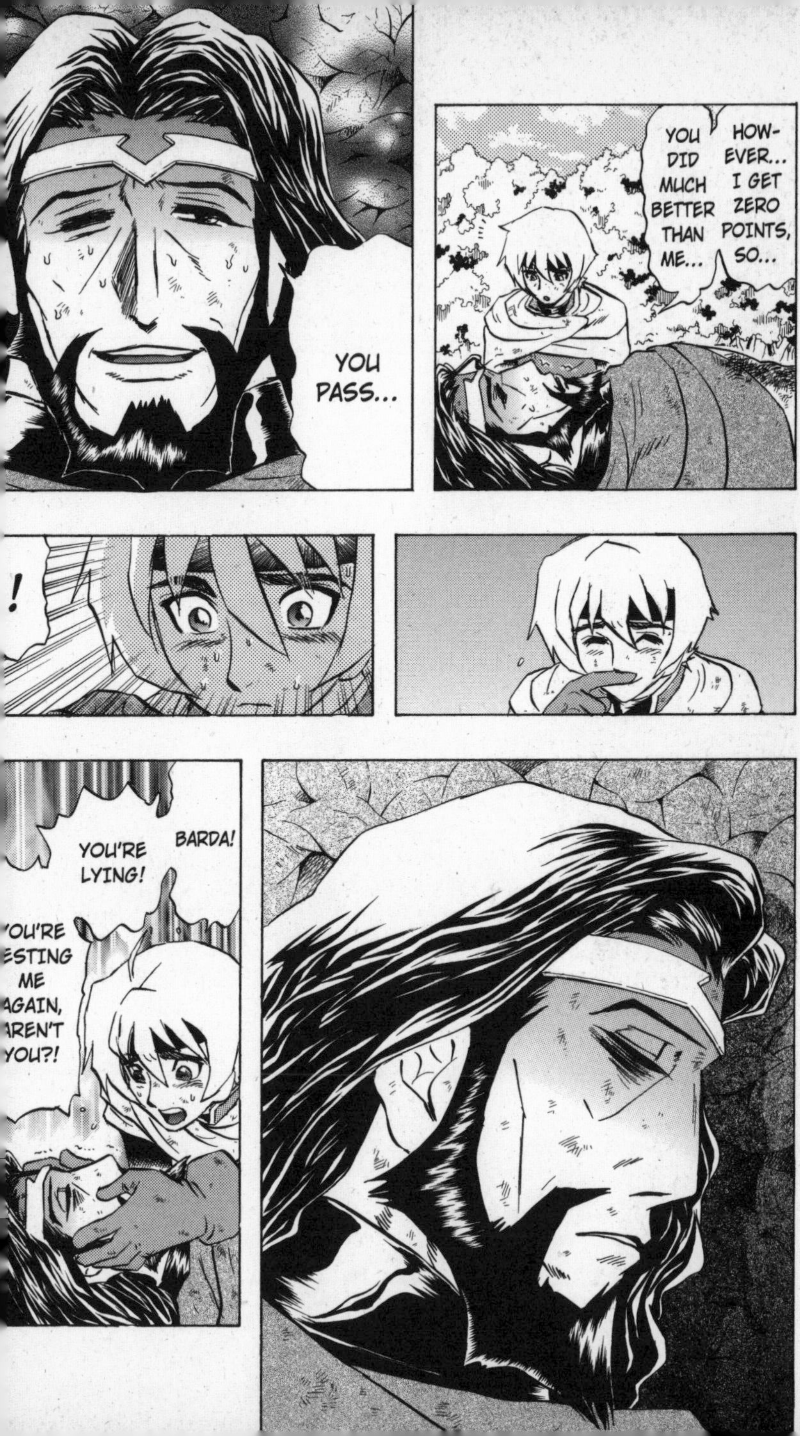
YOU DID MUCH BETTER THAN ME... HOW-EVER... I GET ZERO POINTS, SO...
YOU PASS...
!
BARDA!
YOU'RE LYING!
OU'RE ESTING ME AGAIN, AREN'T YOU?!

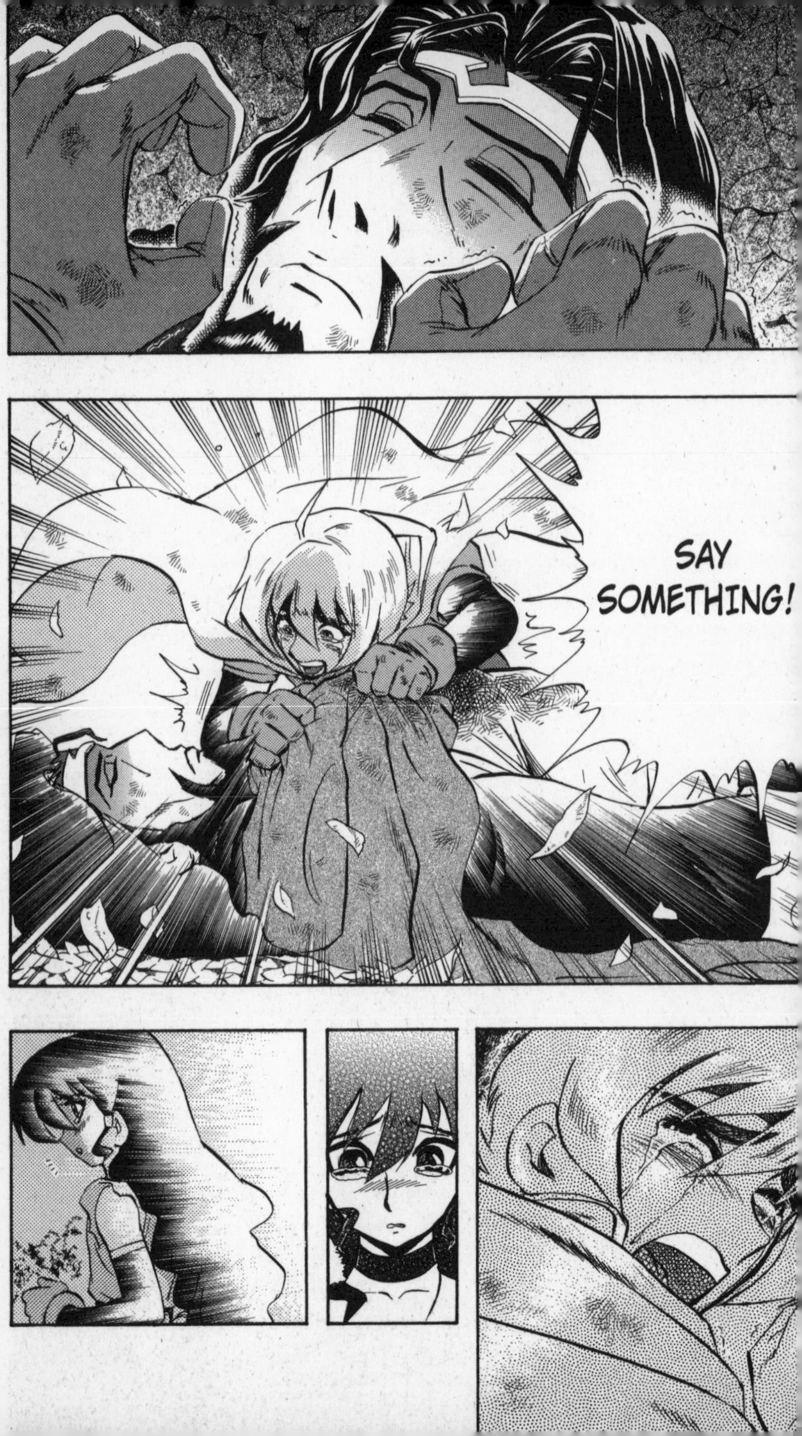
SAY SOMETHING!

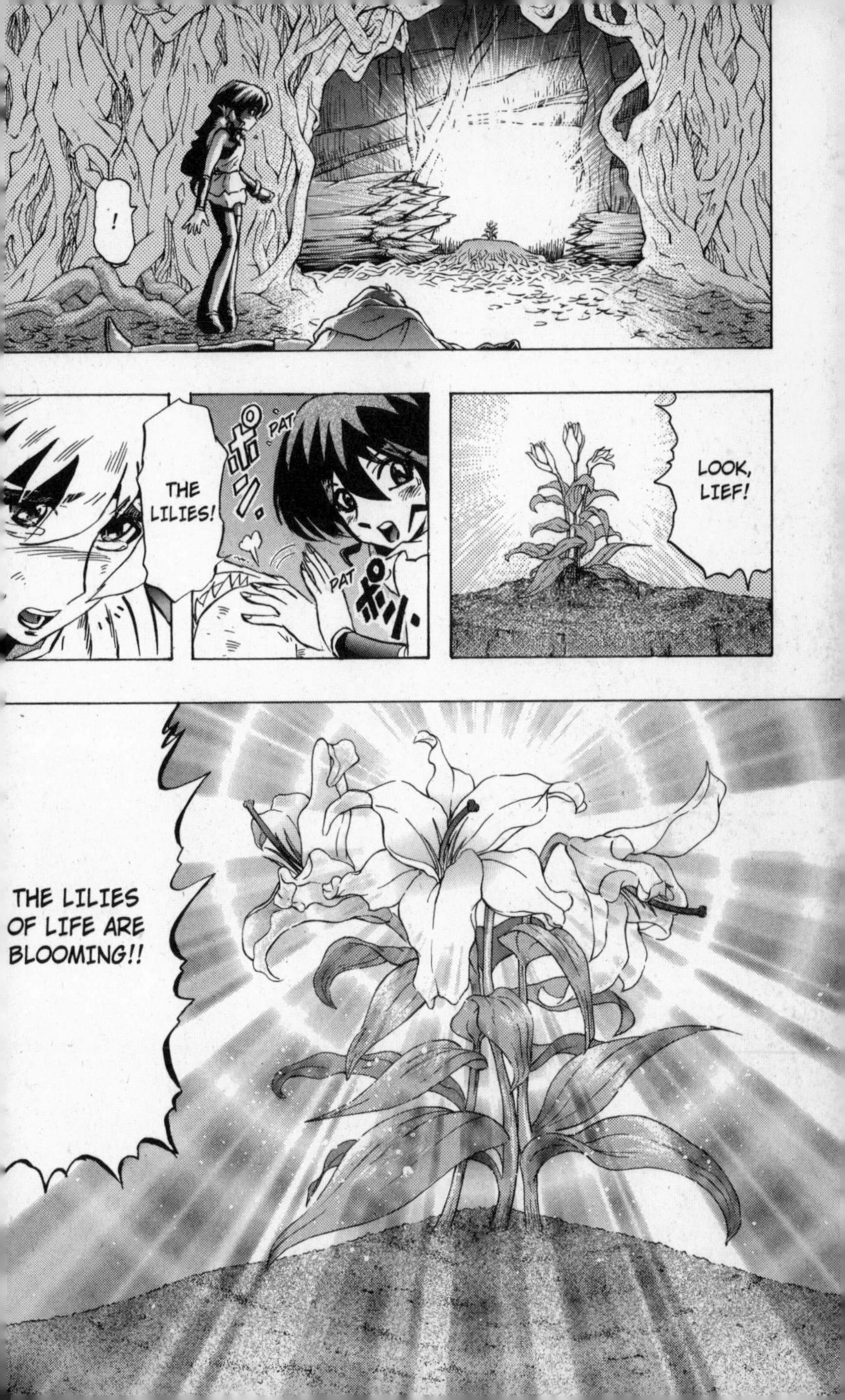
!
LOOK, LIEF!
PAT
PAT
THE LILIES!
THE LILIES OF LIFE ARE BLOOMING!!

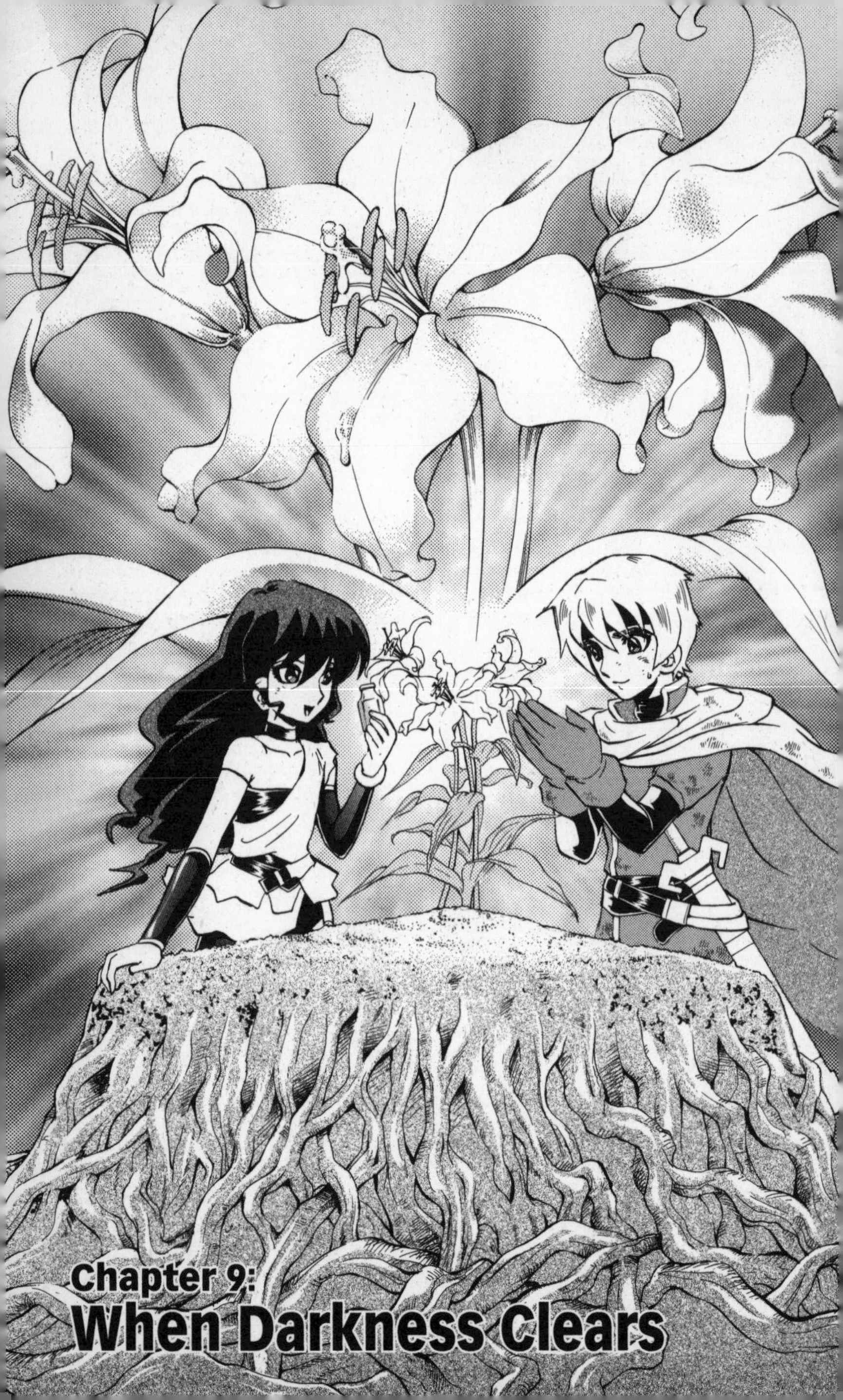
Chapter 9:
When Darkness Clears

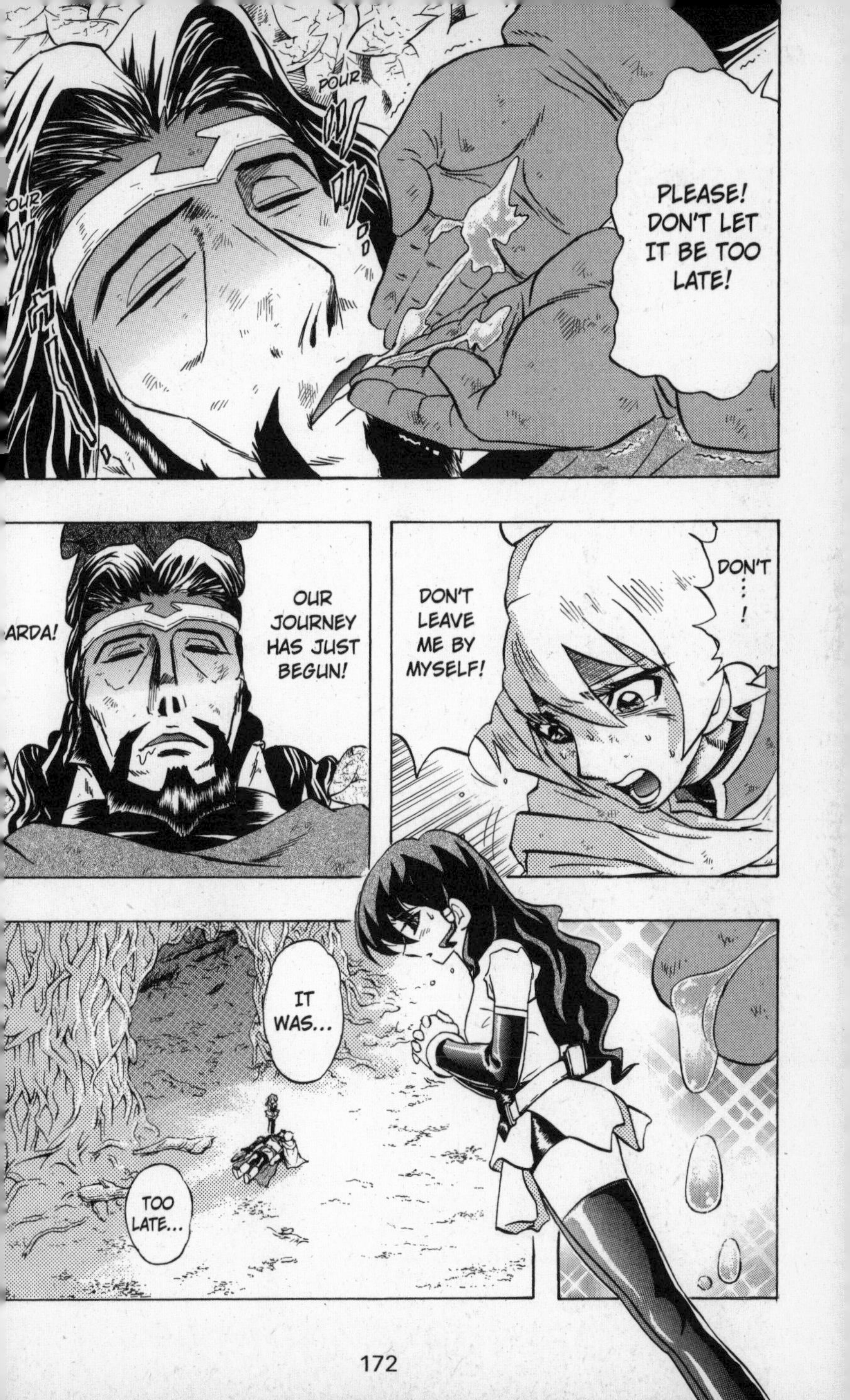
PLEASE! DON'T LET IT BE TOO LATE!
POUR
POUR
DON'T...!
DON'T LEAVE ME BY MYSELF!
OUR JOURNEY HAS JUST BEGUN!
ARDA!
IT WAS...
TOO LATE...

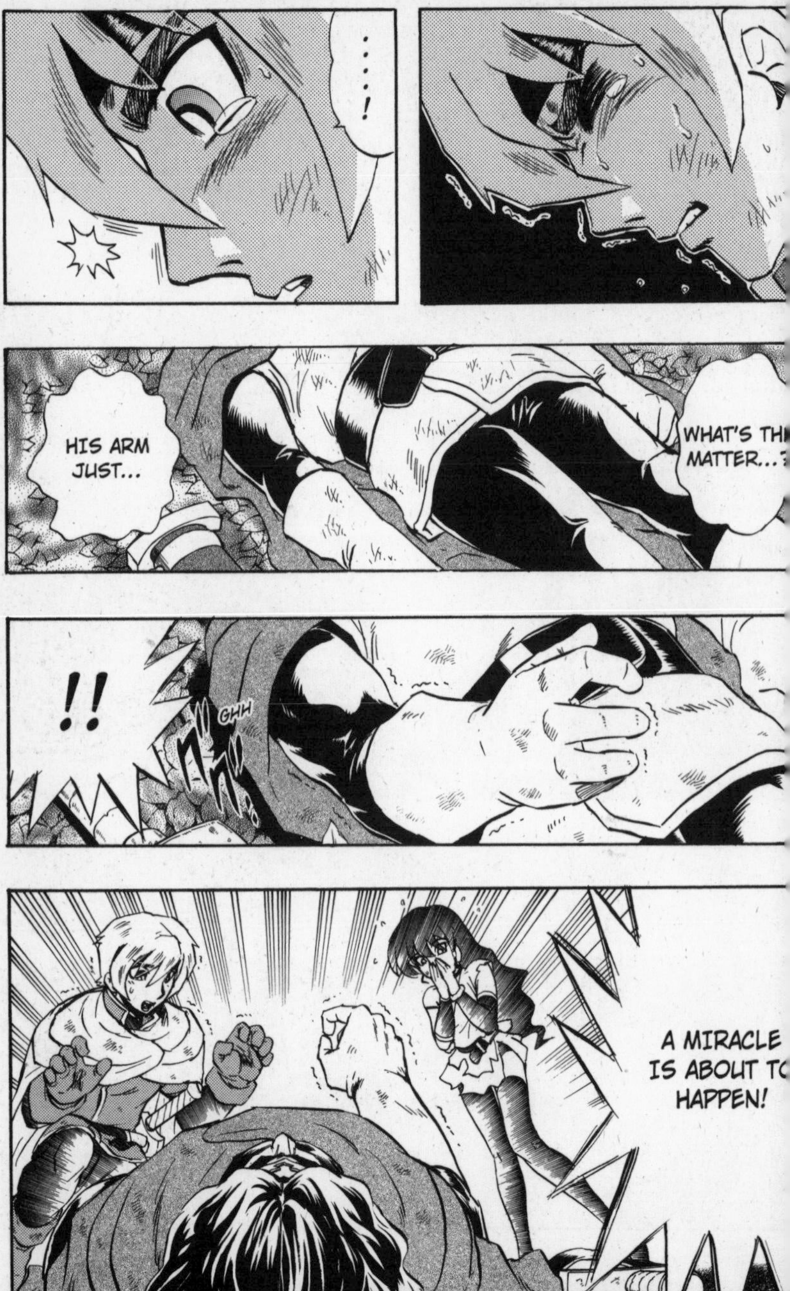
....!
WHAT'S TH
MATTER...
HIS ARM
JUST...
!!
GHH
A MIRACLE
IS ABOUT T
HAPPEN!

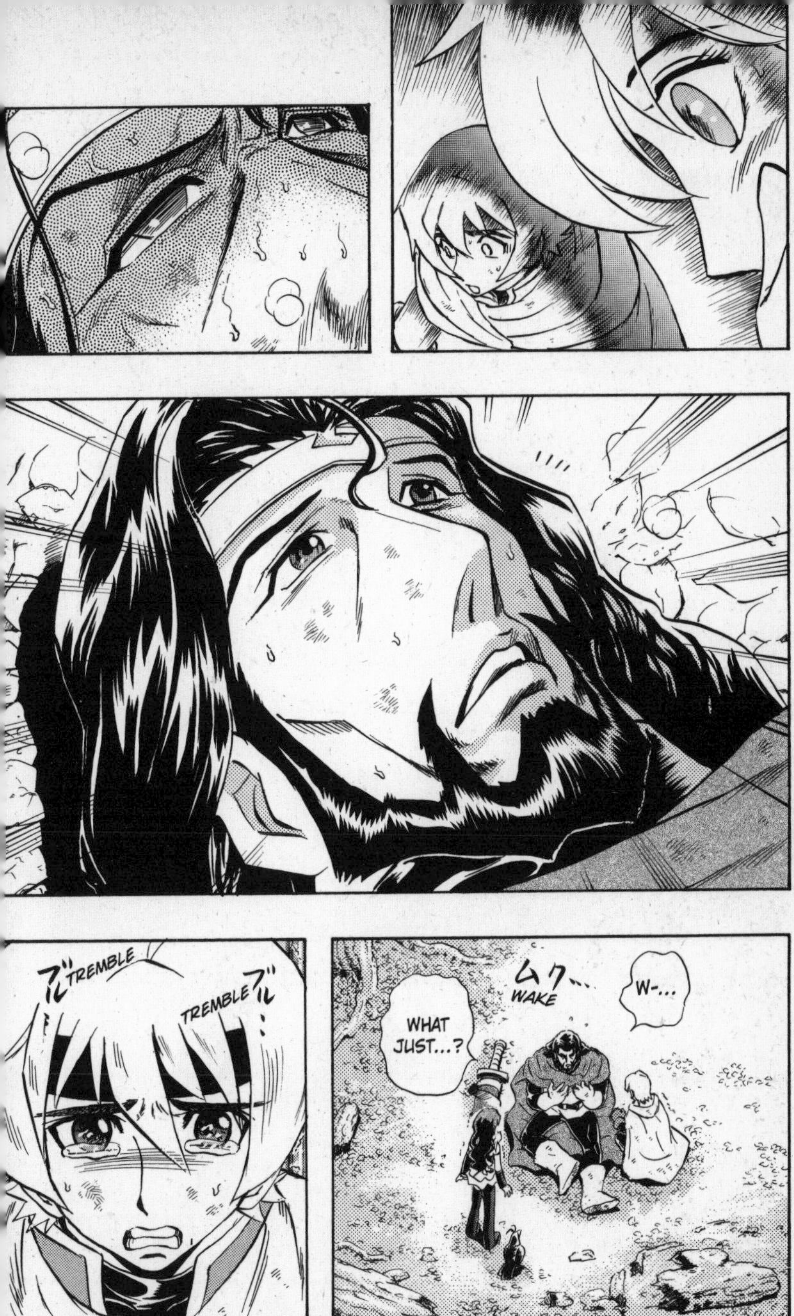
W-...
ムク...
WAKE
WHAT JUST...?
ブル
TREMBLE
ブル
TREMBLE

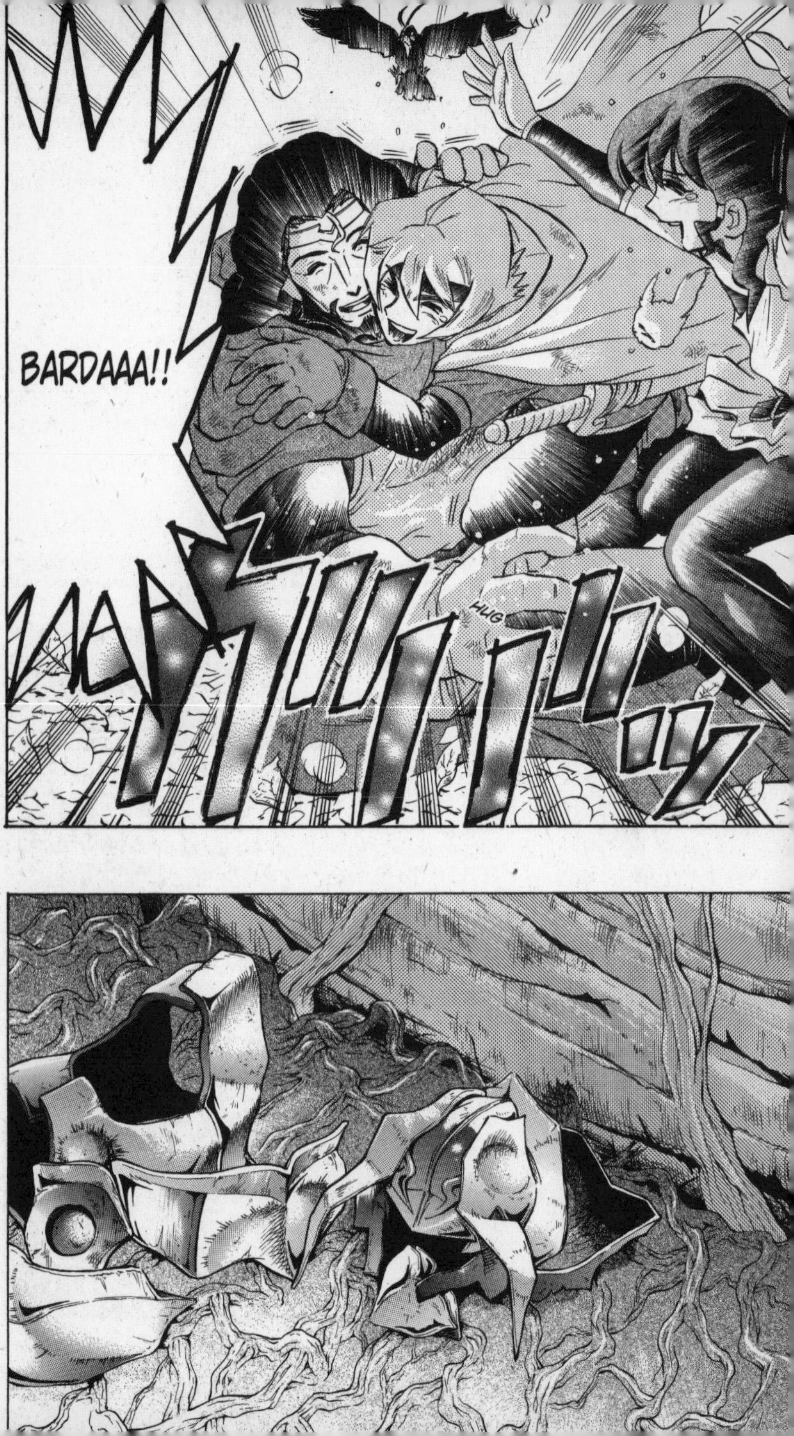
BARDAAA!!
HUG

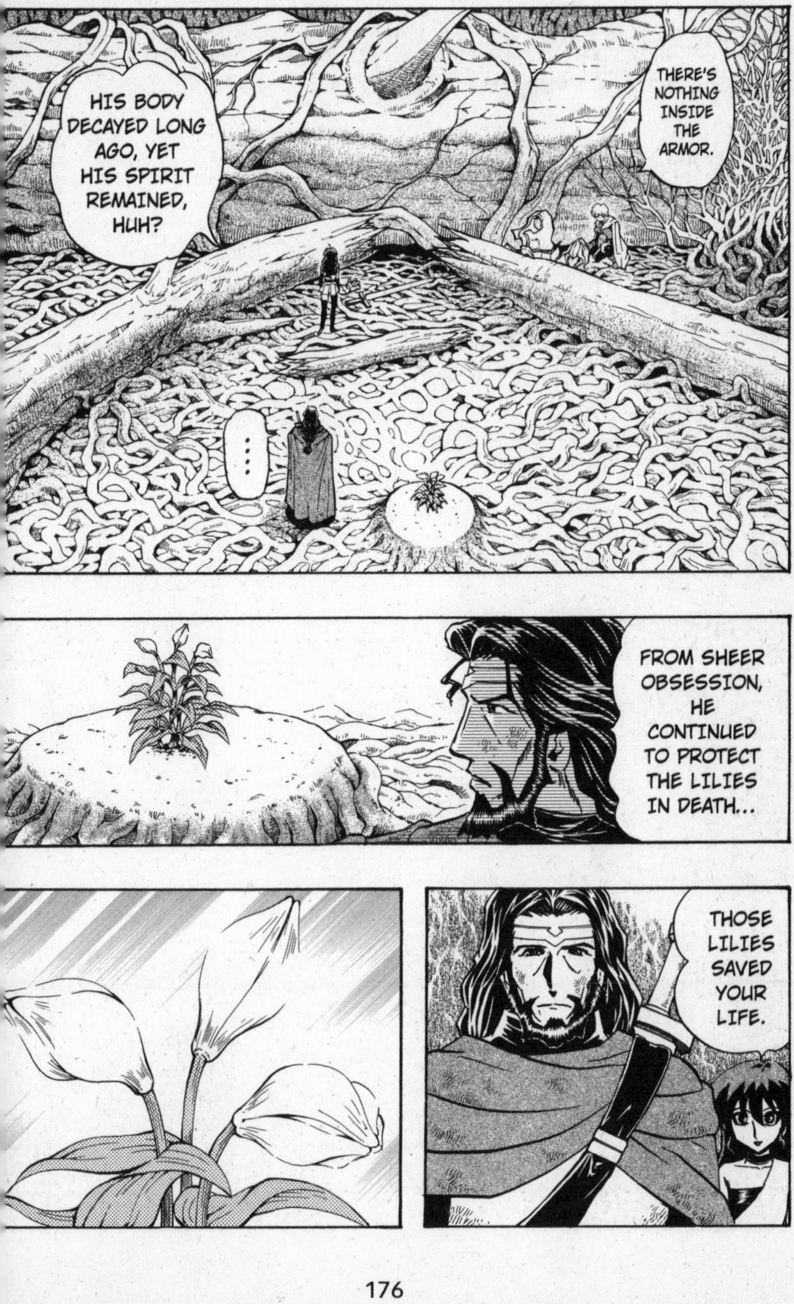
THERE'S NOTHING INSIDE THE ARMOR.
HIS BODY DECAYED LONG AGO, YET HIS SPIRIT REMAINED, HUH?
....
FROM SHEER OBSESSION, HE CONTINUED TO PROTECT THE LILIES IN DEATH...
THOSE LILIES SAVED YOUR LIFE.

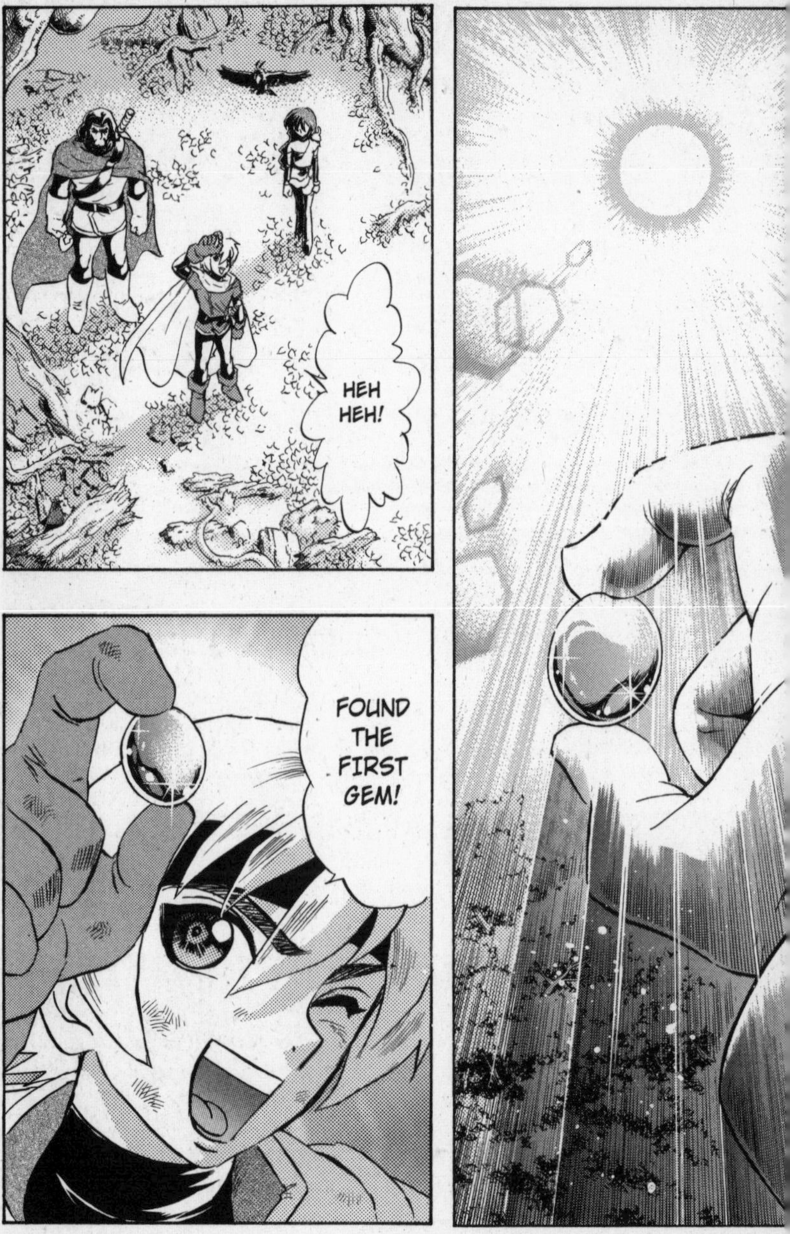
HEH HEH!
FOUND THE FIRST GEM!

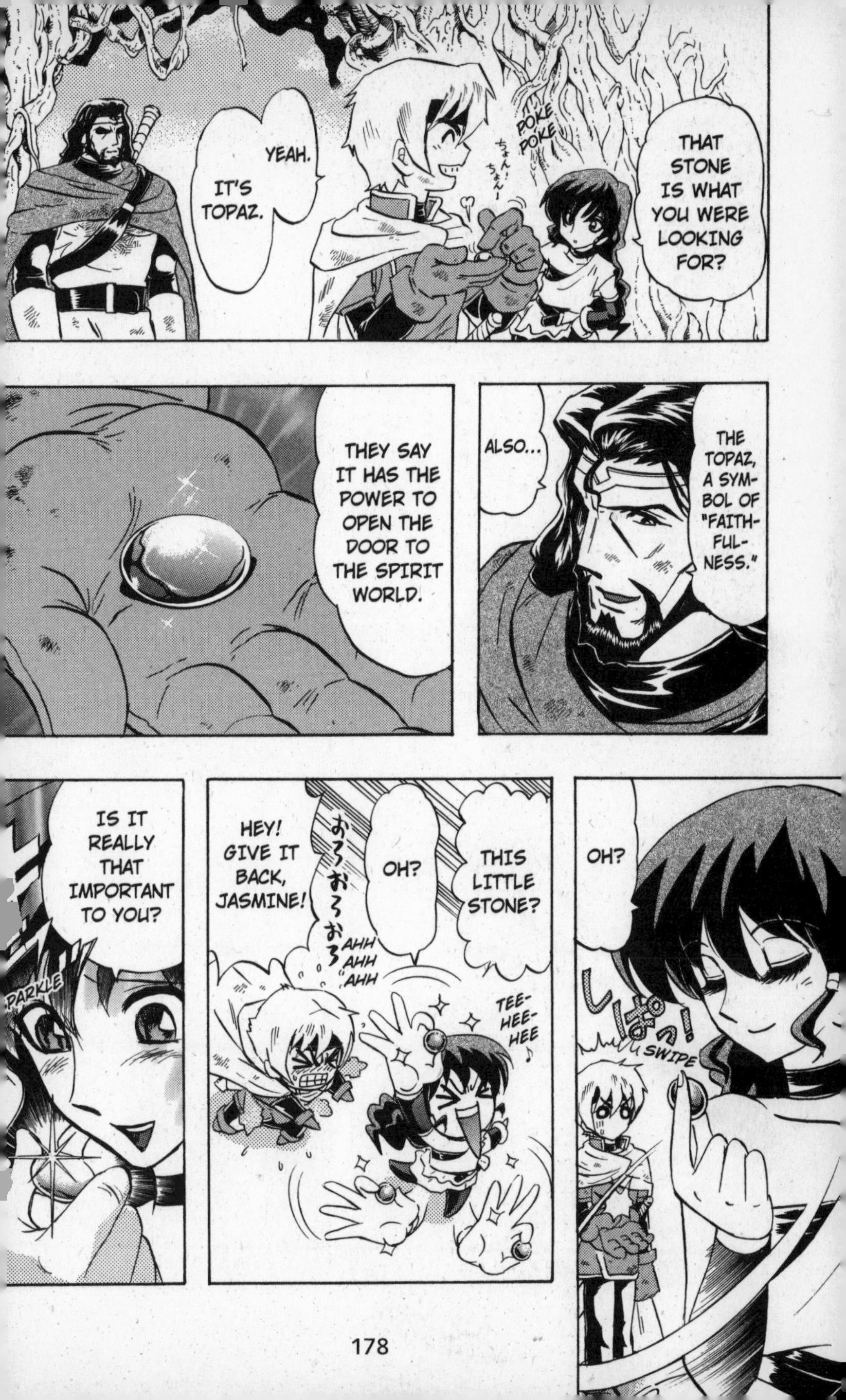
THAT STONE IS WHAT YOU WERE LOOKING FOR?
POKE POKE
ちょん・ちょん
YEAH.
IT'S TOPAZ.
THE TOPAZ, A SYMBOL OF "FAITH-FUL-NESS."
ALSO...
THEY SAY IT HAS THE POWER TO OPEN THE DOOR TO THE SPIRIT WORLD.
OH?
しぽっ!
SWIPE
THIS LITTLE STONE?
OH?
HEY! GIVE IT BACK, JASMINE!
おろおろおろ
AHH AHH AHH
TEE-HEE-HEE ♪
IS IT REALLY THAT IMPORTANT TO YOU?
PARKLE

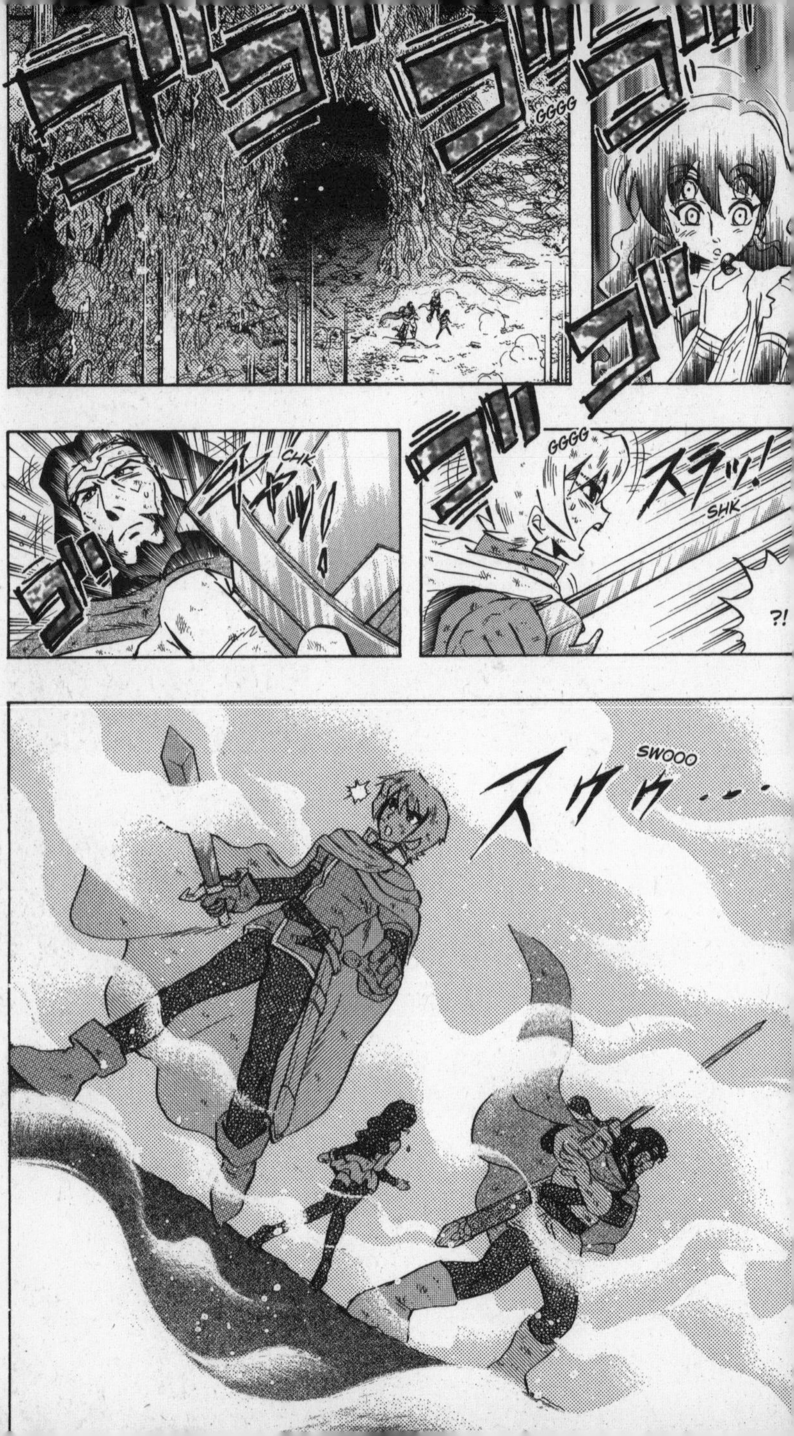
GGGG
GGGG
スラッ!
SHK
?!
CHK
SWOOO
スゥゥ…

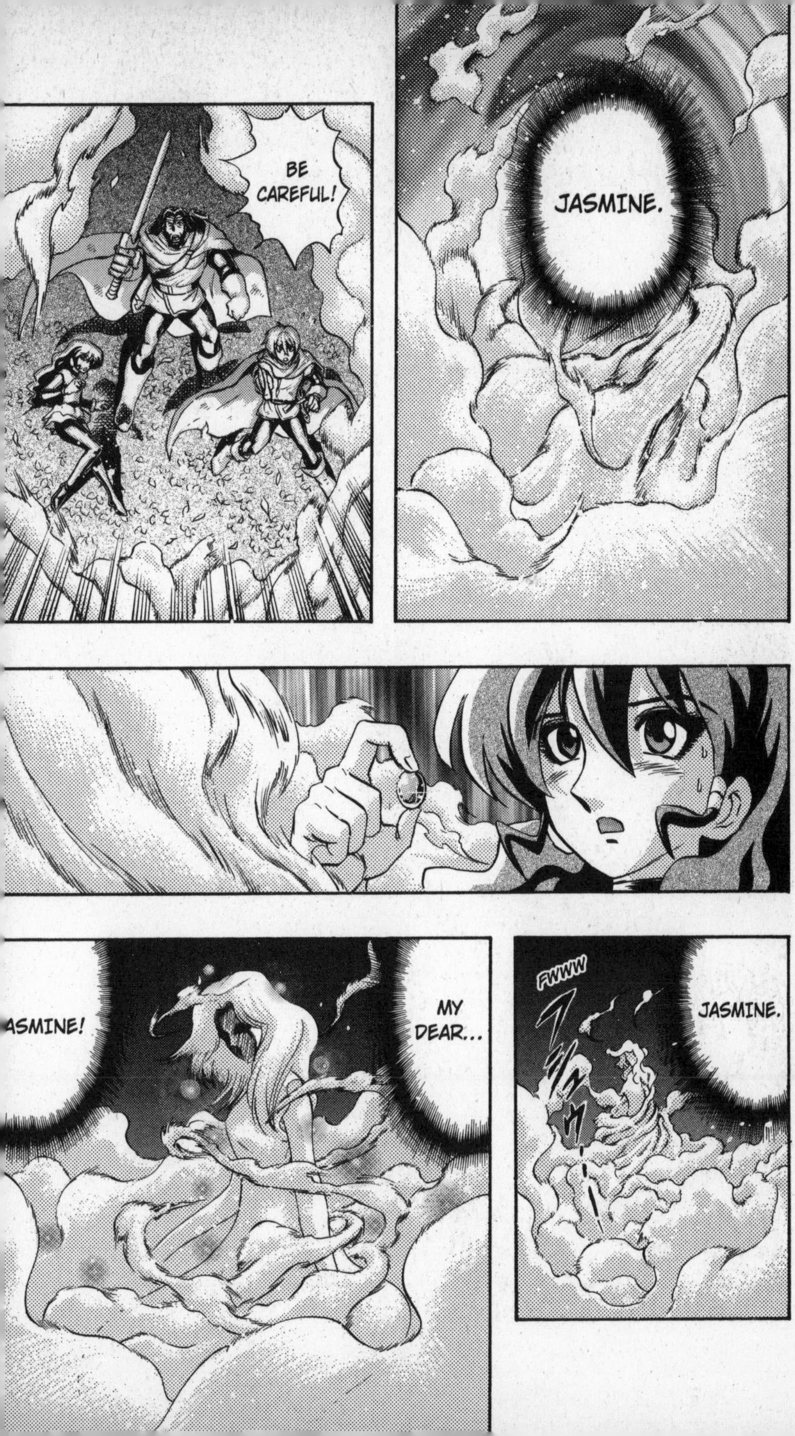
JASMINE.
BE CAREFUL!
JASMINE.
FWWW
MY DEAR...
ASMINE!

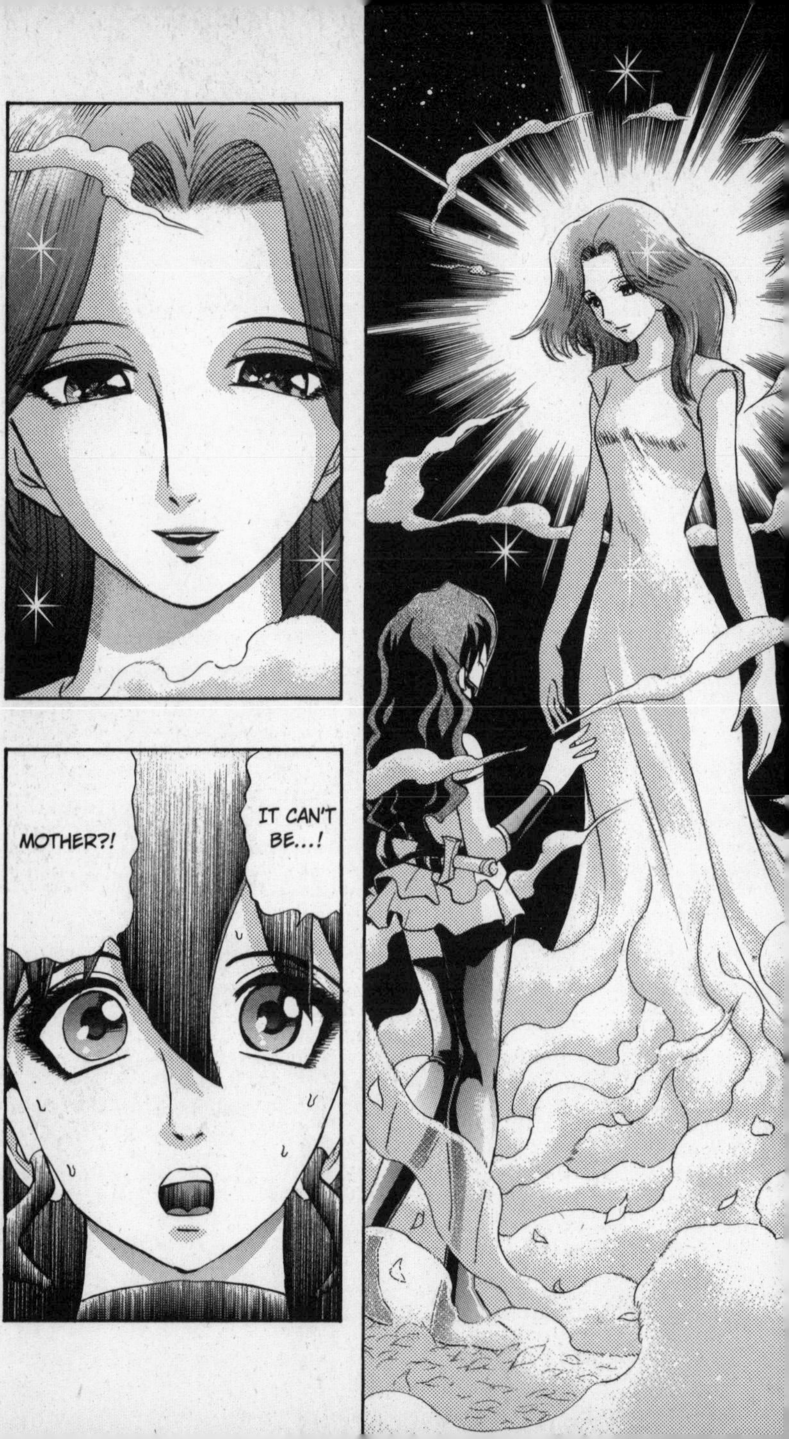
IT CAN'T BE...!
MOTHER?!

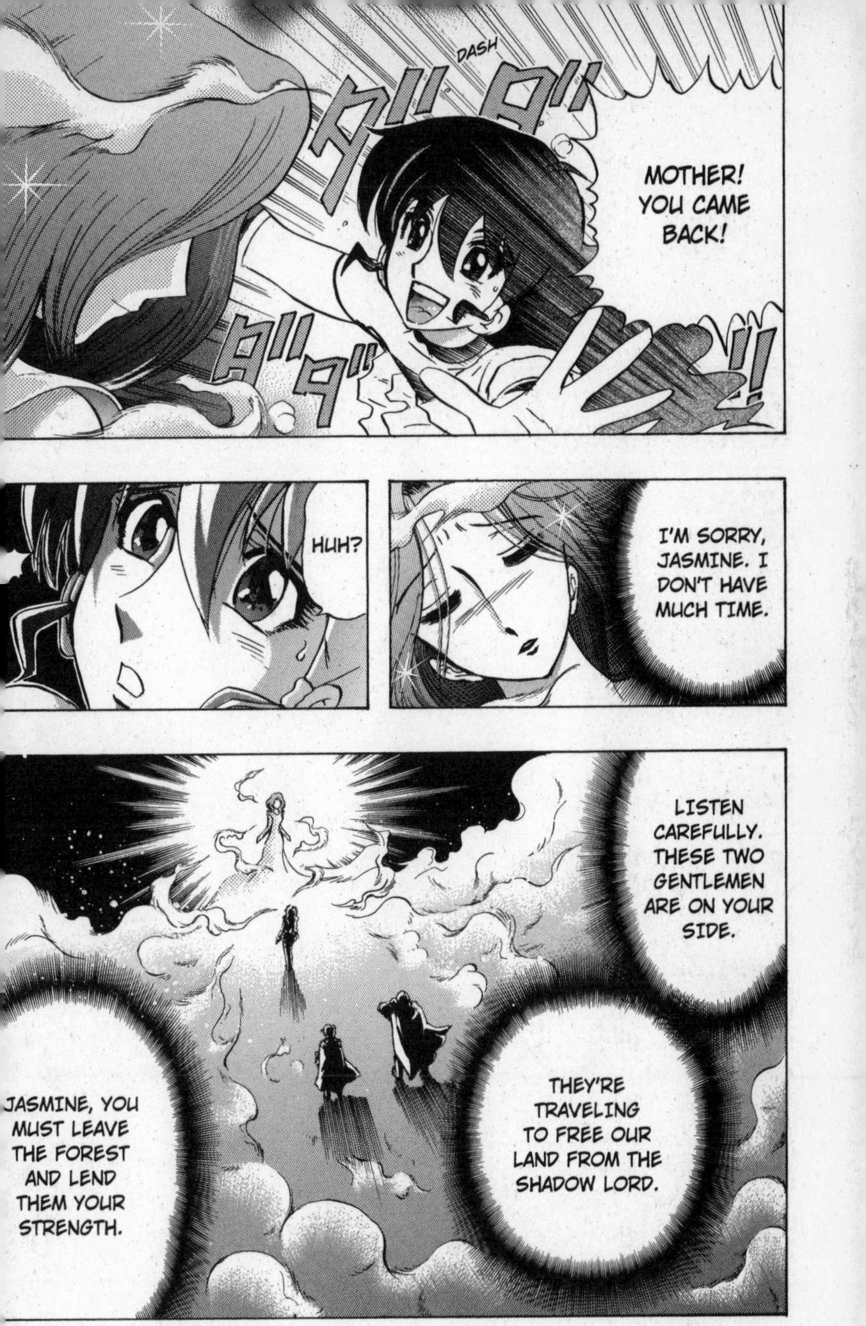
DASH
MOTHER! YOU CAME BACK!
I'M SORRY, JASMINE. I DON'T HAVE MUCH TIME.
HUH?
LISTEN CAREFULLY. THESE TWO GENTLEMEN ARE ON YOUR SIDE.
THEY'RE TRAVELING TO FREE OUR LAND FROM THE SHADOW LORD.
JASMINE, YOU MUST LEAVE THE FOREST AND LEND THEM YOUR STRENGTH.

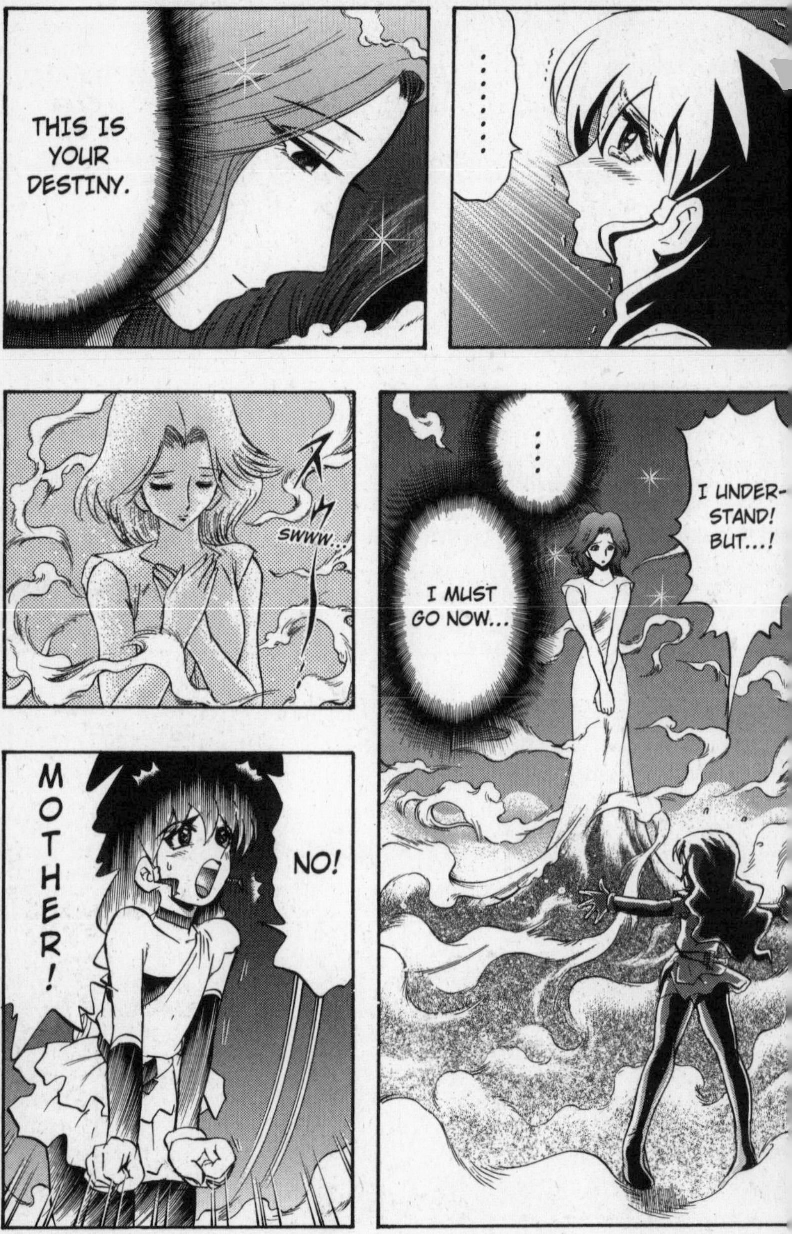
......
THIS IS YOUR DESTINY.
I UNDER-STAND! BUT...!
....
I MUST GO NOW...
SWWW...
NO!
MOTHER!

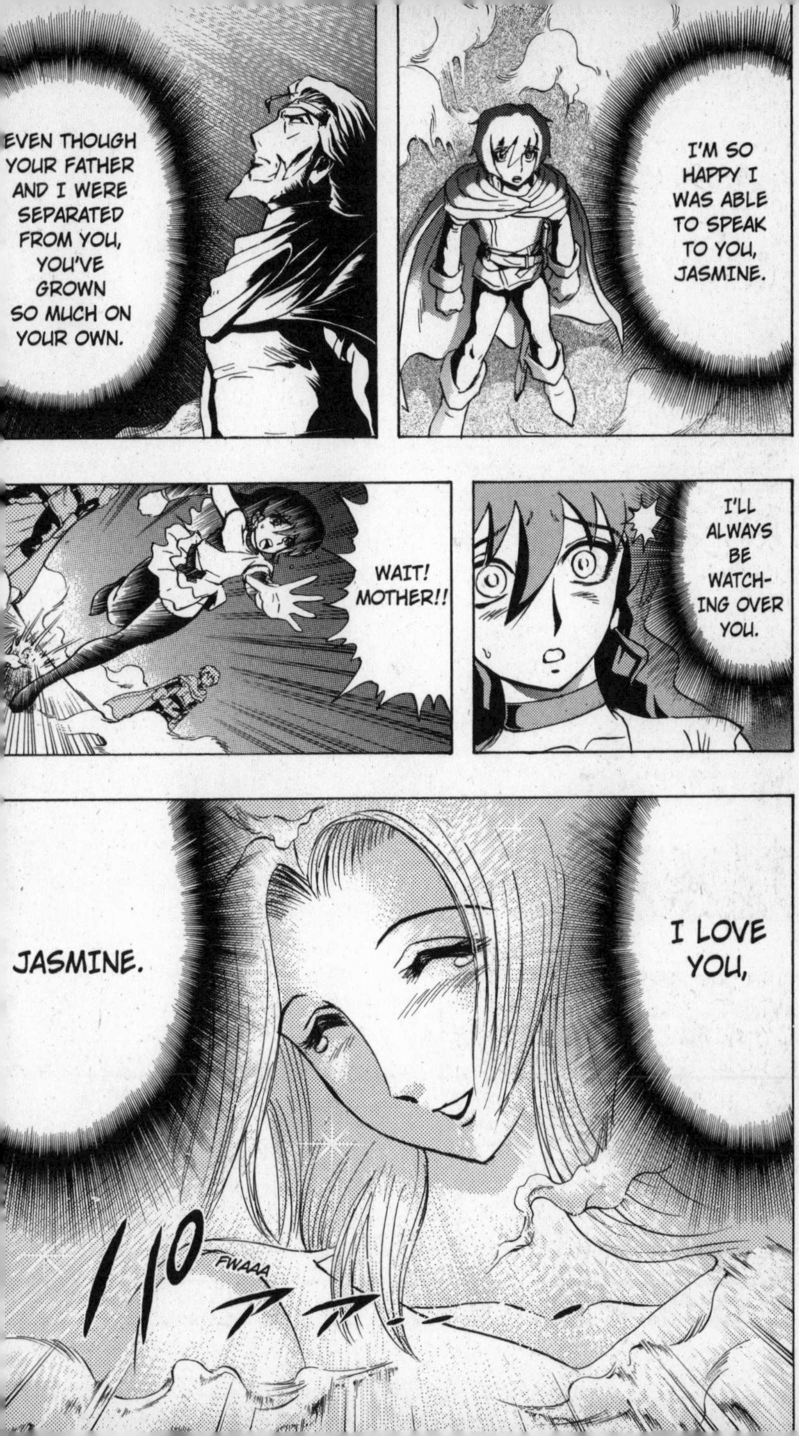
I'M SO HAPPY I WAS ABLE TO SPEAK TO YOU, JASMINE.
EVEN THOUGH YOUR FATHER AND I WERE SEPARATED FROM YOU, YOU'VE GROWN SO MUCH ON YOUR OWN.
I'LL ALWAYS BE WATCHING OVER YOU.
WAIT! MOTHER!!
I LOVE YOU,
JASMINE.
FWAAA

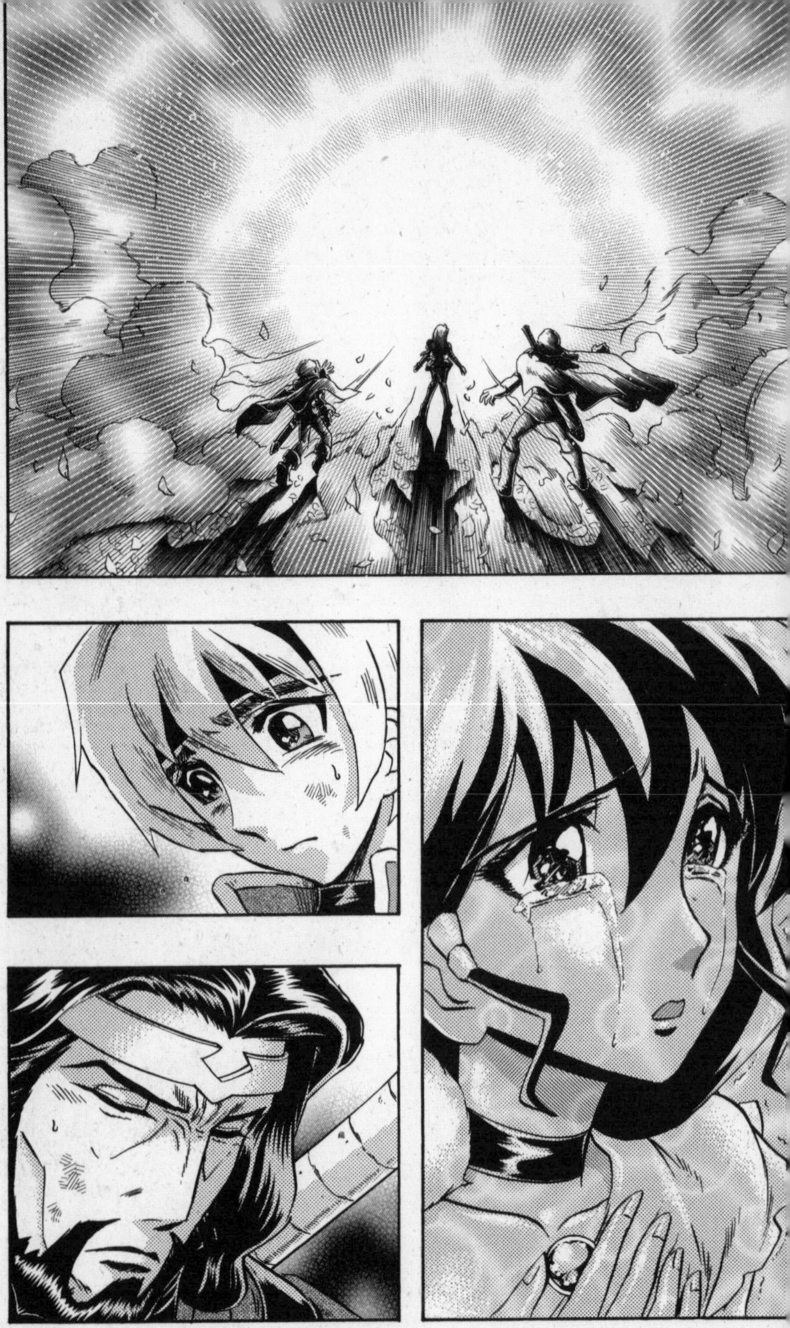

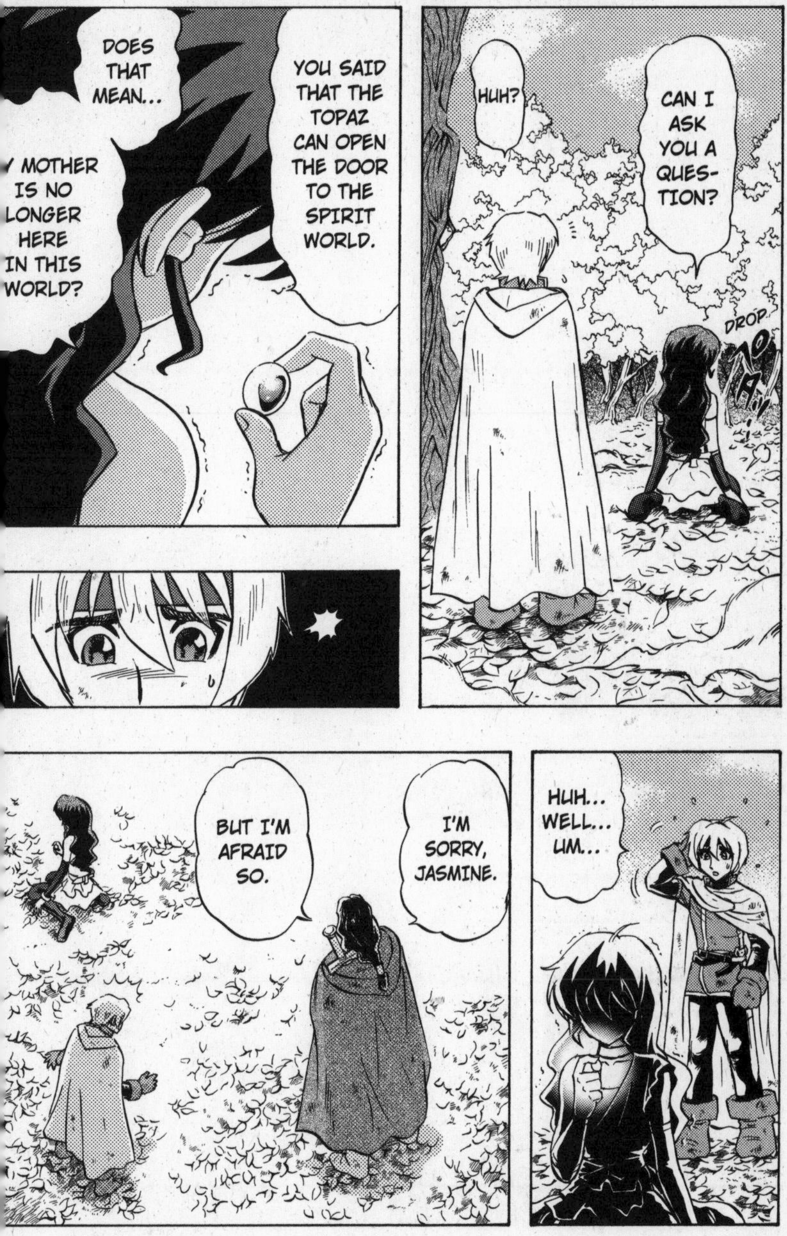
CAN I ASK YOU A QUESTION?
HUH?
DROP
YOU SAID THAT THE TOPAZ CAN OPEN THE DOOR TO THE SPIRIT WORLD.
DOES THAT MEAN...
MOTHER IS NO LONGER HERE IN THIS WORLD?
HUH... WELL... UM...
I'M SORRY, JASMINE.
BUT I'M AFRAID SO.

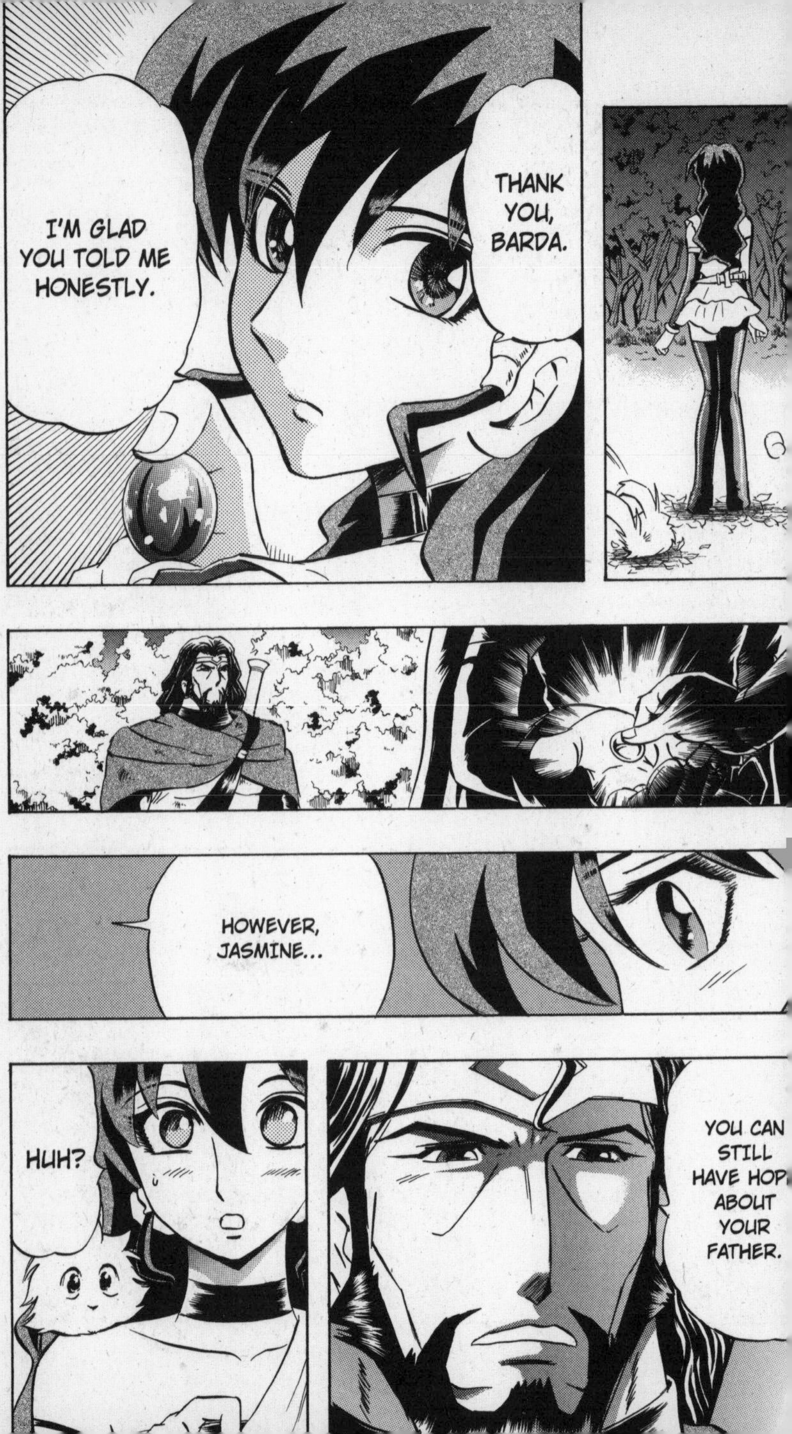
THANK YOU, BARDA.
I'M GLAD YOU TOLD ME HONESTLY.
HOWEVER, JASMINE...
YOU CAN STILL HAVE HOP ABOUT YOUR FATHER.
HUH?

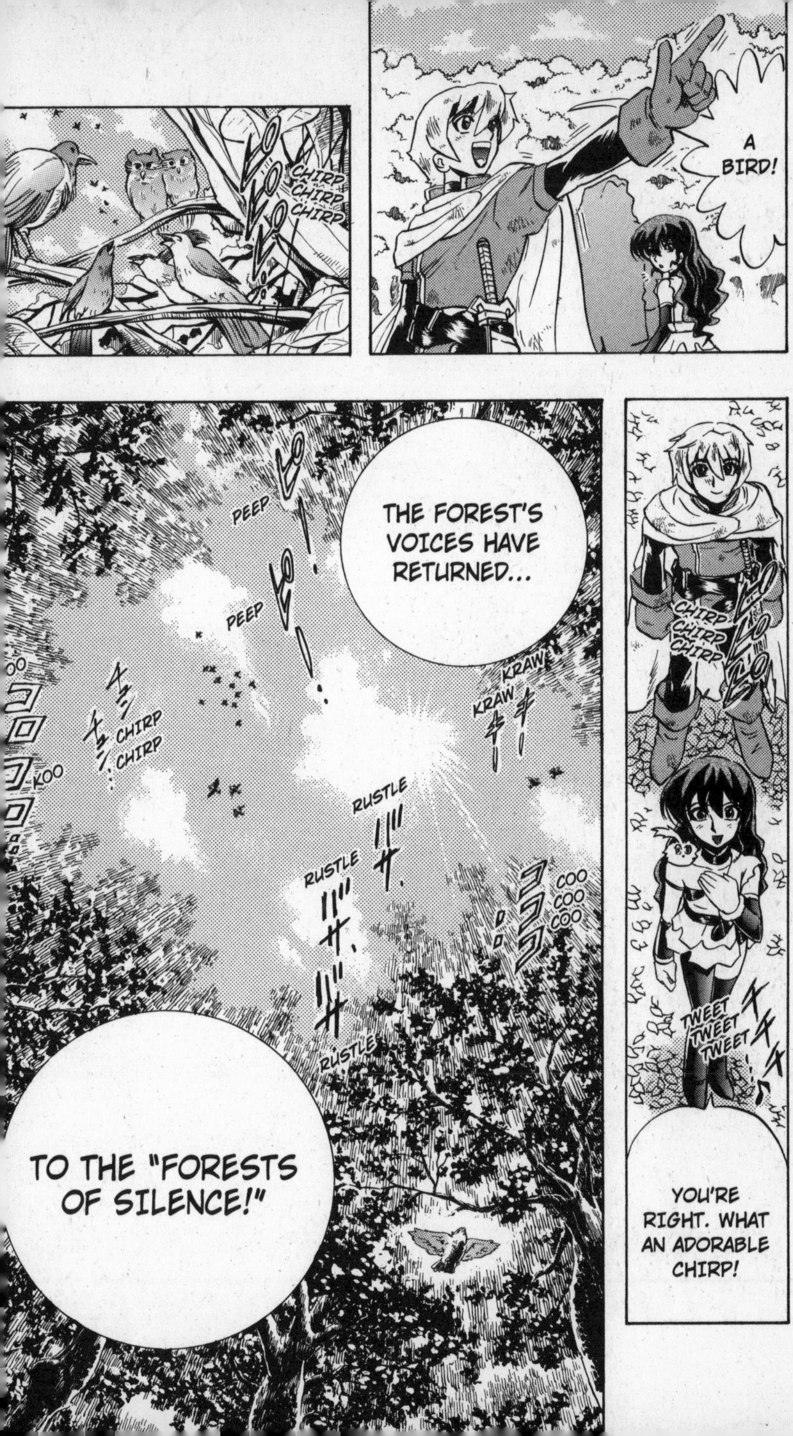
A BIRD!
CHIRP CHIRP CHIRP
CHIRP CHIRP CHIRP
TWEET TWEET TWEET
YOU'RE RIGHT. WHAT AN ADORABLE CHIRP!
THE FOREST'S VOICES HAVE RETURNED...
PEEP
PEEP
KRAW KRAW
CHIRP CHIRP
KOO
COO COO COO
RUSTLE
RUSTLE
RUSTLE
TO THE "FORESTS OF SILENCE!"

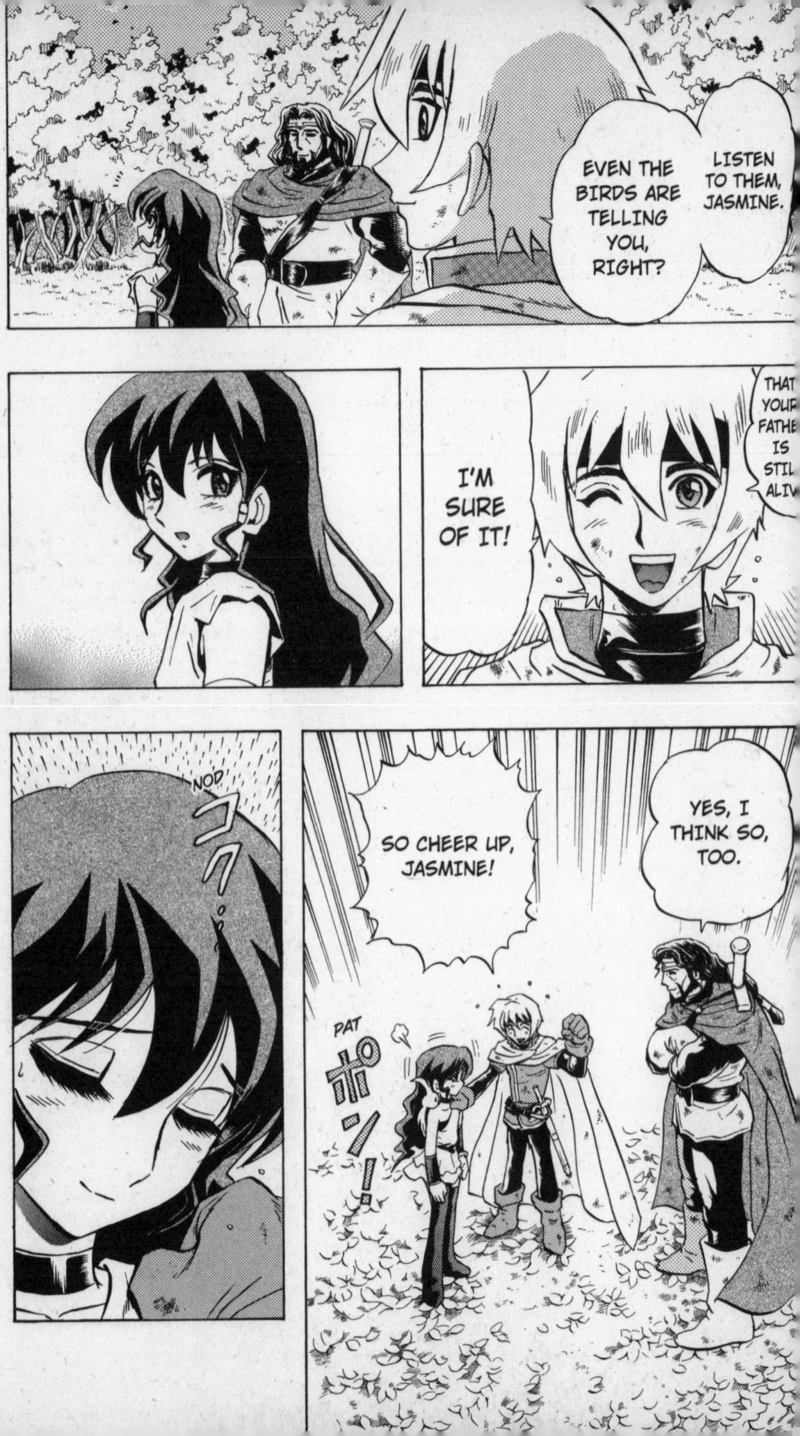
LISTEN TO THEM, JASMINE.
EVEN THE BIRDS ARE TELLING YOU, RIGHT?
THAT YOUR FATHE IS STIL ALIV
I'M SURE OF IT!
YES, I THINK SO, TOO.
SO CHEER UP, JASMINE!
PAT
ポン!!
NOD
コク...

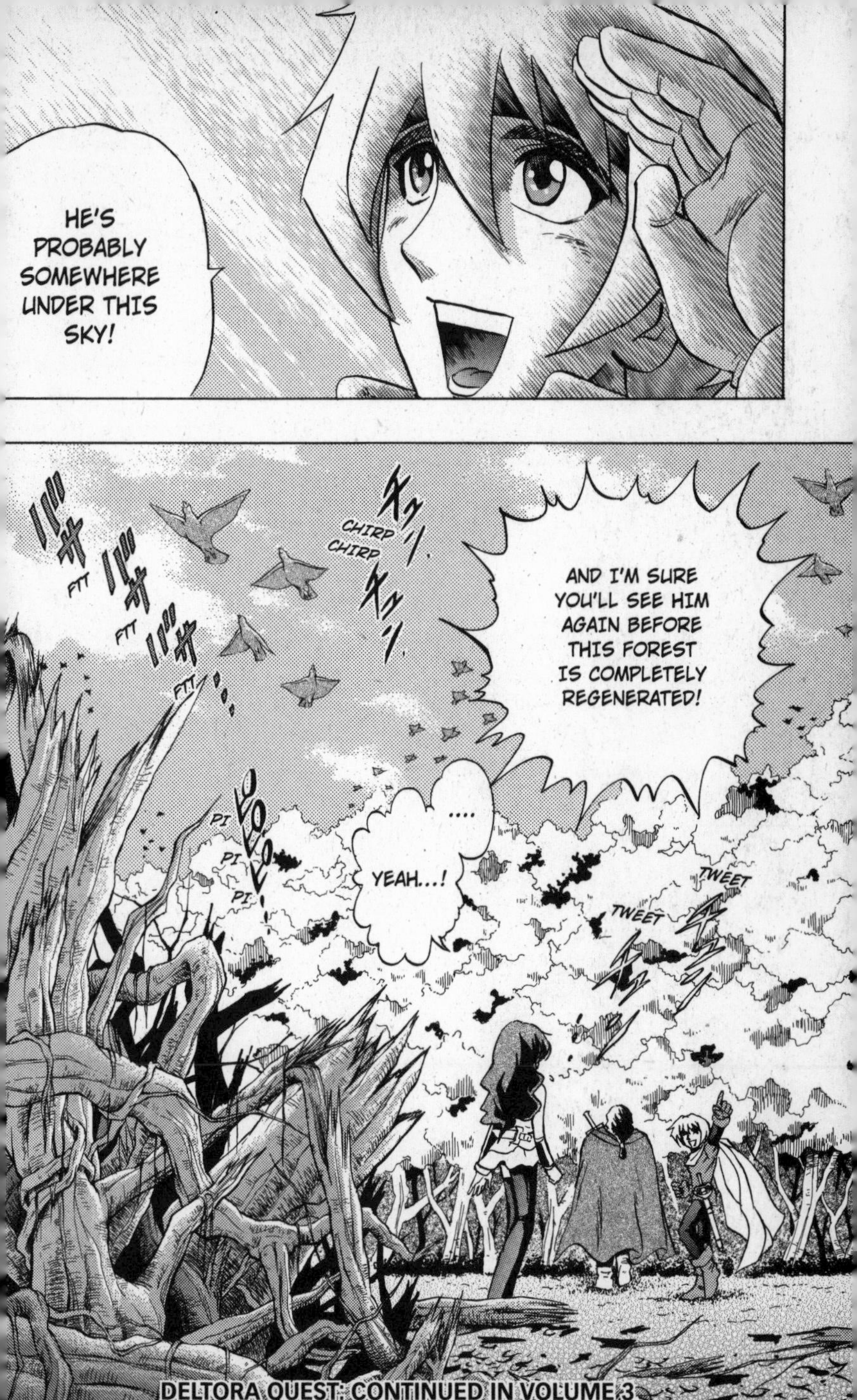
HE'S PROBABLY SOMEWHERE UNDER THIS SKY!
AND I'M SURE YOU'LL SEE HIM AGAIN BEFORE THIS FOREST IS COMPLETELY REGENERATED!
TWEET
TWEET
....
YEAH...!
CHIRP
CHIRP
FTT
FTT
FTT
PI
PI
PI

DELTORA QUEST: CONTINUED IN VOLUME 3

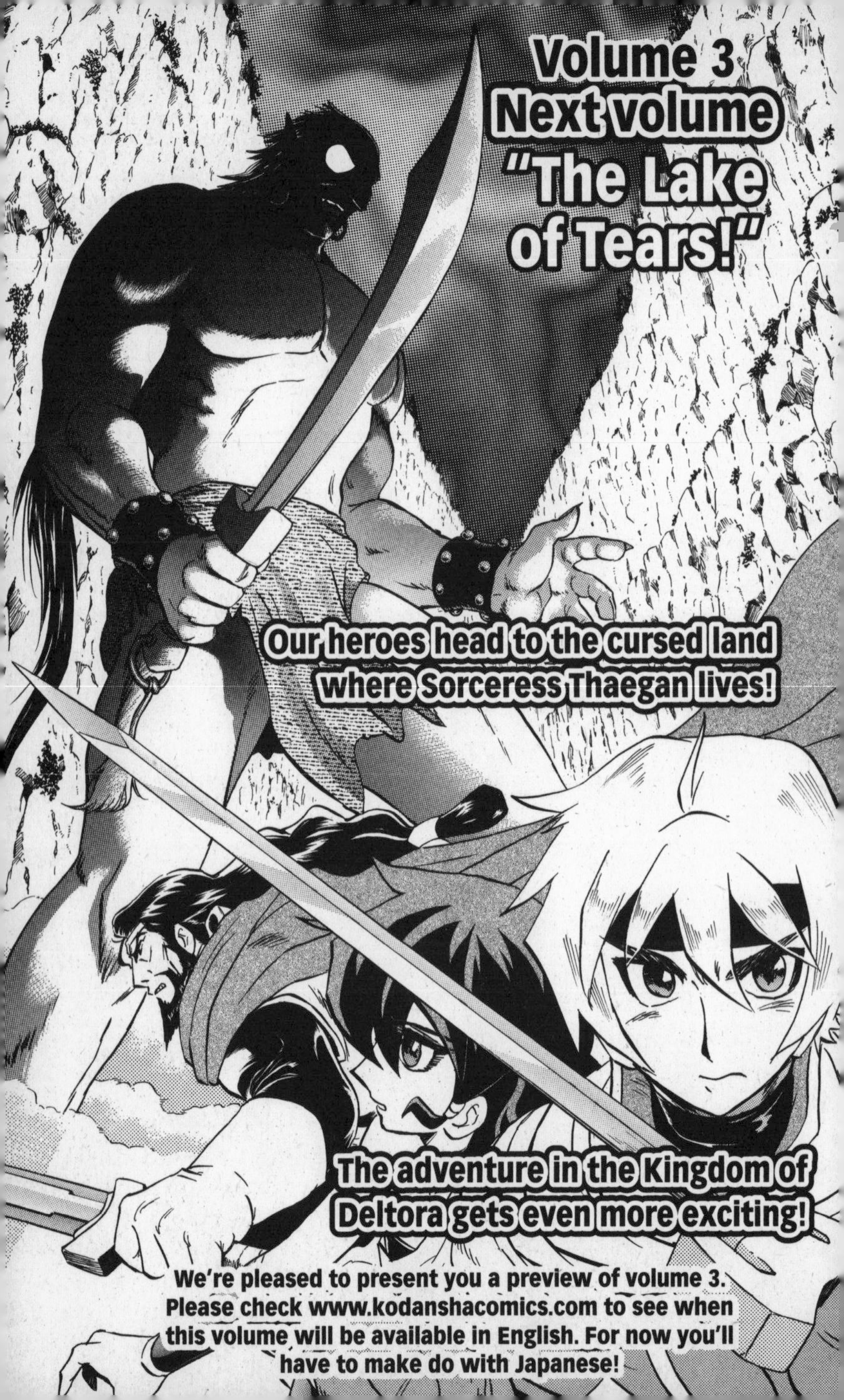
Volume 3
Next volume
"The Lake of Tears!"
Our heroes head to the cursed land where Sorceress Thaegan lives!
The adventure in the Kingdom of Deltora gets even more exciting!
We're pleased to present you a preview of volume 3. Please check www.kodanshacomics.com to see when this volume will be available in English. For now you'll have to make do with Japanese!

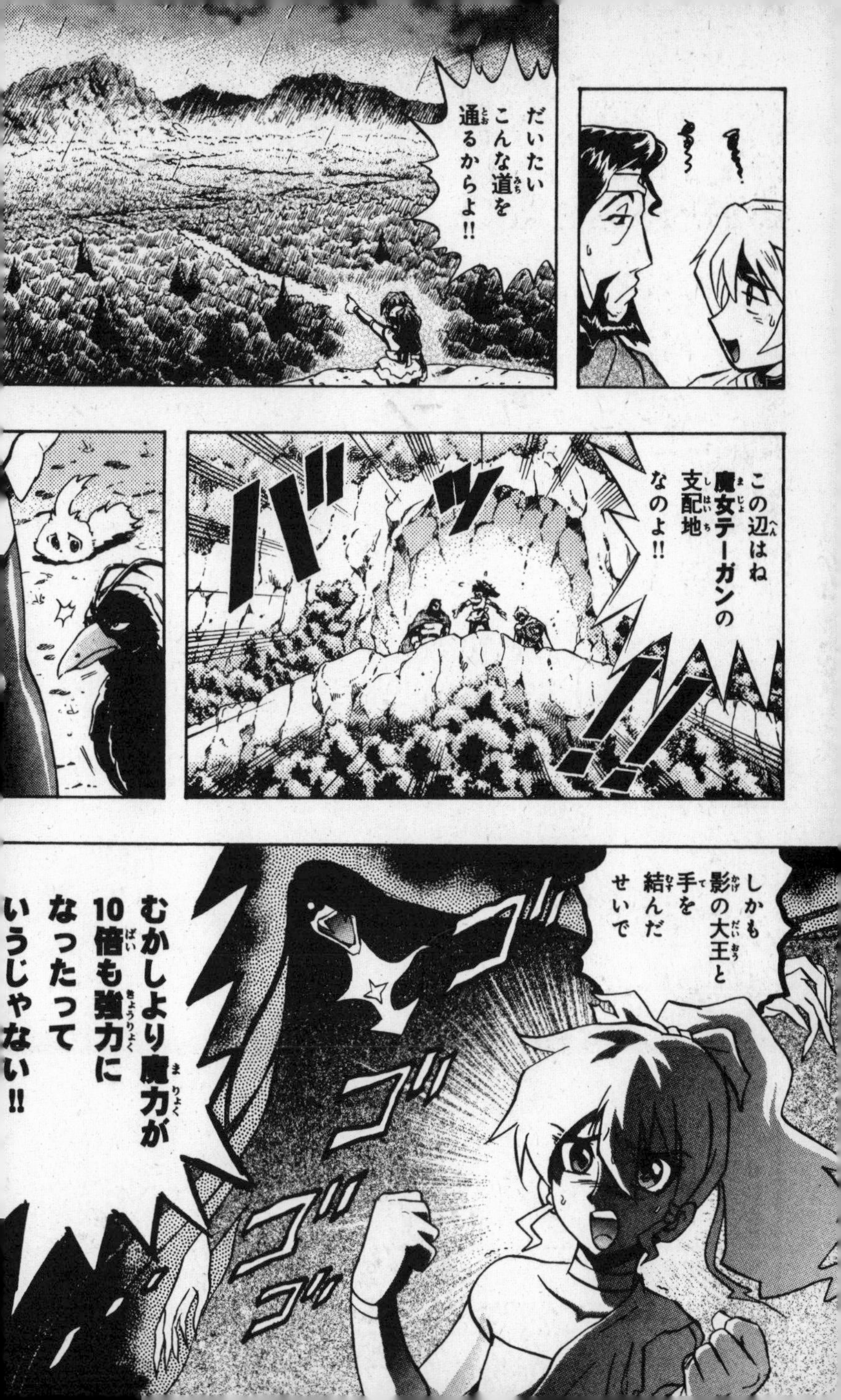
だいたいこんな道を通るからよ!!
この辺はね魔女テーガンの支配地なのよ!!
バッ!!
しかも影の大王と手を結んだせいで
むかしより魔力が10倍も強力になったっていうじゃない!!
ゴゴゴ

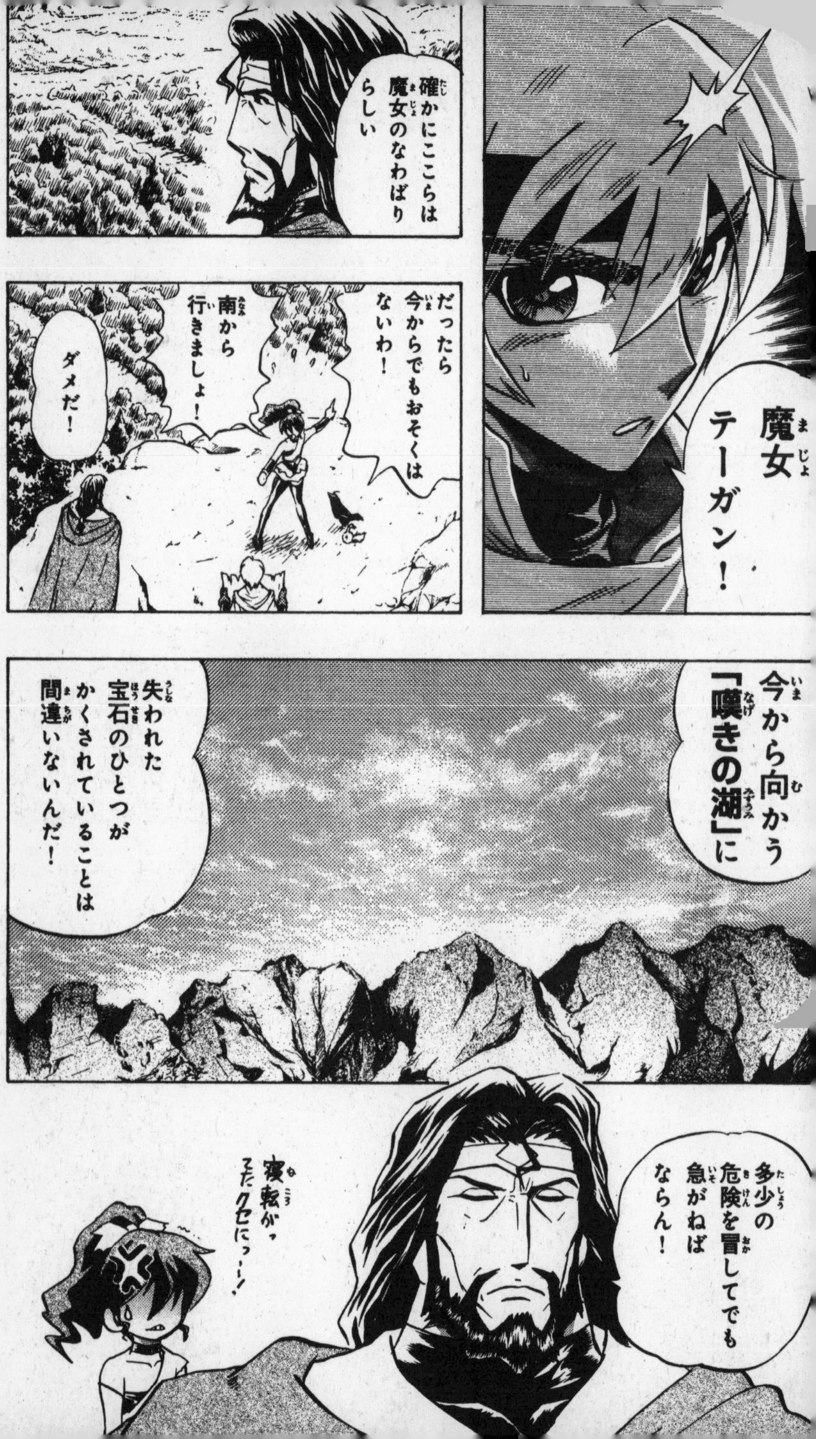
魔女テーガン！
確かにここらは魔女のなわばりらしい
だったら今からでもおそくはないわ！
南から行きましょ！
ダメだ！
今から向かう「嘆きの湖」に
失われた宝石のひとつがかくされていることは間違いないんだ！
多少の危険を冒してでも急がねばならん！
寝転がっ またクセにっ～！

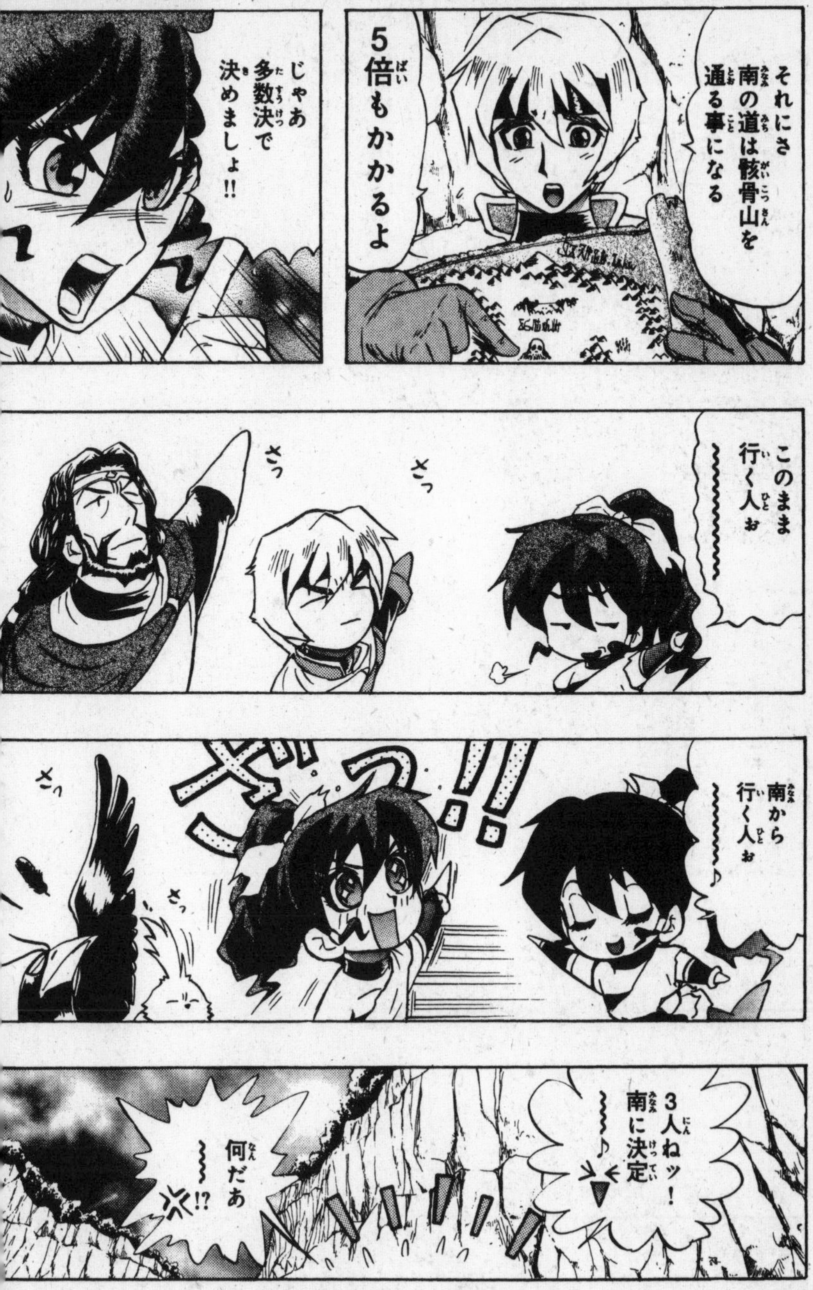
それにさ
南の道は骸骨山を
通る事になる
5倍もかかるよ
じゃあ
多数決で
決めましょ!!
このまま
行く人お〜〜〜
さっ
さっ
南から
行く人お〜〜〜♪
ざっ!!
さっ
さっ
3人ねッ!
南に決定〜〜〜♪
何だあ〜〜〜!?

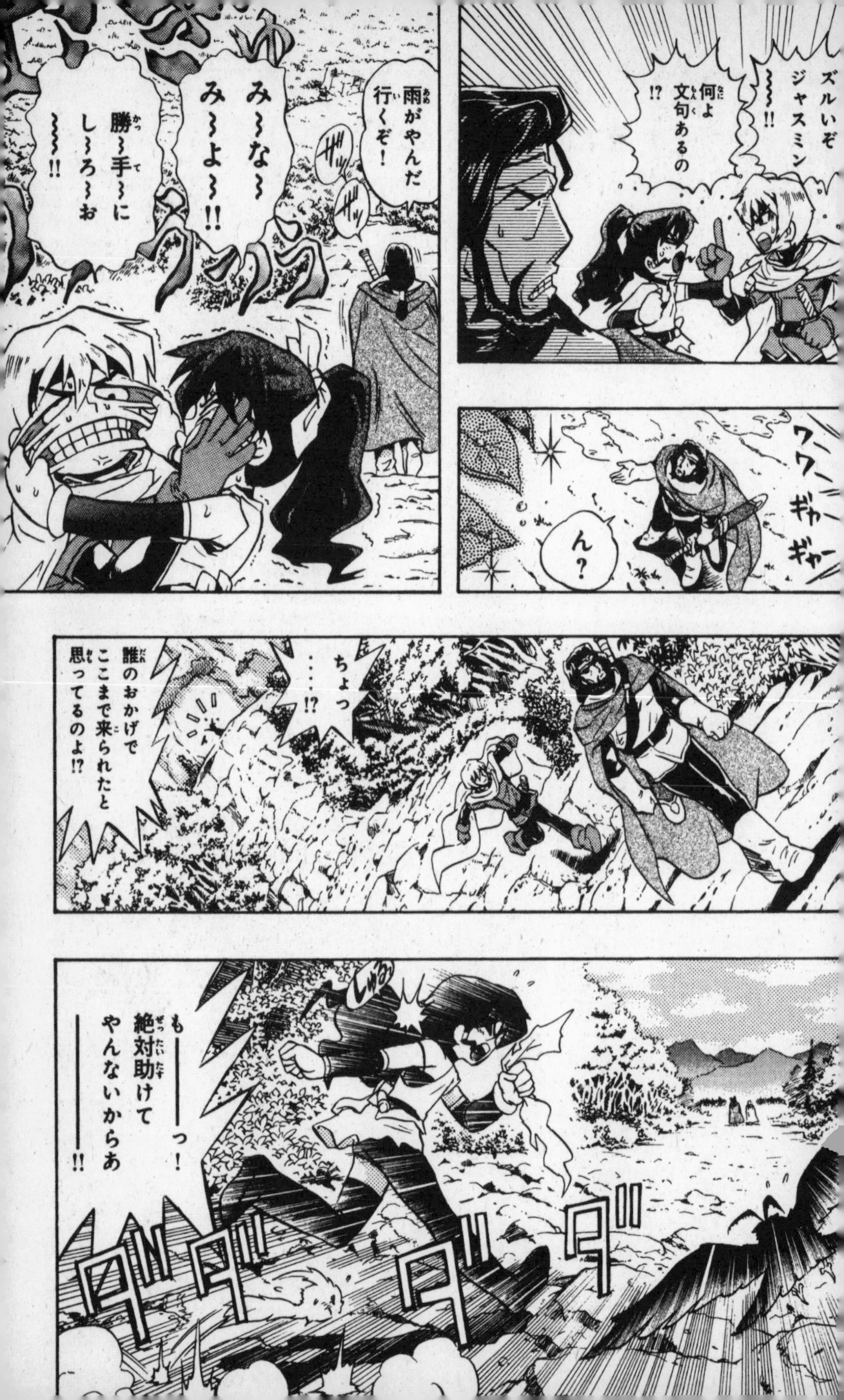
ズルいぞジャスミン〜〜〜!!
何よ文句あるの!?
ワーワーギャーギャー
ん？
雨がやんだ行くぞ！
ザッ
ザッ
み〜な〜み〜よ〜!!
勝〜手〜にし〜ろ〜お〜〜〜!!
ちょっ……!?
誰のおかげでここまで来られたと思ってるのよ!?
も———っ！絶対助けてやんないからあ———!!
ダダダダ

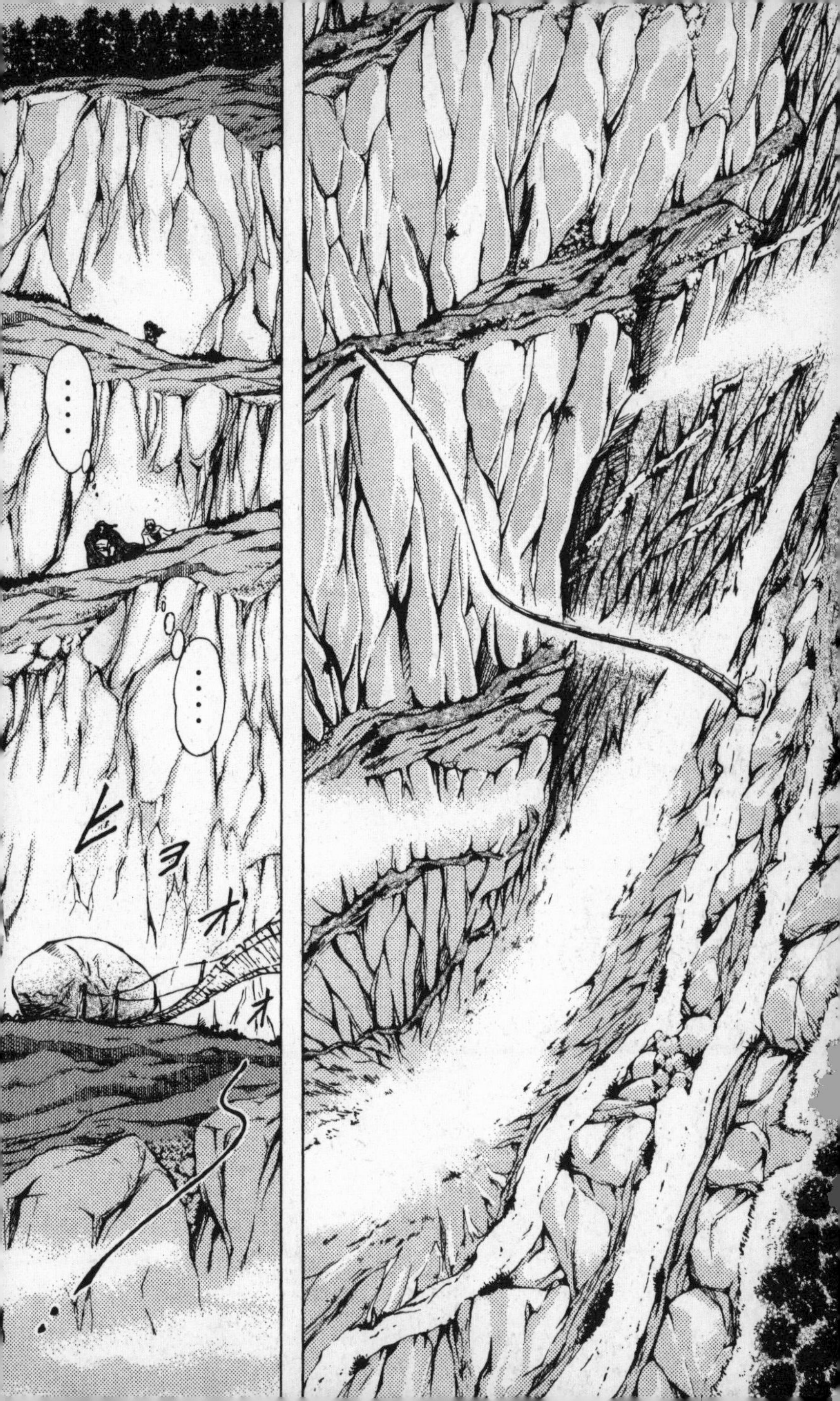
……
……
ヒョオオ

恐ろしく深い谷だなぁ……

ああ あの吊り橋も頼りない

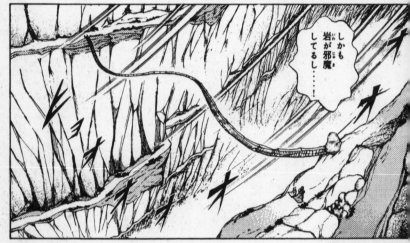

しかも岩が邪魔してるし……！

え!?

……！

……

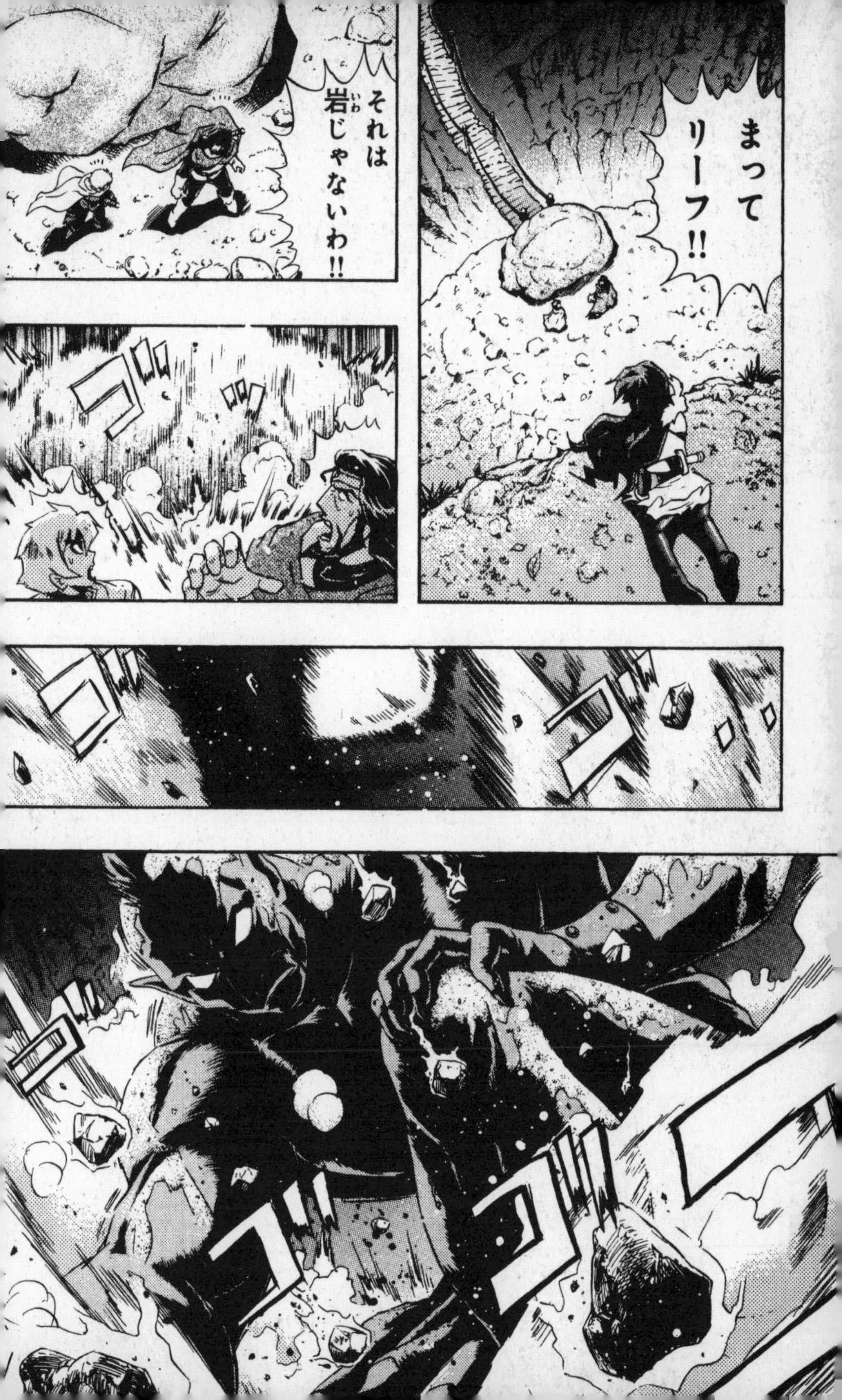
まって
リーフ!!
それは
岩じゃないわ!!

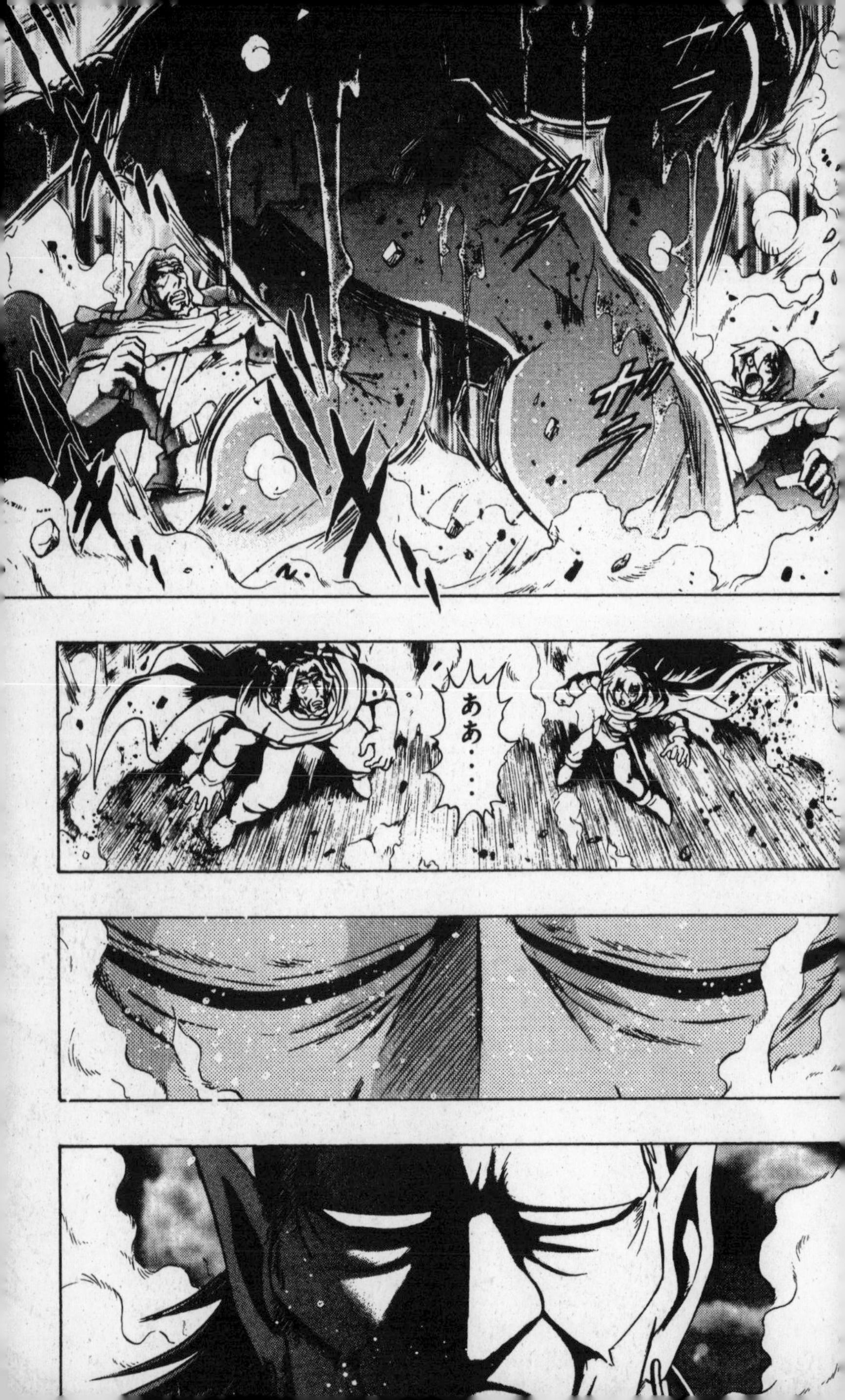
ガラ
ガラ
ガラ
ああ……

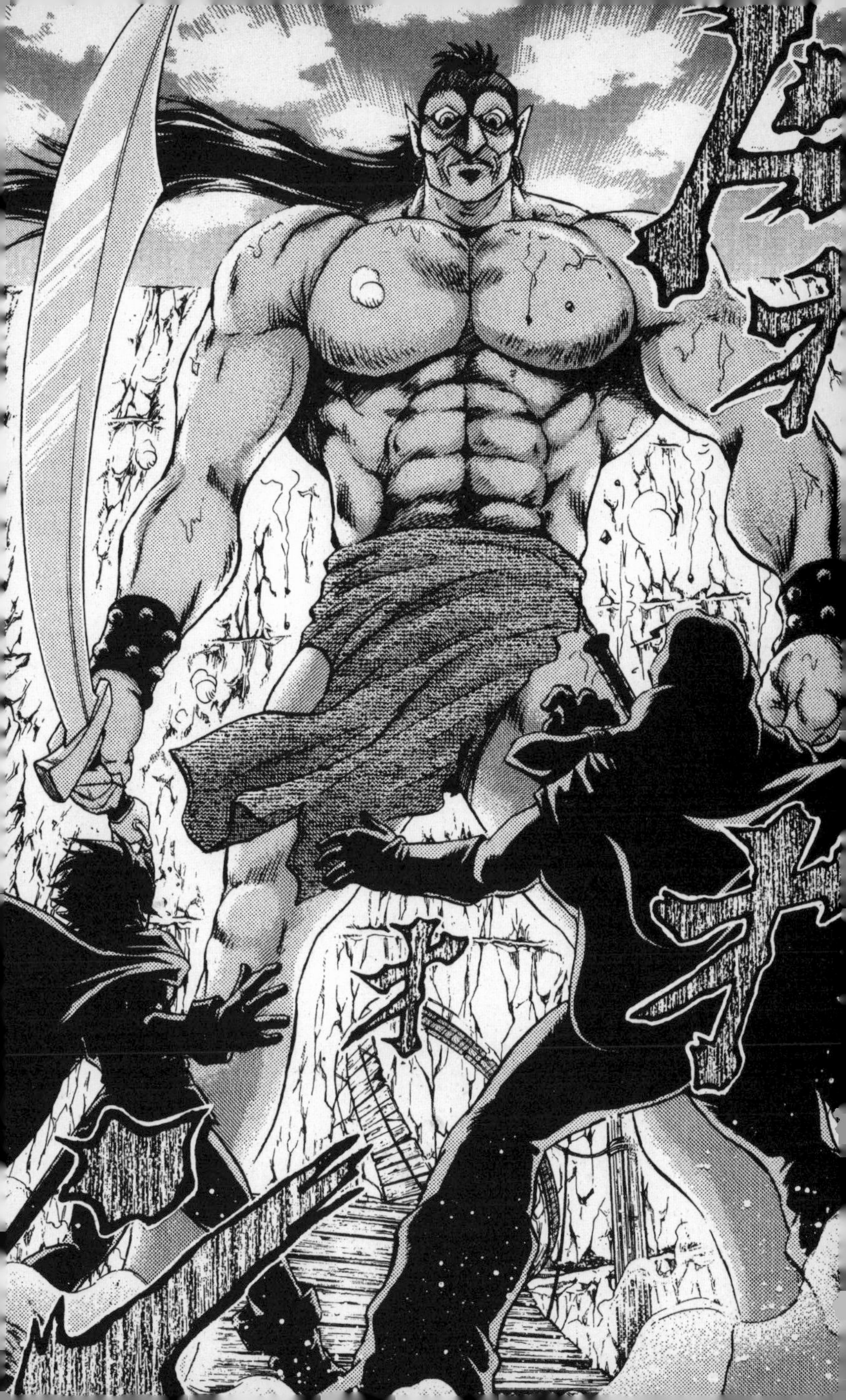

NEGIMA!
MAGISTER NEGI MAGI

BY KEN AKAMATSU

Negi Springfield is a ten-year-old wizard teaching English at an all-girls Japanese school. He dreams of becoming a master wizard like his legendary father, the Thousand Master. At first his biggest concern was concealing his magic powers, because if he's ever caught using them publicly, he thinks he'll be turned into an ermine! But in a world that gets stranger every day, it turns out that the strangest people of all are Negi's students! From a librarian with a magic book to a centuries-old vampire, from a robot to a ninja, Negi will risk his own life to protect the girls in his care!

Ages: 16+

Special extras in each volume! Read them all!

VISIT WWW.KODANSHACOMICS.COM TO:

• View release date calendars for upcoming volumes
• Find out the latest about new Kodansha Comics series

The Pretty Guardians are back!

Kodansha Comics is proud to present *Sailor Moon* with all new translations.

For more information, go to **www.kodanshacomics.com**

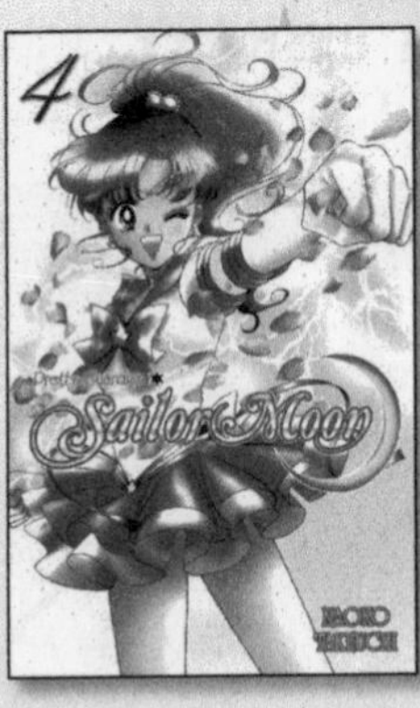
4
Pretty Guardian
Sailor Moon
NAOKO TAKEUCHI
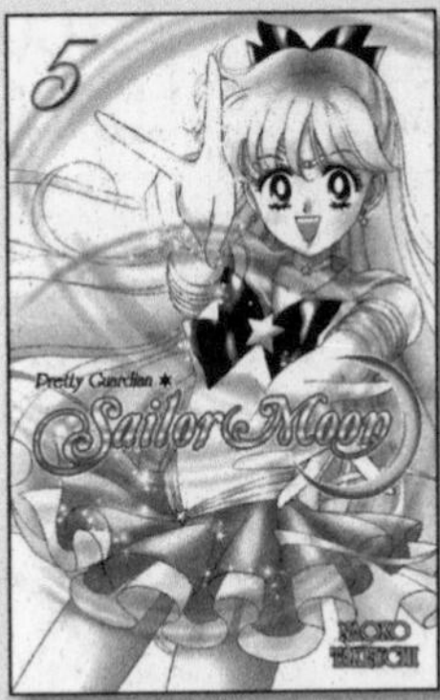
5
Pretty Guardian
Sailor Moon
NAOKO TAKEUCHI
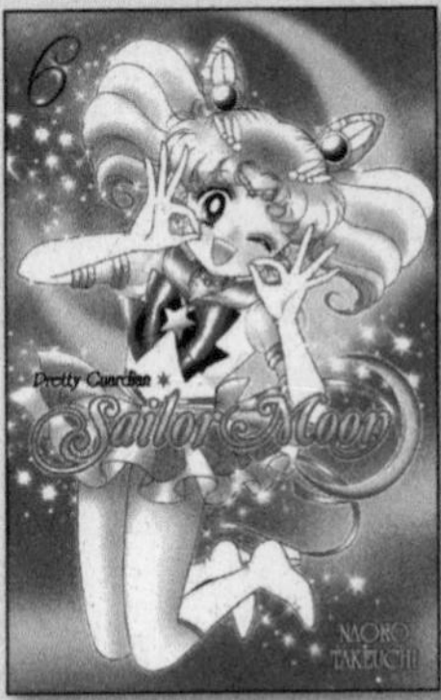
6
Pretty Guardian
Sailor Moon
NAOKO TAKEUCHI
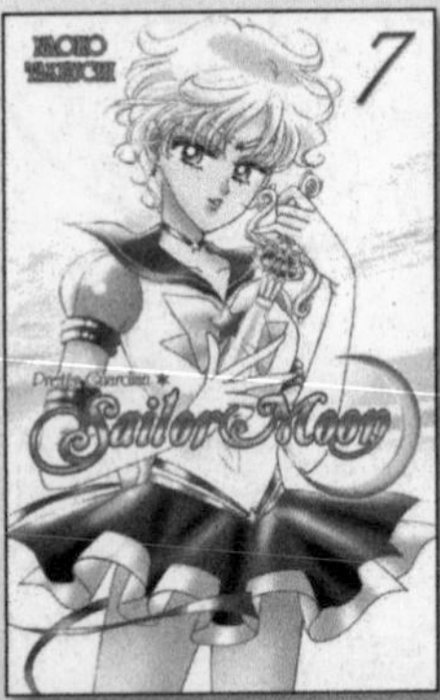
NAOKO TAKEUCHI
7
Pretty Guardian
Sailor Moon
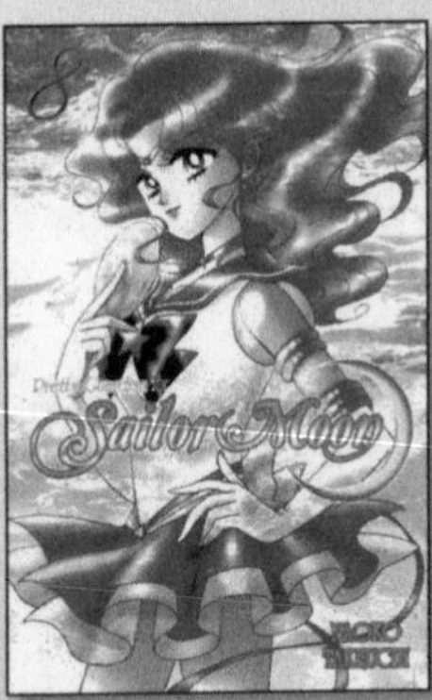
8
Sailor Moon
NAOKO TAKEUCHI
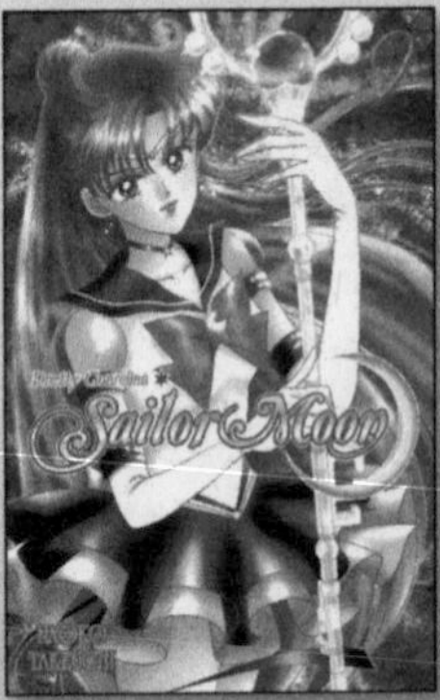
Sailor Moon
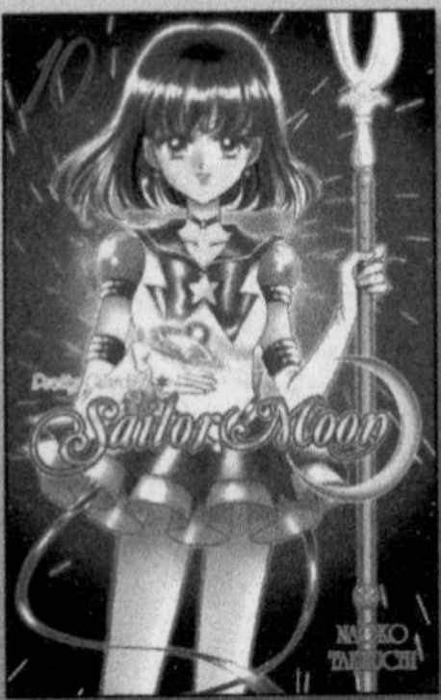
10
Sailor Moon
NAOKO TAKEUCHI
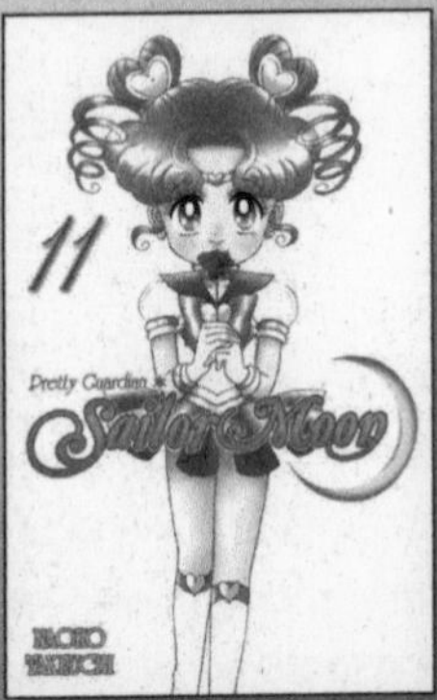
11
Pretty Guardian
Sailor Moon
NAOKO TAKEUCHI
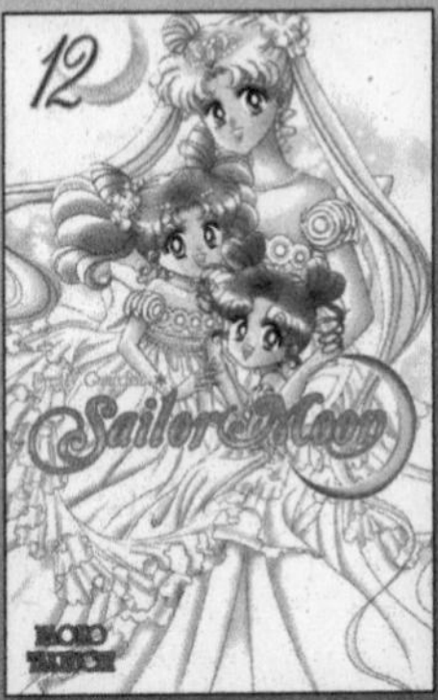
12
Sailor Moon
NAOKO TAKEUCHI

KC
KODANSHA
COMICS

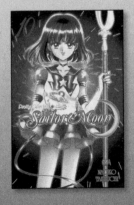

TOMARE!

[STOP!]

You are going the wrong way!

Manga is a completely different type of reading experience.

To start at the *beginning,* go to the *end*!

That's right! Authentic manga is read the traditional Japanese way—from right to left, exactly the opposite of how American books are read. It's easy to follow: Just go to the other end of the book, and read each page—and each panel—from the right side to the left side, starting at the top right. Now you're experiencing manga as it was meant to be.